Honey Hunt

5 story and art by Miki Aihara

CHARACTERS

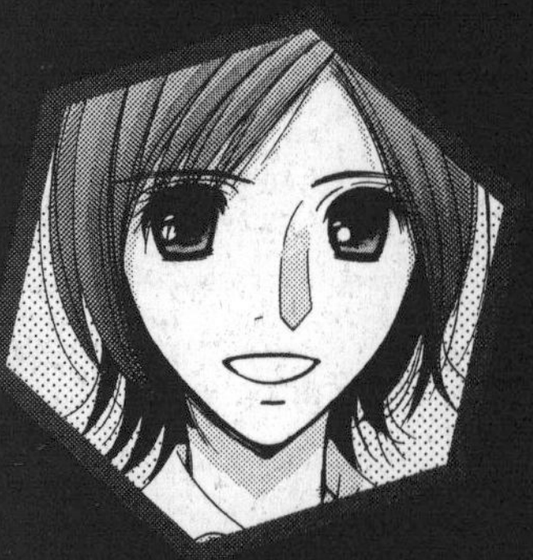

YURA ONOZUKA ★
The only child of celebrity parents. She is a surprisingly average, ordinary girl, considering her father is a world-famous musician and her mother is an award-winning actress.

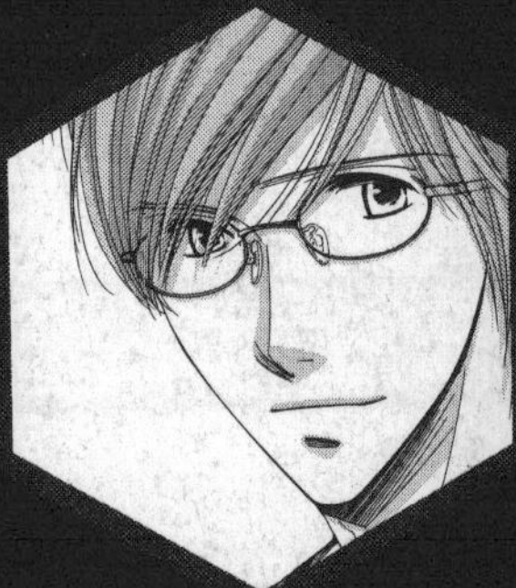

KEIICHI MIZOROGI ★
President of the entertainment company Meteorite Productions. He scouted Yura and became her manager.

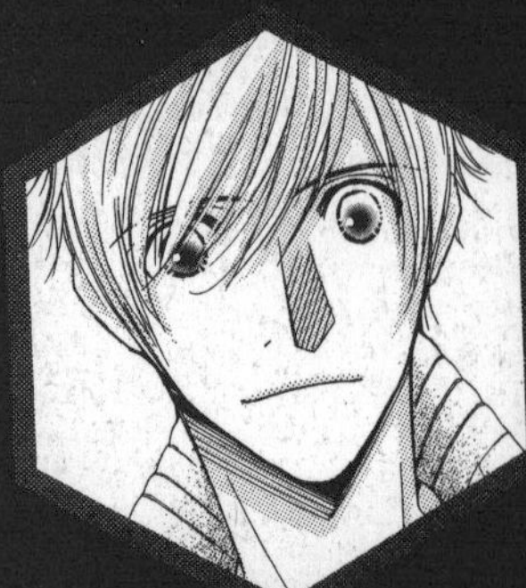

Q-TA MINAMITANI ★
The singer of popular music group Assha (also known as "h.a."). He likes Yura.

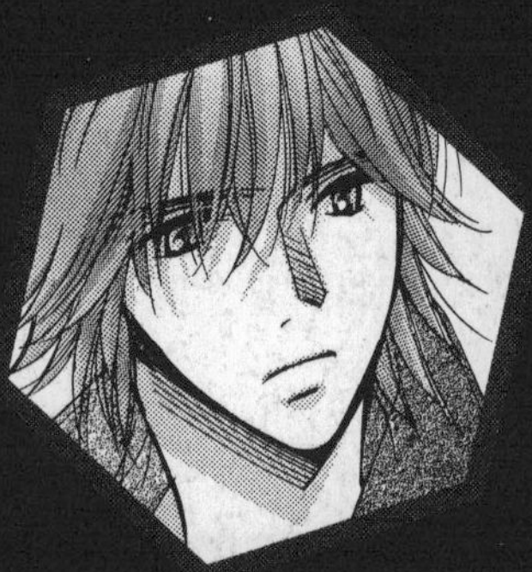

HARUKA ★
A member of the pop idol group KNIGHTS. Q-ta's twin brother and rival.

Honey Hunt 5

STORY

★ Yura knows that growing up as the only child of famous parents isn't as glamorous as it would seem. Because of their busy schedules, Yura was often left home alone. Yura has always been sensitive about being compared to her parents because, unlike them, she is plain, shy and painfully normal.

★ When her parents' love affairs become public, they announce that they will divorce, leaving Yura with no place to go. What's worse, Yura discovers that her mother's lover is her childhood friend Shinsuke.

★ Fed up with how her parents overlook her, Yura decides to start acting in order to compete with her mother. Keiichi sees promise in the unpolished Yura and invites her to stay at his house and work with him. Here she will begin her new life.

★ When Yura is chosen as the lead actress in the "Noodle Girl" project, she finally finds herself a working actress. She also finds herself developing a crush on Q-ta. But her attraction to Q-ta starts interfering with her work, and Mizorogi bans her from any relationships until she is an established actress.

★ However, Yura is unable to contain her feelings, and on the night that her drama is to premiere on TV, she sneaks off with Q-ta on an overnight trip to a hot springs resort...

Honey Hunt 5

CONTENTS

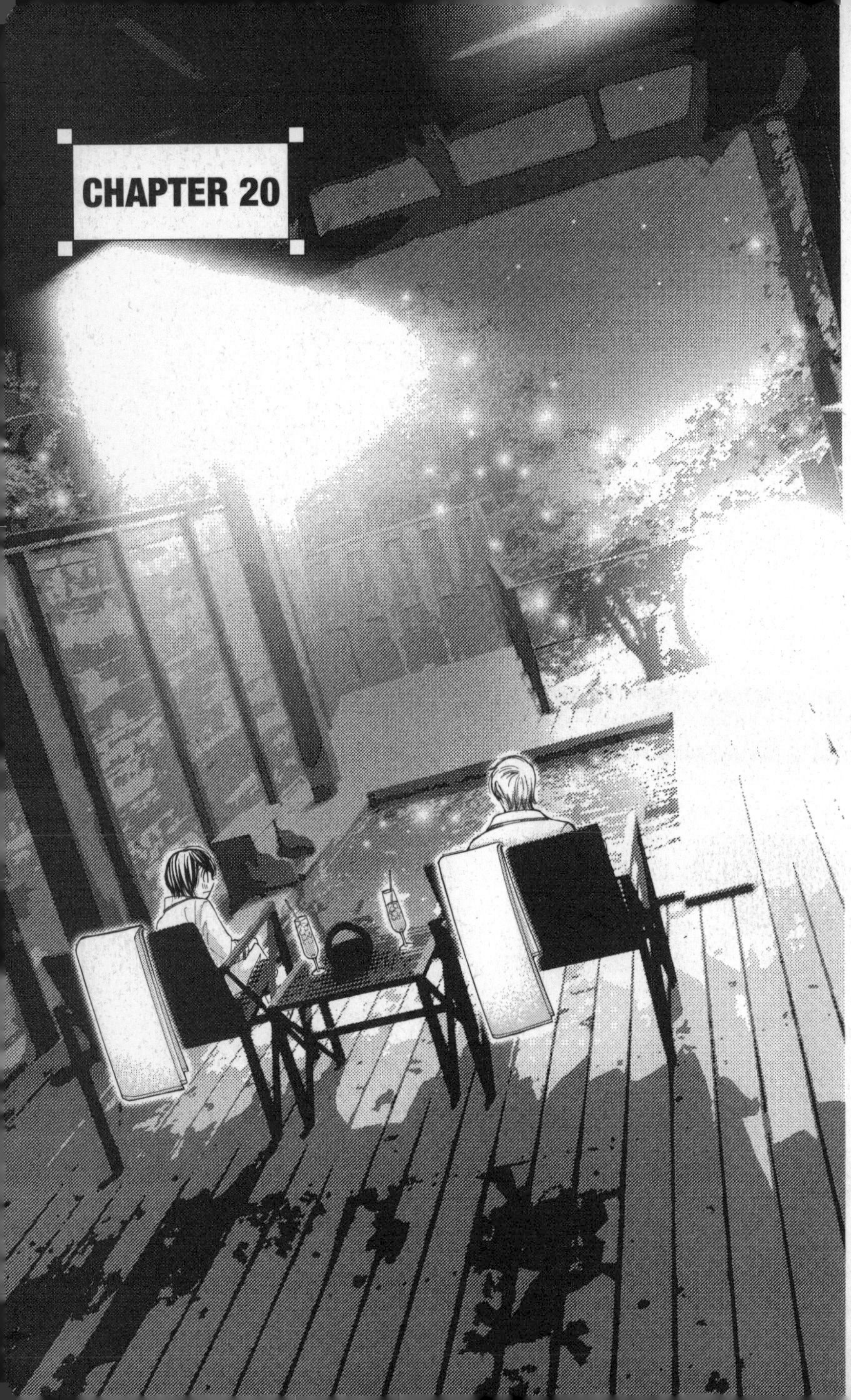
CHAPTER 20

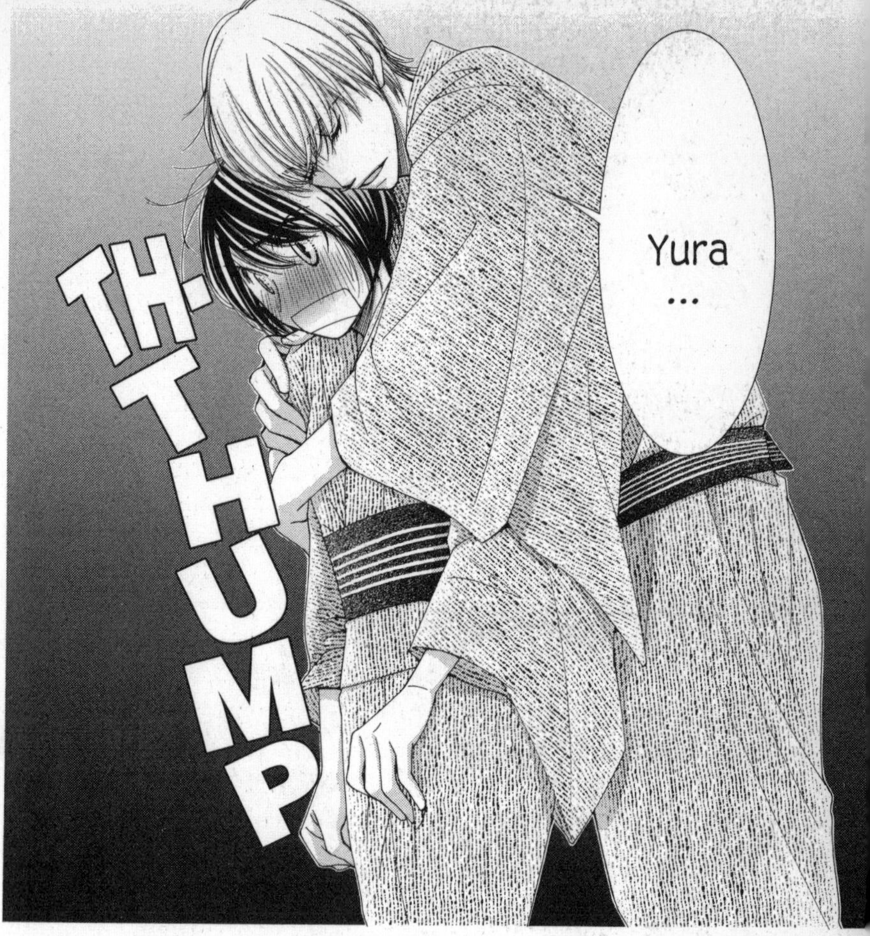
Yura
...
TH-THUMP

Honey Hunt

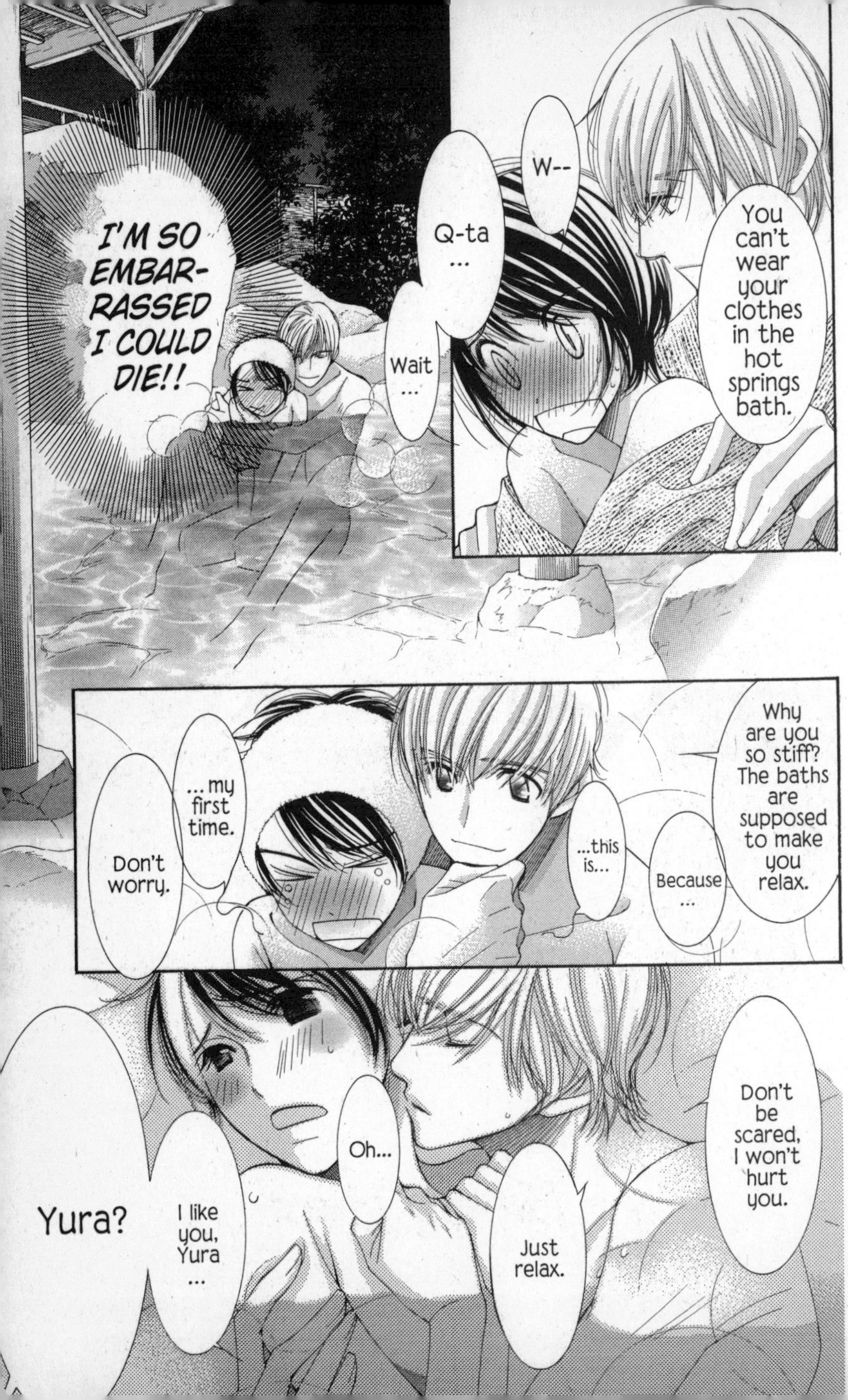
You can't wear your clothes in the hot springs bath.
W--
Q-ta ...
Wait ...
I'M SO EMBARRASSED I COULD DIE!!
Why are you so stiff? The baths are supposed to make you relax.
Because ...
...this is...
...my first time.
Don't worry.
Don't be scared, I won't hurt you.
Just relax.
Oh...
I like you, Yura ...
Yura?

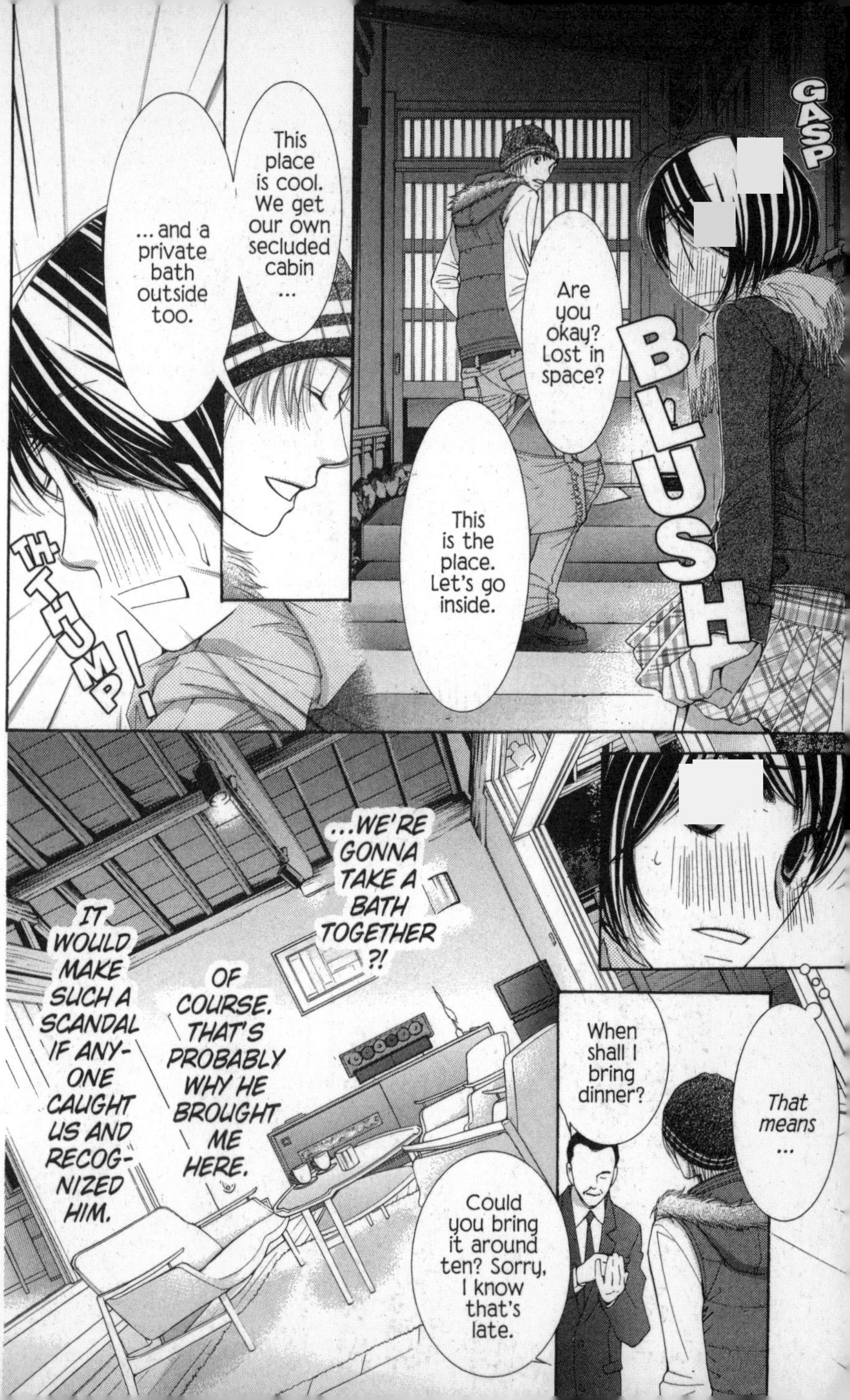
GASP
BLUSH
Are you okay? Lost in space?
This is the place. Let's go inside.
This place is cool. We get our own secluded cabin ...
...and a private bath outside too.
TH-THUMP
That means ...
When shall I bring dinner?
Could you bring it around ten? Sorry, I know that's late.
...WE'RE GONNA TAKE A BATH TOGETHER?!
OF COURSE. THAT'S PROBABLY WHY HE BROUGHT ME HERE.
IT WOULD MAKE SUCH A SCANDAL IF ANY-ONE CAUGHT US AND RECOG-NIZED HIM.

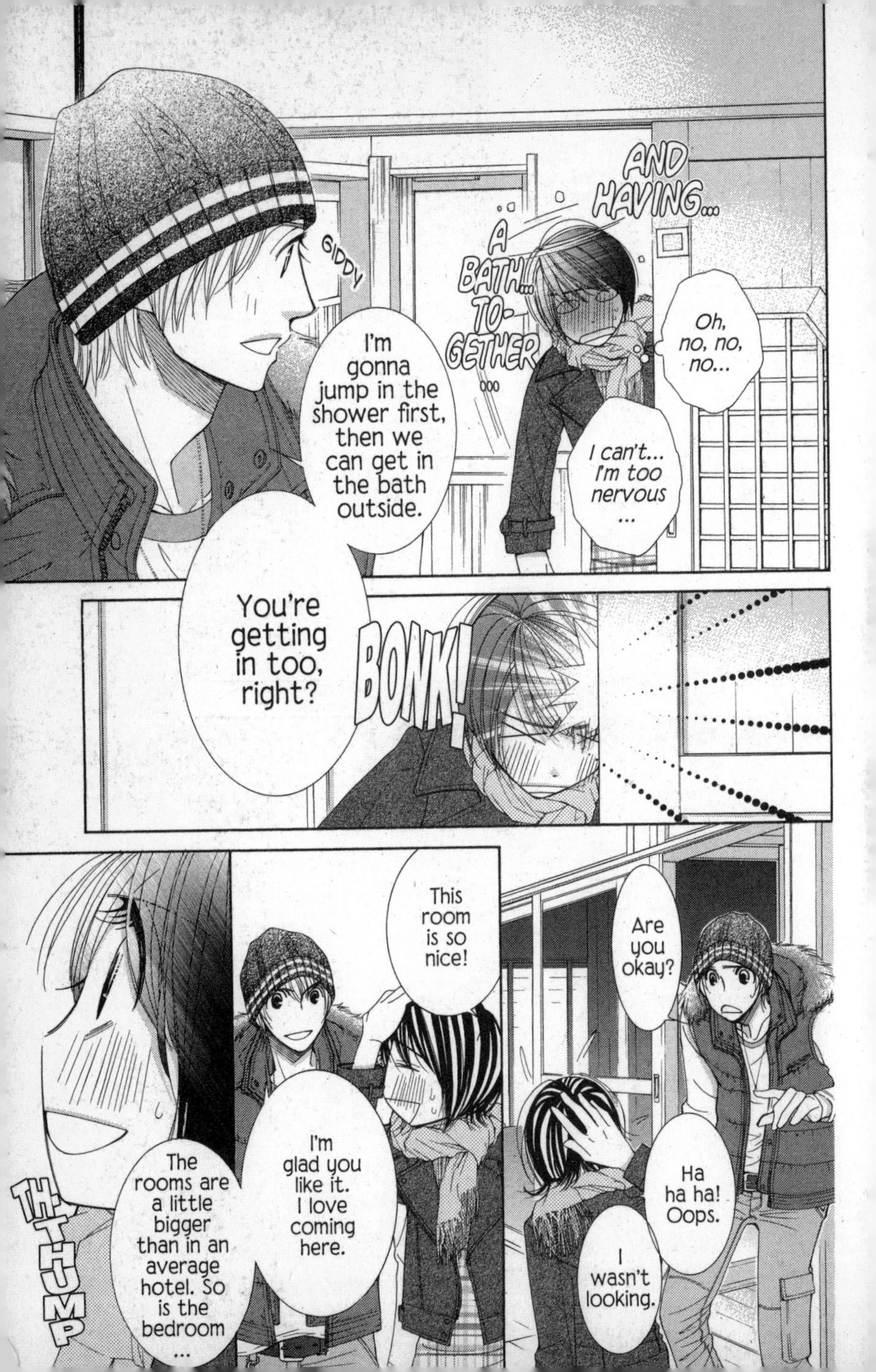
AND HAVING...
A BATH... TO-GETHER...
Oh, no, no, no...
I can't... I'm too nervous...
I'm gonna jump in the shower first, then we can get in the bath outside.
GIDDY
You're getting in too, right?
BONK!
Are you okay?
Ha ha ha! Oops.
I wasn't looking.
This room is so nice!
I'm glad you like it. I love coming here.
The rooms are a little bigger than in an average hotel. So is the bedroom...
THTHUMP

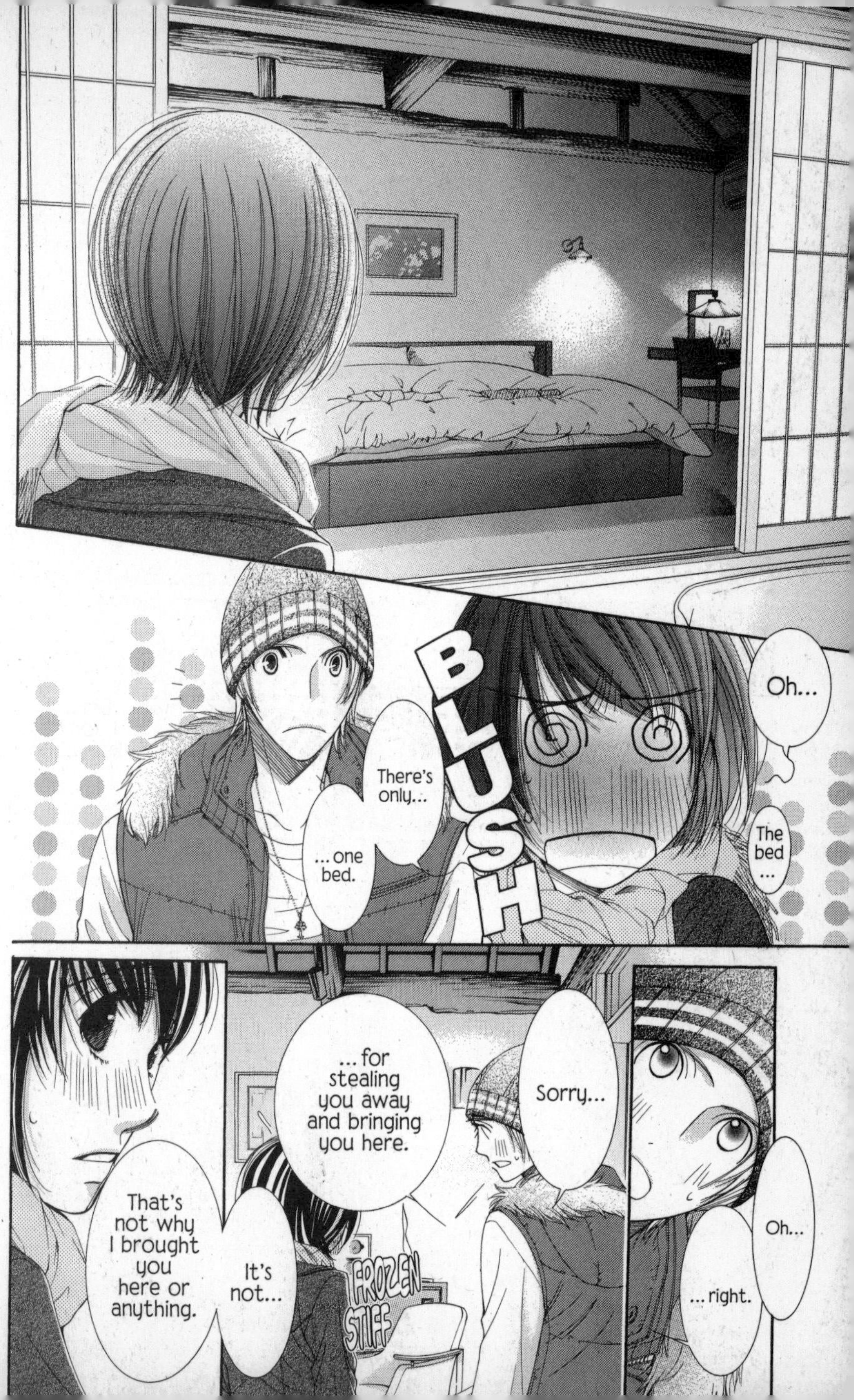
Oh...
The bed ...
BLUSH
There's only...
...one bed.
Oh...
...right.
Sorry...
...for stealing you away and bringing you here.
FROZEN STIFF
It's not...
That's not why I brought you here or anything.

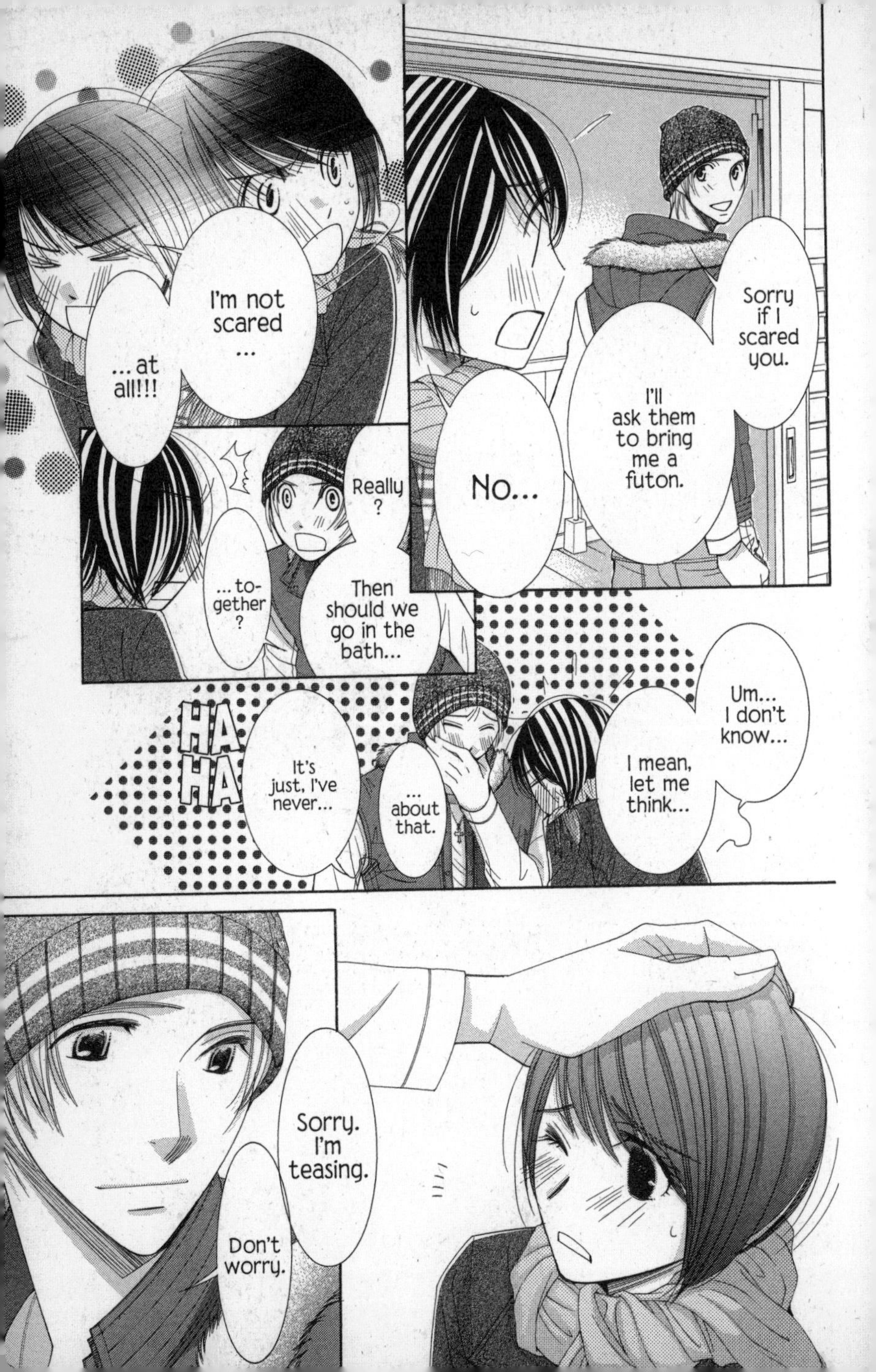
Sorry if I scared you.
I'll ask them to bring me a futon.
No...
I'm not scared ...
... at all!!!
Really?
Then should we go in the bath...
... together?
Um... I don't know...
I mean, let me think...
... about that.
It's just, I've never...
HA HA
Sorry. I'm teasing.
Don't worry.

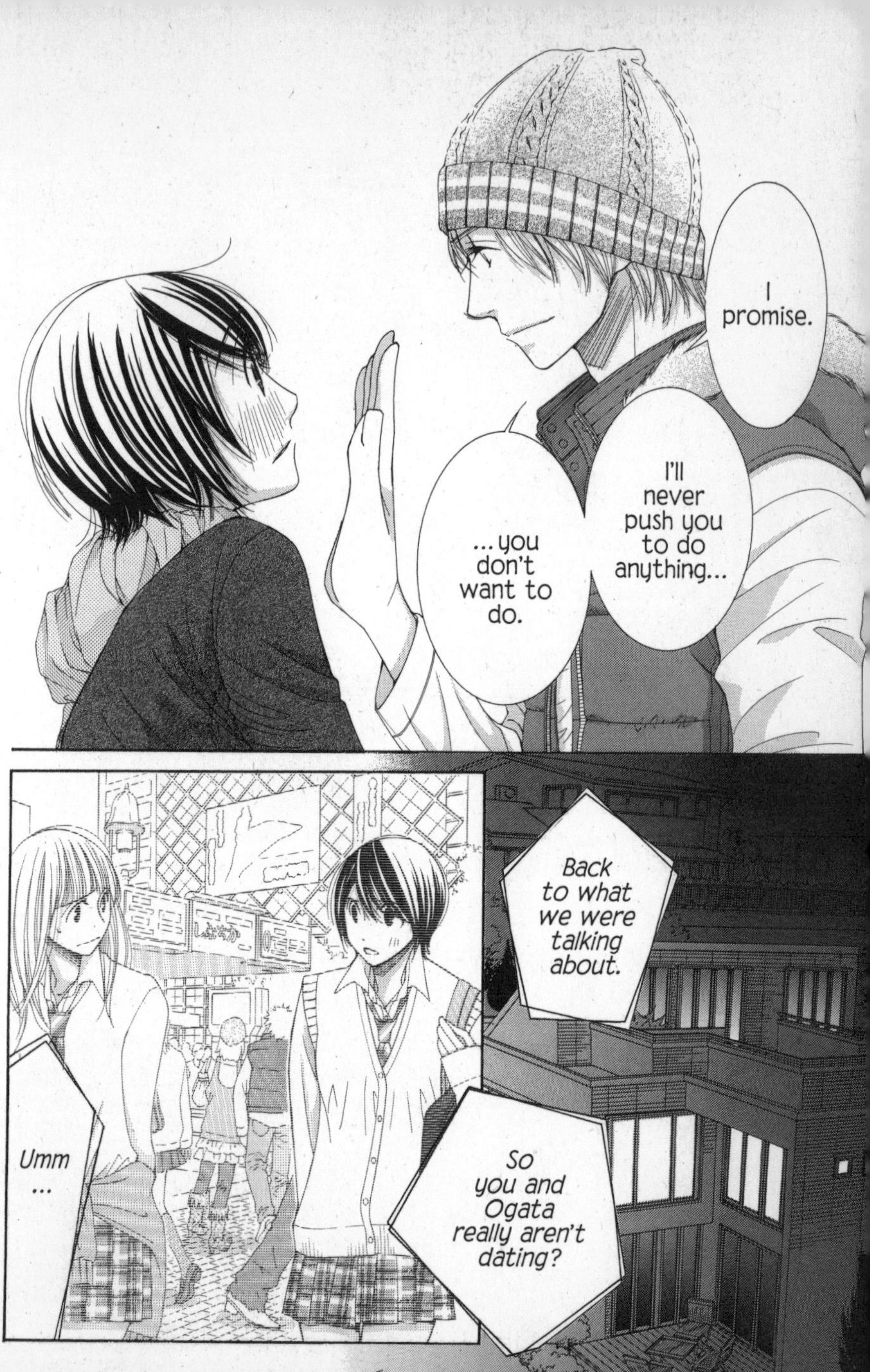
I promise.
I'll never push you to do anything...
...you don't want to do.
Back to what we were talking about.
So you and Ogata really aren't dating?
Umm ...

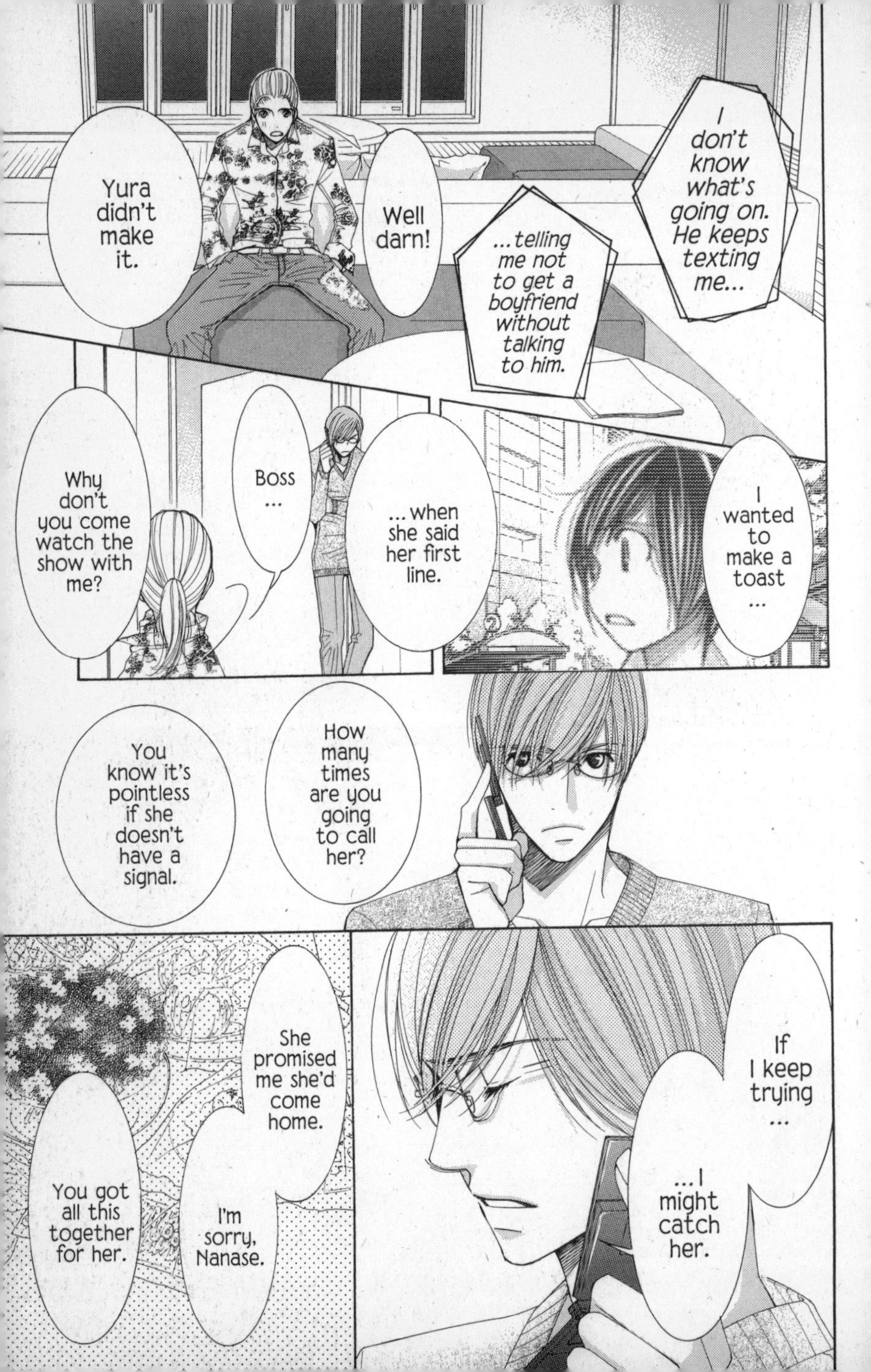

I don't know what's going on. He keeps texting me...
...telling me not to get a boyfriend without talking to him.
Well darn!
Yura didn't make it.
I wanted to make a toast...
...when she said her first line.
Boss...
Why don't you come watch the show with me?
How many times are you going to call her?
You know it's pointless if she doesn't have a signal.
If I keep trying...
...I might catch her.
She promised me she'd come home.
I'm sorry, Nanase.
You got all this together for her.

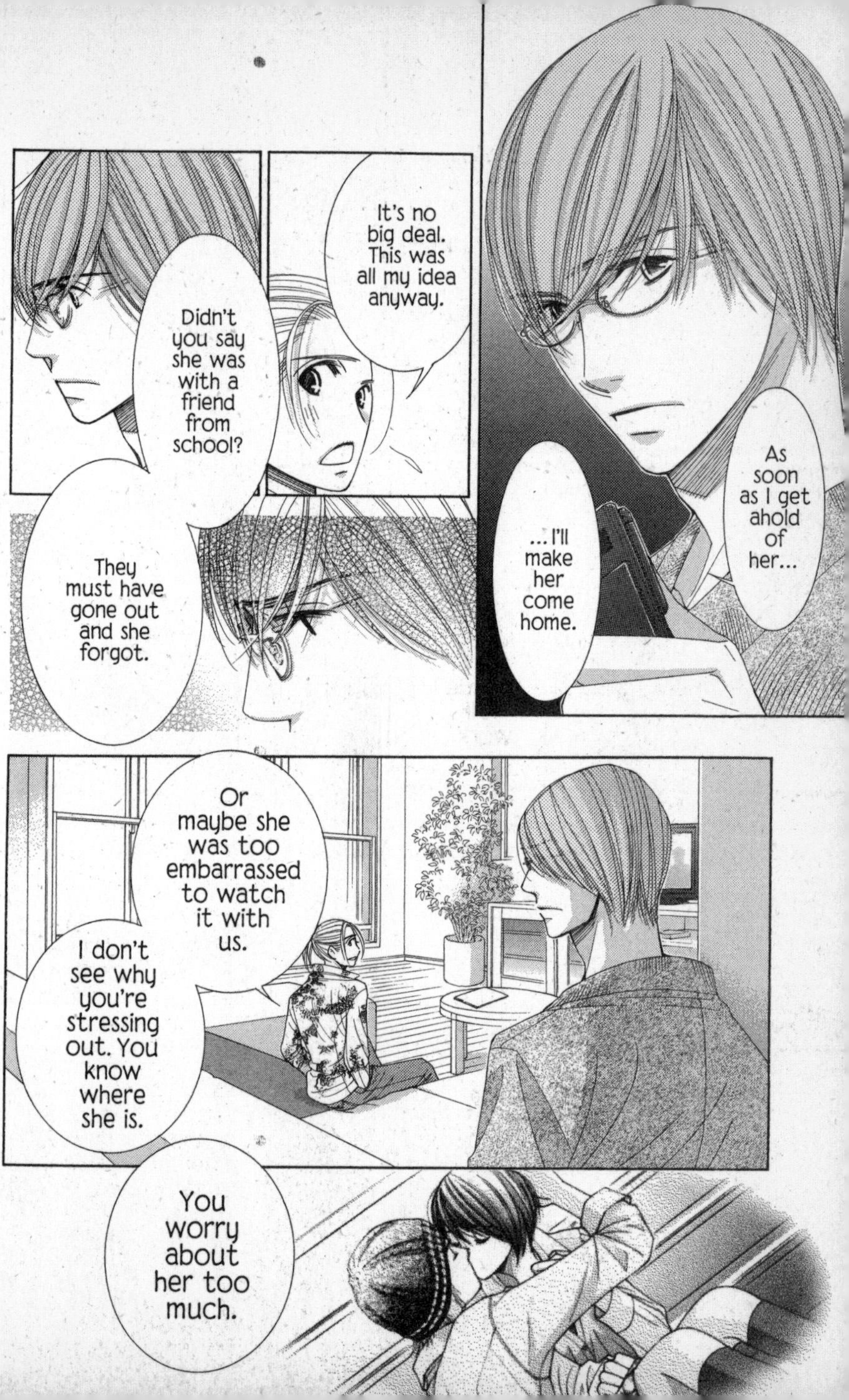
As soon as I get ahold of her...
...I'll make her come home.
It's no big deal. This was all my idea anyway.
Didn't you say she was with a friend from school?
They must have gone out and she forgot.
Or maybe she was too embarrassed to watch it with us.
I don't see why you're stressing out. You know where she is.
You worry about her too much.

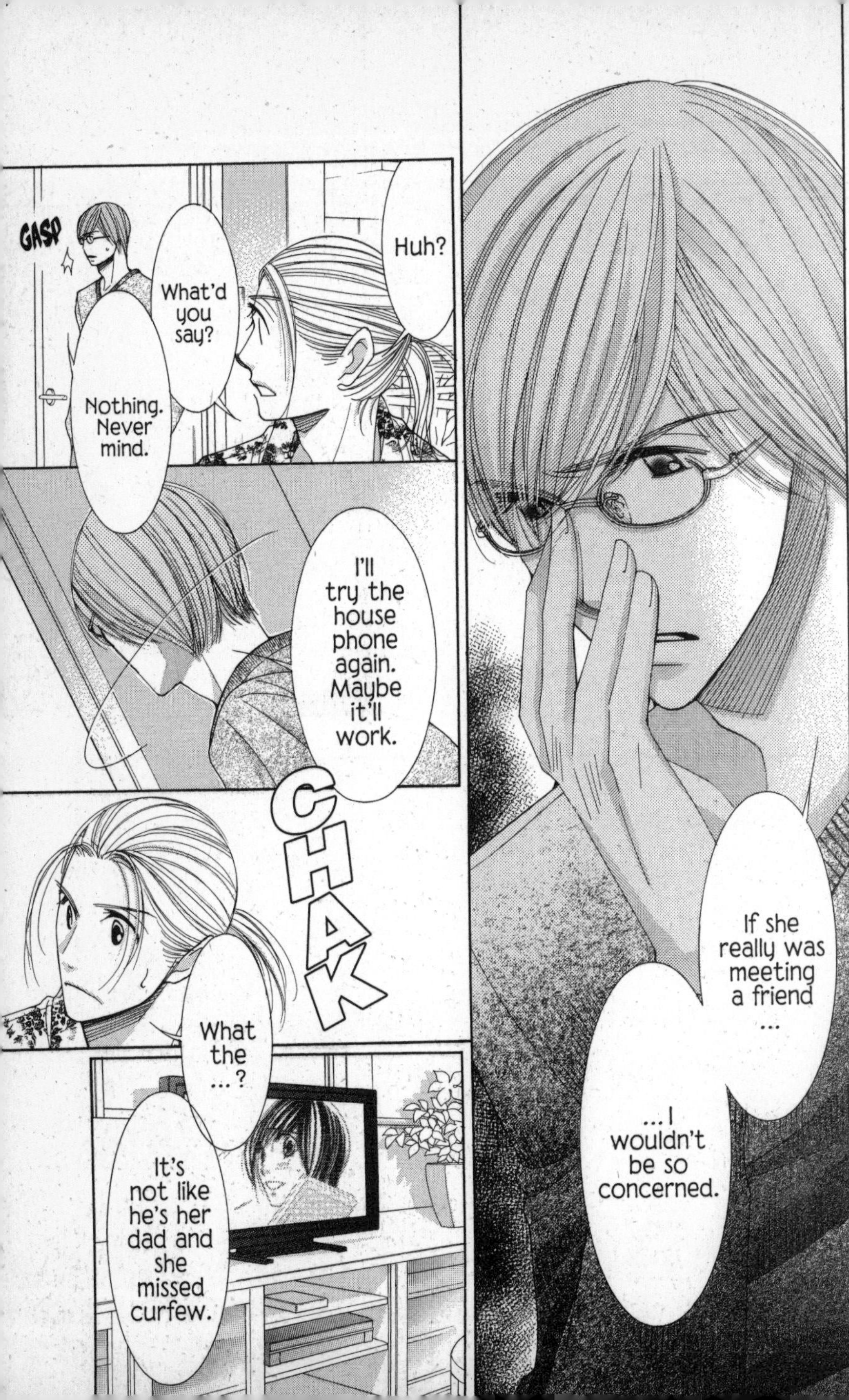
If she really was meeting a friend ...
... I wouldn't be so concerned.
Huh?
What'd you say?
GASP
Nothing. Never mind.
I'll try the house phone again. Maybe it'll work.
CHAK
What the ...?
It's not like he's her dad and she missed curfew.

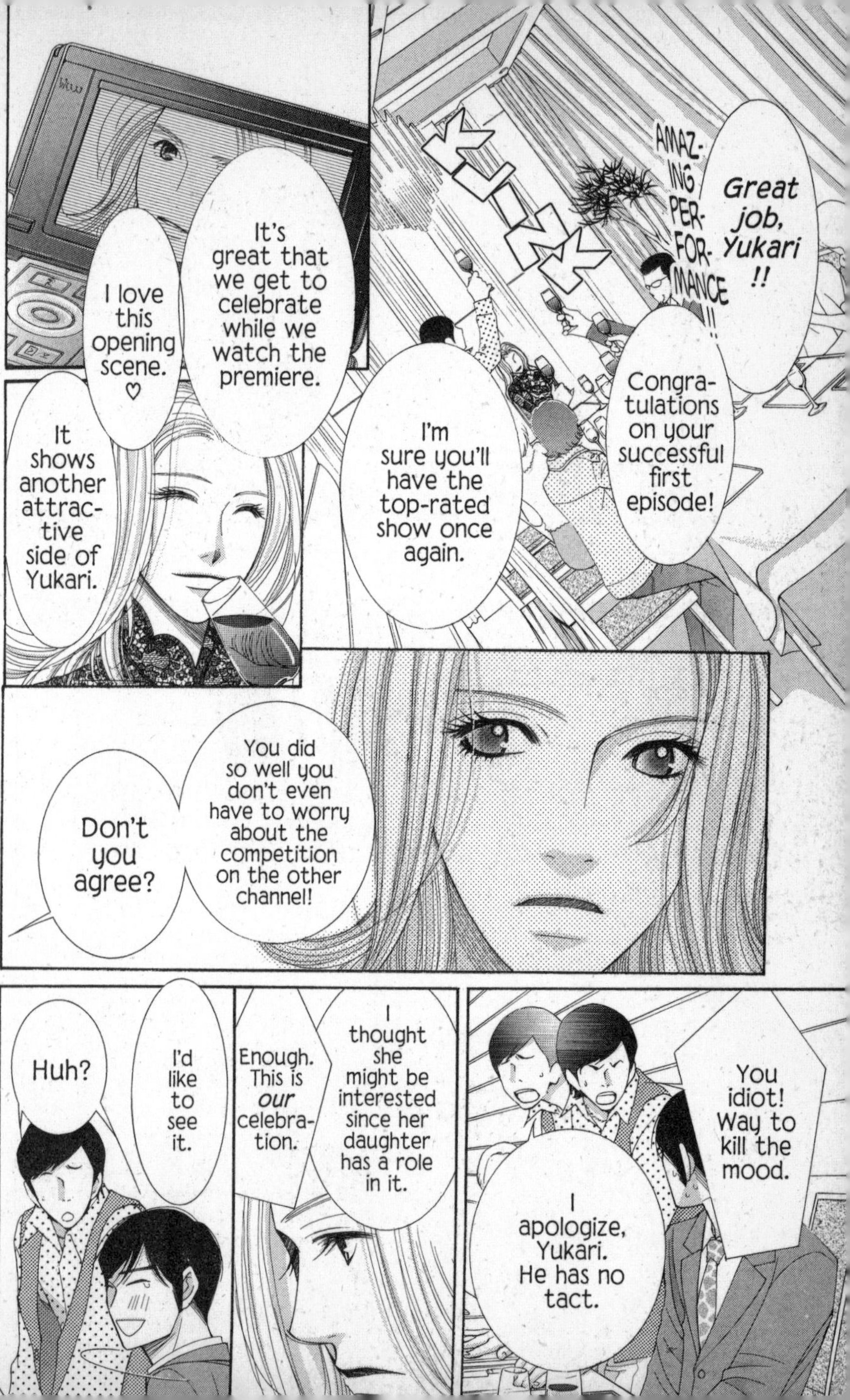
Great job, Yukari!!
AMAZING PERFORMANCE!!
KLINK
Congratulations on your successful first episode!
I'm sure you'll have the top-rated show once again.
It's great that we get to celebrate while we watch the premiere.
I love this opening scene. ♡
It shows another attractive side of Yukari.
You did so well you don't even have to worry about the competition on the other channel!
Don't you agree?
You idiot! Way to kill the mood.
I apologize, Yukari. He has no tact.
I thought she might be interested since her daughter has a role in it.
Enough. This is *our* celebration.
I'd like to see it.
Huh?

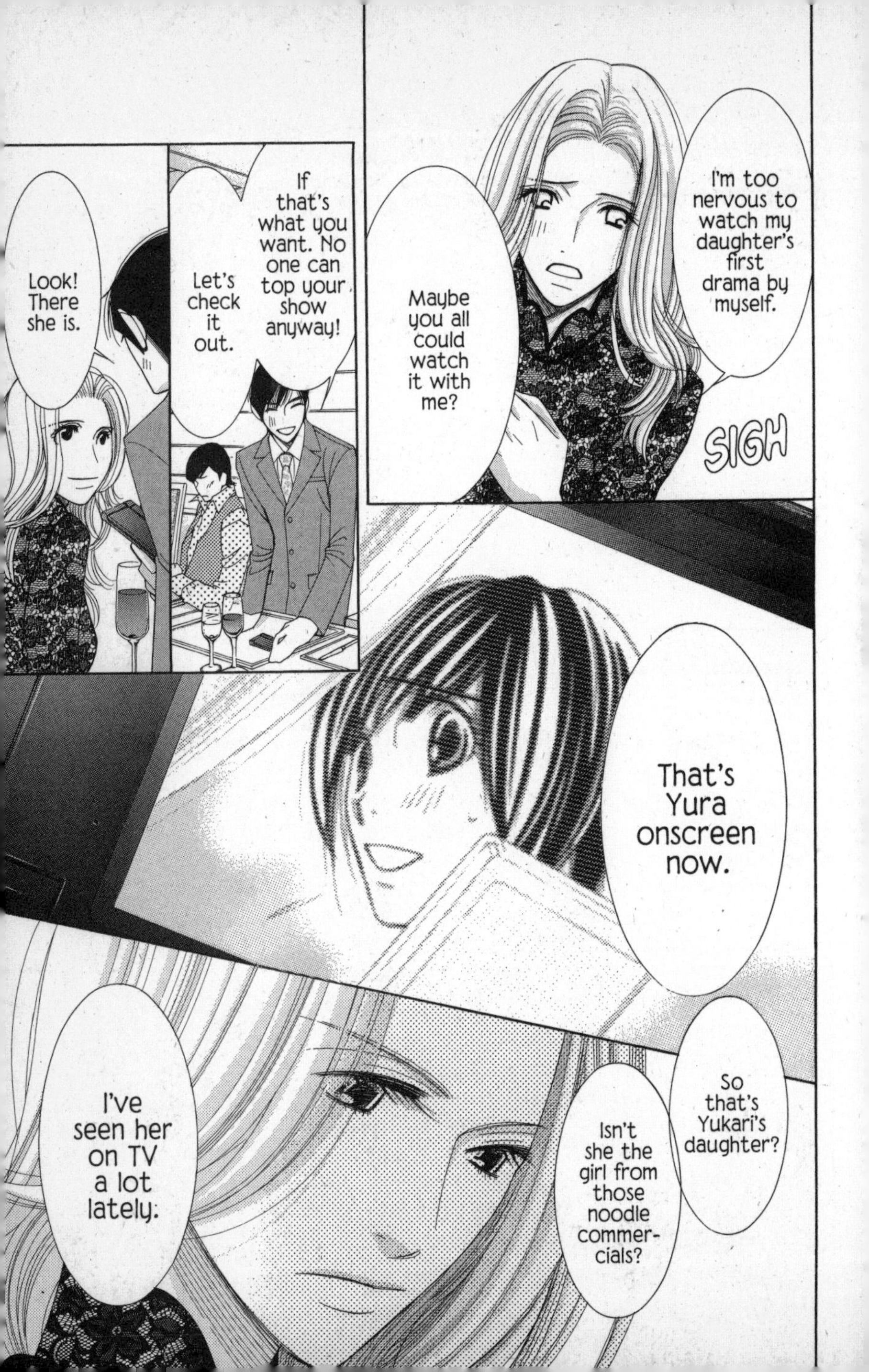
I'm too nervous to watch my daughter's first drama by myself.
Maybe you all could watch it with me?
SIGH
If that's what you want. No one can top your show anyway!
Let's check it out.
Look! There she is.
That's Yura onscreen now.
So that's Yukari's daughter?
Isn't she the girl from those noodle commercials?
I've seen her on TV a lot lately.

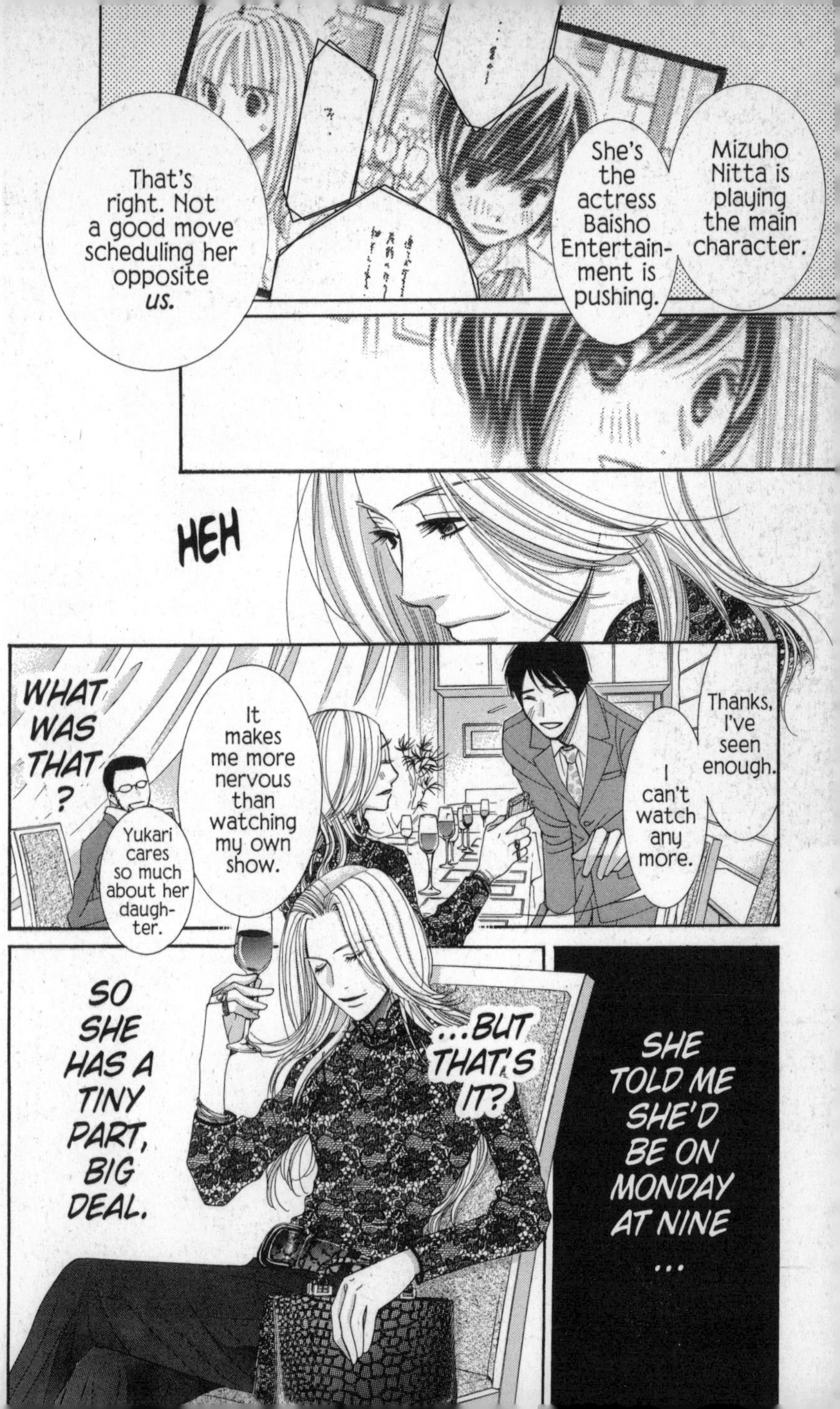
Mizuho Nitta is playing the main character.
She's the actress Baisho Entertainment is pushing.
That's right. Not a good move scheduling her opposite *us*.
HEH
Thanks, I've seen enough.
I can't watch any more.
It makes me more nervous than watching my own show.
WHAT WAS THAT?
Yukari cares so much about her daughter.
SHE TOLD ME SHE'D BE ON MONDAY AT NINE ...
...BUT THAT'S IT?
SO SHE HAS A TINY PART, BIG DEAL.

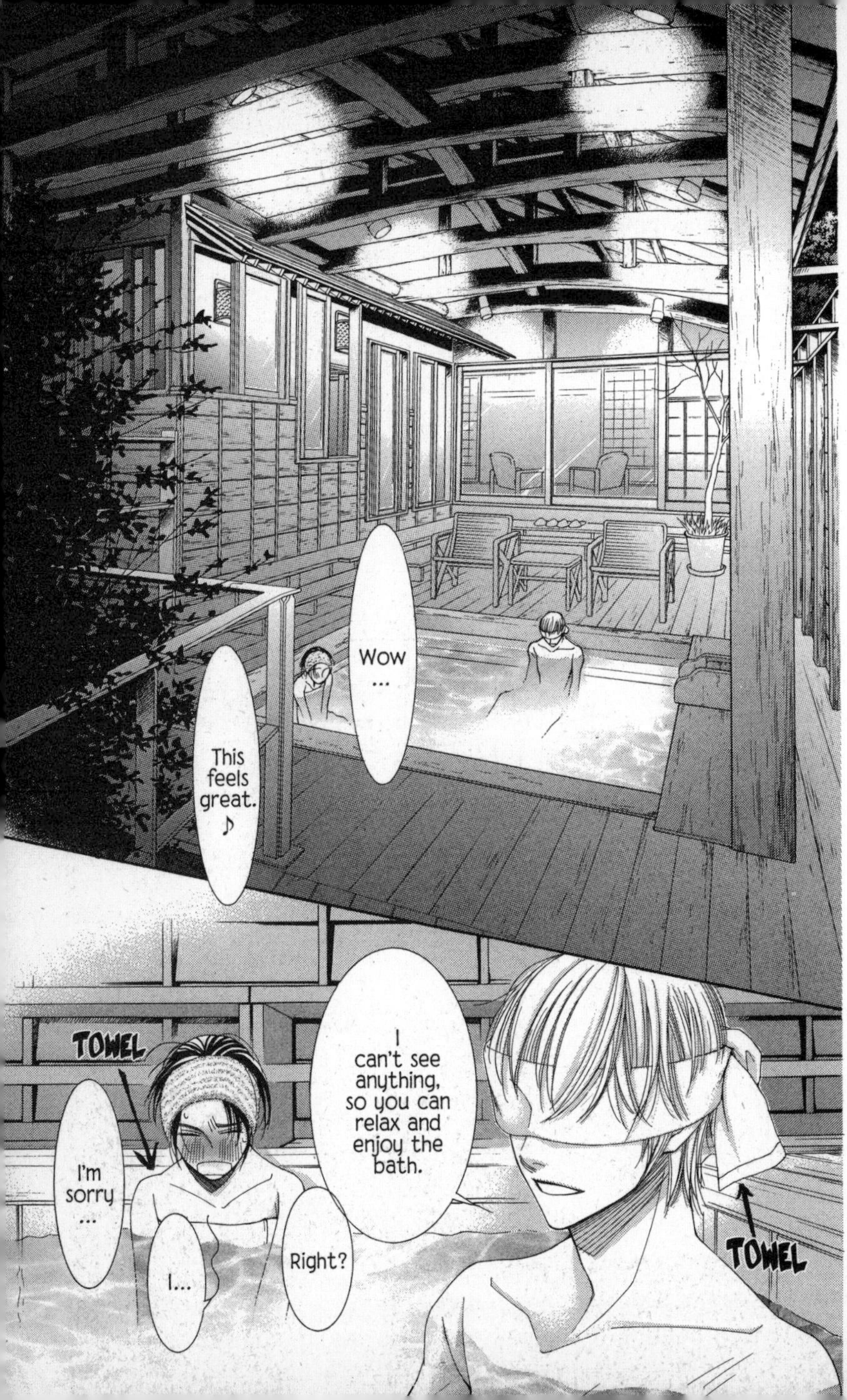
Wow...
This feels great. ♪
I can't see anything, so you can relax and enjoy the bath.
TOWEL
Right?
I'm sorry...
I...
TOWEL

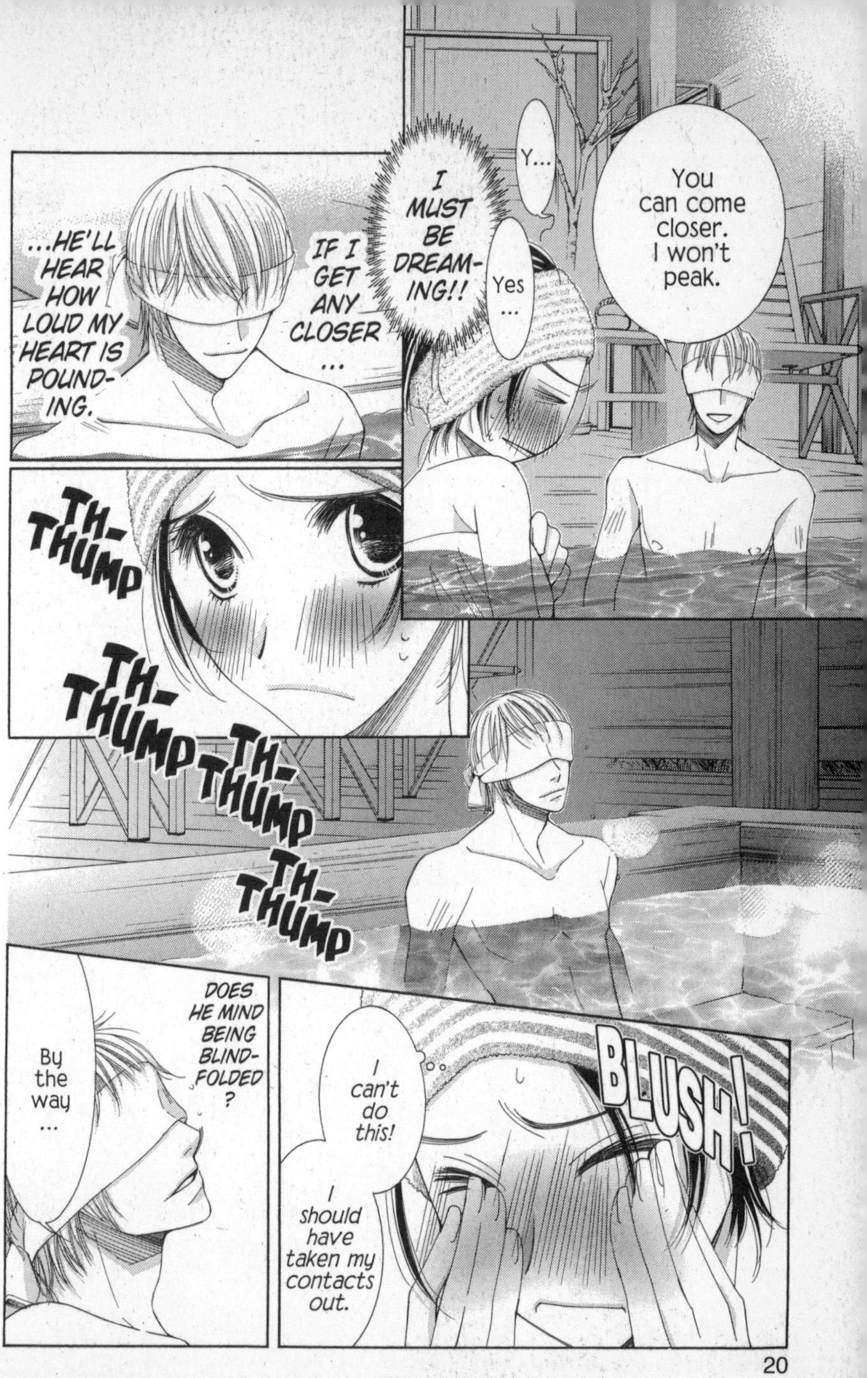
You can come closer. I won't peak.
Y...
Yes...
I MUST BE DREAMING!!
IF I GET ANY CLOSER...
...HE'LL HEAR HOW LOUD MY HEART IS POUNDING.
TH-THUMP
TH-THUMP
TH-THUMP
TH-THUMP
BLUSH!
I can't do this!
I should have taken my contacts out.
DOES HE MIND BEING BLINDFOLDED?
By the way...

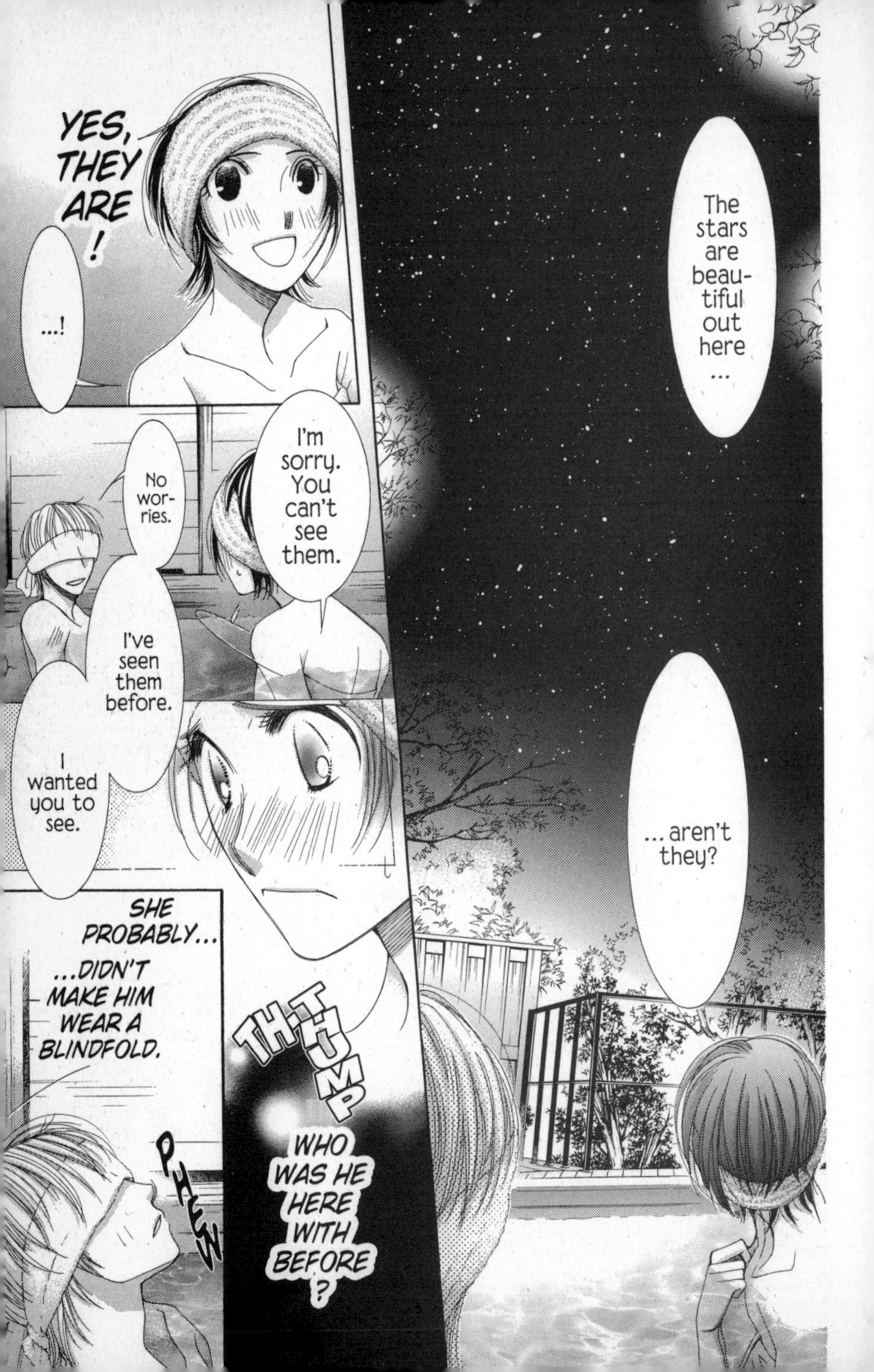

The stars are beautiful out here...
...aren't they?
YES, THEY ARE!
...!
I'm sorry. You can't see them.
No worries.
I've seen them before.
I wanted you to see.
THTHUMP
SHE PROBABLY...
...DIDN'T MAKE HIM WEAR A BLINDFOLD.
WHO WAS HE HERE WITH BEFORE?
PHEW

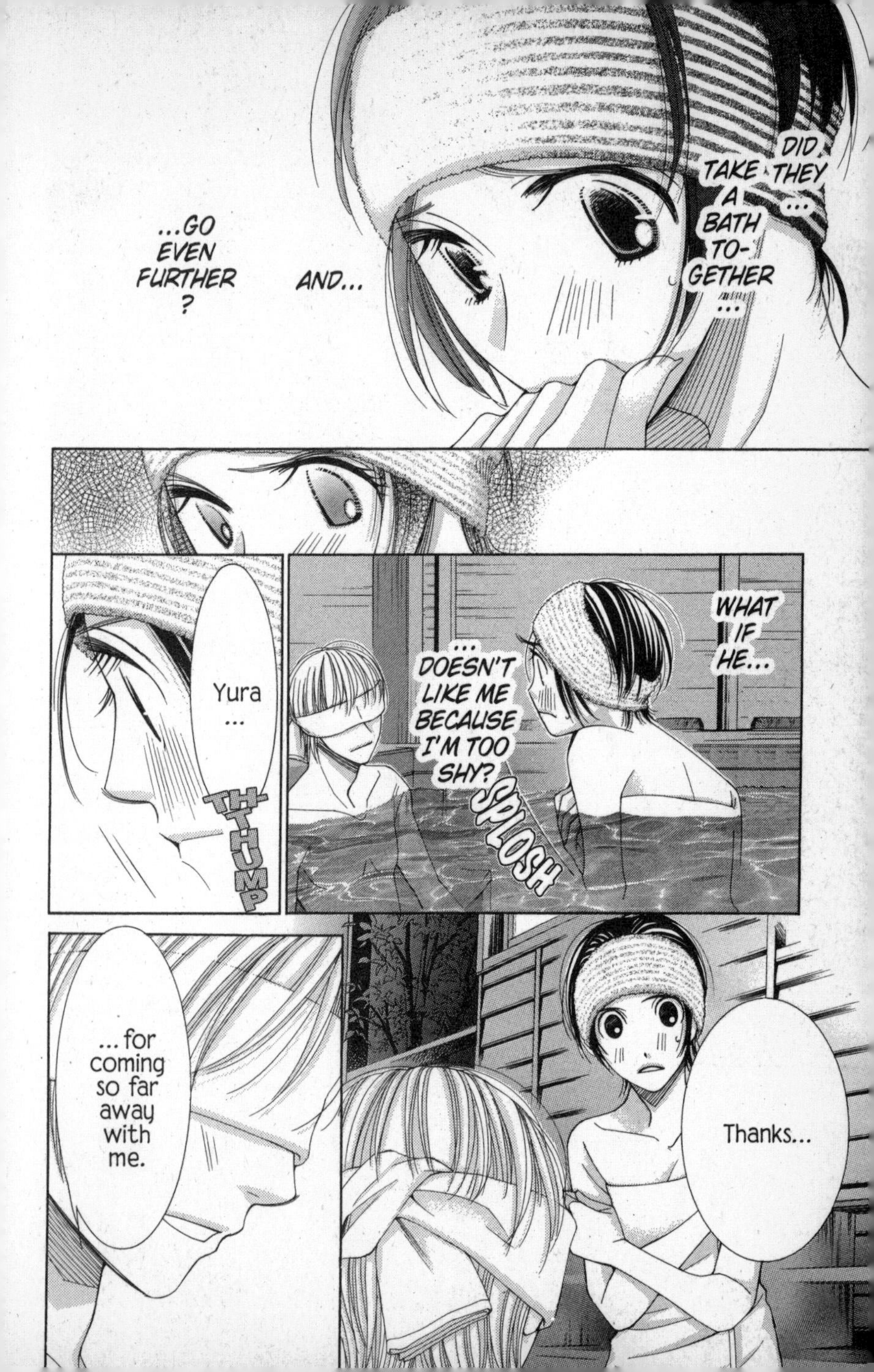
DID THEY...
TAKE A BATH TOGETHER...
AND...
...GO EVEN FURTHER?
WHAT IF HE...
...DOESN'T LIKE ME BECAUSE I'M TOO SHY?
SPLOSH
Yura...
TH-THUMP
Thanks...
...for coming so far away with me.

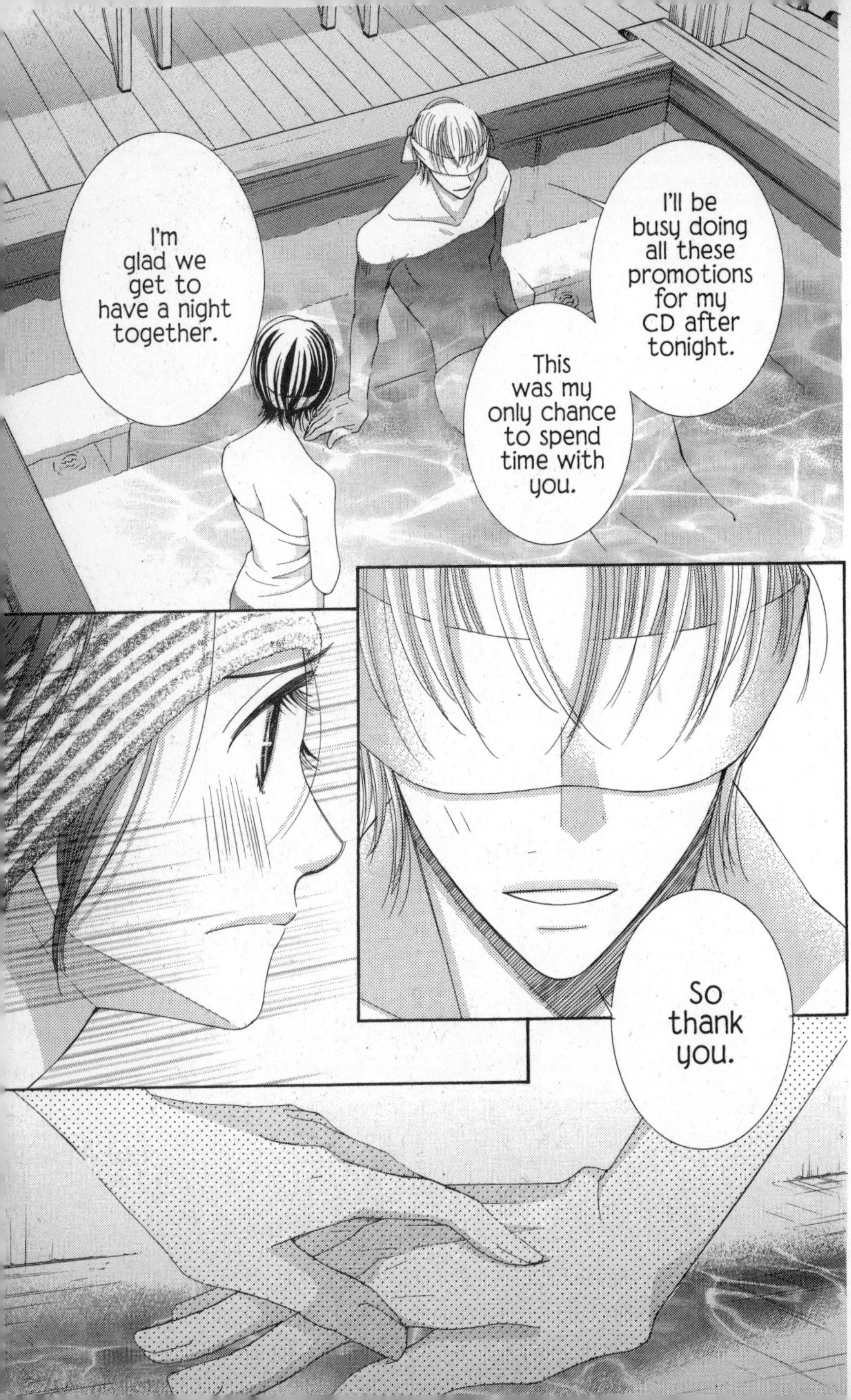
I'll be busy doing all these promotions for my CD after tonight.
This was my only chance to spend time with you.
I'm glad we get to have a night together.
So thank you.

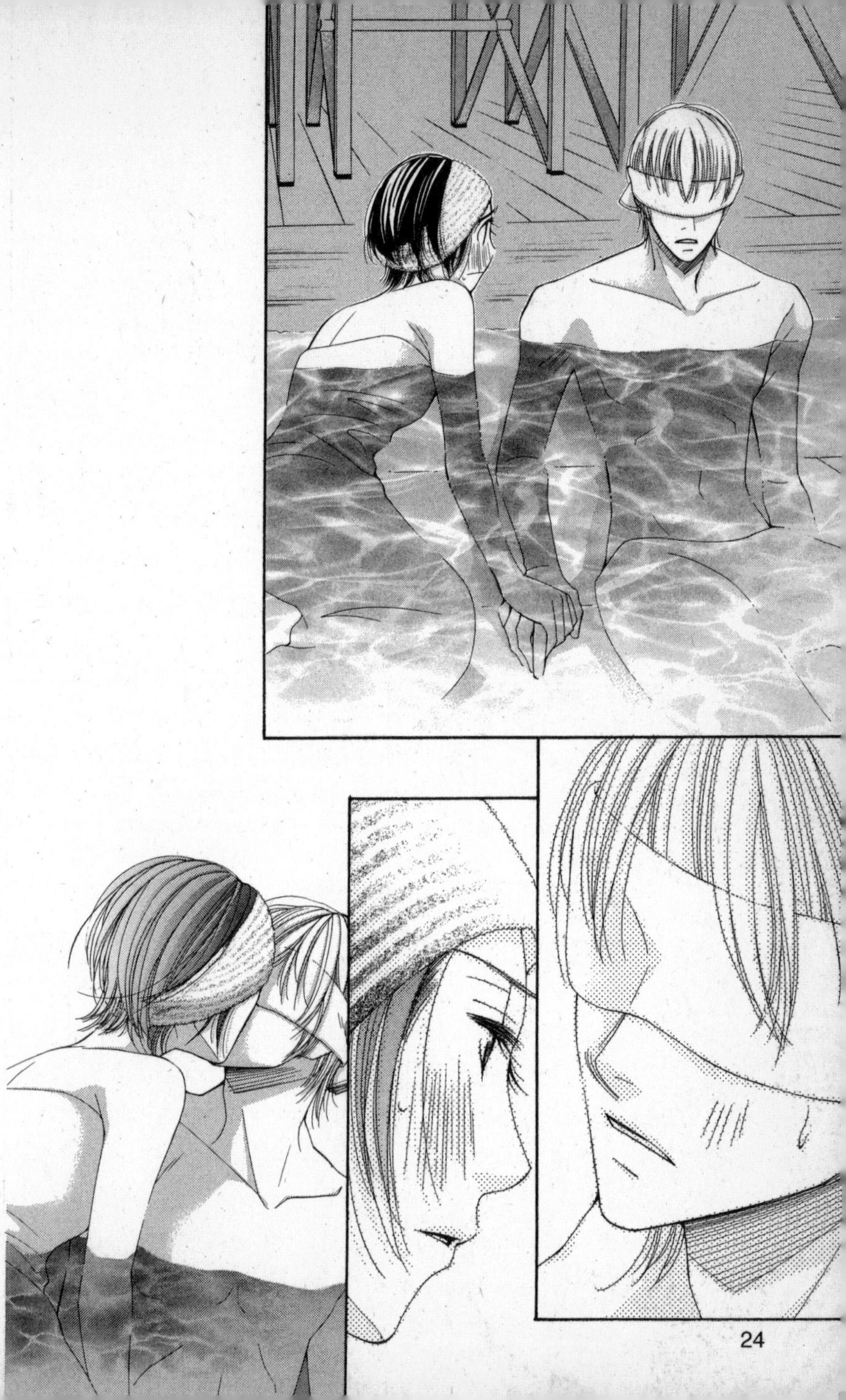

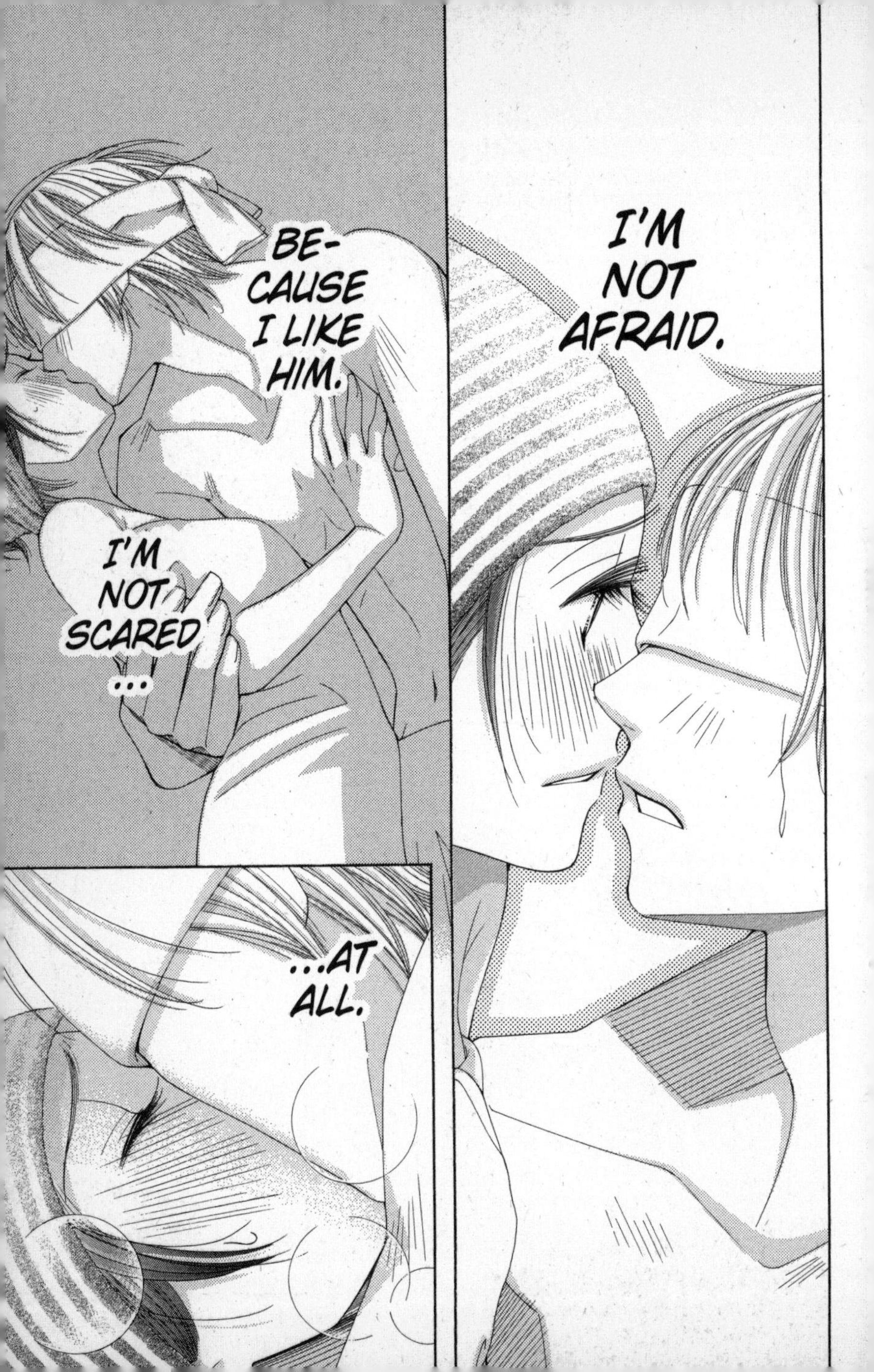
I'M NOT AFRAID.
BE-CAUSE I LIKE HIM.
I'M NOT SCARED ...
...AT ALL.

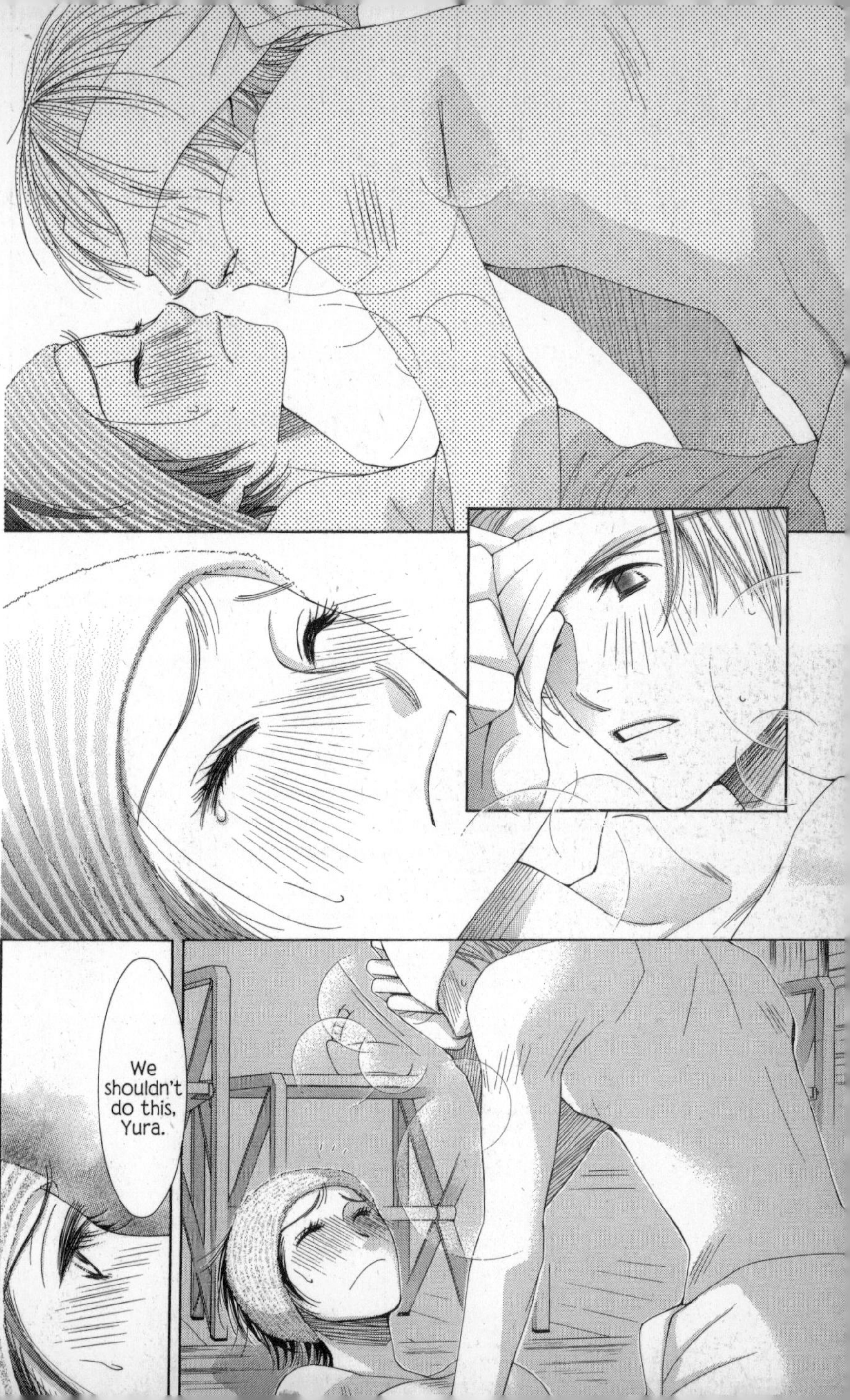
We shouldn't do this, Yura.

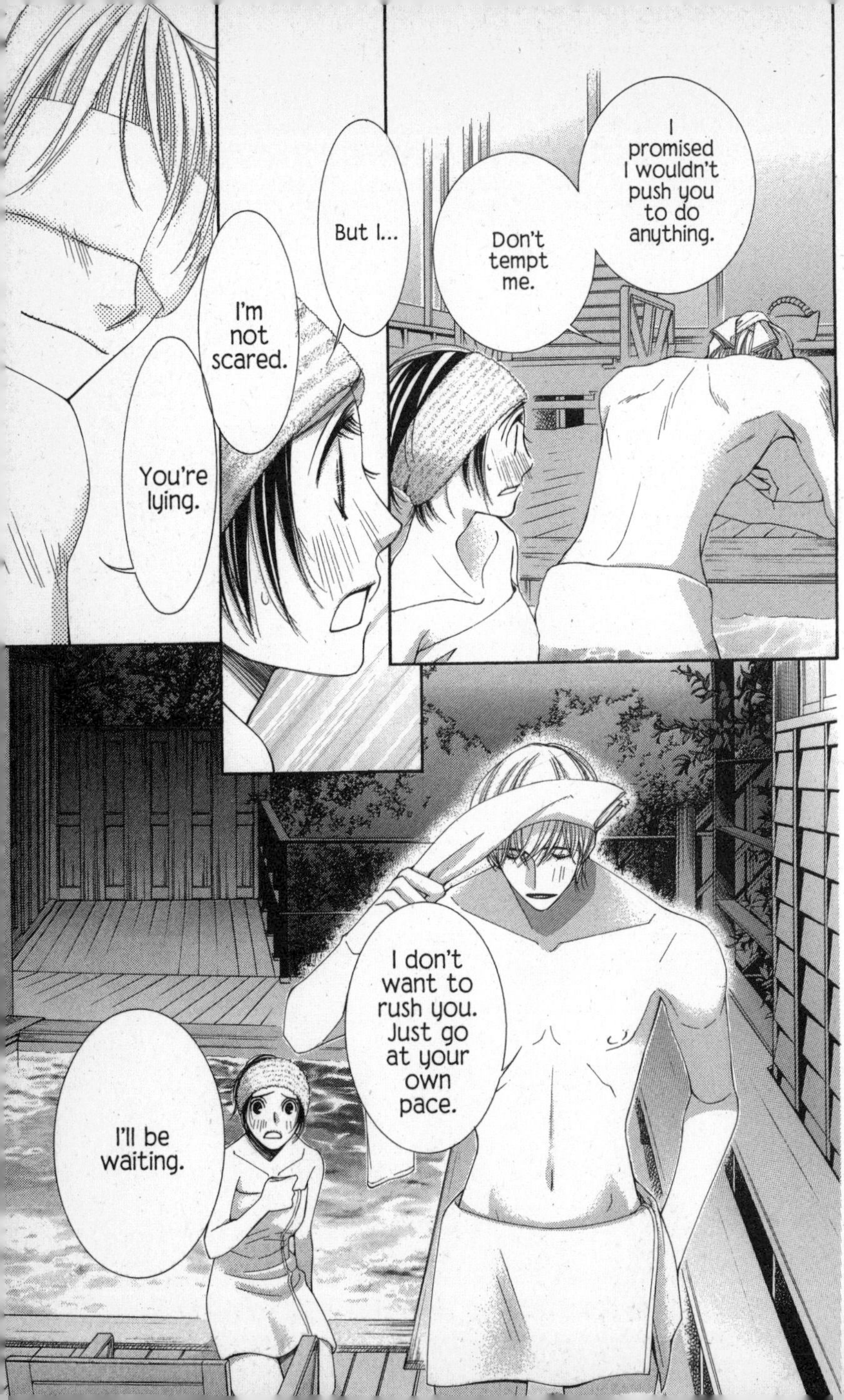
I promised I wouldn't push you to do anything.
Don't tempt me.
But I...
I'm not scared.
You're lying.
I don't want to rush you. Just go at your own pace.
I'll be waiting.

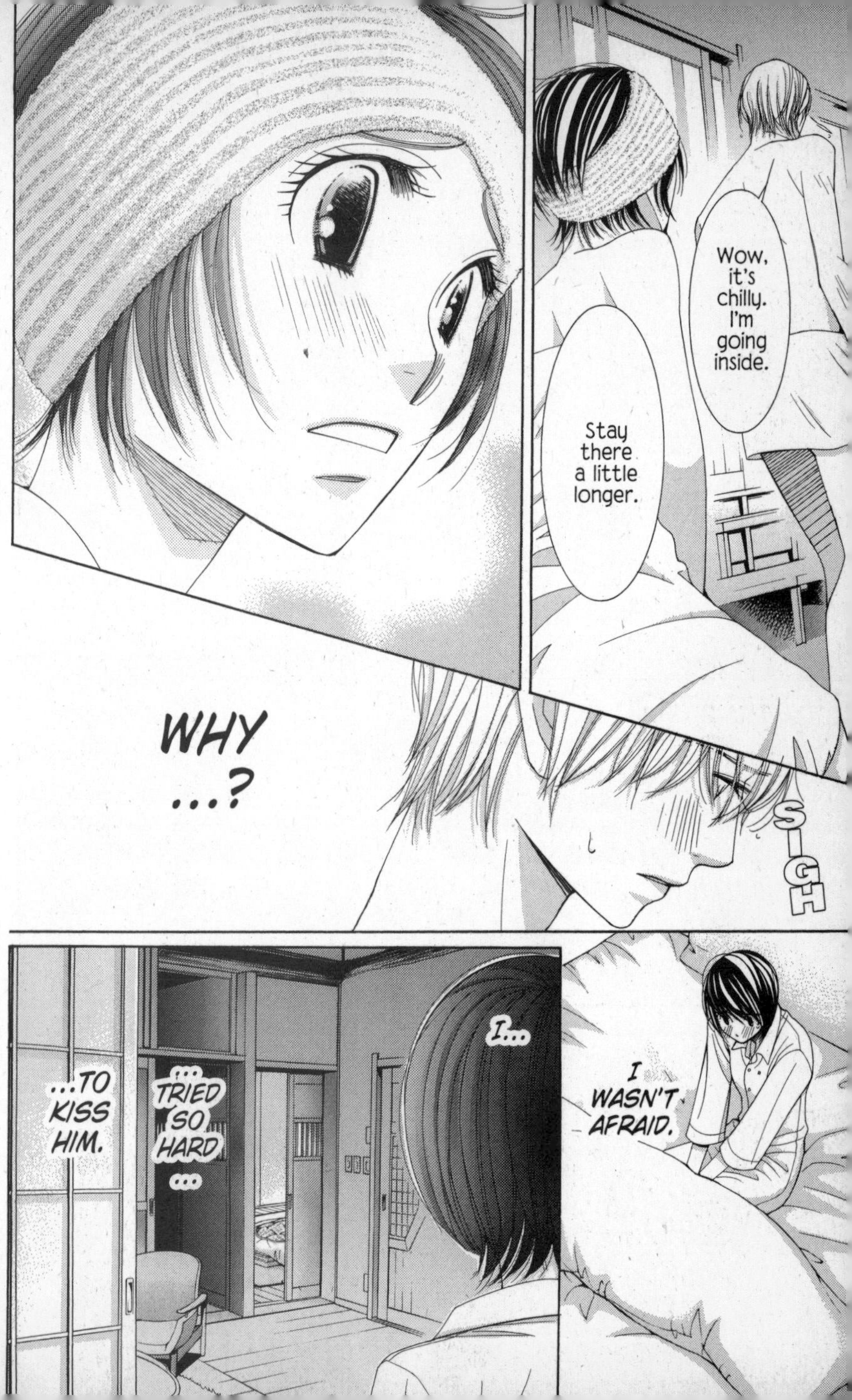
Wow, it's chilly. I'm going inside.
Stay there a little longer.
SIGH
WHY ...?
I WASN'T AFRAID.
I...
...TRIED SO HARD...
...TO KISS HIM.

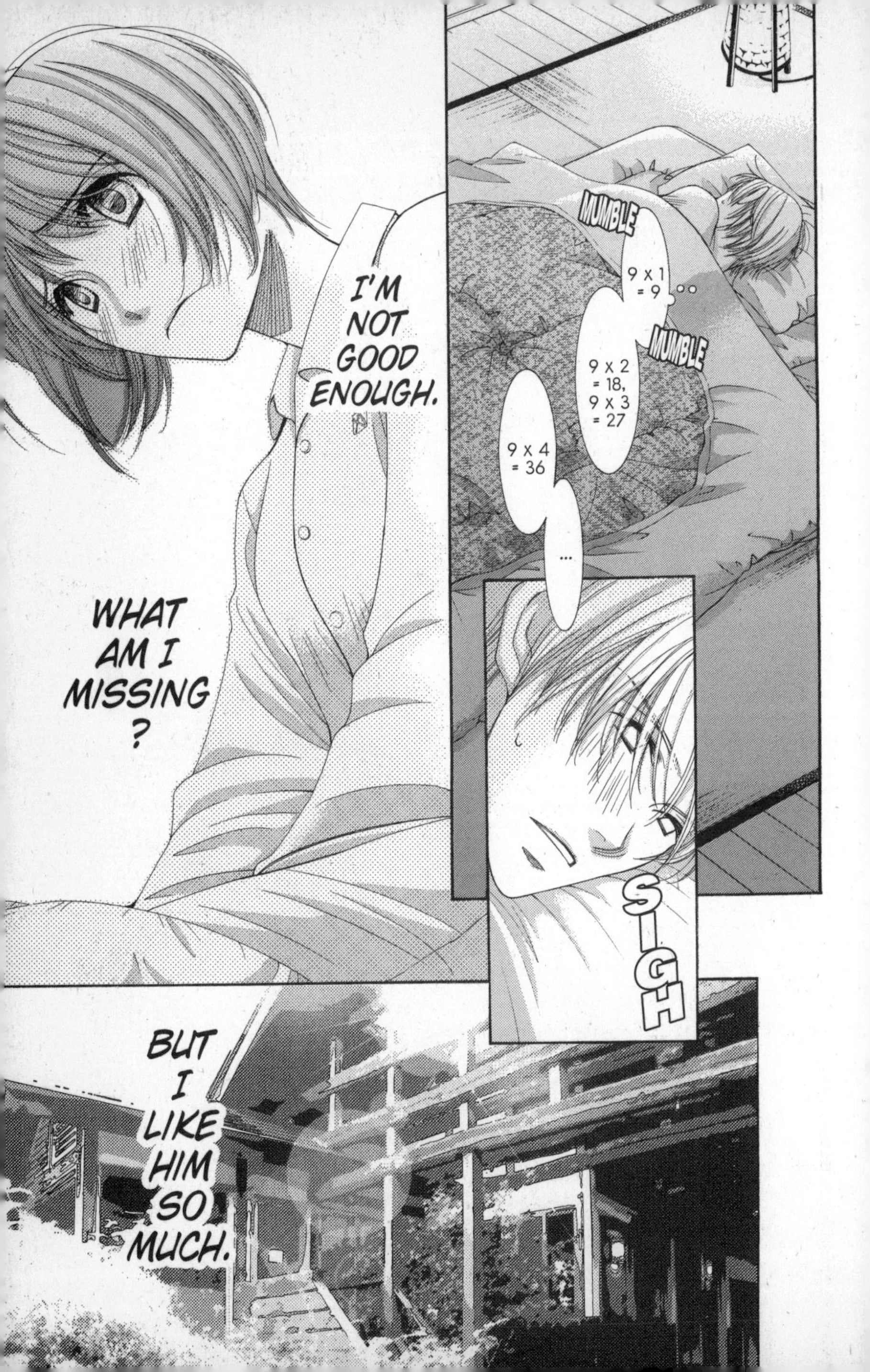
MUMBLE
9 x 1 = 9 ...
MUMBLE
9 x 2 = 18, 9 x 3 = 27
9 x 4 = 36
...
SIGH
I'M NOT GOOD ENOUGH.
WHAT AM I MISSING?
BUT I LIKE HIM SO MUCH.

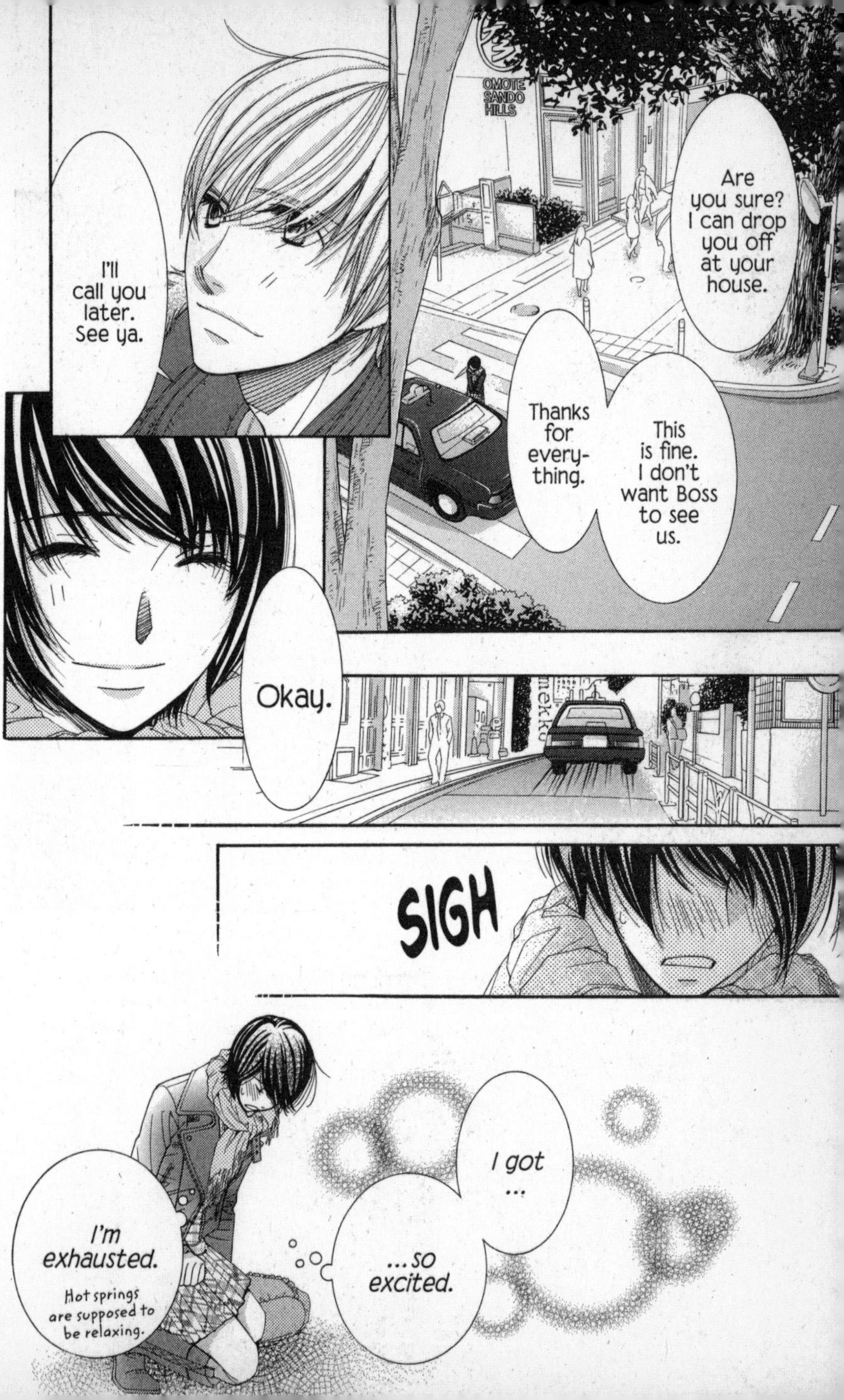
OMOTE SANDO HILLS
Are you sure? I can drop you off at your house.
This is fine. I don't want Boss to see us.
Thanks for every-thing.
I'll call you later. See ya.
Okay.
SIGH
I got ...
...so excited.
I'm exhausted.
Hot springs are supposed to be relaxing.

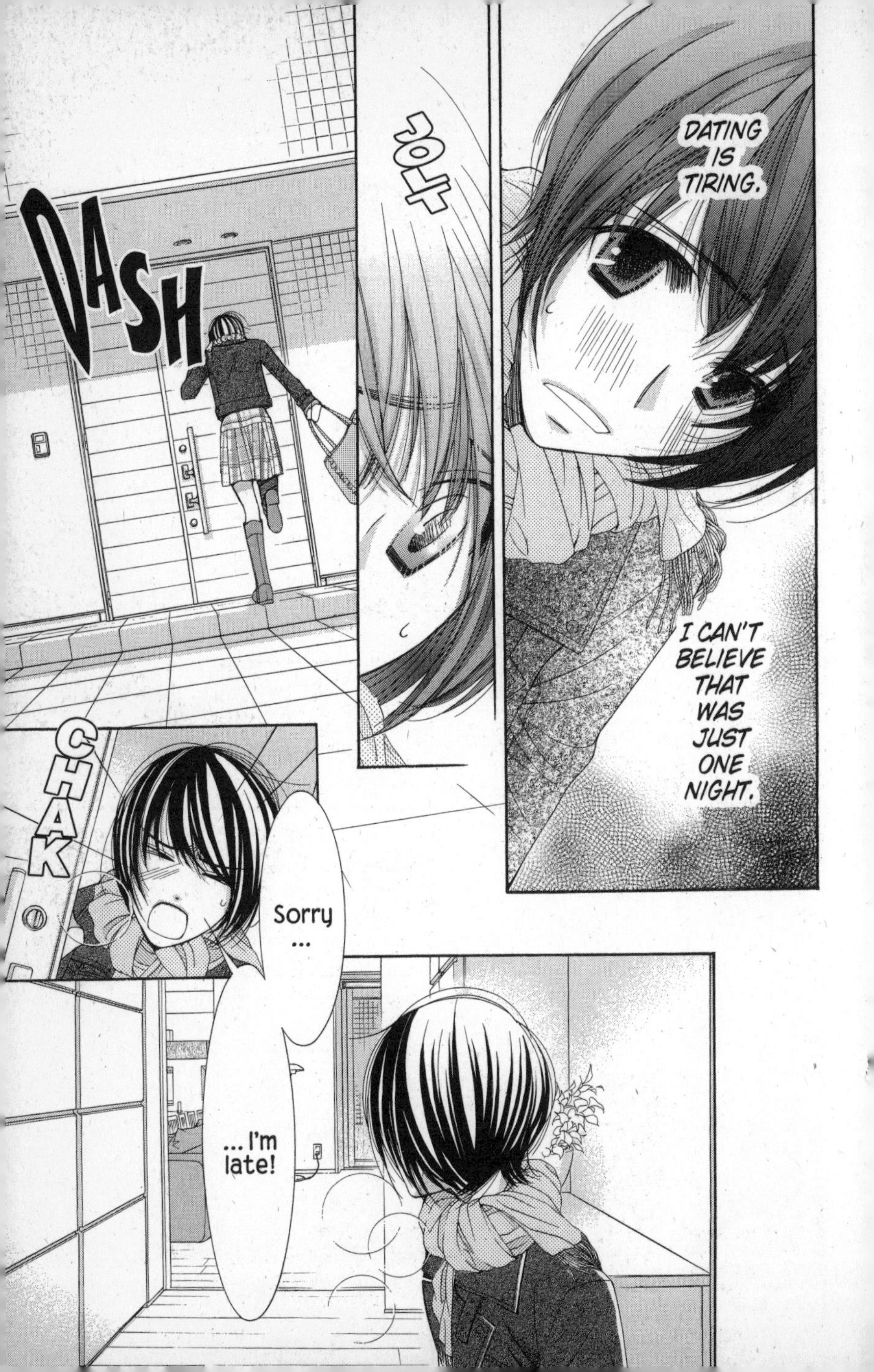
DATING IS TIRING.
I CAN'T BELIEVE THAT WAS JUST ONE NIGHT.
JOLT
DASH
CHAK
Sorry ...
... I'm late!

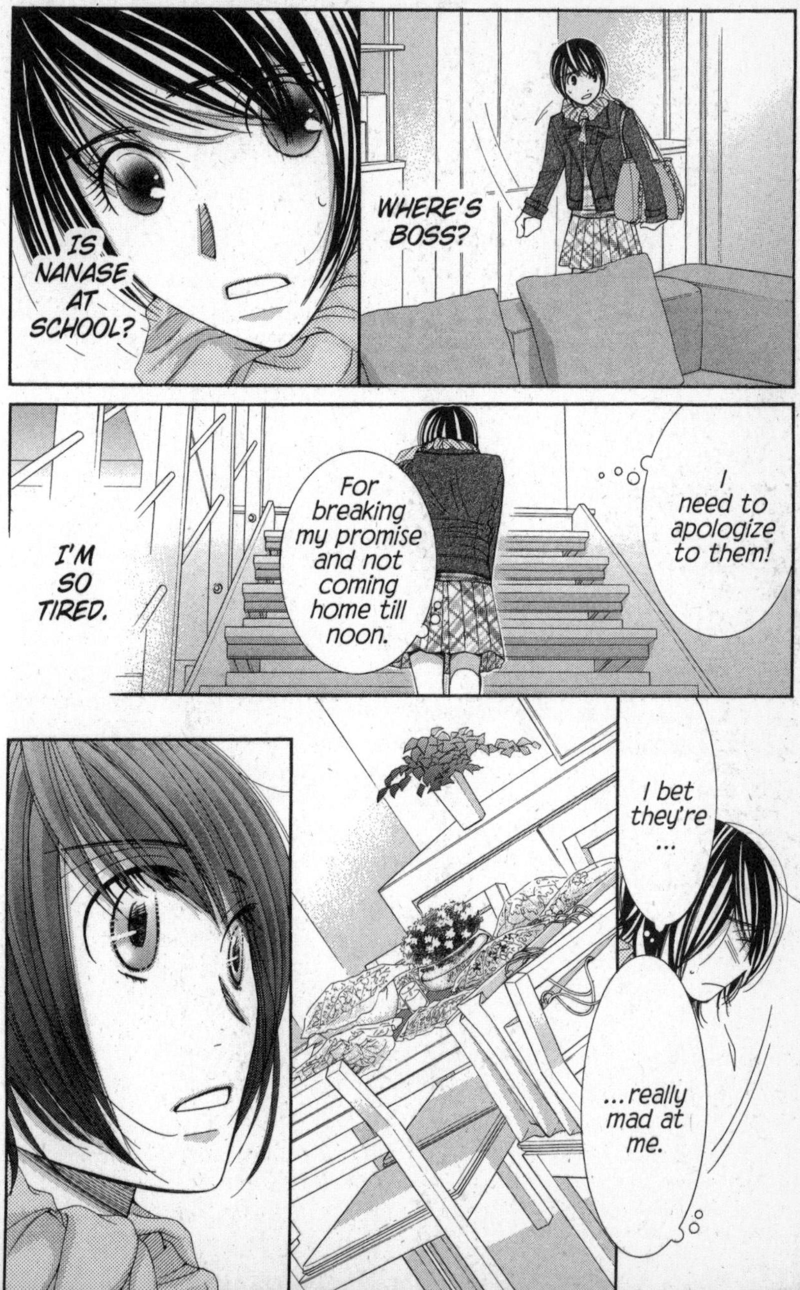
WHERE'S BOSS?
IS NANASE AT SCHOOL?
I need to apologize to them!
For breaking my promise and not coming home till noon.
I'M SO TIRED.
I bet they're ...
...really mad at me.

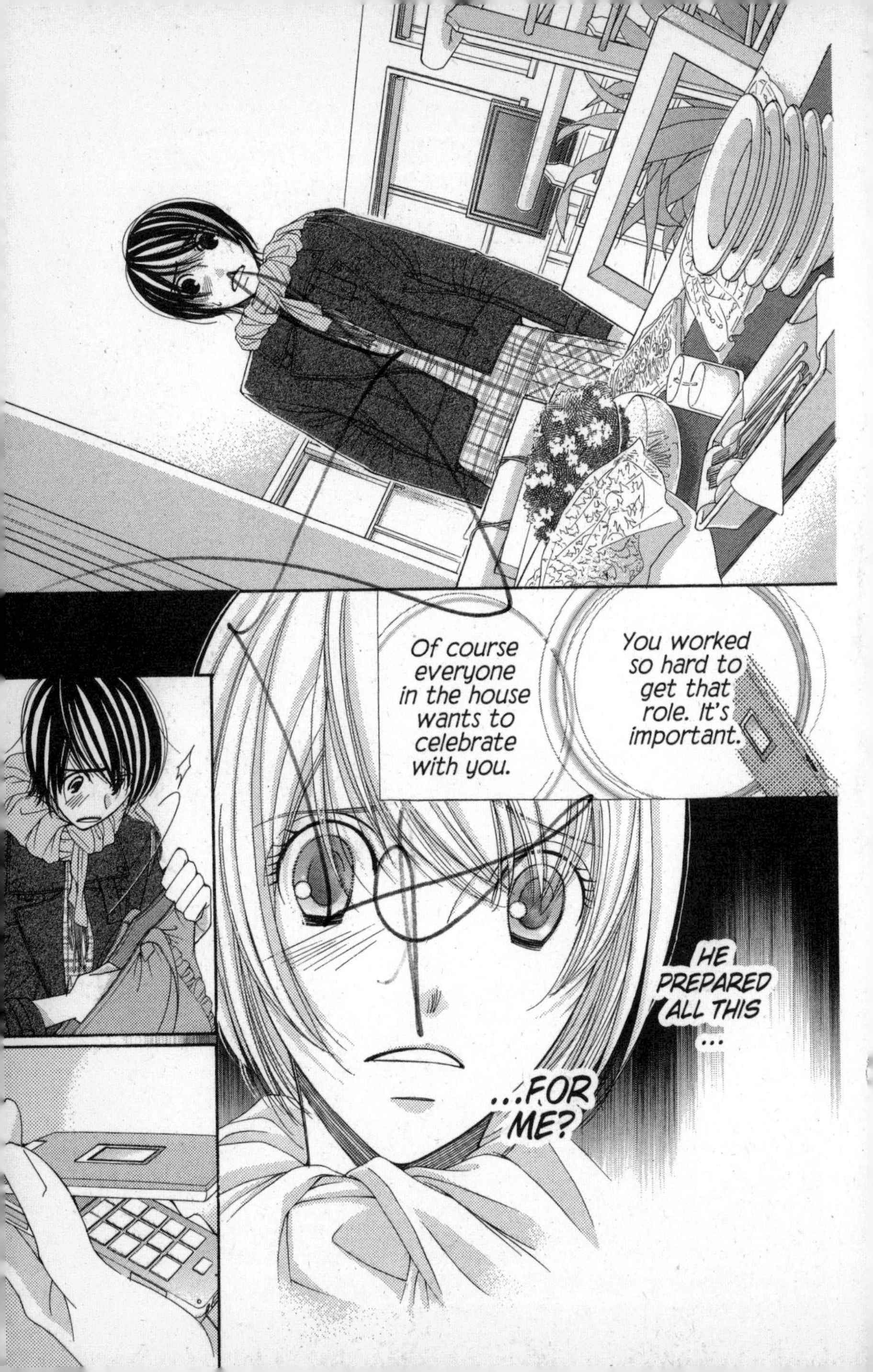
You worked so hard to get that role. It's important.
Of course everyone in the house wants to celebrate with you.
HE PREPARED ALL THIS ...
...FOR ME?

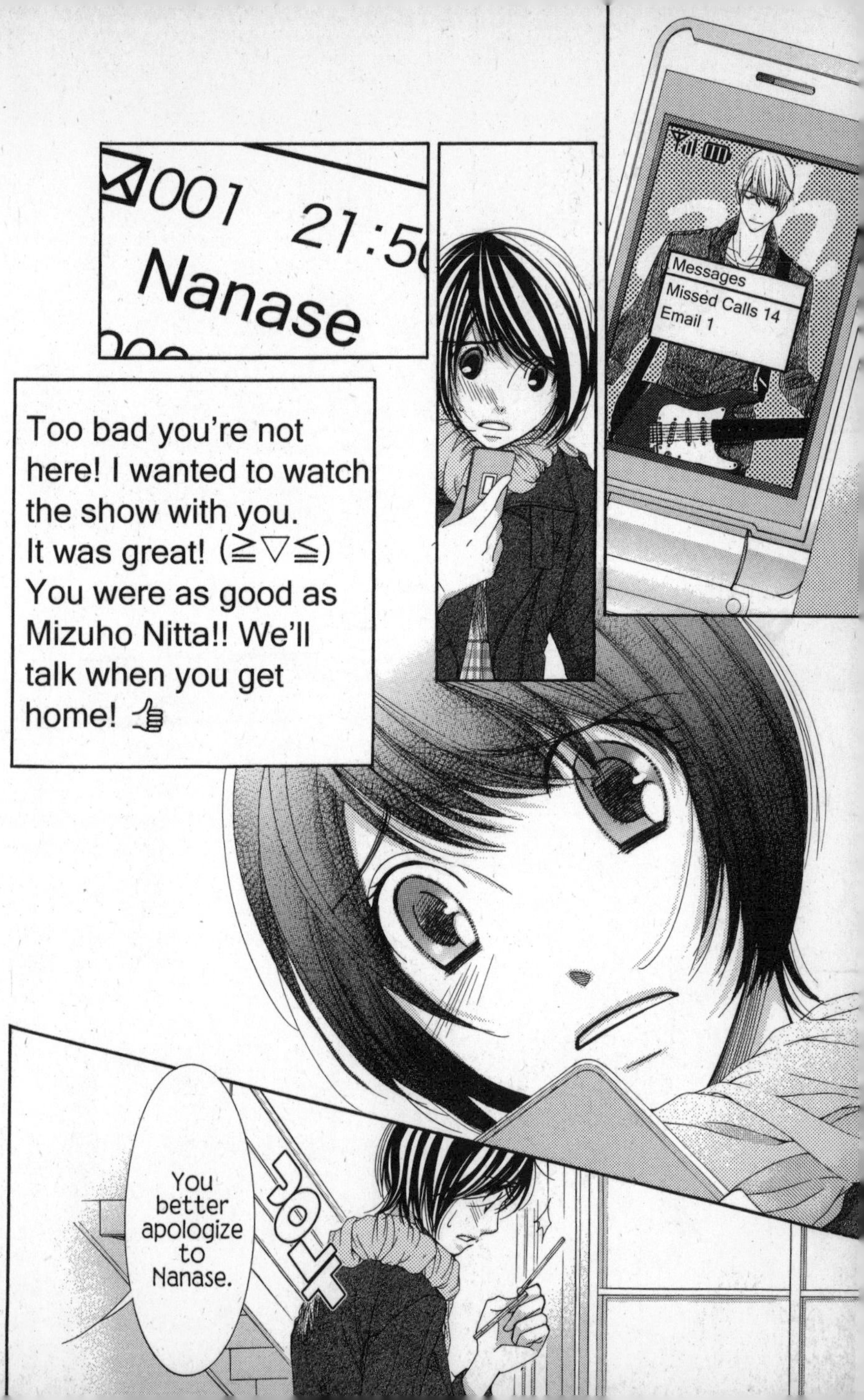
Messages
Missed Calls 14
Email 1
001 21:5
Nanase
Too bad you're not here! I wanted to watch the show with you. It was great! (≧▽≦) You were as good as Mizuho Nitta!! We'll talk when you get home!
JOLT
You better apologize to Nanase.

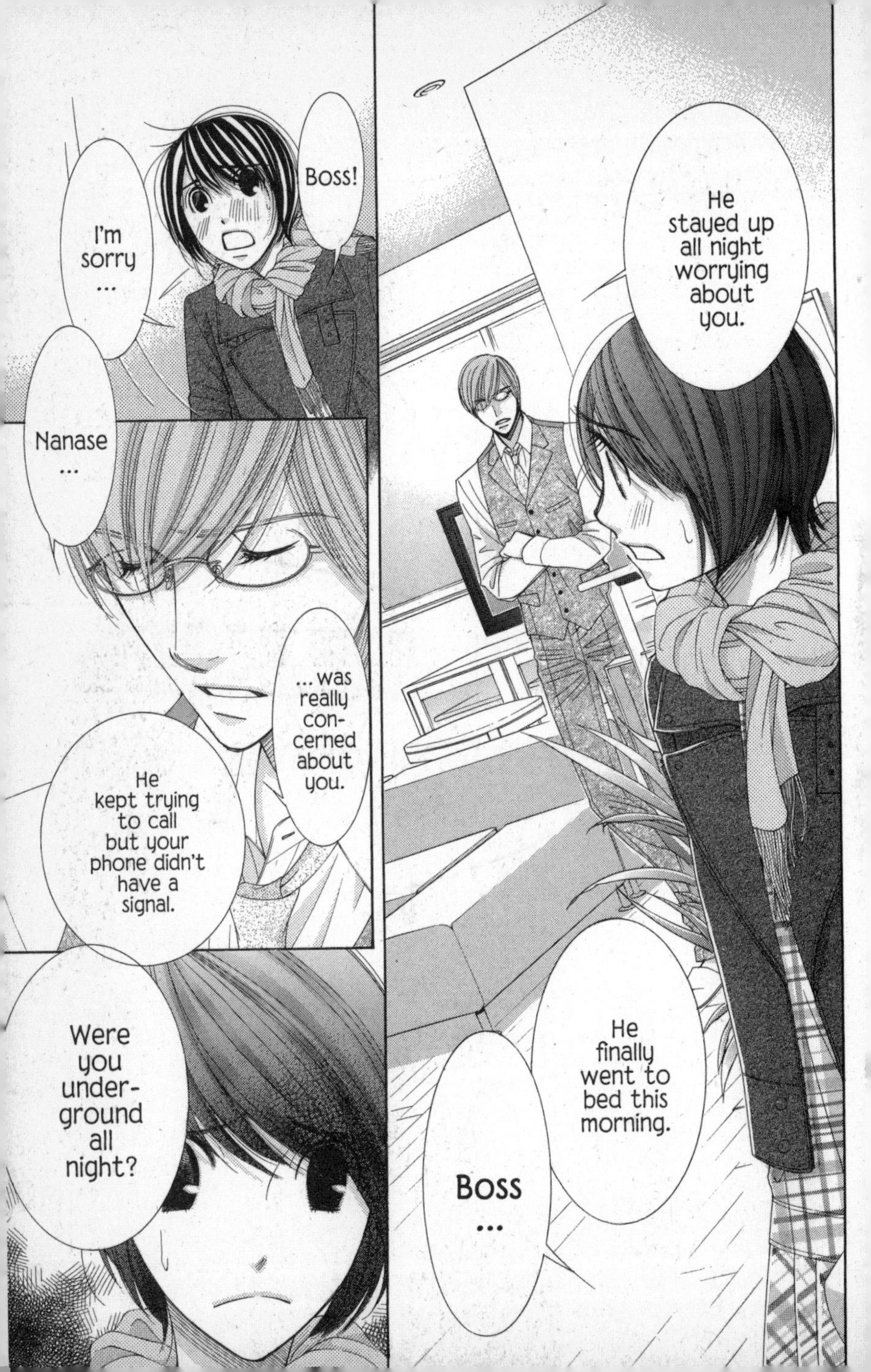
He stayed up all night worrying about you.
He finally went to bed this morning.
Boss ...
Boss!
I'm sorry ...
Nanase ...
... was really concerned about you.
He kept trying to call but your phone didn't have a signal.
Were you under-ground all night?

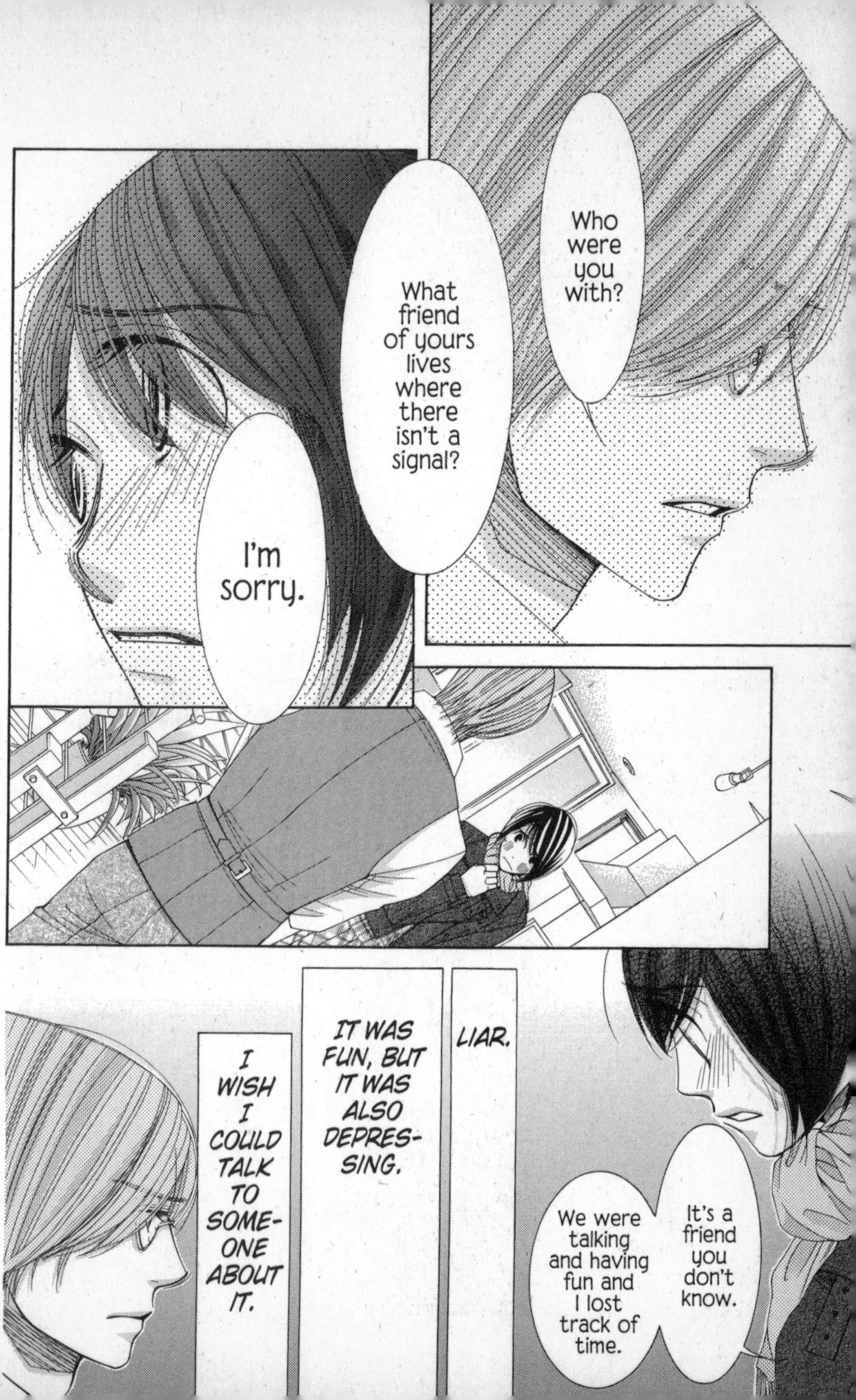
Who were you with?
What friend of yours lives where there isn't a signal?
I'm sorry.
LIAR.
IT WAS FUN, BUT IT WAS ALSO DEPRESSING.
I WISH I COULD TALK TO SOMEONE ABOUT IT.
It's a friend you don't know.
We were talking and having fun and I lost track of time.

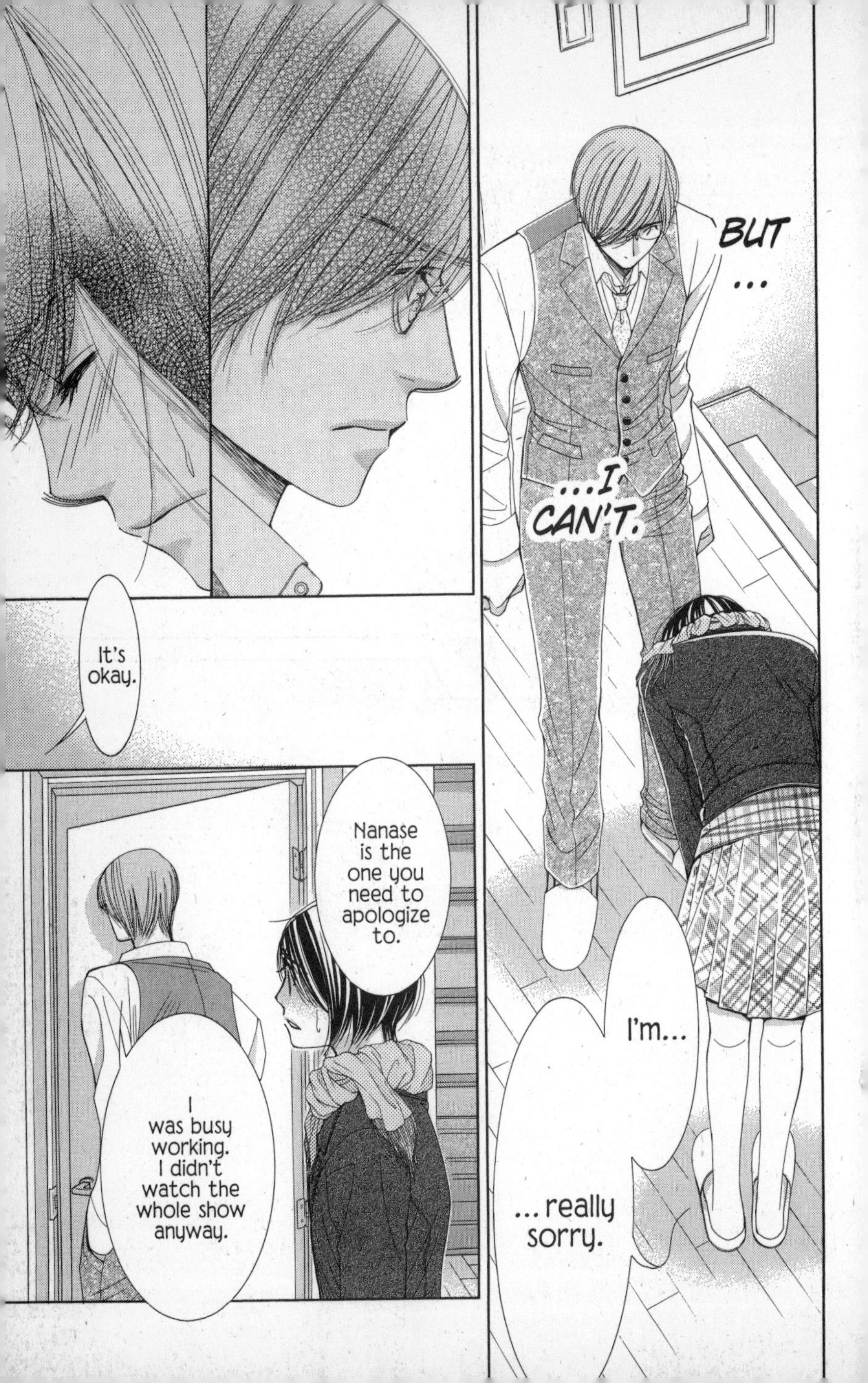
BUT ...
...I CAN'T.
I'm...
...really sorry.
It's okay.
Nanase is the one you need to apologize to.
I was busy working. I didn't watch the whole show anyway.

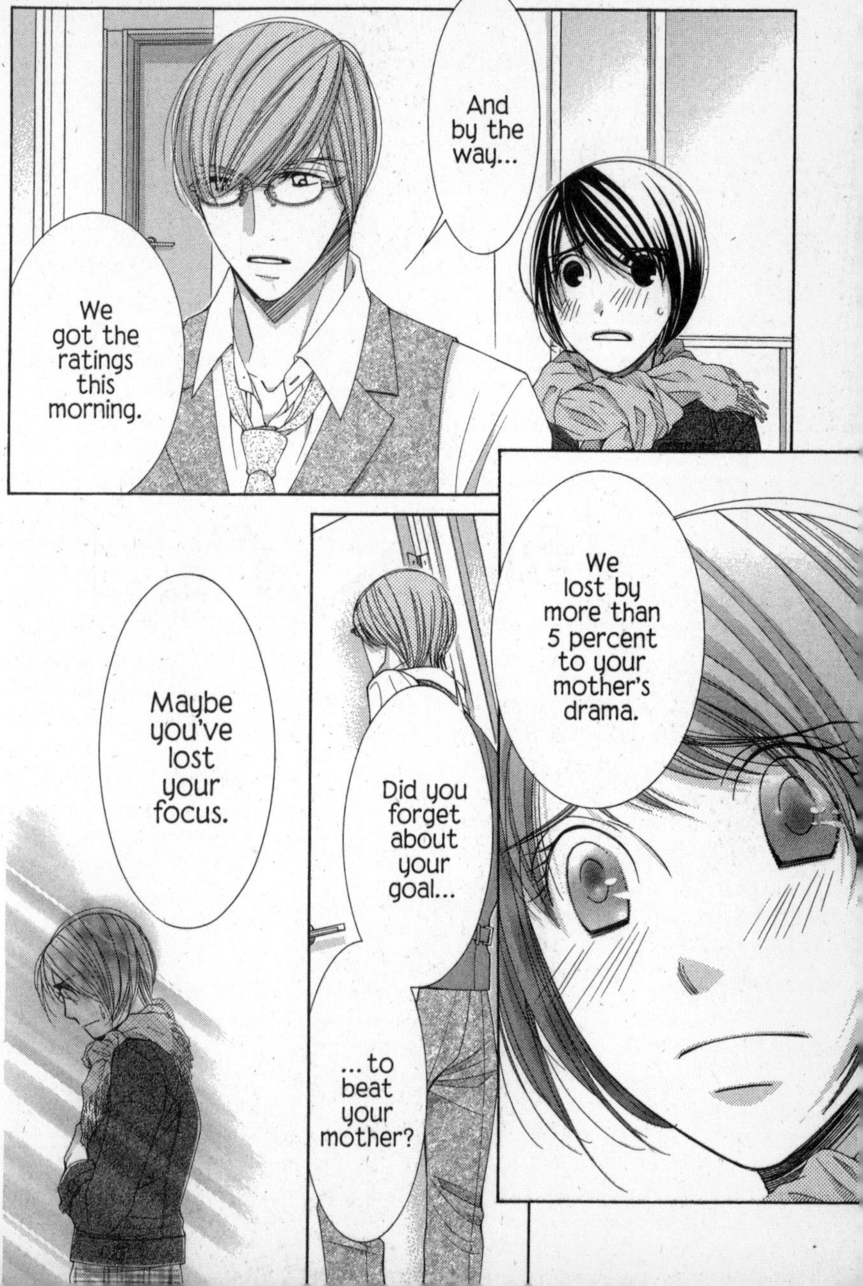
And by the way...
We got the ratings this morning.
We lost by more than 5 percent to your mother's drama.
Did you forget about your goal...
...to beat your mother?
Maybe you've lost your focus.

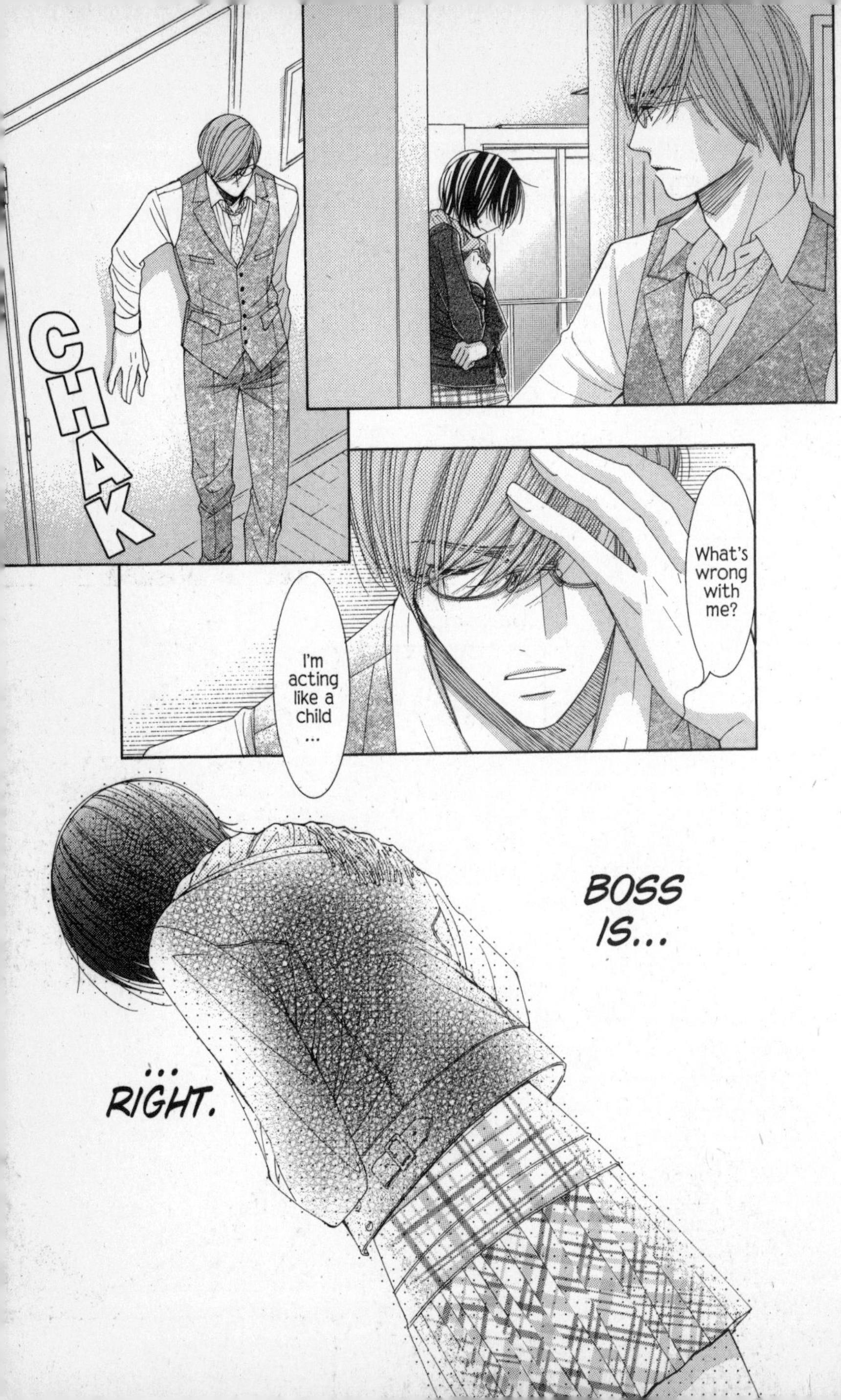
CHAK
What's wrong with me?
I'm acting like a child ...
BOSS IS...
... RIGHT.

Honey Hunt 05

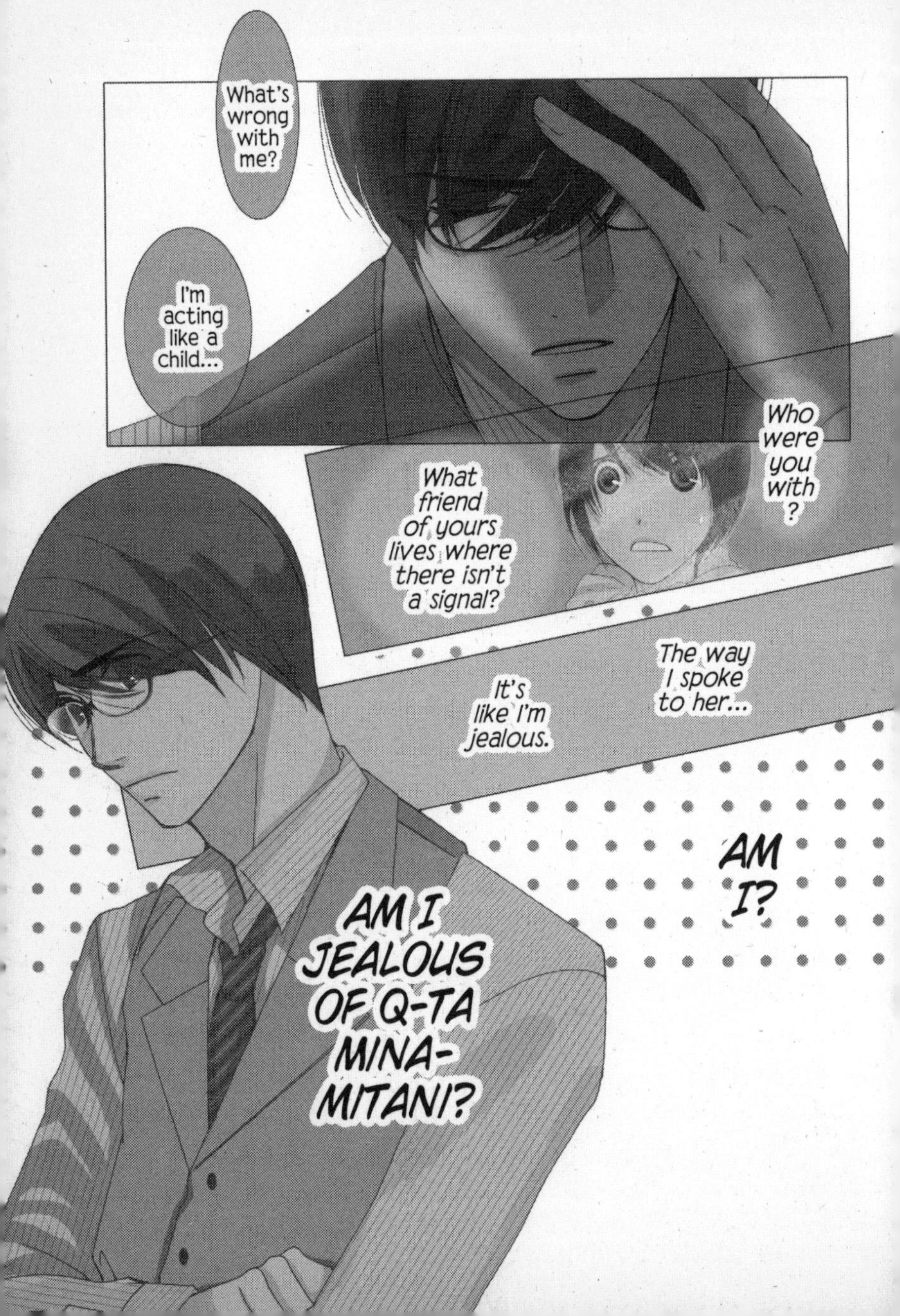
What's wrong with me?
I'm acting like a child...
Who were you with?
What friend of yours lives where there isn't a signal?
The way I spoke to her...
It's like I'm jealous.
AM I?
AM I JEALOUS OF Q-TA MINA-MITANI?

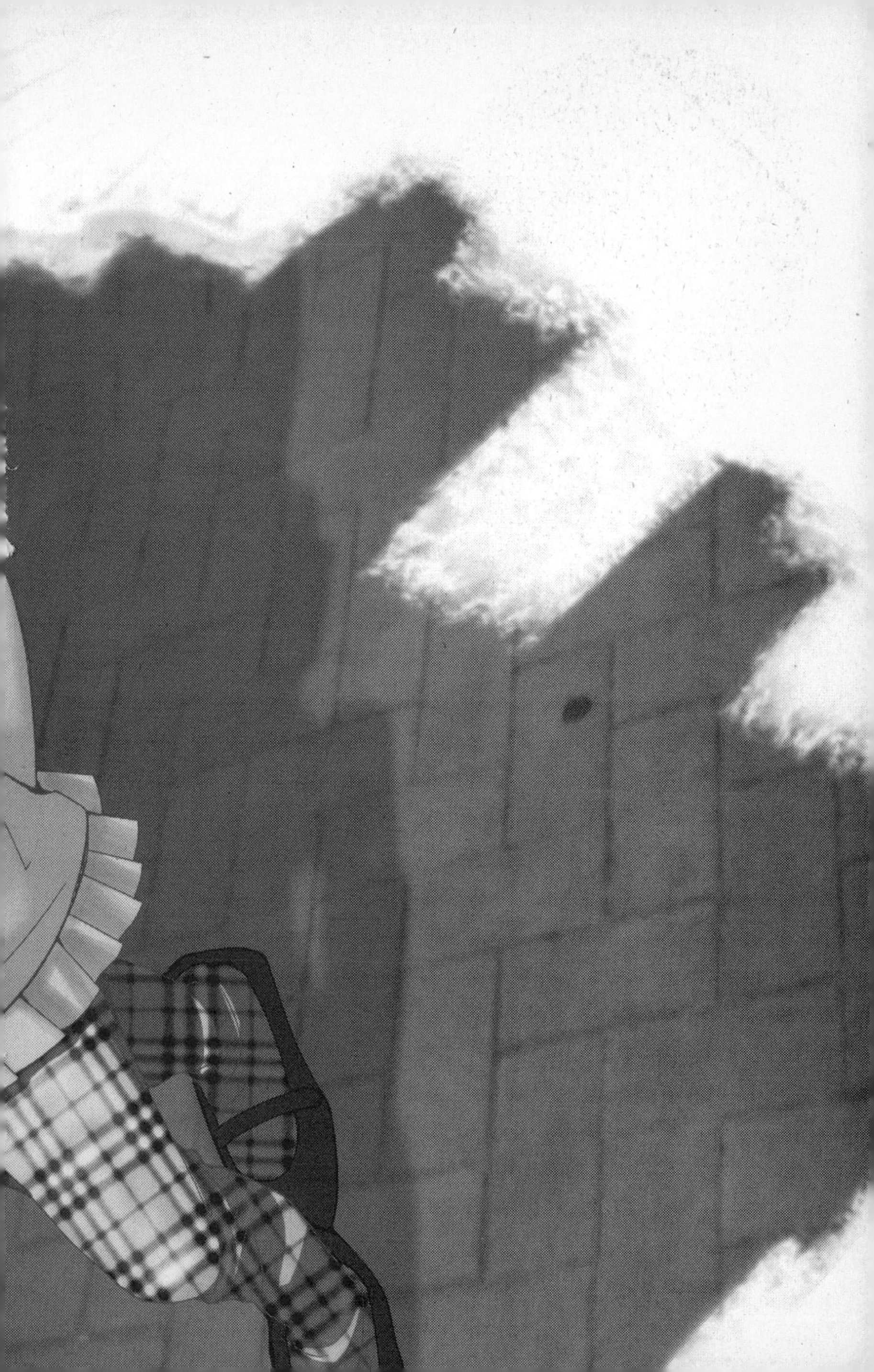

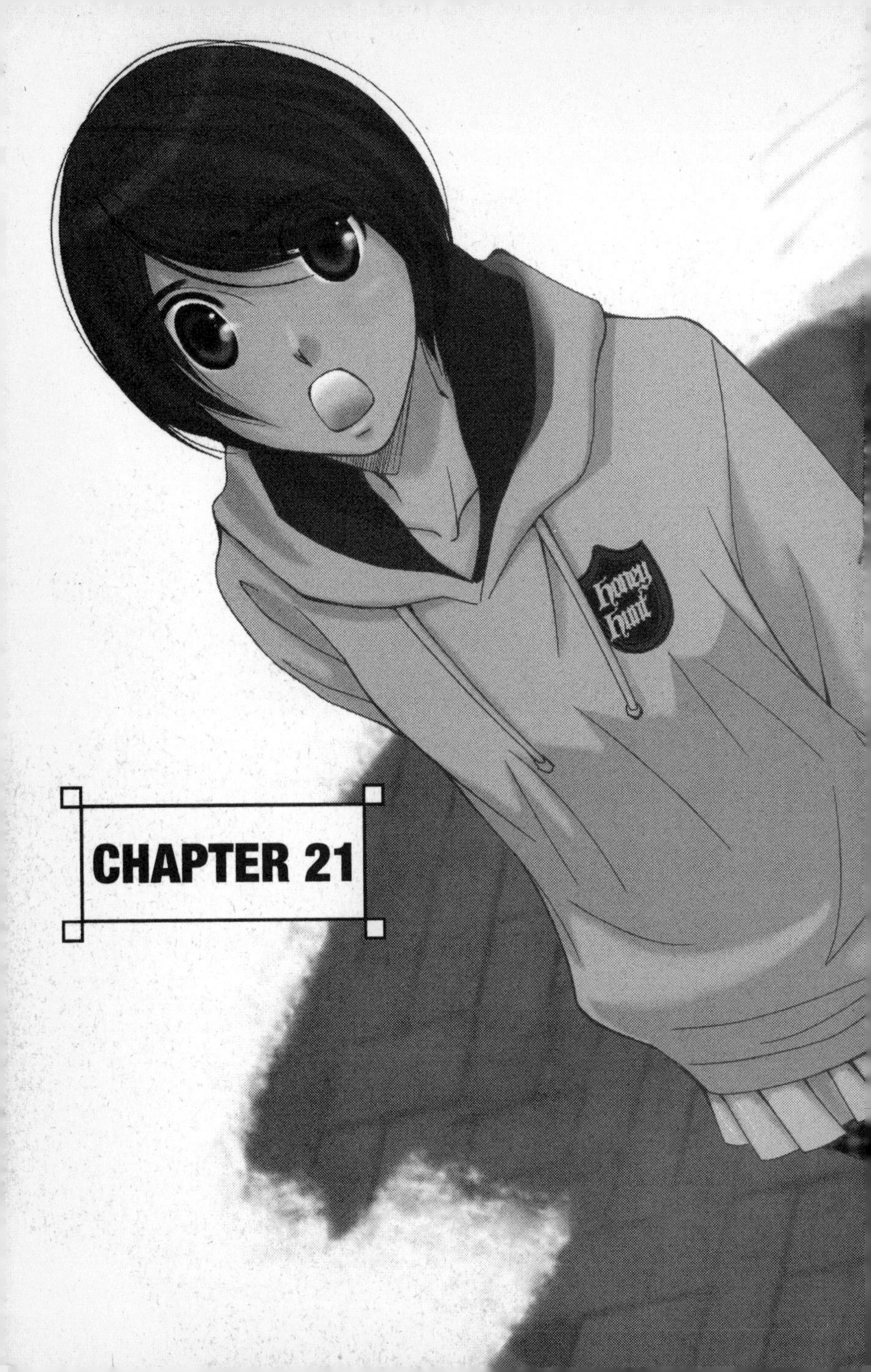
CHAPTER 21
Honey Hunt

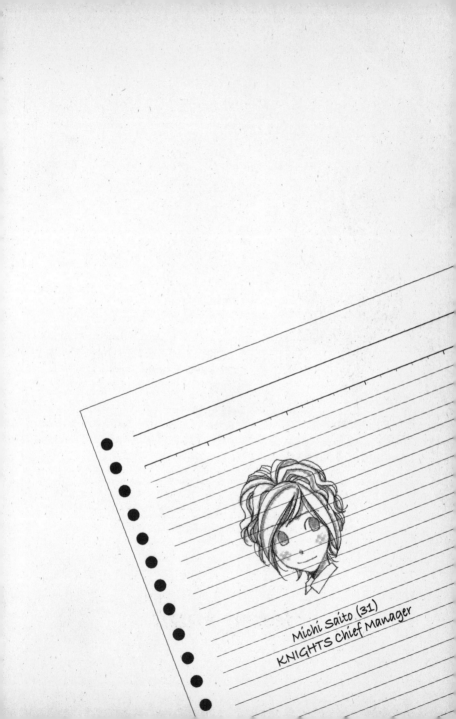

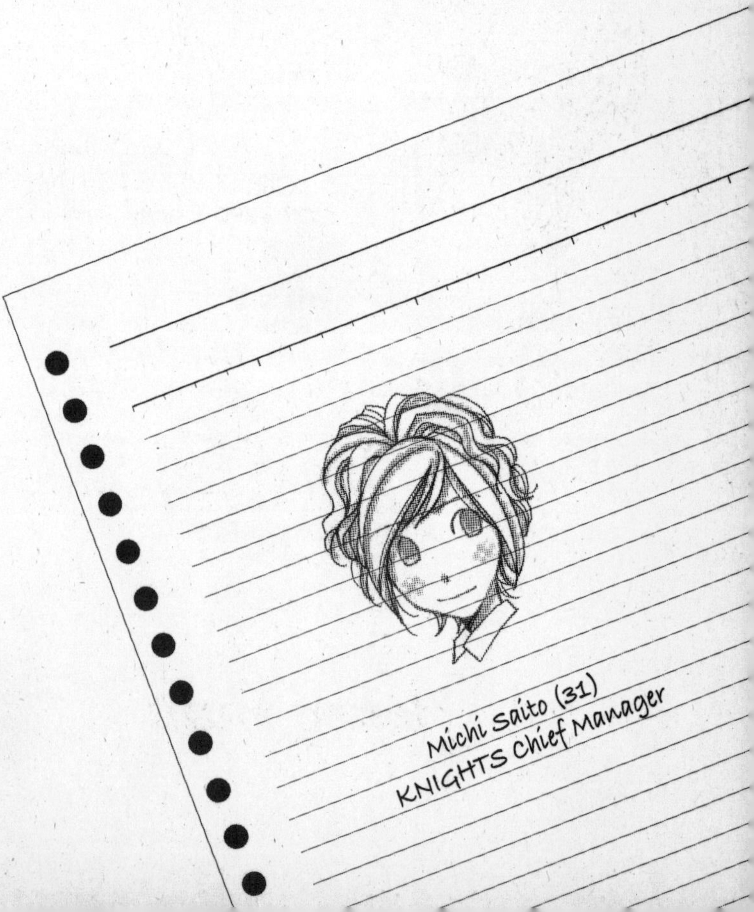
Michi Saito (31)
KNIGHTS Chief Manager

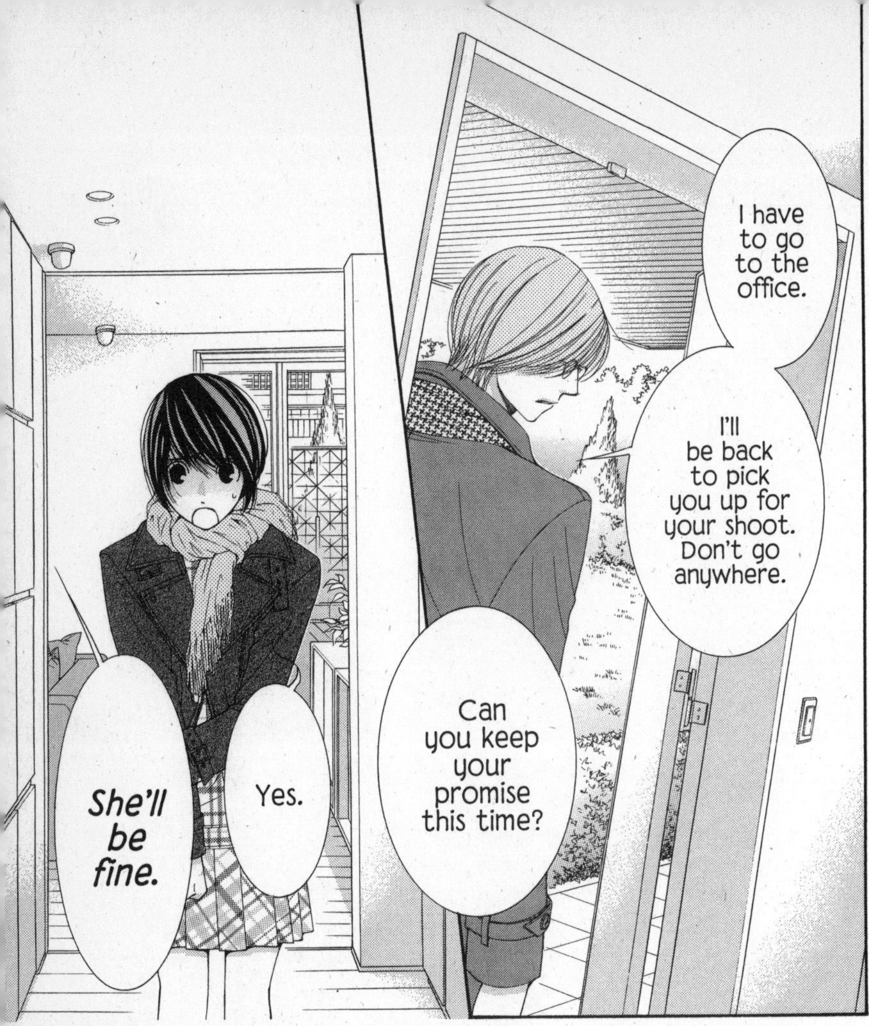
I have to go to the office.
I'll be back to pick you up for your shoot. Don't go anywhere.
Can you keep your promise this time?
Yes.
She'll be fine.

Honey Hunt

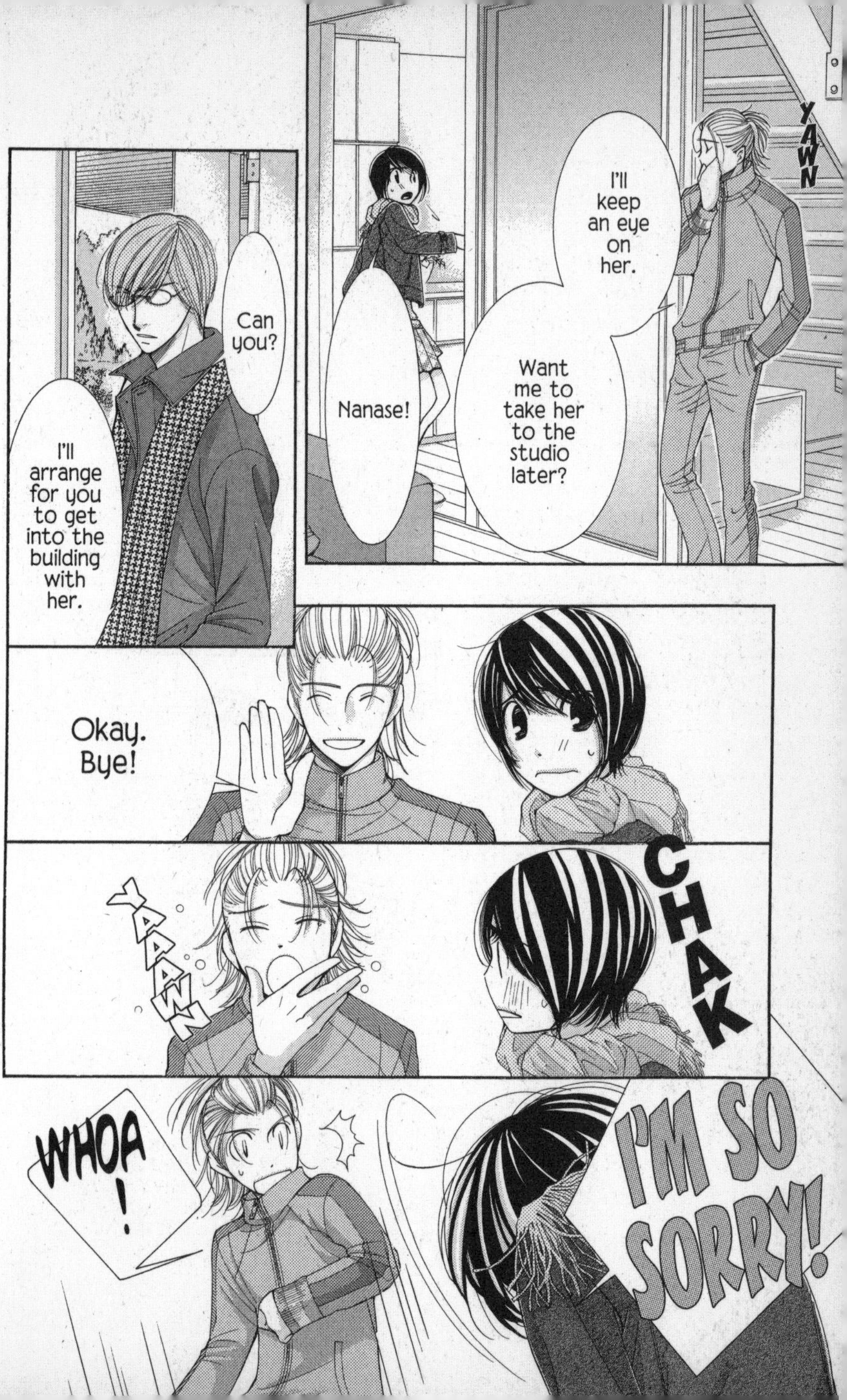
YAWN
I'll keep an eye on her.
Want me to take her to the studio later?
Nanase!
Can you?
I'll arrange for you to get into the building with her.
Okay. Bye!
CHAK
YAAAWN
I'M SO SORRY!
WHOA!

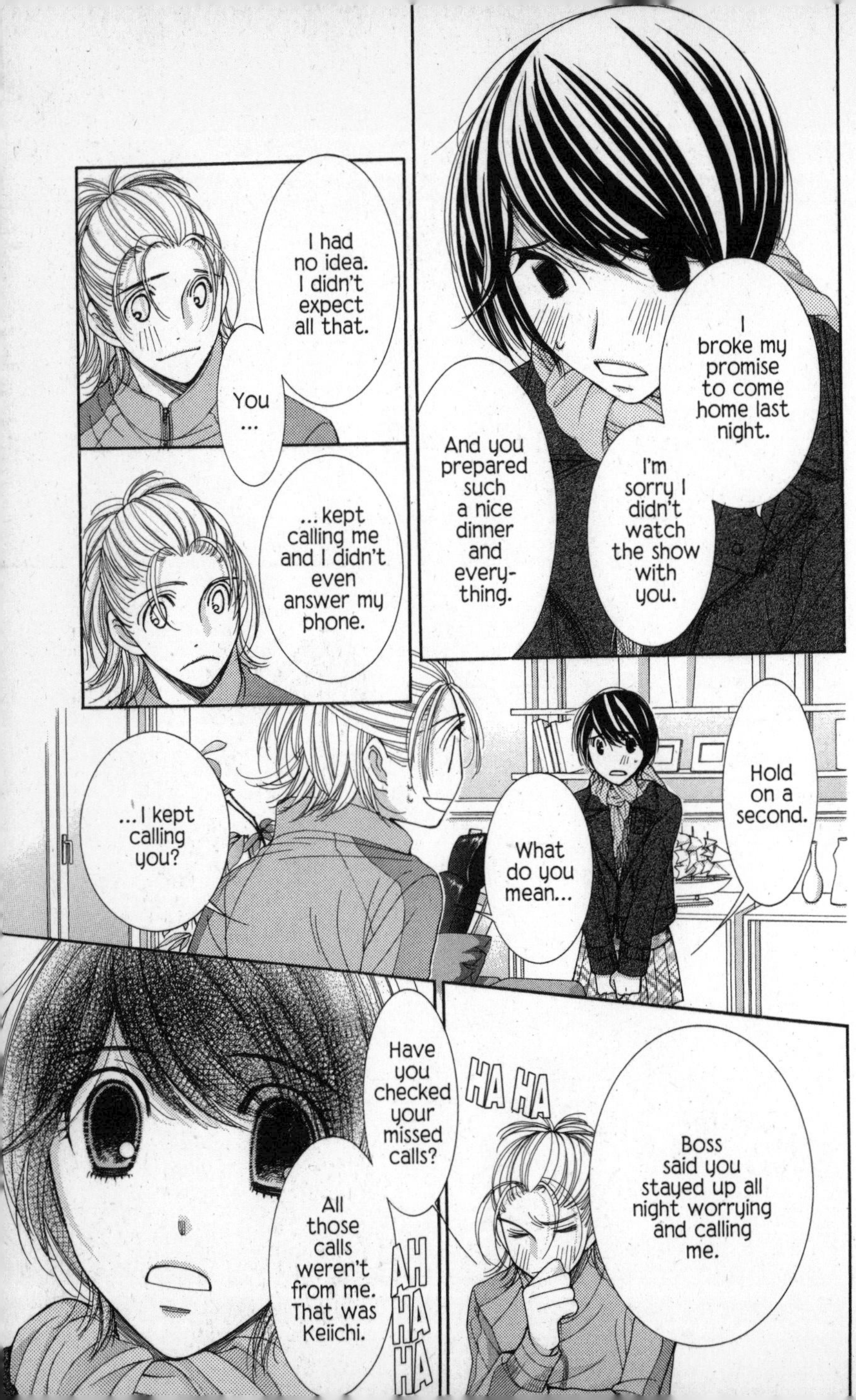
I broke my promise to come home last night.
I'm sorry I didn't watch the show with you.
And you prepared such a nice dinner and everything.
I had no idea. I didn't expect all that.
You ...
...kept calling me and I didn't even answer my phone.
Hold on a second.
What do you mean...
...I kept calling you?
Boss said you stayed up all night worrying and calling me.
HA HA
Have you checked your missed calls?
All those calls weren't from me. That was Keiichi.
AH HA HA HA

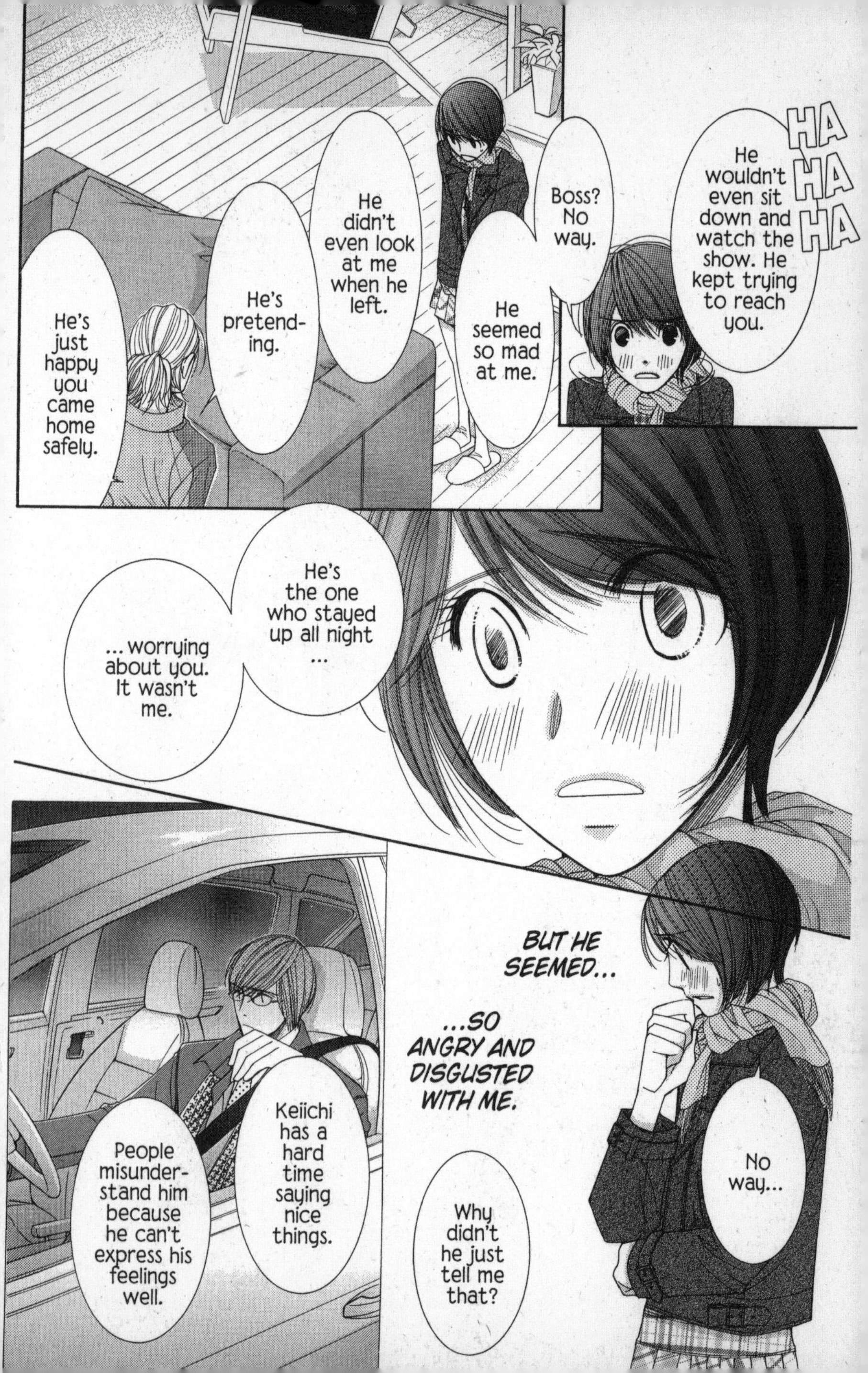
He wouldn't even sit down and watch the show. He kept trying to reach you.
HA HA HA
Boss? No way.
He seemed so mad at me.
He didn't even look at me when he left.
He's pretend-ing.
He's just happy you came home safely.
He's the one who stayed up all night ...
...worrying about you. It wasn't me.
BUT HE SEEMED...
...SO ANGRY AND DISGUSTED WITH ME.
No way...
Why didn't he just tell me that?
Keiichi has a hard time saying nice things.
People misunder-stand him because he can't express his feelings well.

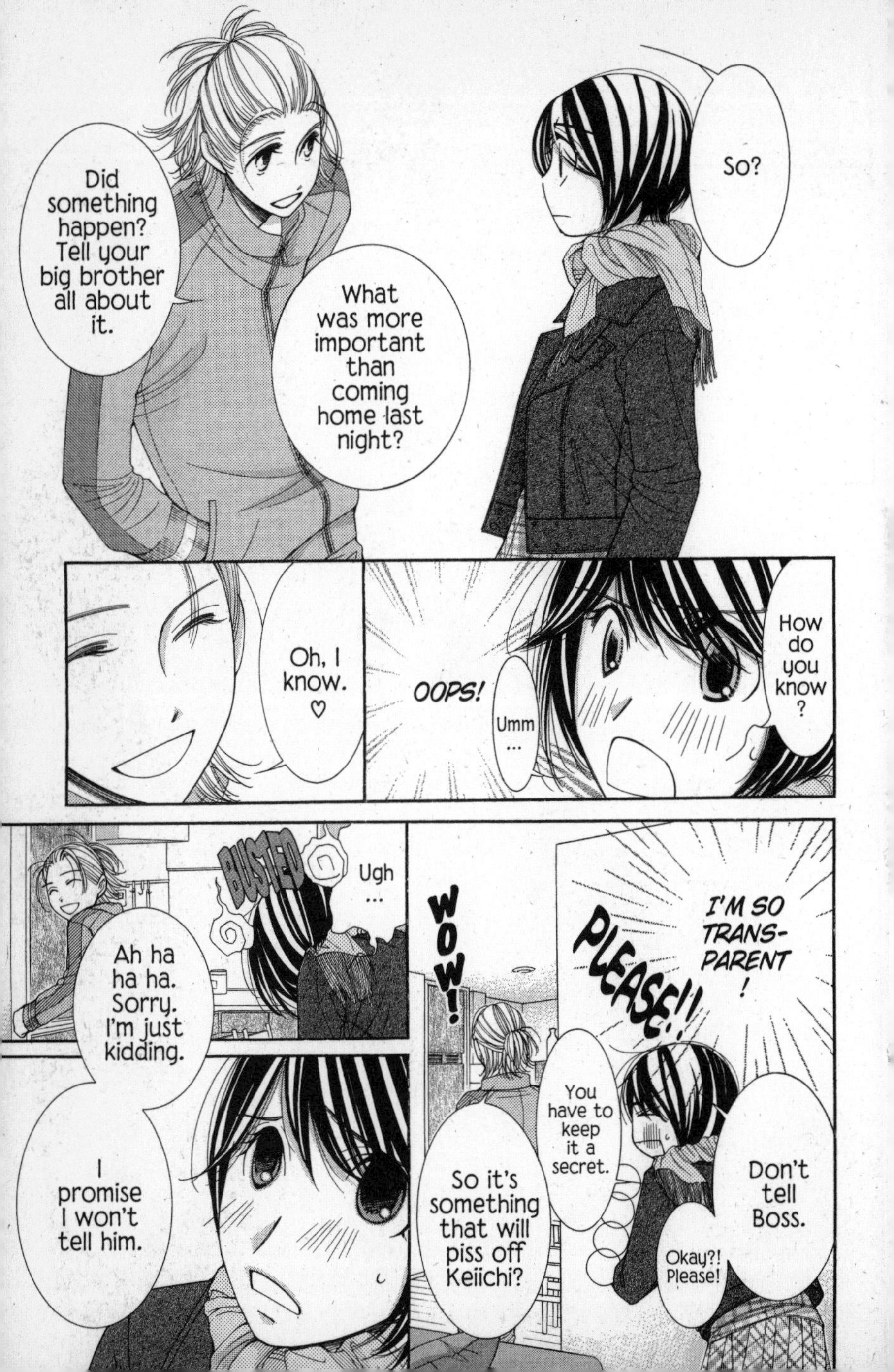
So?
Did something happen? Tell your big brother all about it.
What was more important than coming home last night?
How do you know?
Umm...
OOPS!
Oh, I know. ♡
I'M SO TRANS-PARENT!
PLEASE!!
WOW!
Don't tell Boss.
You have to keep it a secret.
Okay?! Please!
So it's something that will piss off Keiichi?
BUSTED
Ugh...
Ah ha ha ha. Sorry. I'm just kidding.
I promise I won't tell him.

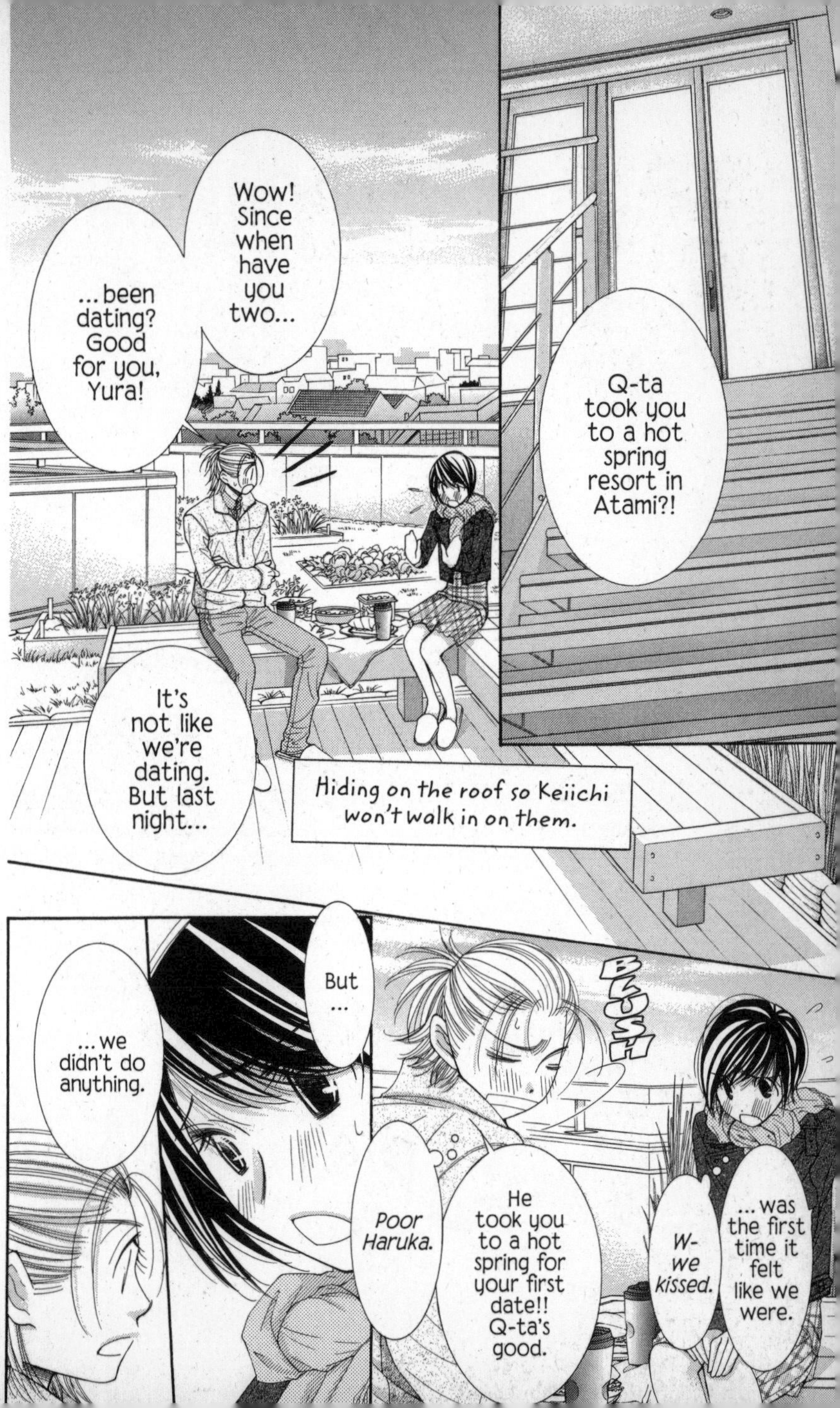
Q-ta took you to a hot spring resort in Atami?!
Wow! Since when have you two...
...been dating? Good for you, Yura!
Hiding on the roof so Keiichi won't walk in on them.
It's not like we're dating. But last night...
BLUSH
...was the first time it felt like we were.
W-we kissed.
He took you to a hot spring for your first date!! Q-ta's good.
Poor Haruka.
But...
...we didn't do anything.

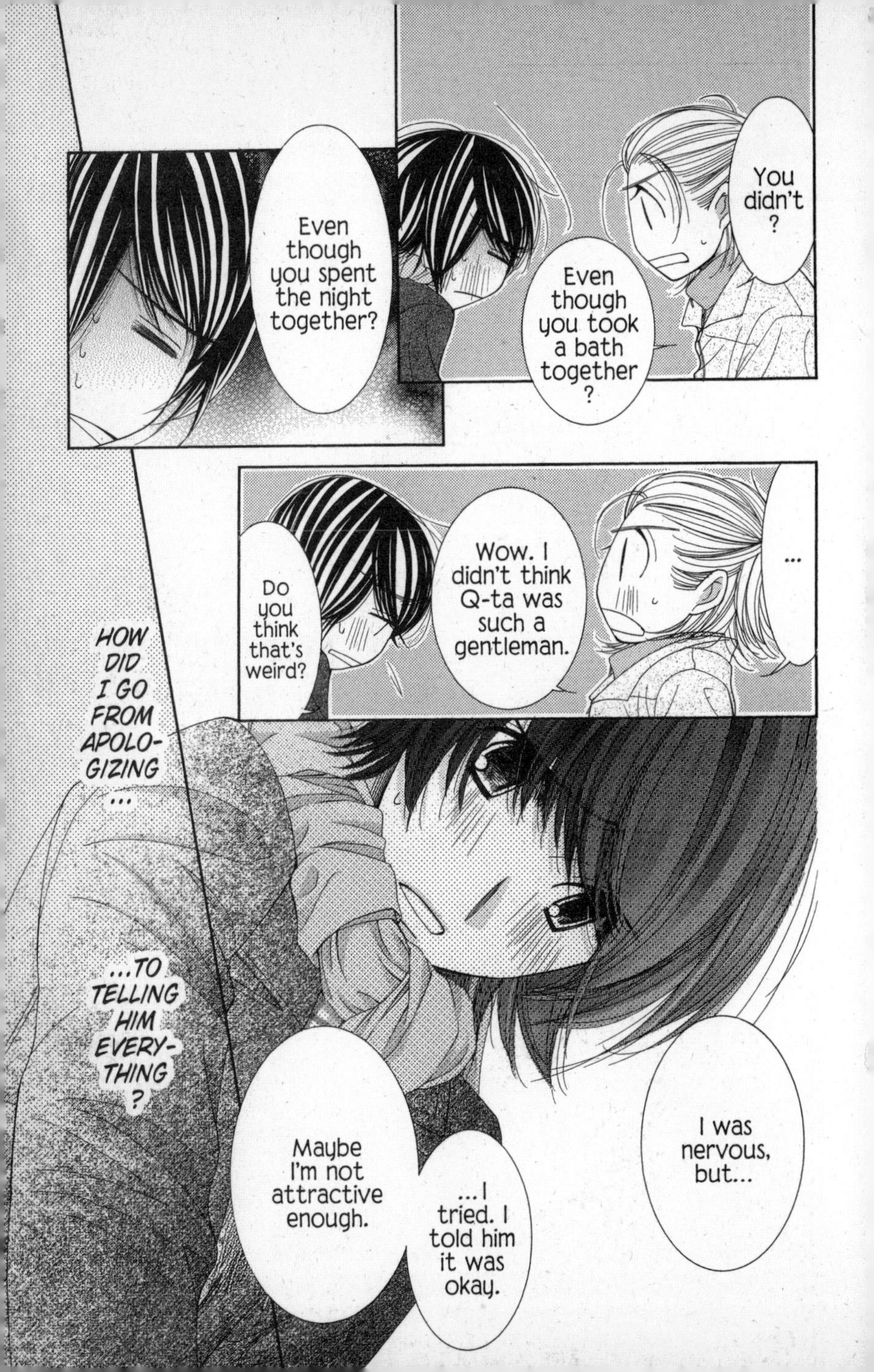
You didn't ?
Even though you took a bath together ?
Even though you spent the night together?
...
Wow. I didn't think Q-ta was such a gentleman.
Do you think that's weird?
I was nervous, but...
...I tried. I told him it was okay.
Maybe I'm not attractive enough.
HOW DID I GO FROM APOLOGIZING...
...TO TELLING HIM EVERYTHING?

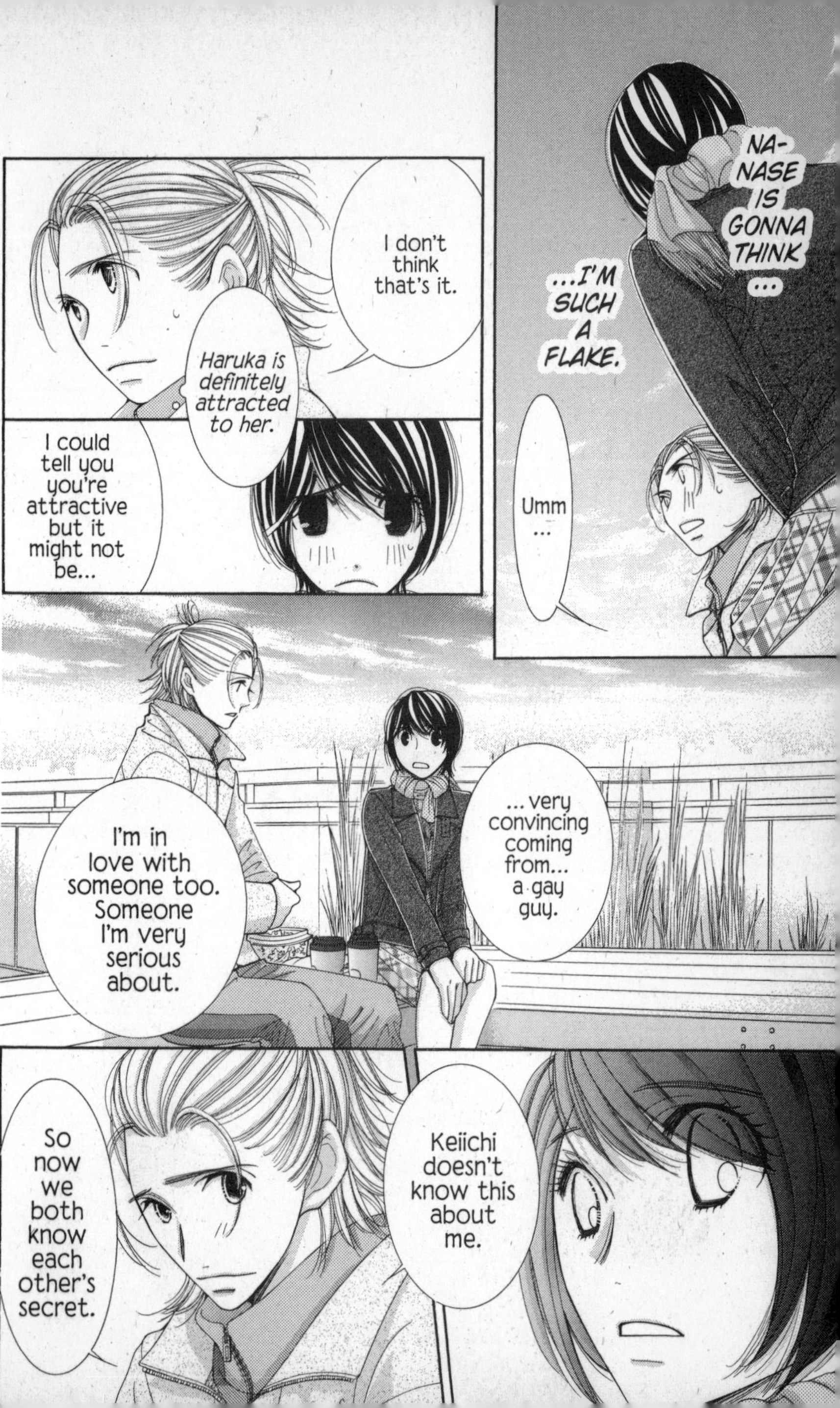
NA-NASE IS GONNA THINK ...
...I'M SUCH A FLAKE.
Umm ...
I don't think that's it.
Haruka is definitely attracted to her.
I could tell you you're attractive but it might not be...
... very convincing coming from... a gay guy.
I'm in love with someone too. Someone I'm very serious about.
Keiichi doesn't know this about me.
So now we both know each other's secret.

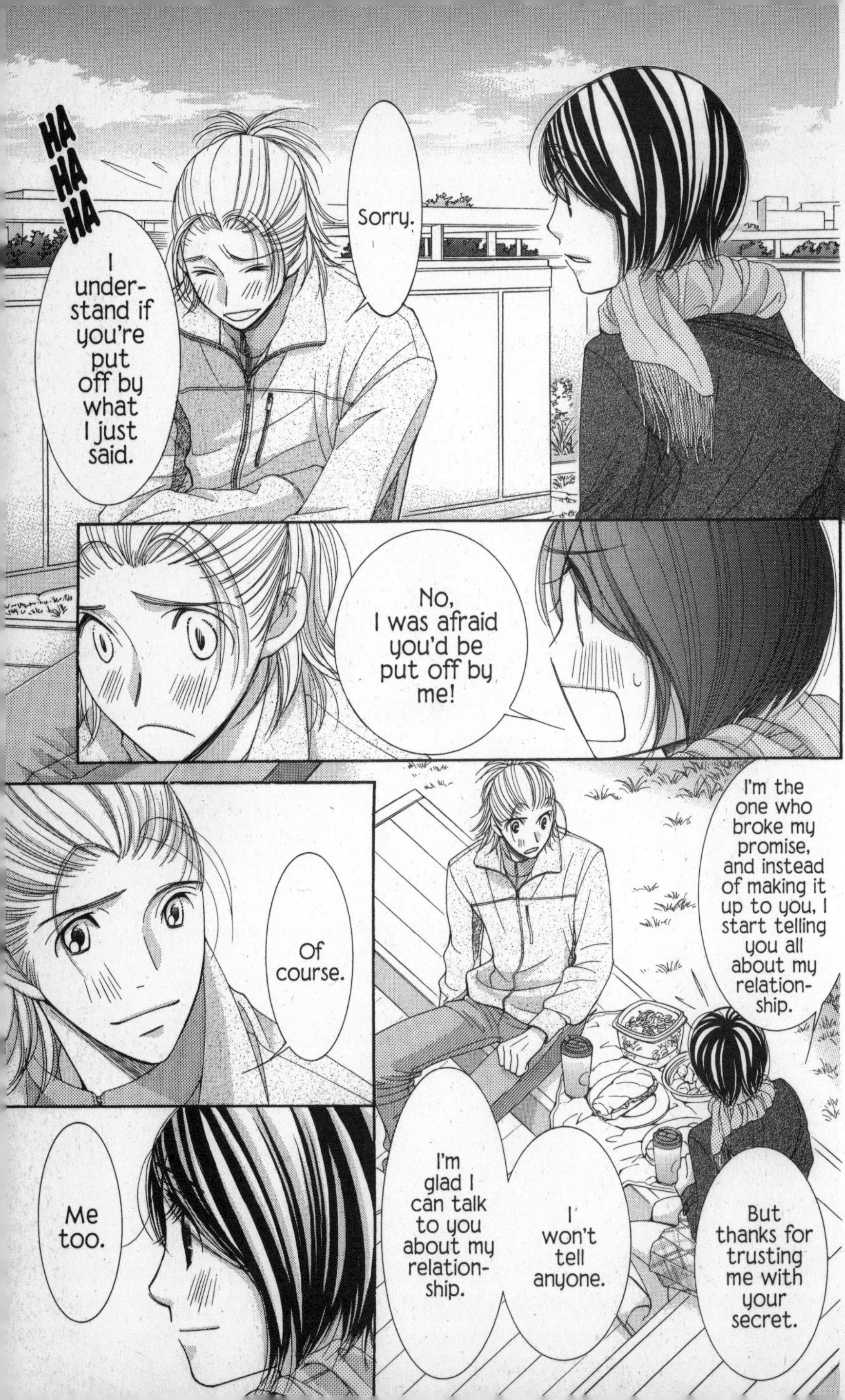
Sorry.
HA HA HA
I understand if you're put off by what I just said.
No, I was afraid you'd be put off by me!
I'm the one who broke my promise, and instead of making it up to you, I start telling you all about my relationship.
But thanks for trusting me with your secret.
I won't tell anyone.
I'm glad I can talk to you about my relationship.
Of course.
Me too.

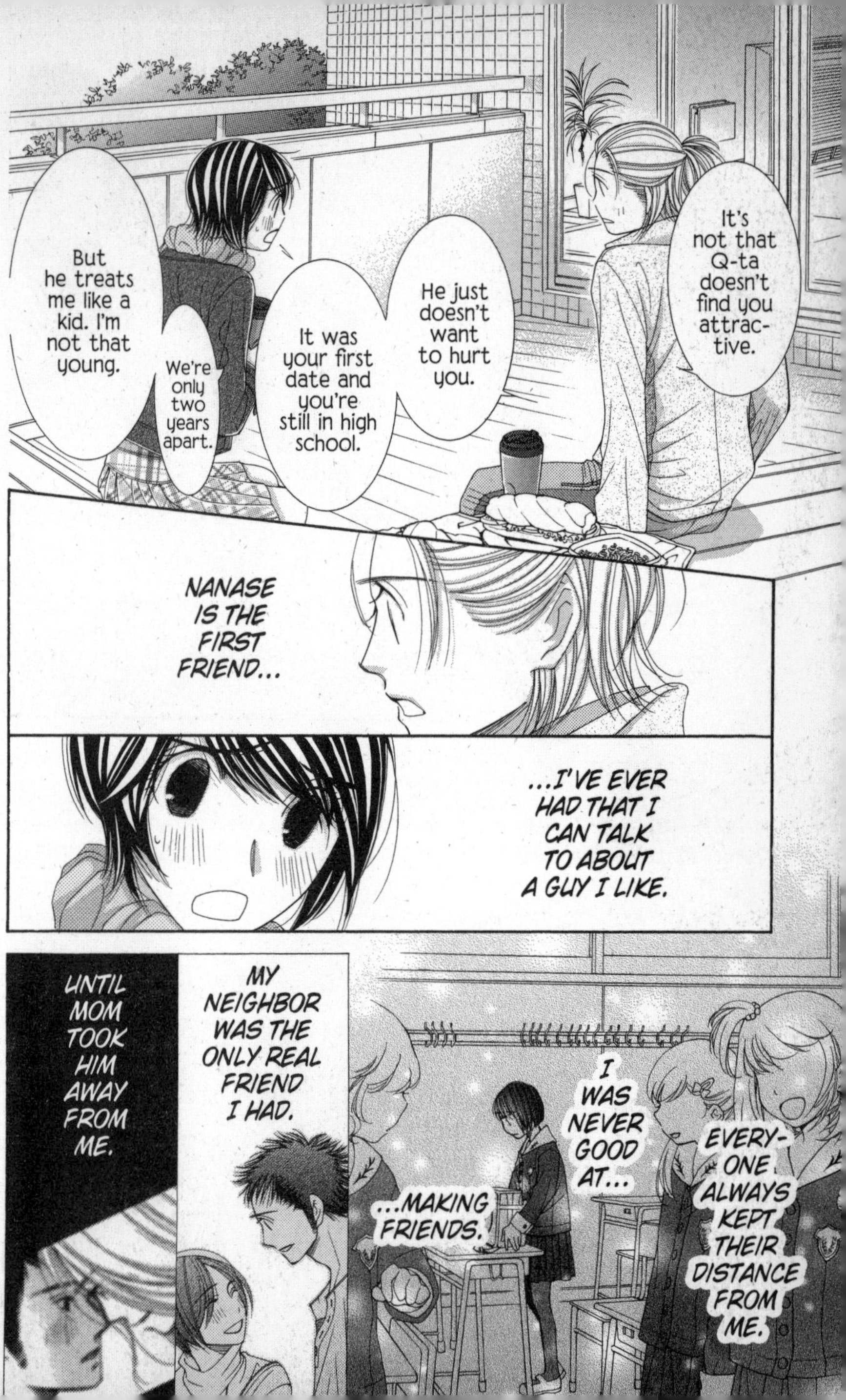
It's not that Q-ta doesn't find you attractive.
He just doesn't want to hurt you.
It was your first date and you're still in high school.
But he treats me like a kid. I'm not that young.
We're only two years apart.
NANASE IS THE FIRST FRIEND...
...I'VE EVER HAD THAT I CAN TALK TO ABOUT A GUY I LIKE.
EVERY-ONE ALWAYS KEPT THEIR DISTANCE FROM ME.
I WAS NEVER GOOD AT...
...MAKING FRIENDS.
MY NEIGHBOR WAS THE ONLY REAL FRIEND I HAD.
UNTIL MOM TOOK HIM AWAY FROM ME.

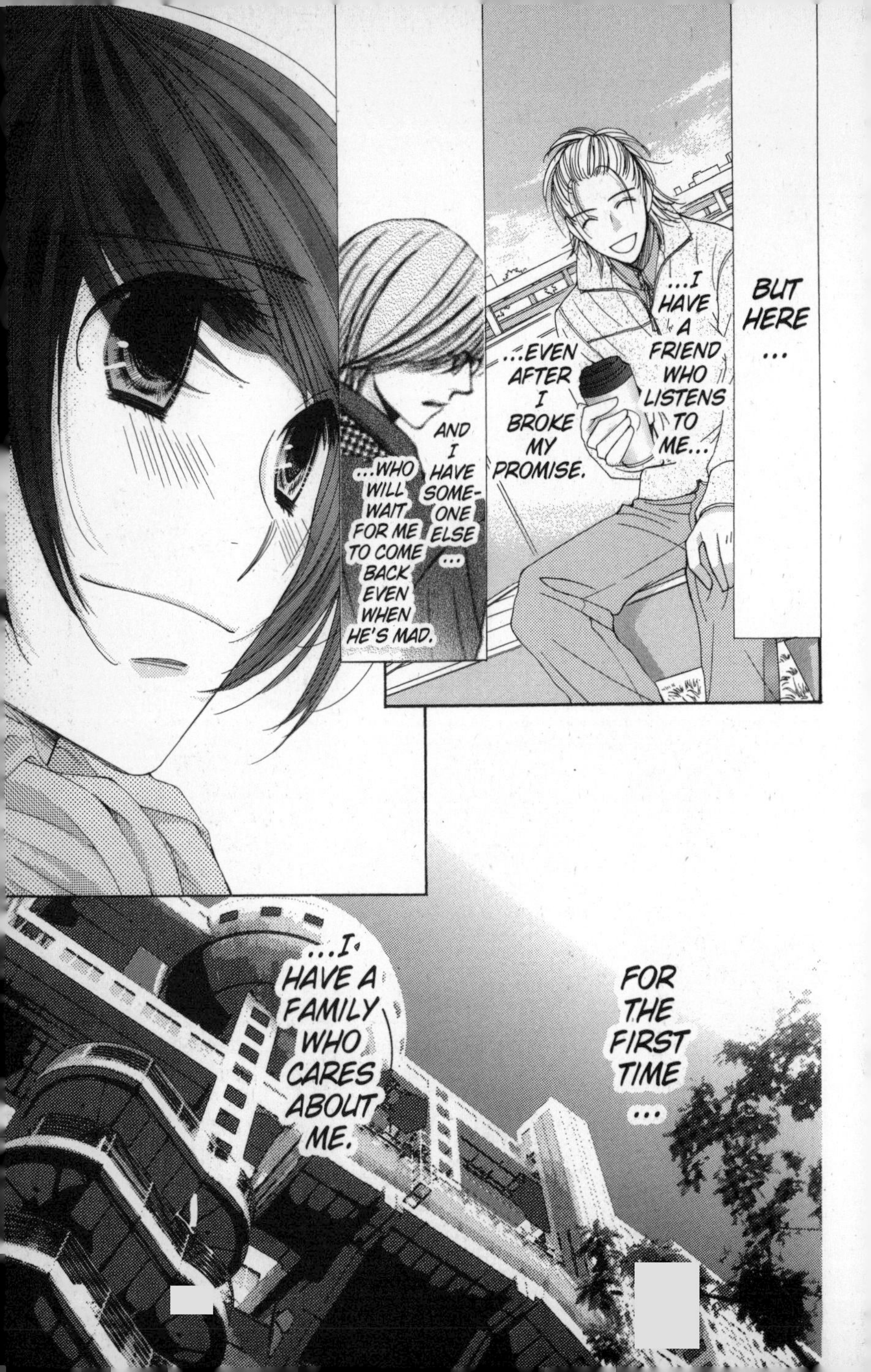
BUT HERE...
...I HAVE A FRIEND WHO LISTENS TO ME...
...EVEN AFTER I BROKE MY PROMISE.
AND I HAVE SOMEONE ELSE...
...WHO WILL WAIT FOR ME TO COME BACK EVEN WHEN HE'S MAD.
FOR THE FIRST TIME...
...I HAVE A FAMILY WHO CARES ABOUT ME.

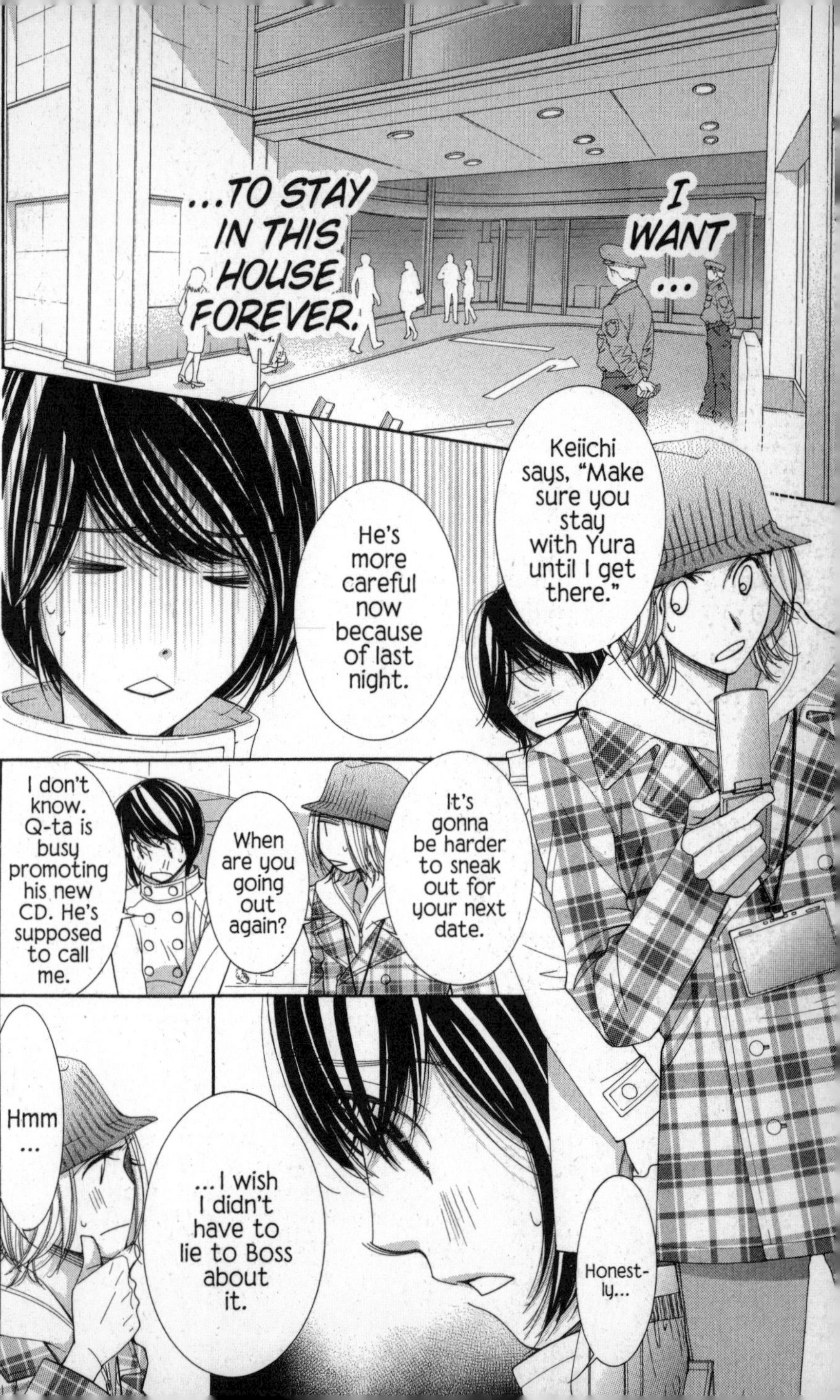
I WANT ...
...TO STAY IN THIS HOUSE FOREVER.
Keiichi says, "Make sure you stay with Yura until I get there."
Honestly...
He's more careful now because of last night.
It's gonna be harder to sneak out for your next date.
When are you going out again?
I don't know. Q-ta is busy promoting his new CD. He's supposed to call me.
...I wish I didn't have to lie to Boss about it.
Hmm ...

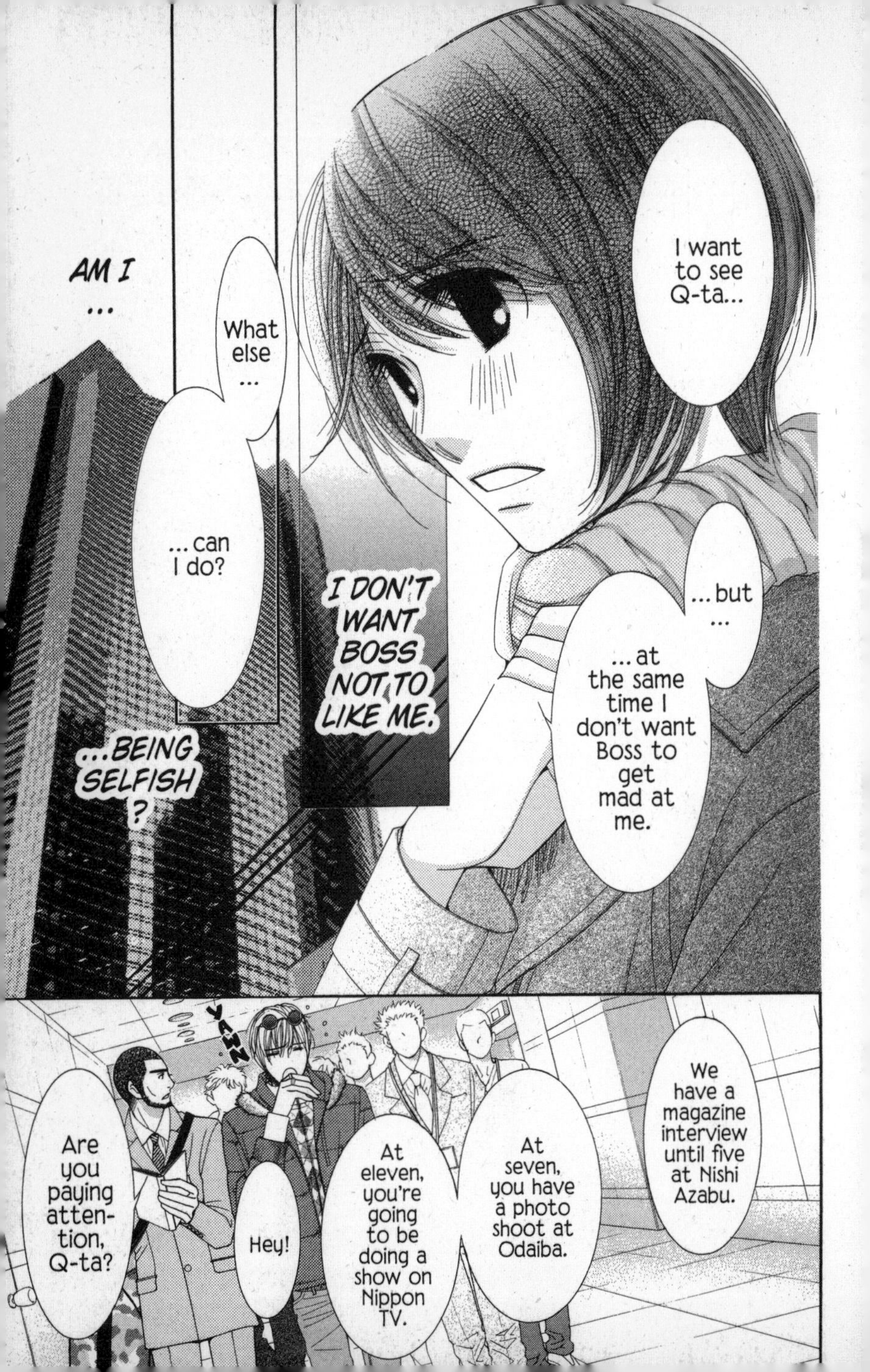
I want to see Q-ta...
...but...
...at the same time I don't want Boss to get mad at me.
I DON'T WANT BOSS NOT TO LIKE ME.
What else...
...can I do?
AM I ...
...BEING SELFISH?
We have a magazine interview until five at Nishi Azabu.
At seven, you have a photo shoot at Odaiba.
At eleven, you're going to be doing a show on Nippon TV.
YAWN
Hey!
Are you paying atten-tion, Q-ta?

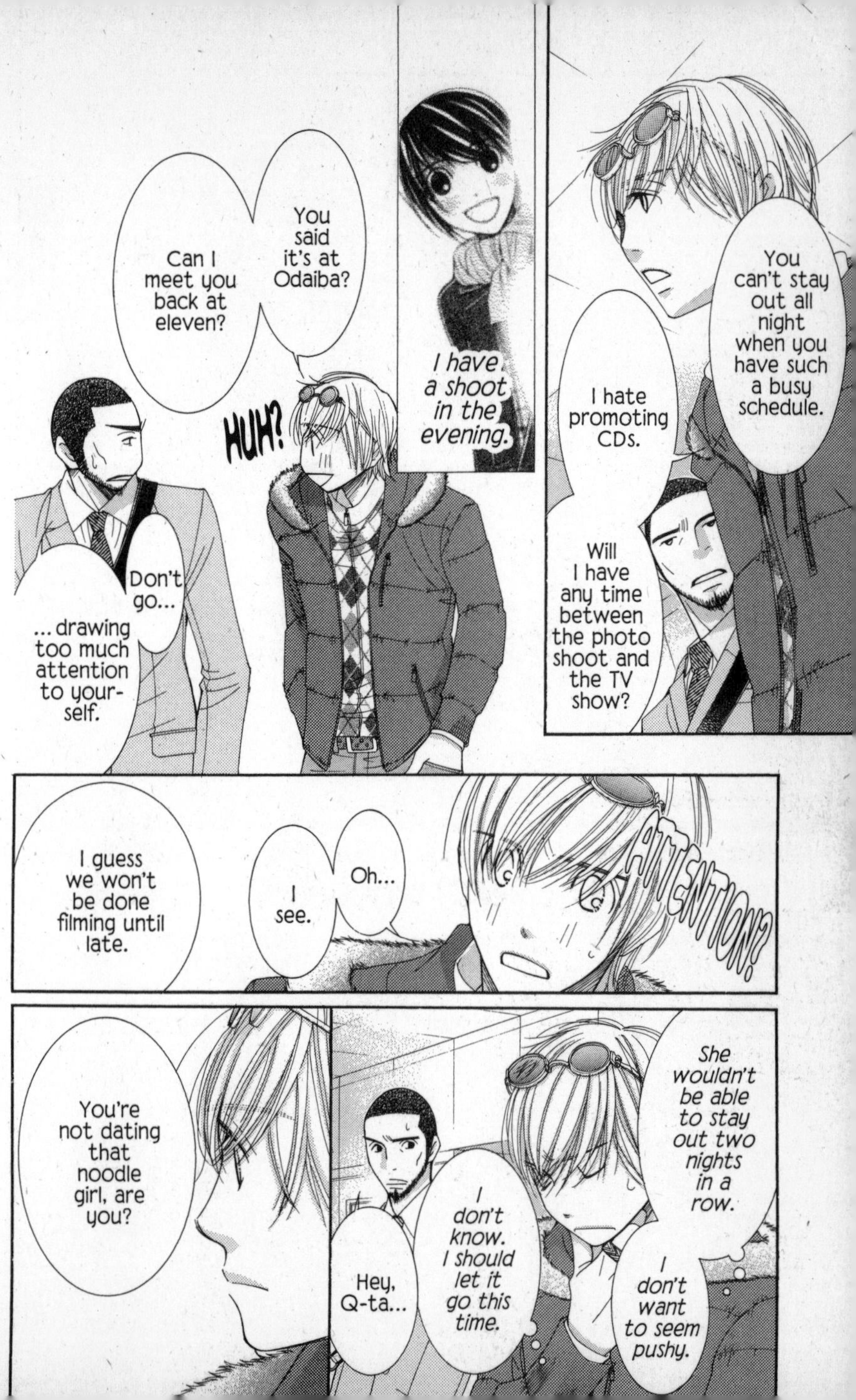
You can't stay out all night when you have such a busy schedule.
I hate promoting CDs.
Will I have any time between the photo shoot and the TV show?
I have a shoot in the evening.
You said it's at Odaiba?
Can I meet you back at eleven?
HUH?
Don't go...
...drawing too much attention to your-self.
ATTENTION?
Oh...
I see.
I guess we won't be done filming until late.
She wouldn't be able to stay out two nights in a row.
I don't want to seem pushy.
I don't know. I should let it go this time.
Hey, Q-ta...
You're not dating that noodle girl, are you?

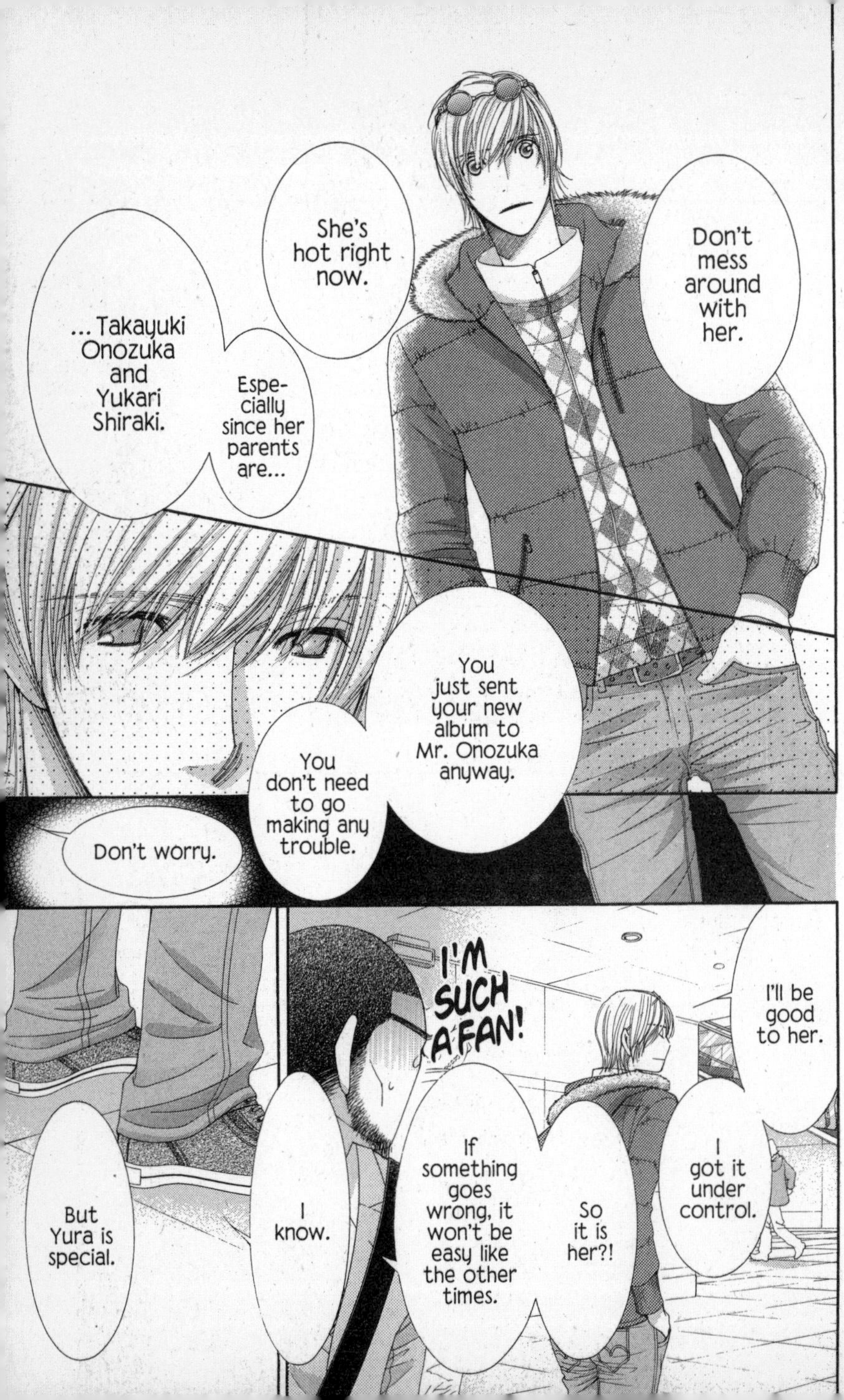

Don't mess around with her.
She's hot right now.
Especially since her parents are...
...Takayuki Onozuka and Yukari Shiraki.
You just sent your new album to Mr. Onozuka anyway.
You don't need to go making any trouble.
Don't worry.
I'll be good to her.
I'M SUCH A FAN!
I got it under control.
So it is her?!
If something goes wrong, it won't be easy like the other times.
I know.
But Yura is special.

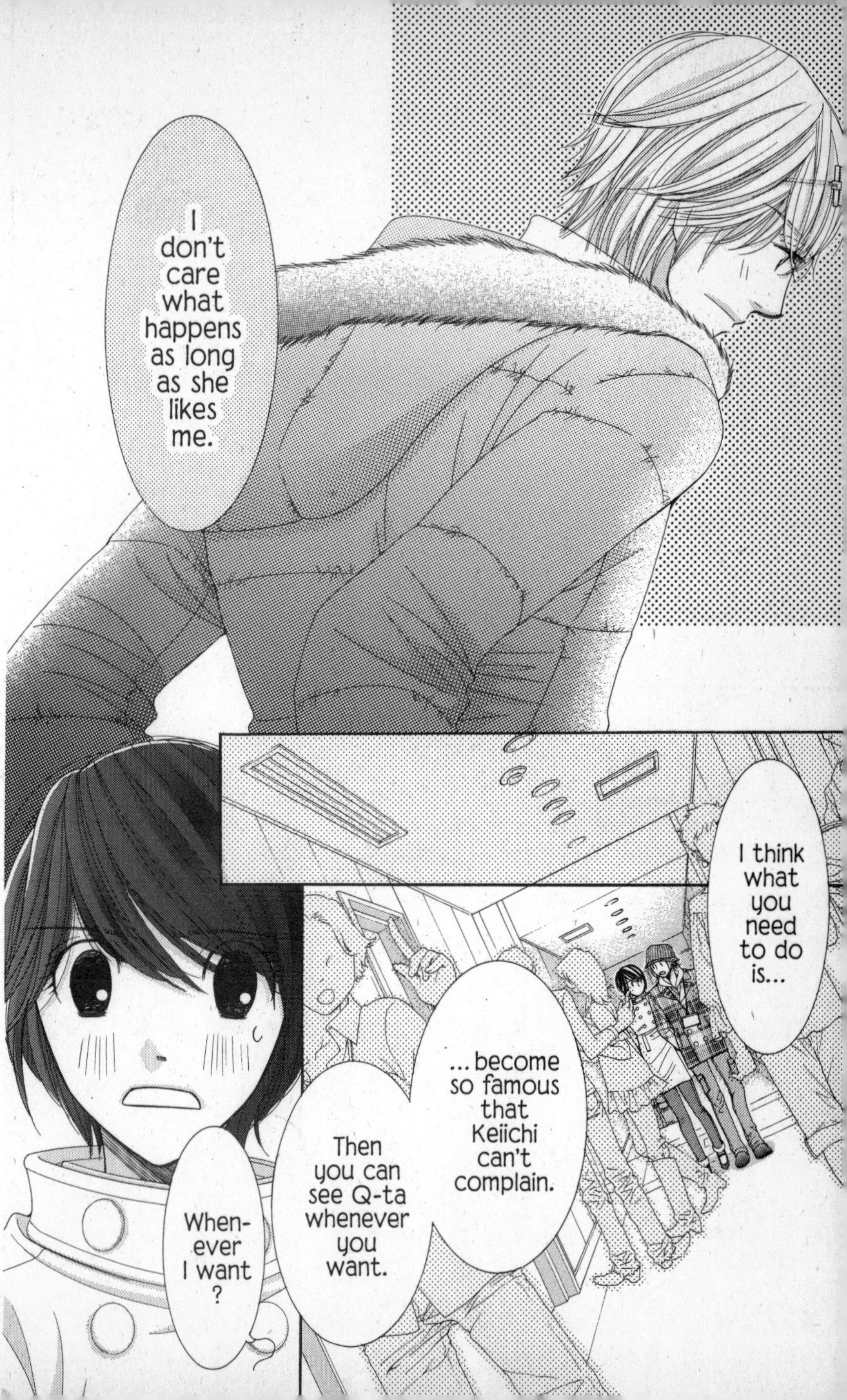
I don't care what happens as long as she likes me.
I think what you need to do is...
...become so famous that Keiichi can't complain.
Then you can see Q-ta whenever you want.
Whenever I want?

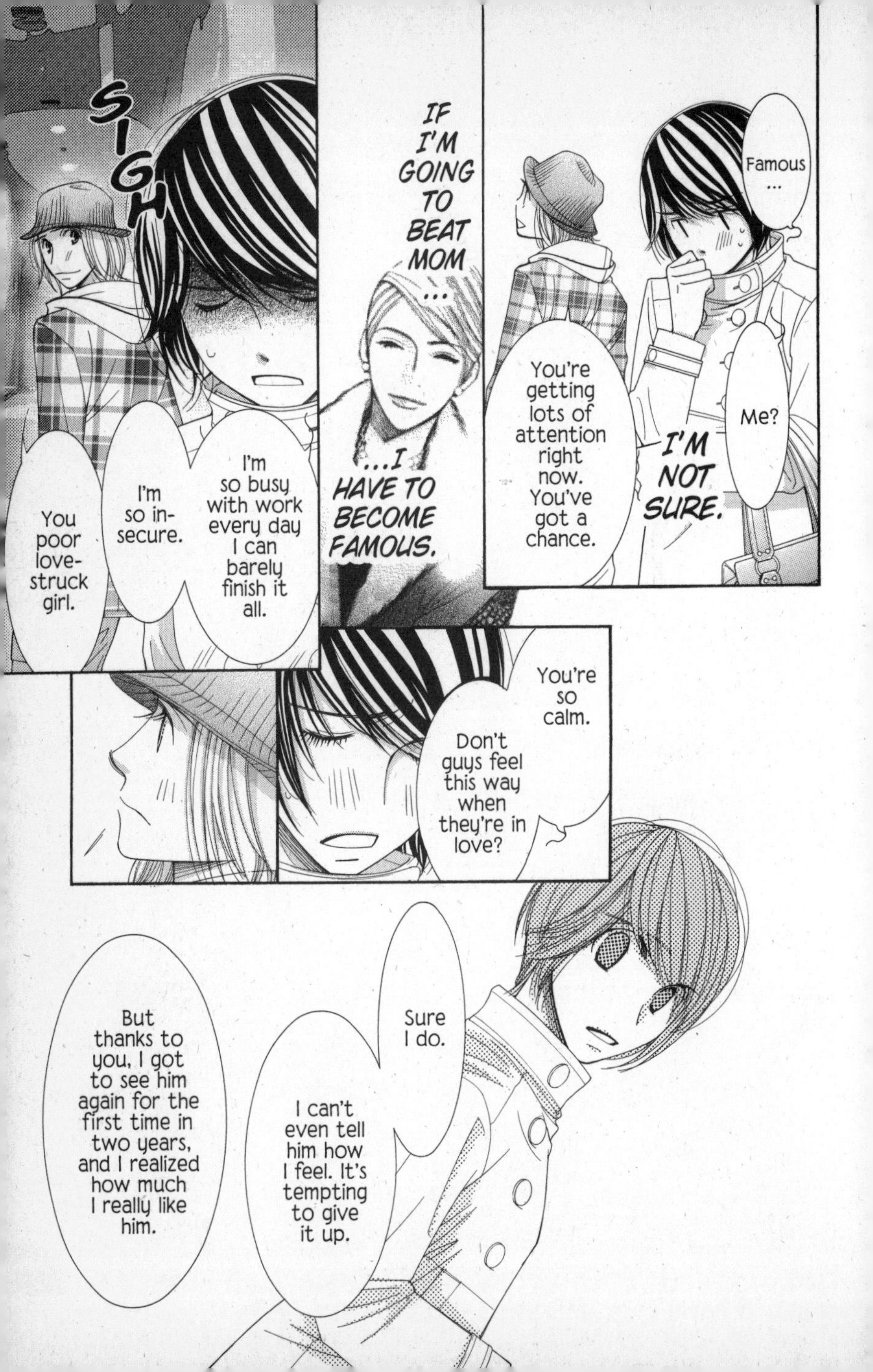
Famous ...
Me?
I'M NOT SURE.
You're getting lots of attention right now. You've got a chance.
IF I'M GOING TO BEAT MOM ...
...I HAVE TO BECOME FAMOUS.
SIGH
I'm so busy with work every day I can barely finish it all.
I'm so in-secure.
You poor love-struck girl.
You're so calm.
Don't guys feel this way when they're in love?
Sure I do.
I can't even tell him how I feel. It's tempting to give it up.
But thanks to you, I got to see him again for the first time in two years, and I realized how much I really like him.

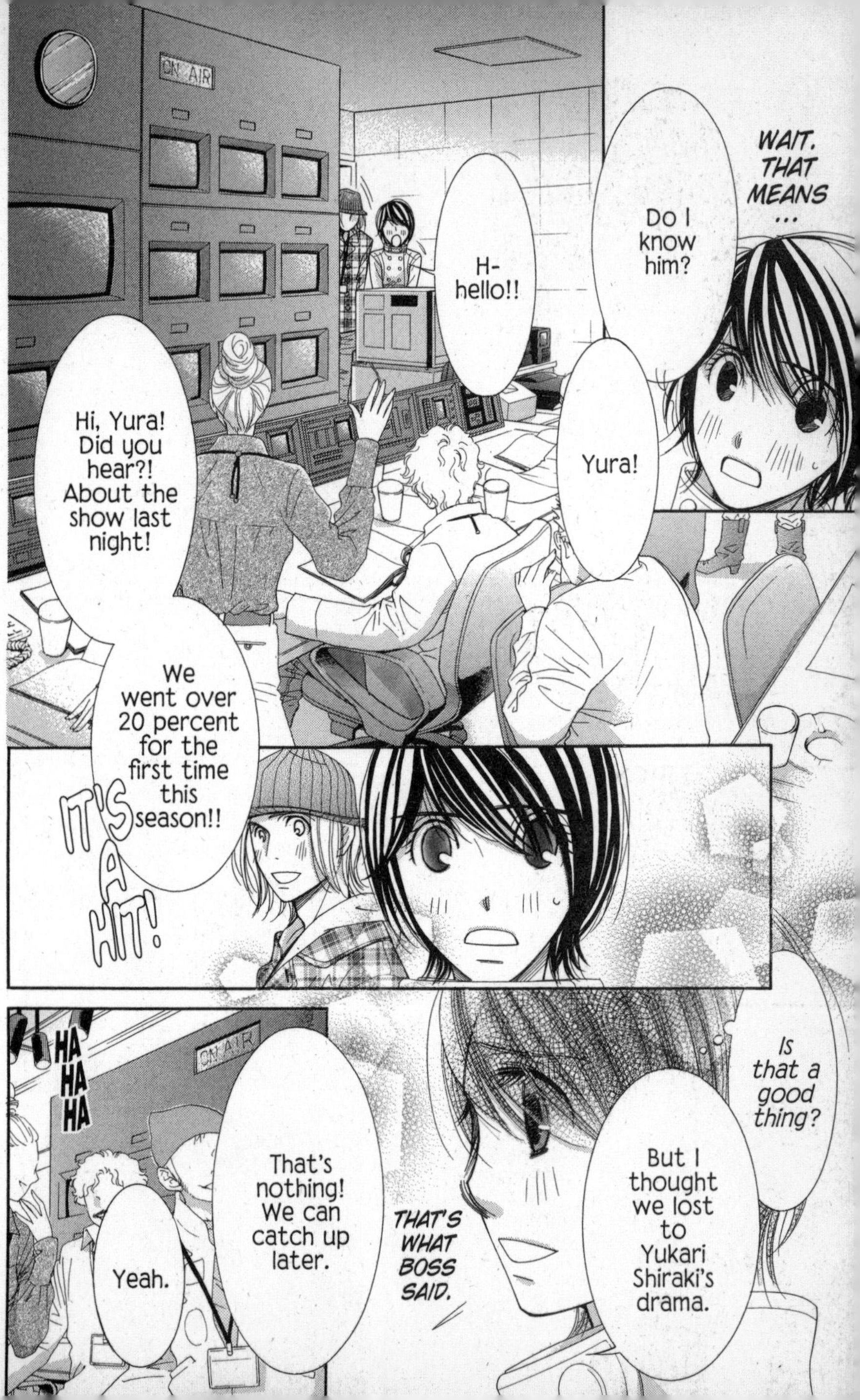
WAIT. THAT MEANS ...
Do I know him?
H- hello!!
Yura!
Hi, Yura! Did you hear?! About the show last night!
We went over 20 percent for the first time this season!!
IT'S A HIT!
Is that a good thing?
But I thought we lost to Yukari Shiraki's drama.
THAT'S WHAT BOSS SAID.
HA HA HA
That's nothing! We can catch up later.
Yeah.
ON AIR

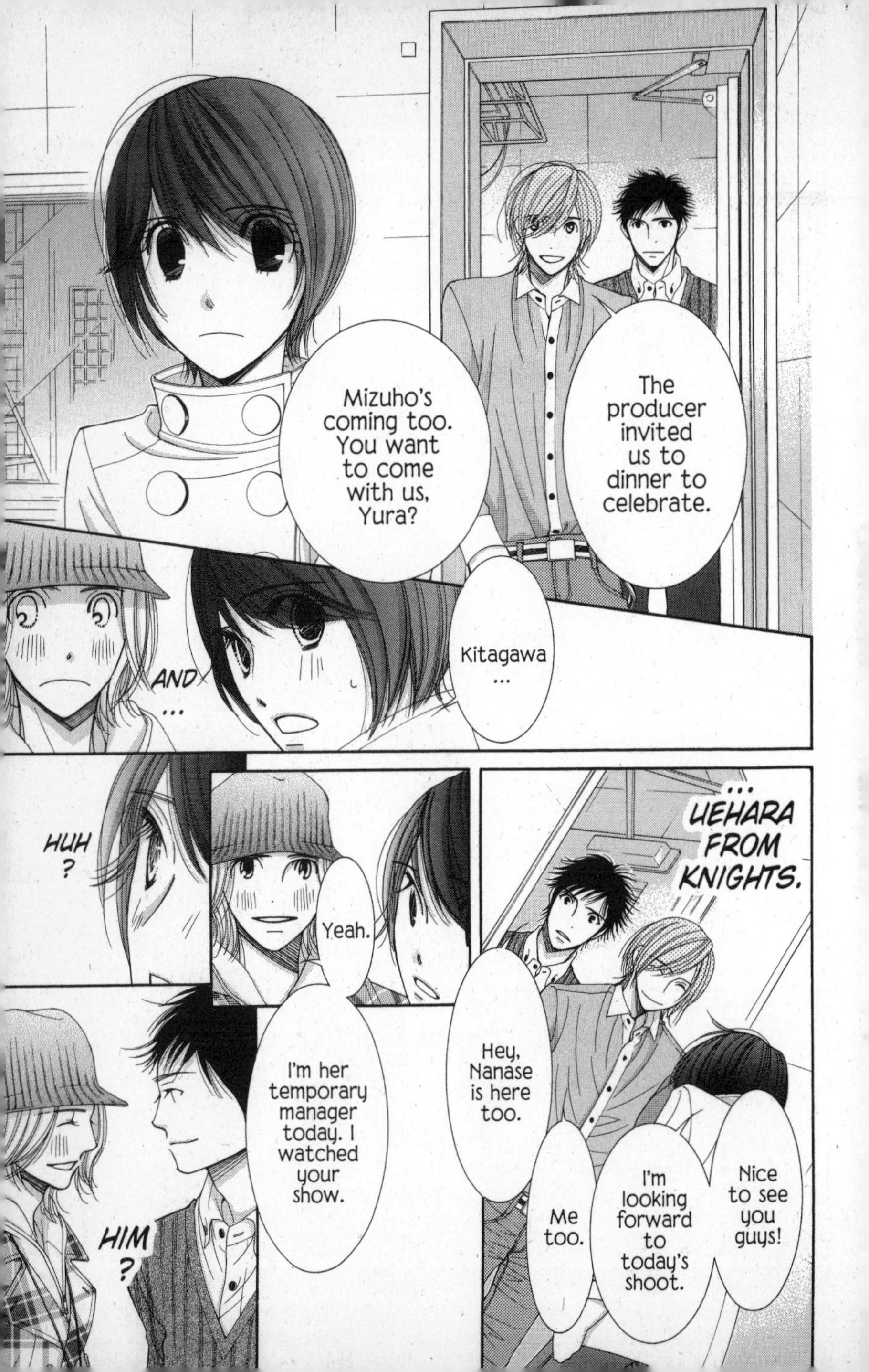
The producer invited us to dinner to celebrate.
Mizuho's coming too. You want to come with us, Yura?
Kitagawa ...
AND ...
... UEHARA FROM KNIGHTS.
Nice to see you guys!
I'm looking forward to today's shoot.
Me too.
Hey, Nanase is here too.
Yeah.
HUH ?
I'm her temporary manager today. I watched your show.
HIM ?

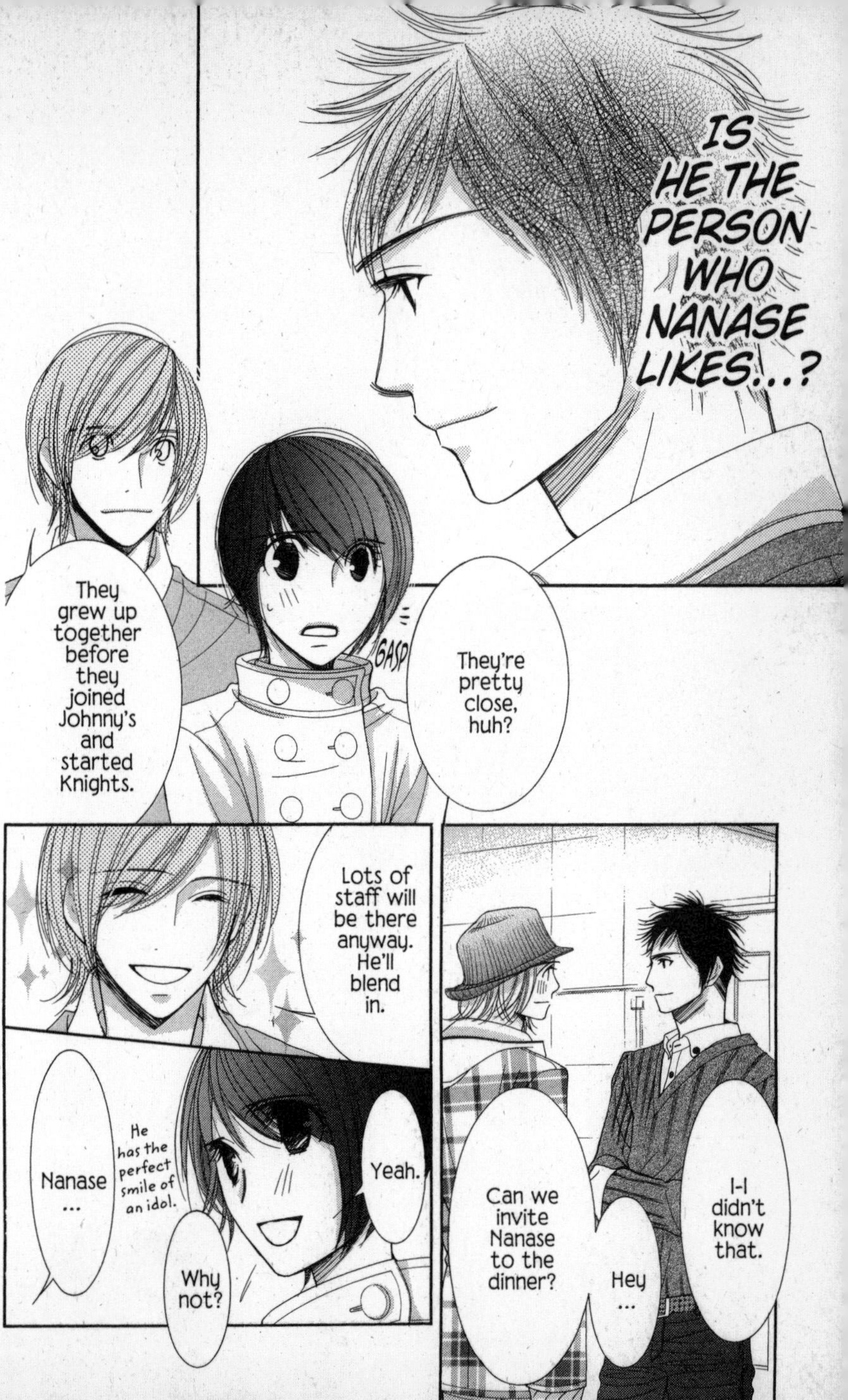
IS HE THE PERSON WHO NANASE LIKES...?
They're pretty close, huh?
GASP
They grew up together before they joined Johnny's and started Knights.
I-I didn't know that.
Hey...
Can we invite Nanase to the dinner?
Lots of staff will be there anyway. He'll blend in.
Yeah.
Why not?
He has the perfect smile of an idol.
Nanase...

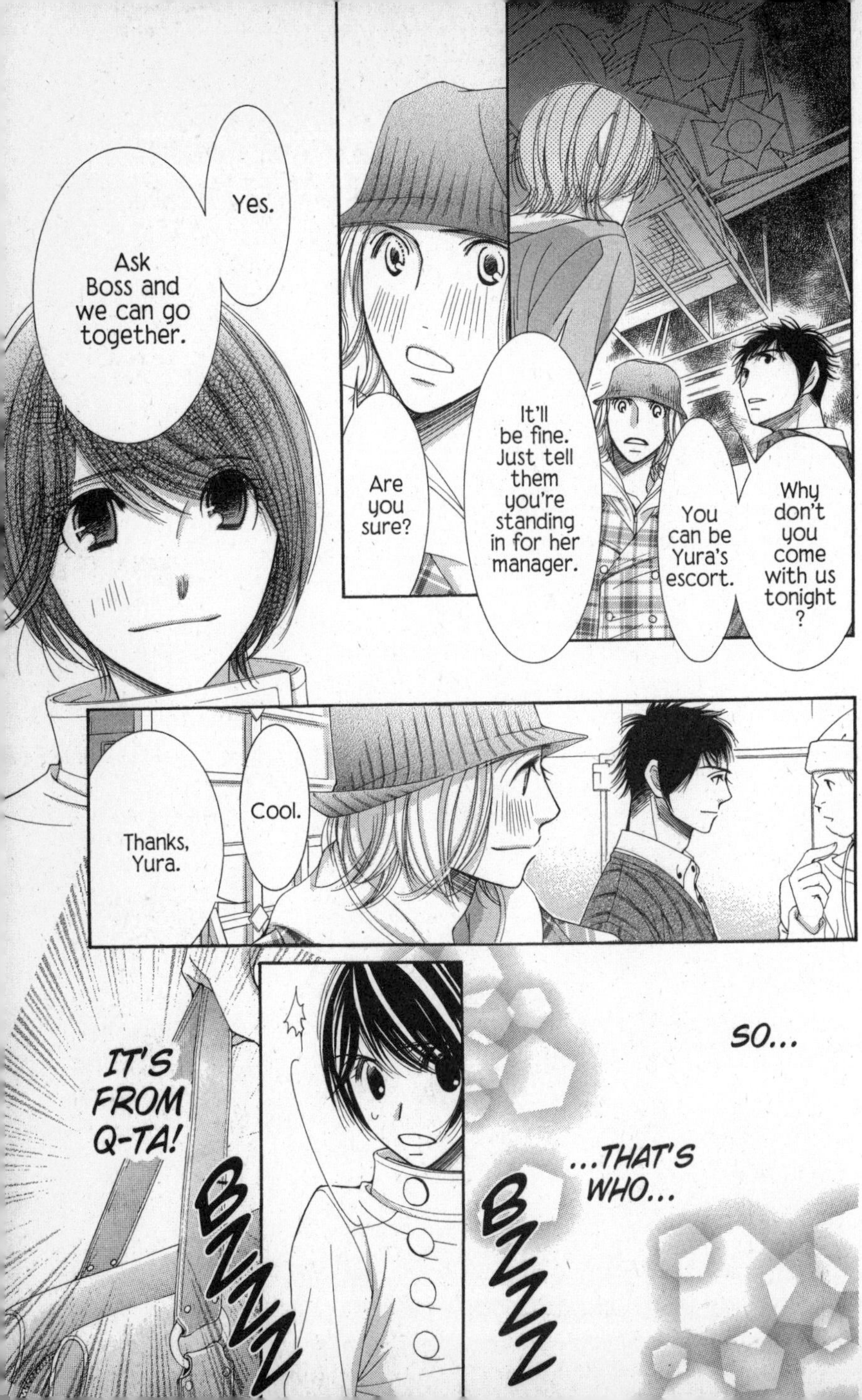

Why don't you come with us tonight?
You can be Yura's escort.
Are you sure?
It'll be fine. Just tell them you're standing in for her manager.
Yes.
Ask Boss and we can go together.
Cool.
Thanks, Yura.
SO...
...THAT'S WHO...
BZZZ
IT'S FROM Q-TA!
BZZZZ

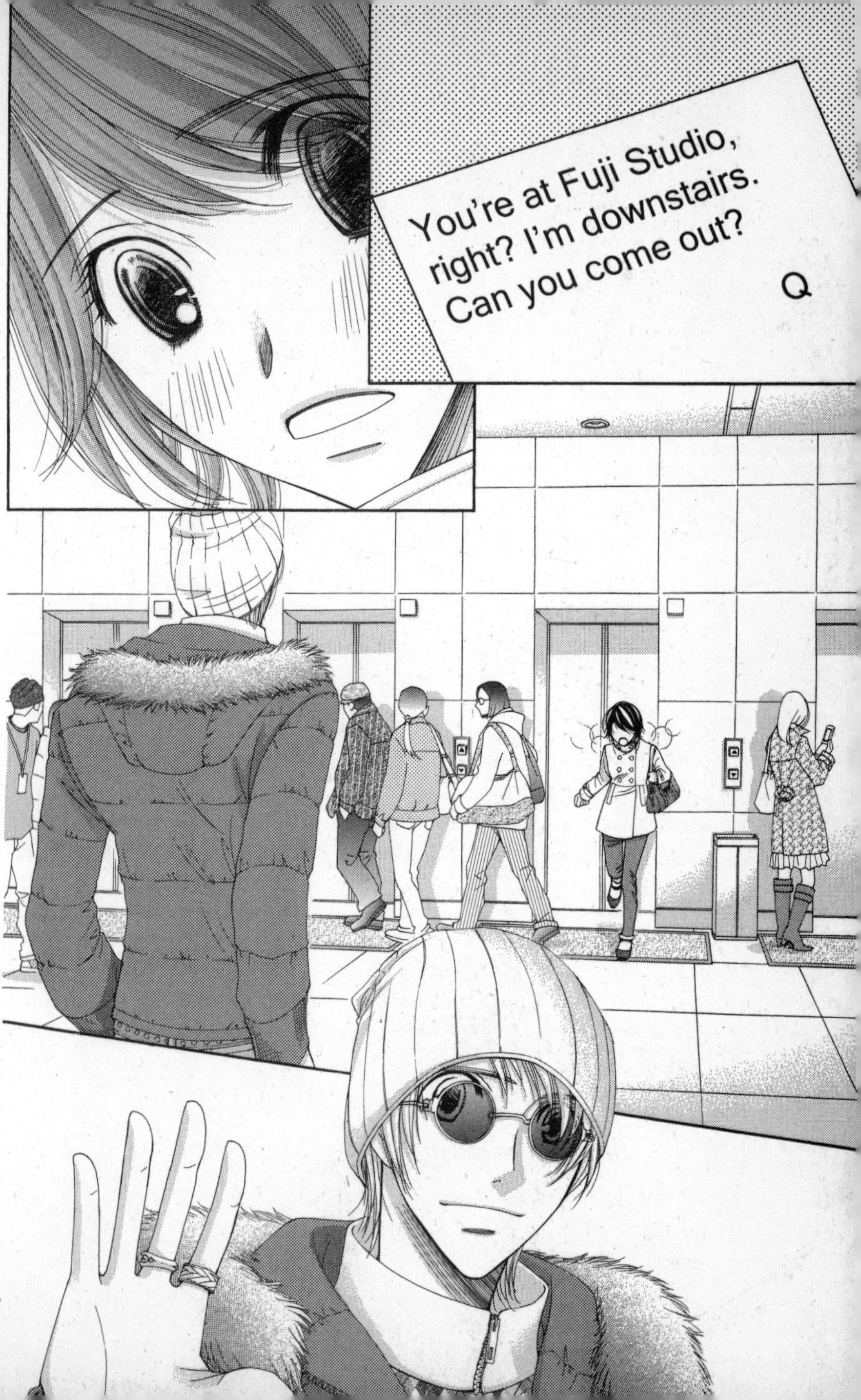
You're at Fuji Studio, right? I'm downstairs. Can you come out?
Q

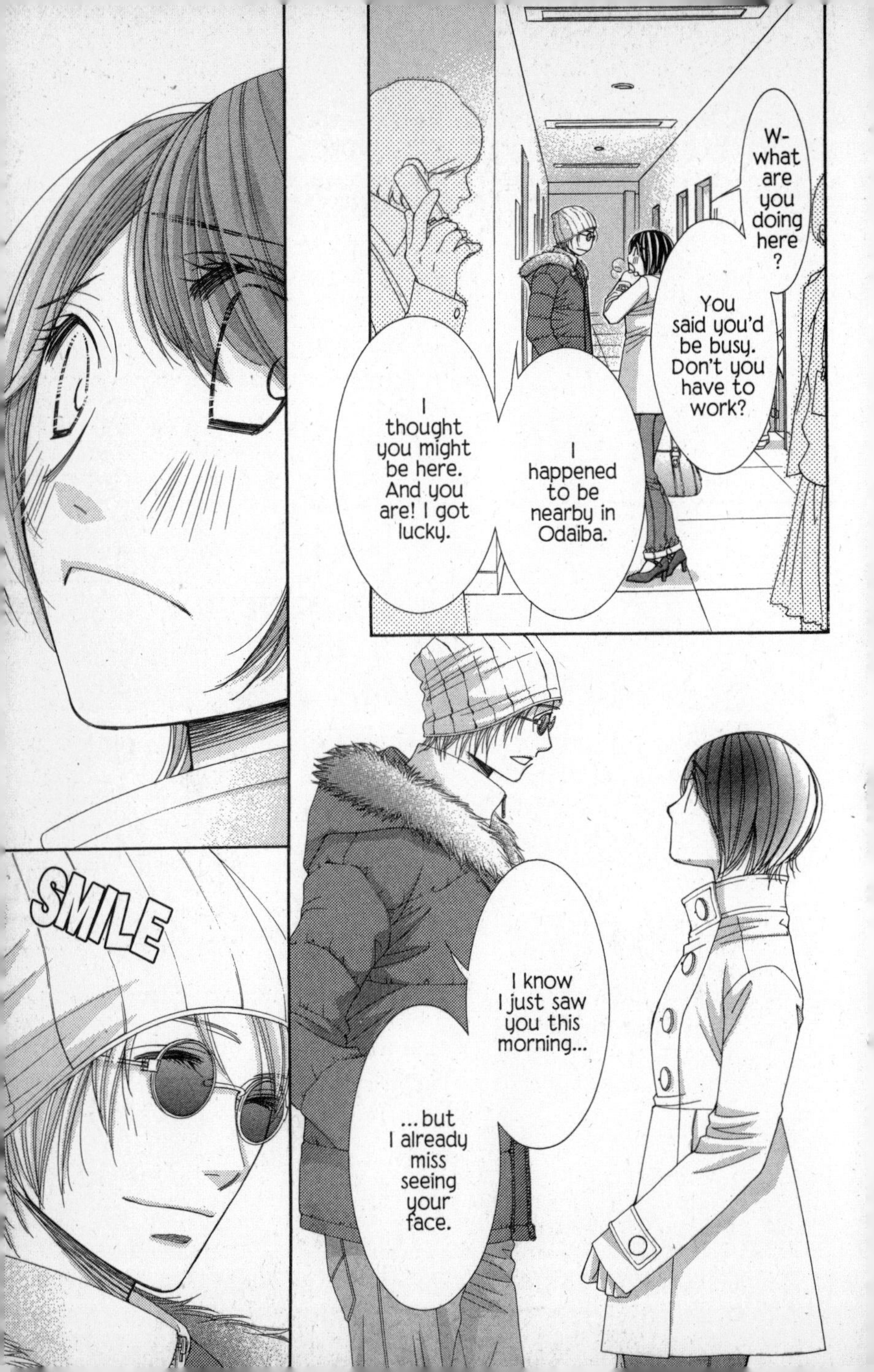
W-what are you doing here?
You said you'd be busy. Don't you have to work?
I happened to be nearby in Odaiba.
I thought you might be here. And you are! I got lucky.
I know I just saw you this morning...
...but I already miss seeing your face.
SMILE

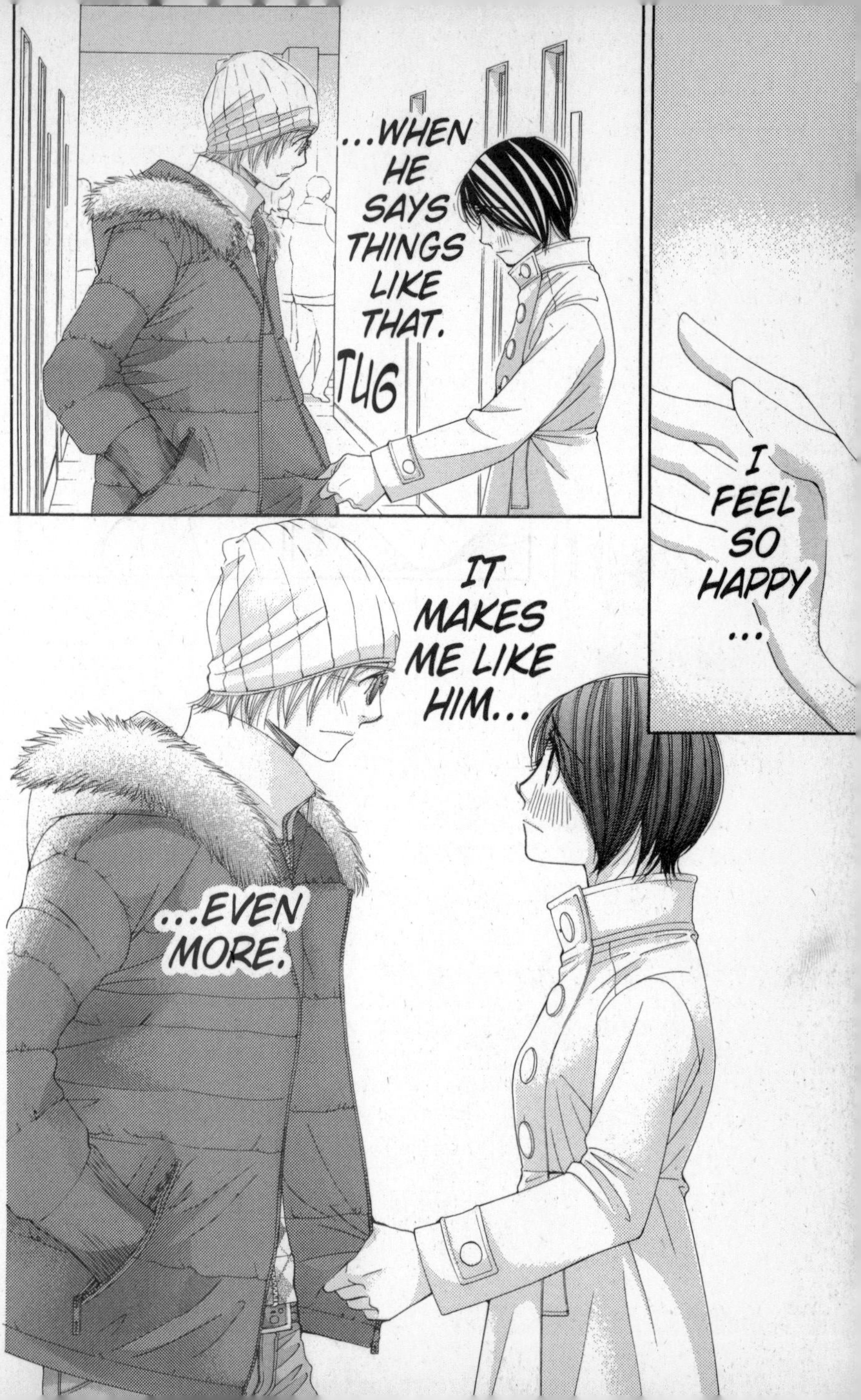
I FEEL SO HAPPY...
...WHEN HE SAYS THINGS LIKE THAT.
TUG
IT MAKES ME LIKE HIM...
...EVEN MORE.

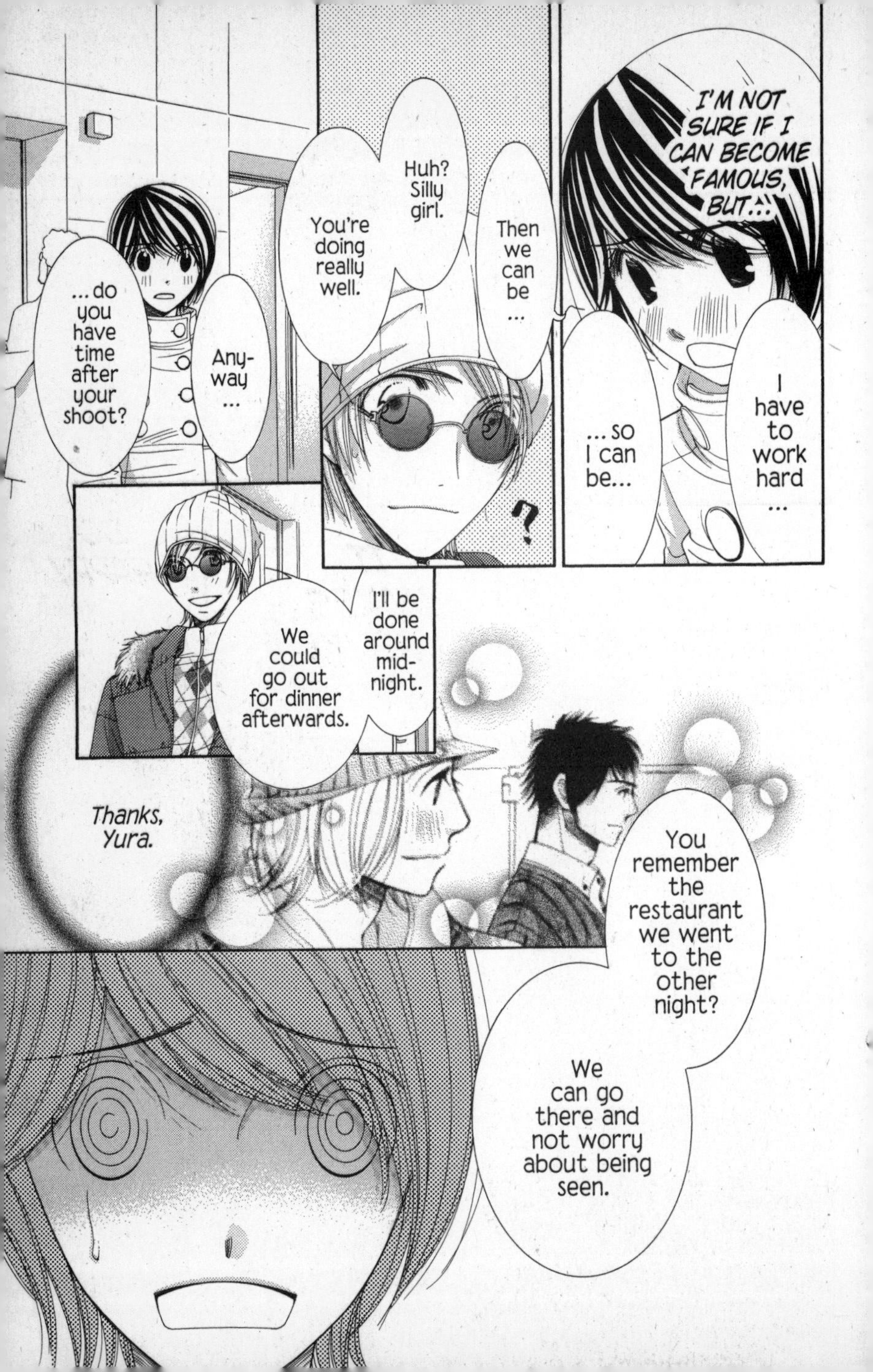
I'M NOT SURE IF I CAN BECOME FAMOUS, BUT...
I have to work hard ...
...so I can be...
Then we can be ...
Huh? Silly girl.
You're doing really well.
Anyway ...
...do you have time after your shoot?
I'll be done around midnight.
We could go out for dinner afterwards.
Thanks, Yura.
You remember the restaurant we went to the other night?
We can go there and not worry about being seen.

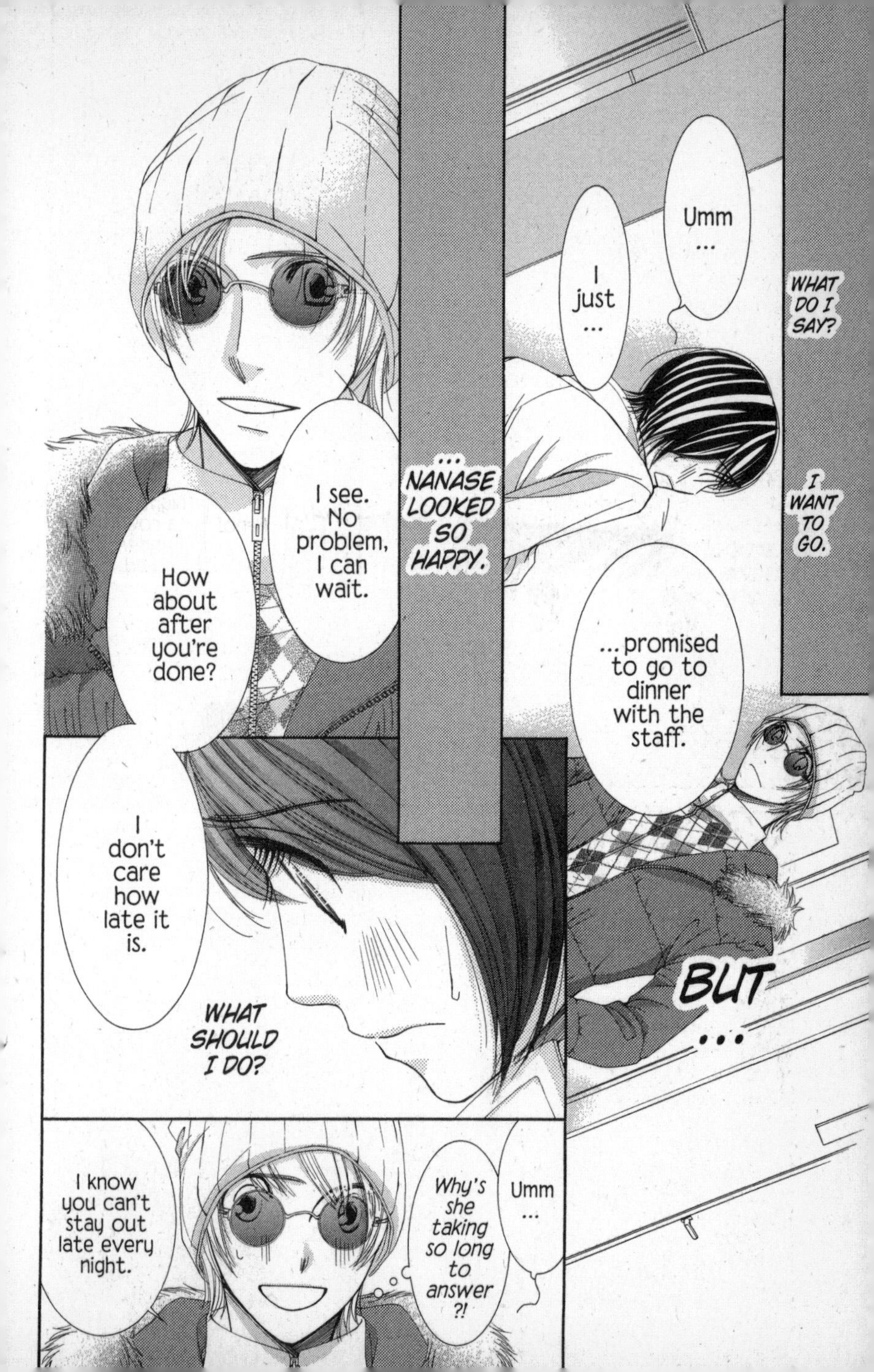
WHAT DO I SAY?
Umm ...
I just ...
I WANT TO GO.
... promised to go to dinner with the staff.
BUT ...
... NANASE LOOKED SO HAPPY.
I see. No problem, I can wait.
How about after you're done?
I don't care how late it is.
WHAT SHOULD I DO?
Umm ...
Why's she taking so long to answer ?!
I know you can't stay out late every night.

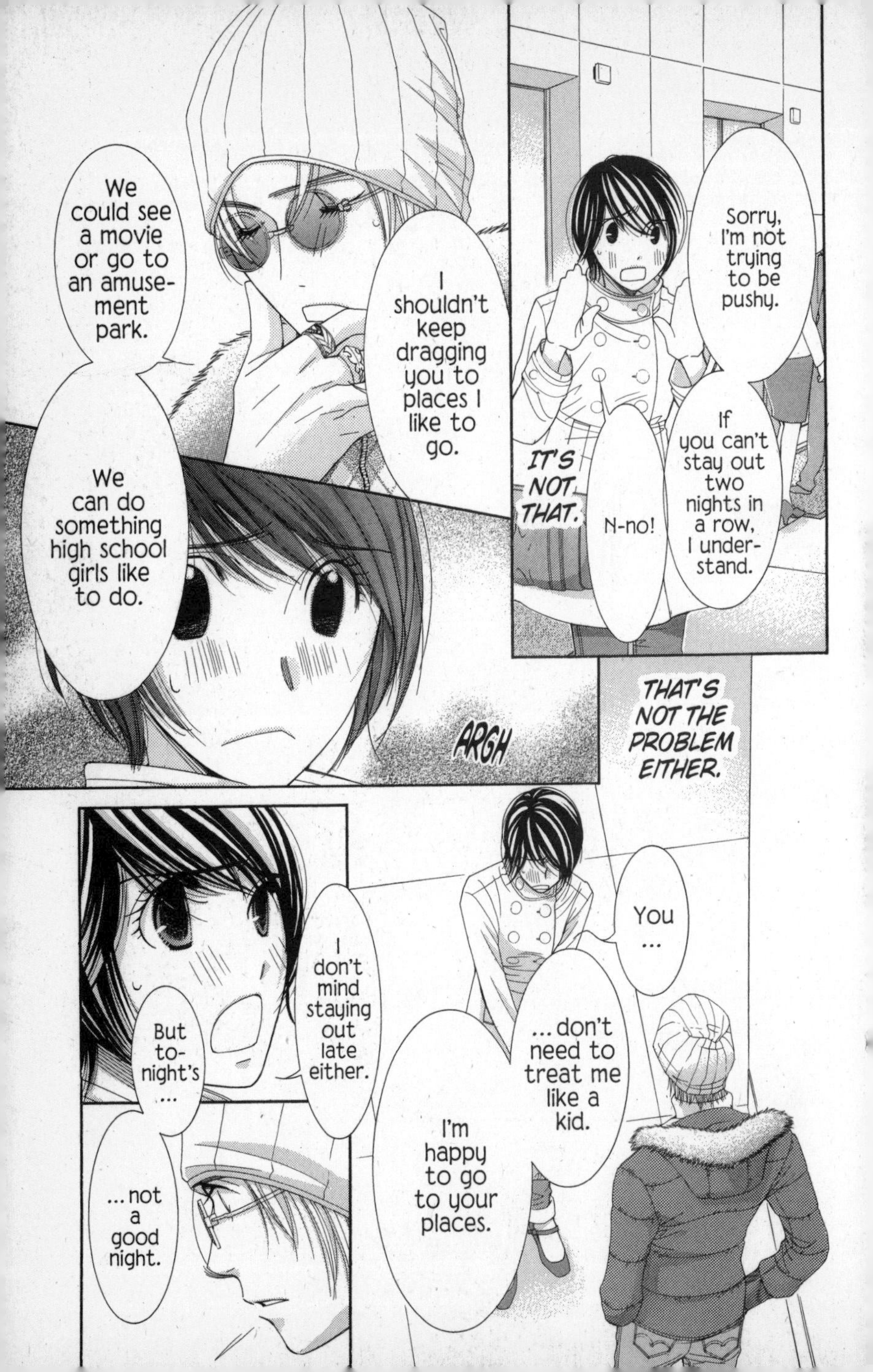
Sorry, I'm not trying to be pushy.
If you can't stay out two nights in a row, I understand.
N-no!
IT'S NOT THAT.
I shouldn't keep dragging you to places I like to go.
We could see a movie or go to an amusement park.
We can do something high school girls like to do.
ARGH
THAT'S NOT THE PROBLEM EITHER.
You ...
... don't need to treat me like a kid.
I'm happy to go to your places.
I don't mind staying out late either.
But to-night's ...
... not a good night.

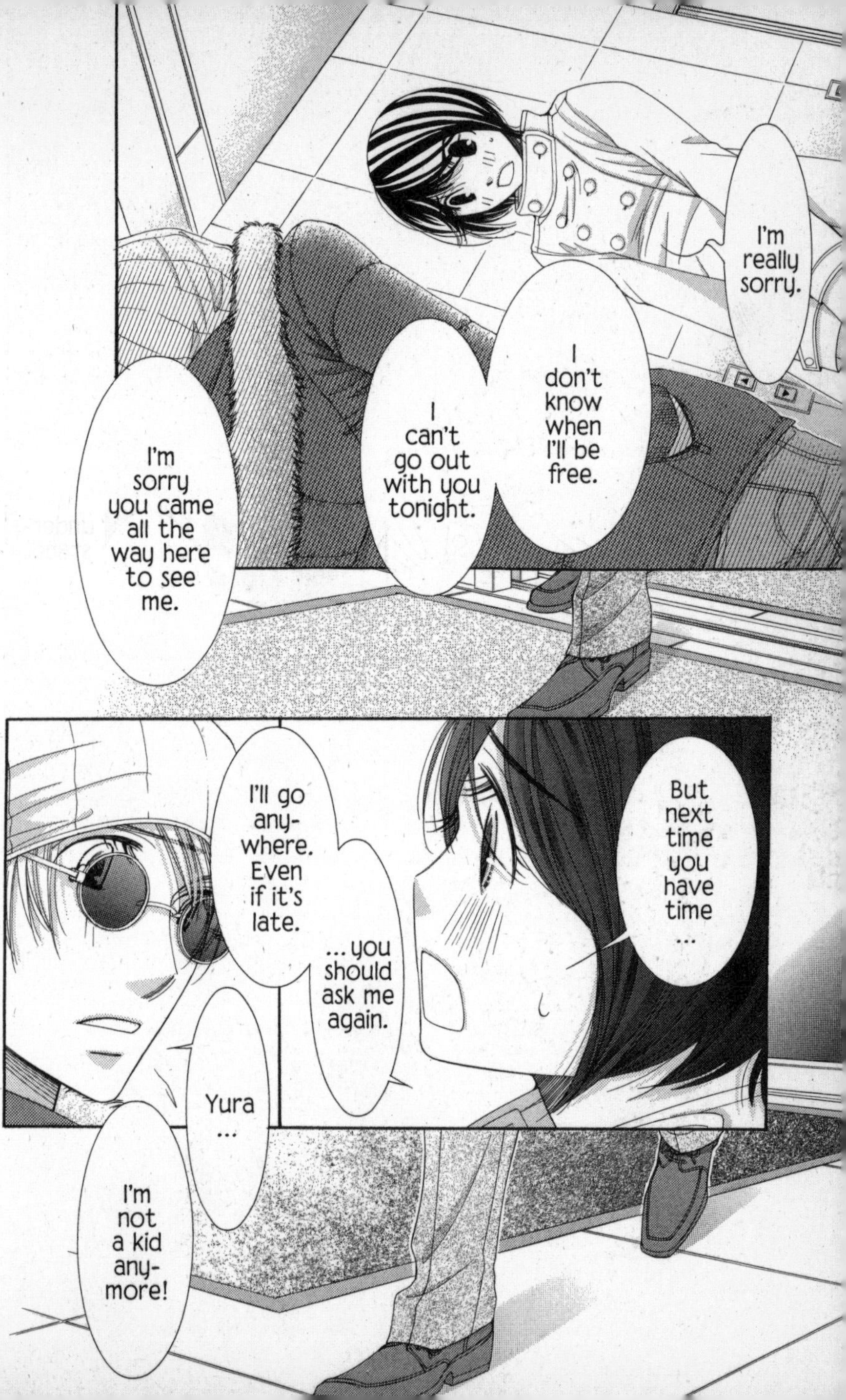
I'm really sorry.
I don't know when I'll be free.
I can't go out with you tonight.
I'm sorry you came all the way here to see me.
But next time you have time ...
I'll go any-where. Even if it's late.
... you should ask me again.
Yura ...
I'm not a kid any-more!

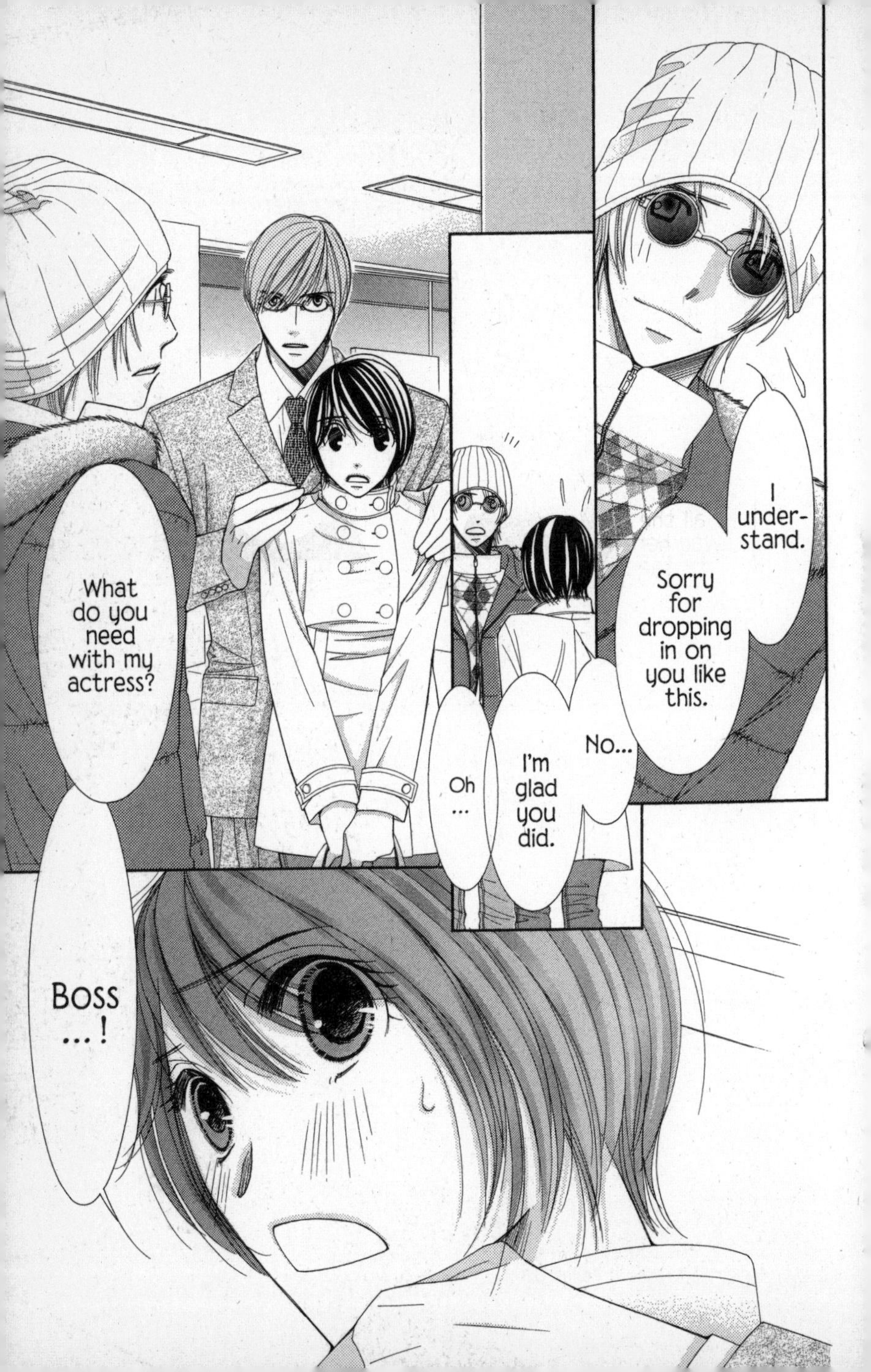
I under-stand.
Sorry for dropping in on you like this.
No...
I'm glad you did.
Oh ...
What do you need with my actress?
Boss ...!

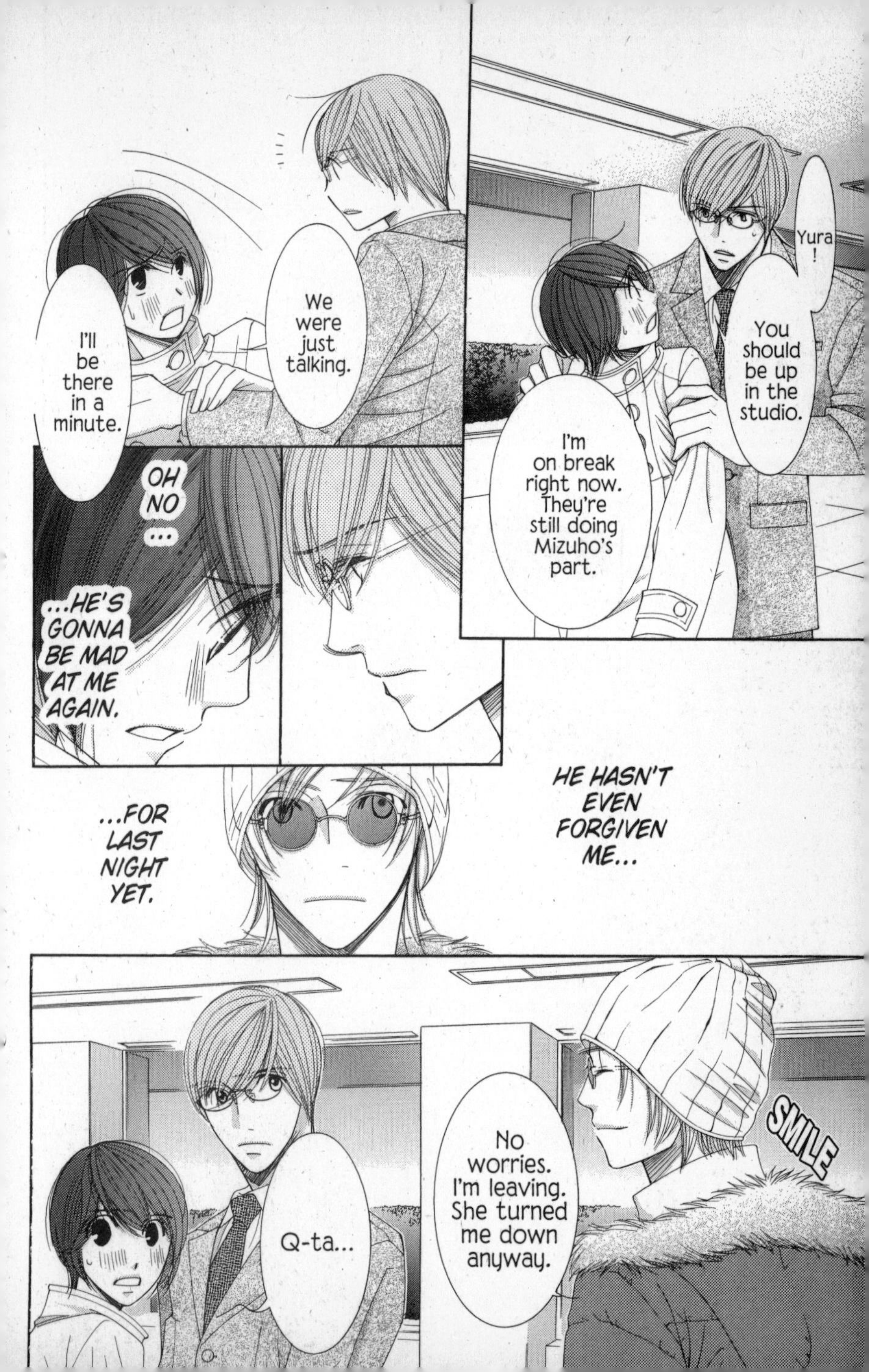
Yura!
You should be up in the studio.
I'm on break right now. They're still doing Mizuho's part.
We were just talking.
I'll be there in a minute.
OH NO...
...HE'S GONNA BE MAD AT ME AGAIN.
HE HASN'T EVEN FORGIVEN ME...
...FOR LAST NIGHT YET.
SMILE
No worries. I'm leaving. She turned me down anyway.
Q-ta...

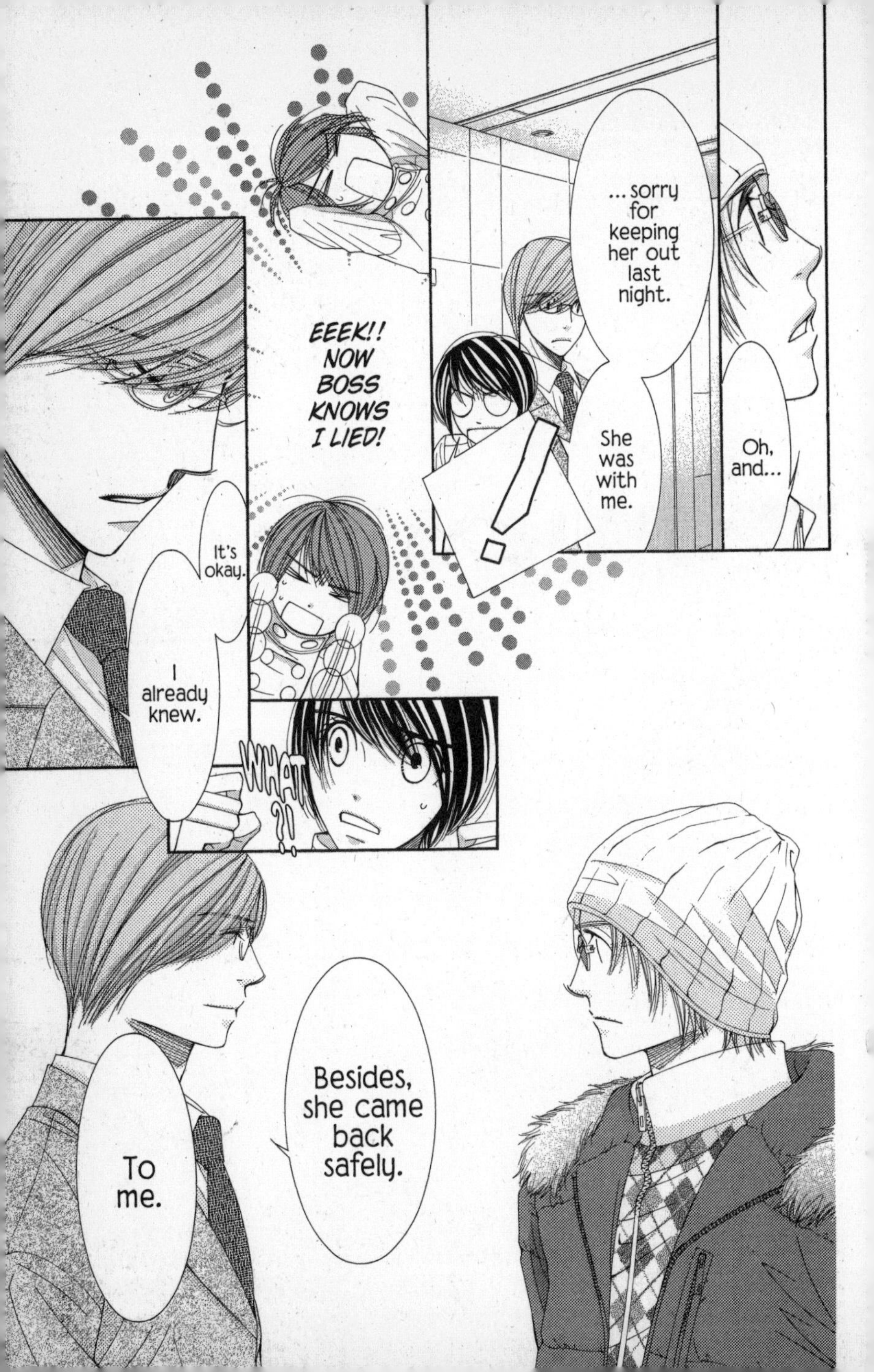
Oh, and...
...sorry for keeping her out last night.
She was with me.
EEEK!! NOW BOSS KNOWS I LIED!
It's okay.
I already knew.
WHAT?!
Besides, she came back safely.
To me.

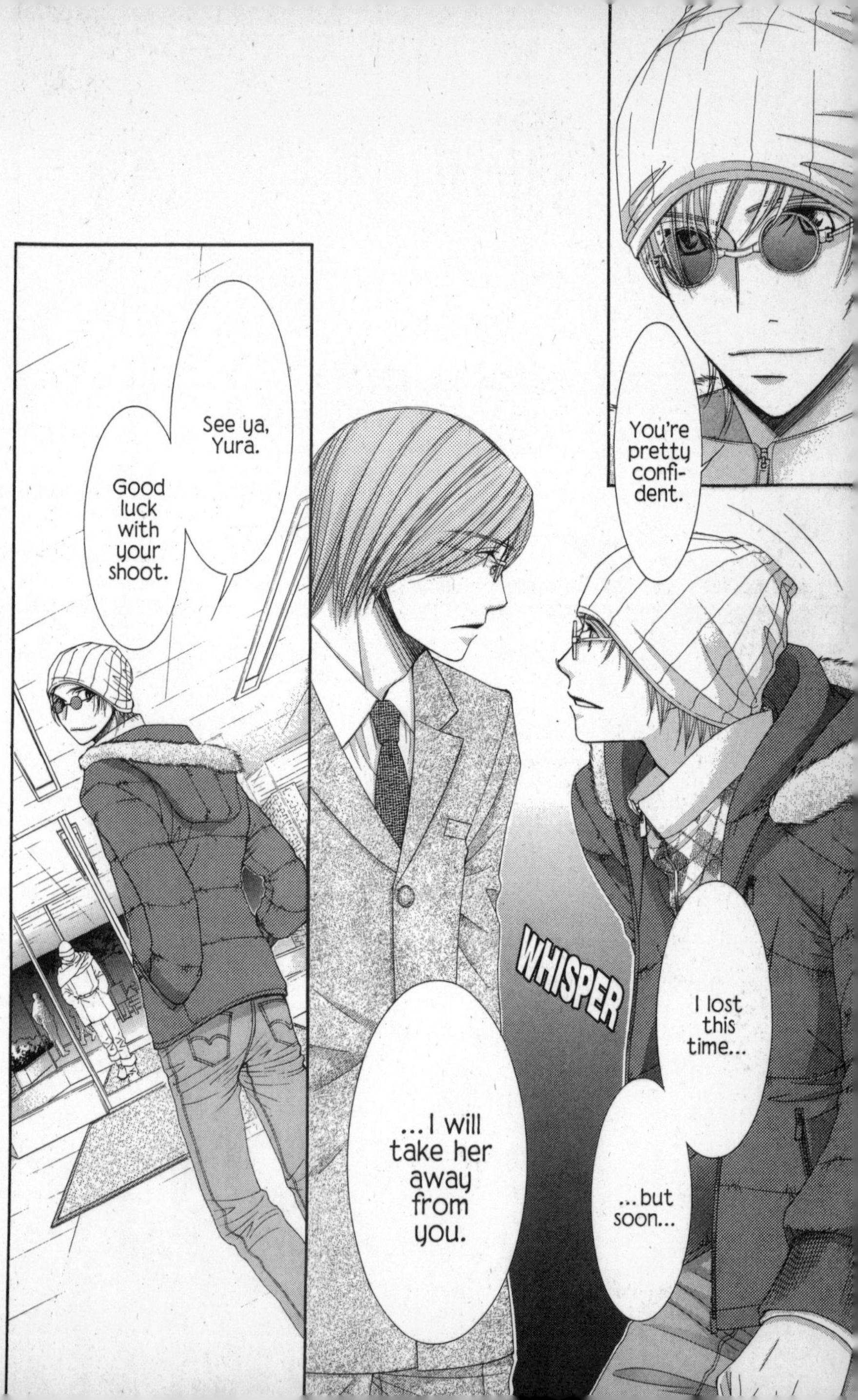
You're pretty confi-dent.
WHISPER
I lost this time...
...but soon...
...I will take her away from you.
See ya, Yura.
Good luck with your shoot.

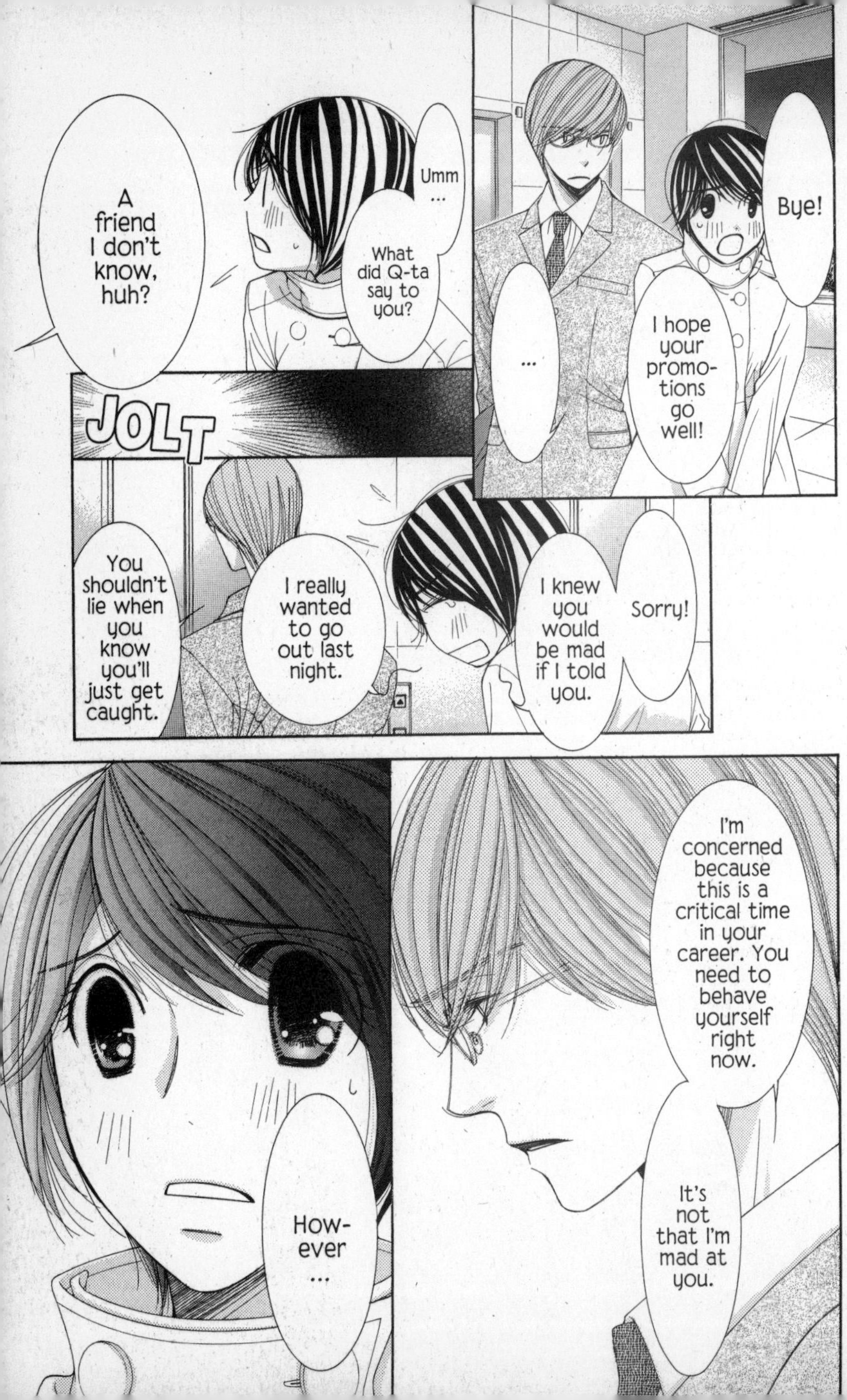
Bye!
I hope your promotions go well!
...
Umm ...
What did Q-ta say to you?
A friend I don't know, huh?
JOLT
Sorry!
I knew you would be mad if I told you.
I really wanted to go out last night.
You shouldn't lie when you know you'll just get caught.
I'm concerned because this is a critical time in your career. You need to behave yourself right now.
It's not that I'm mad at you.
How-ever ...

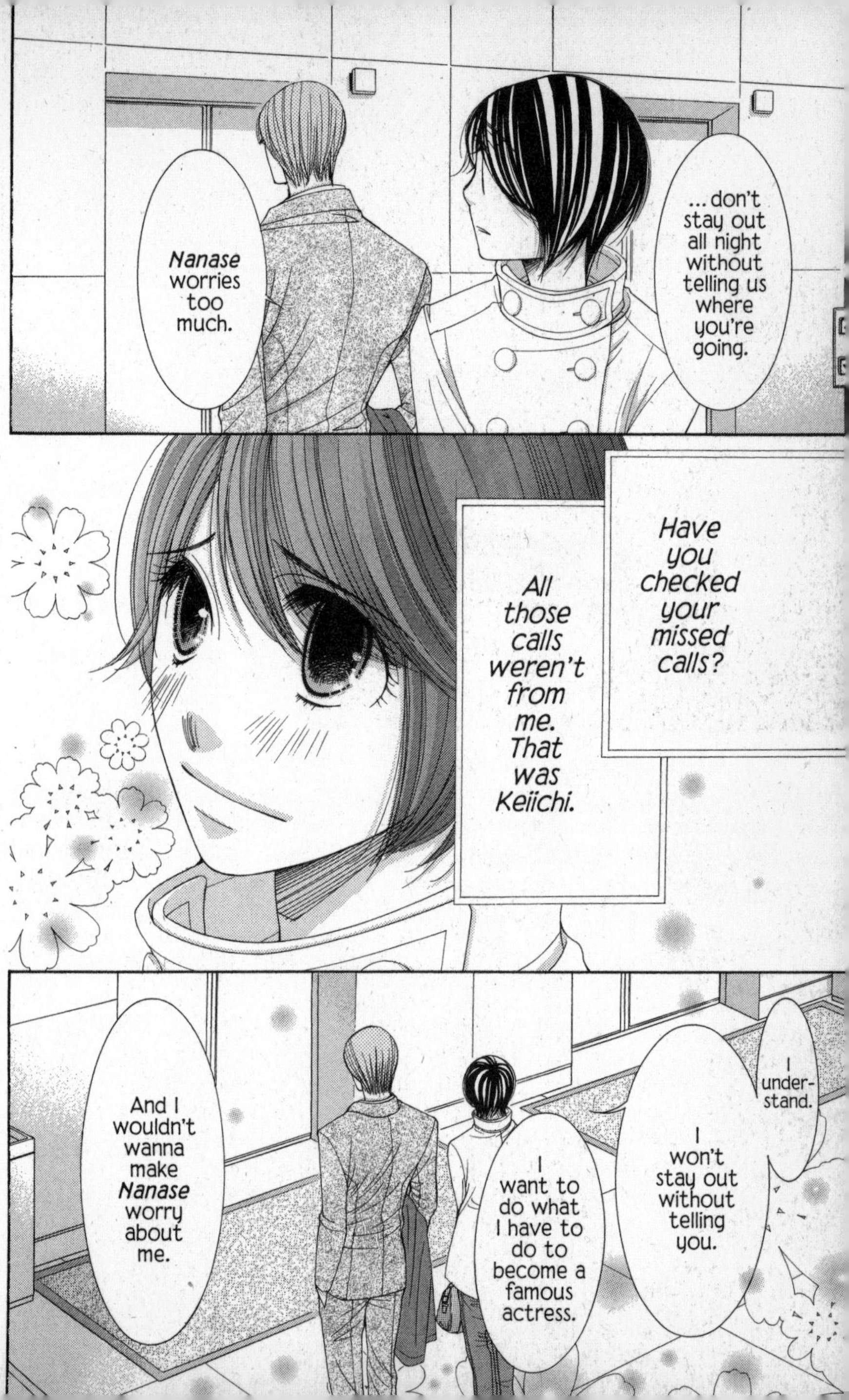
...don't stay out all night without telling us where you're going.
Nanase worries too much.
Have you checked your missed calls?
All those calls weren't from me. That was Keiichi.
I under-stand.
I won't stay out without telling you.
I want to do what I have to do to become a famous actress.
And I wouldn't wanna make Nanase worry about me.

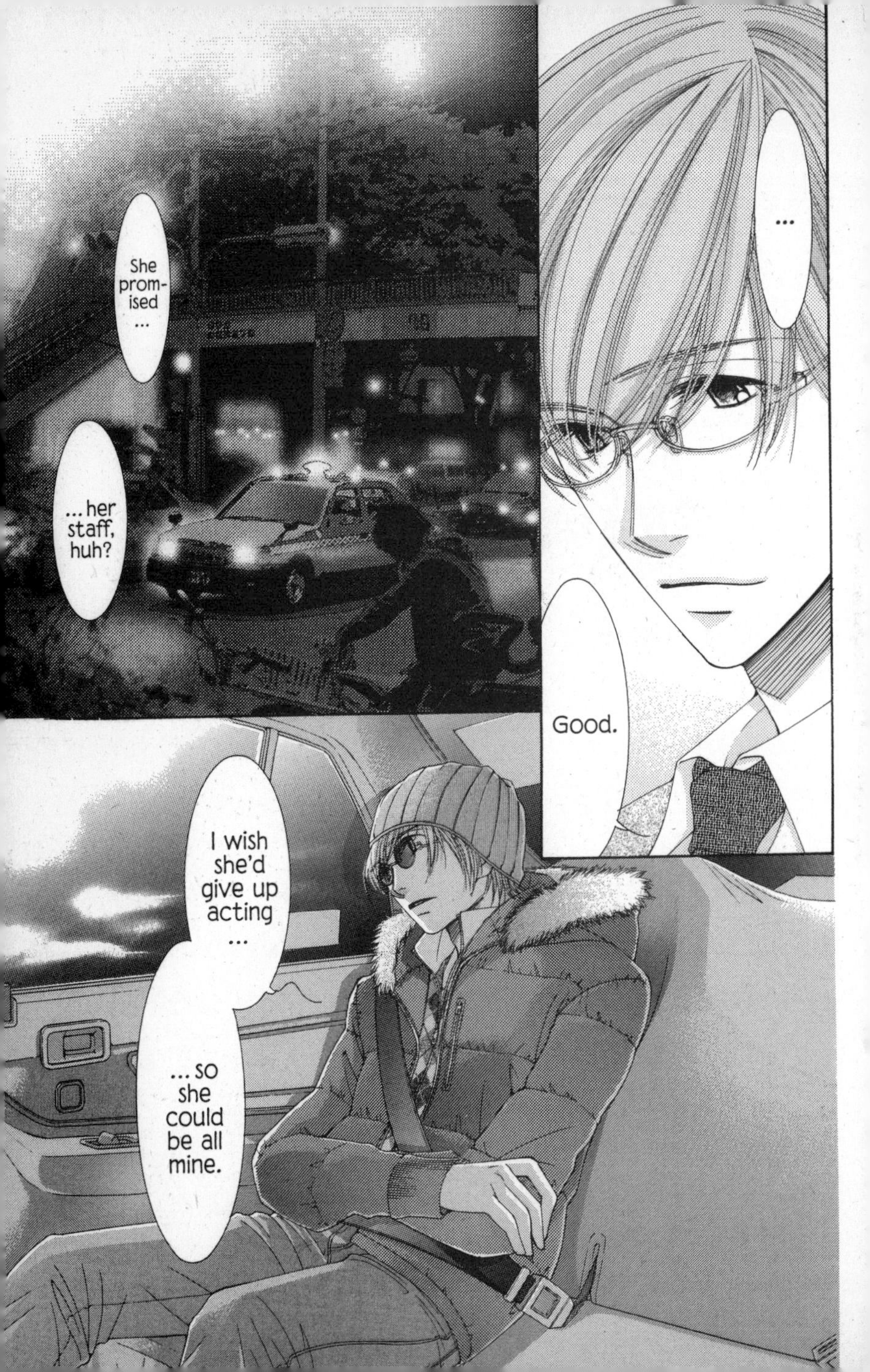
...
Good.
She promised...
...her staff, huh?
I wish she'd give up acting...
...so she could be all mine.

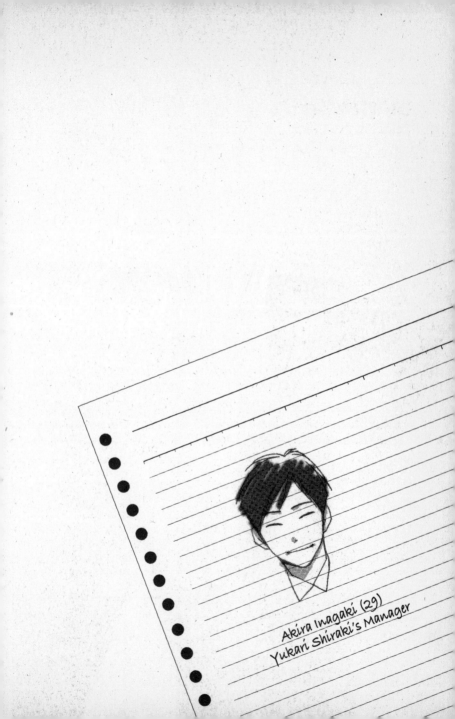

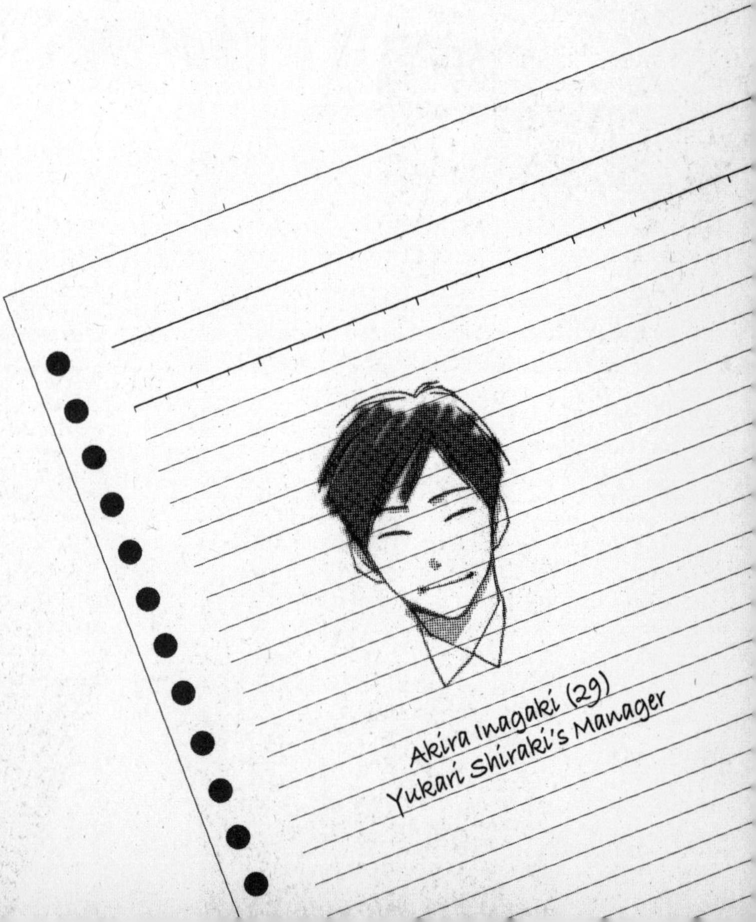
Akira Inagaki (29)
Yukari Shiraki's Manager

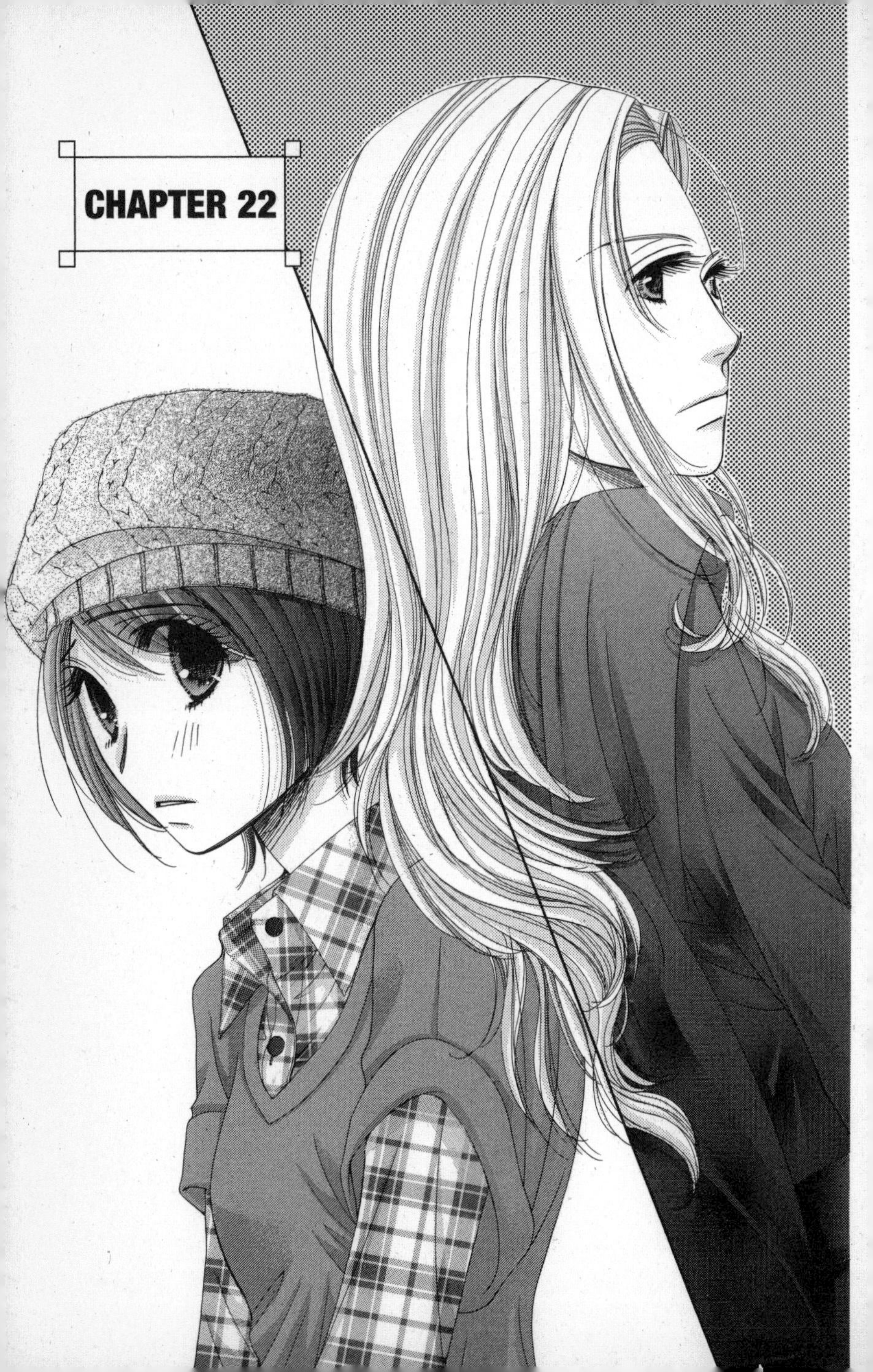
CHAPTER 22

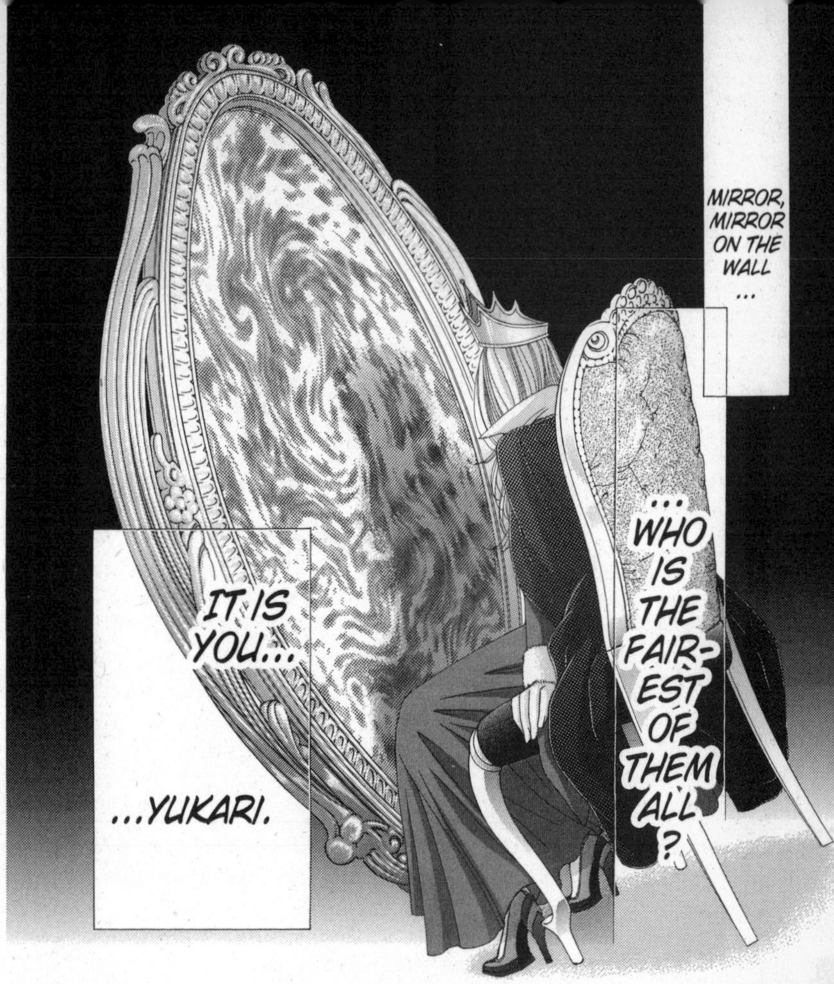
MIRROR, MIRROR ON THE WALL ...
... WHO IS THE FAIREST OF THEM ALL ?
IT IS YOU...
...YUKARI.

Honey Hunt

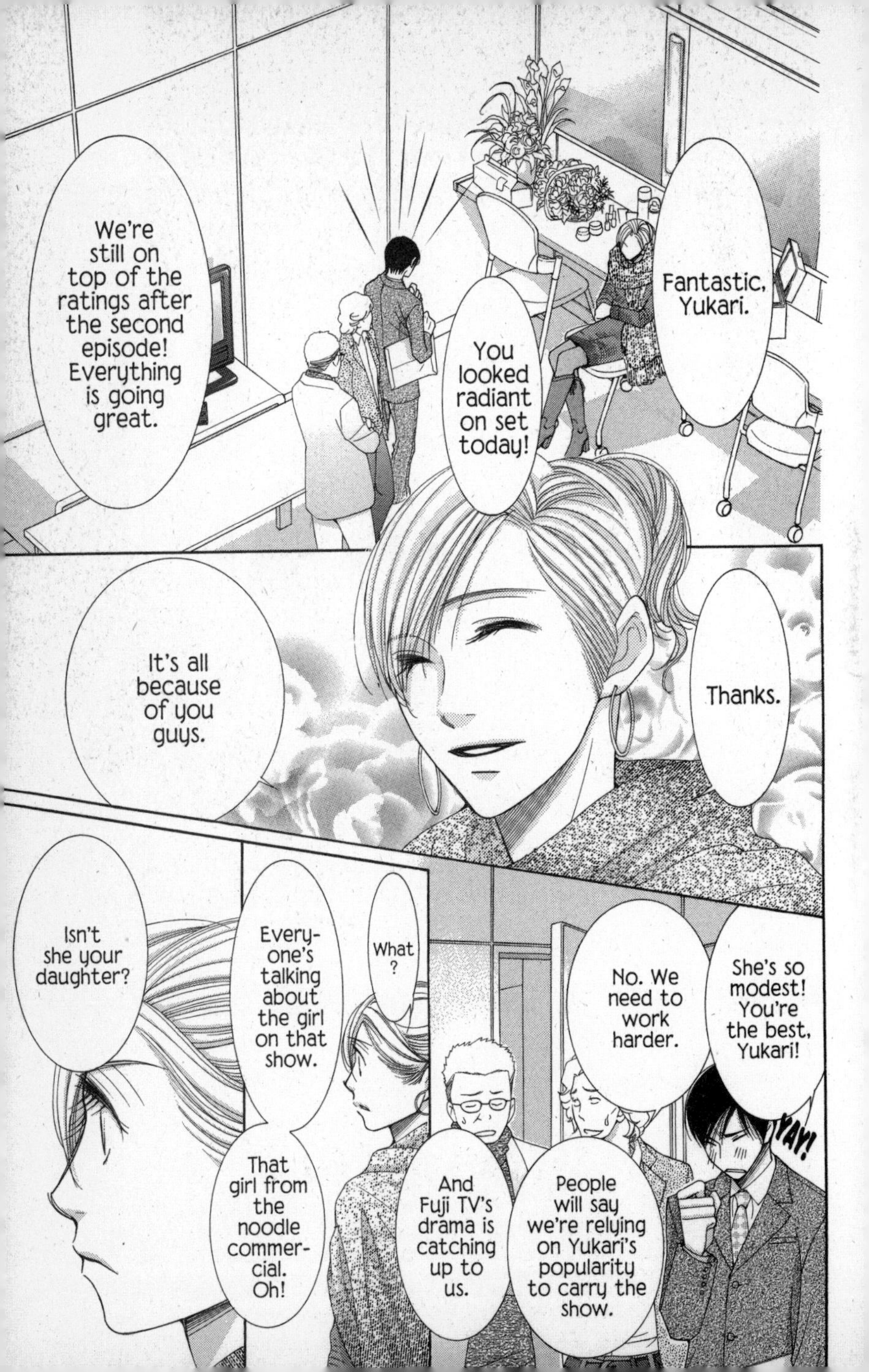
Fantastic, Yukari.
You looked radiant on set today!
We're still on top of the ratings after the second episode! Everything is going great.
Thanks.
It's all because of you guys.
She's so modest! You're the best, Yukari!
YAY!
No. We need to work harder.
People will say we're relying on Yukari's popularity to carry the show.
And Fuji TV's drama is catching up to us.
What?
Every-one's talking about the girl on that show.
That girl from the noodle commer-cial. Oh!
Isn't she your daughter?

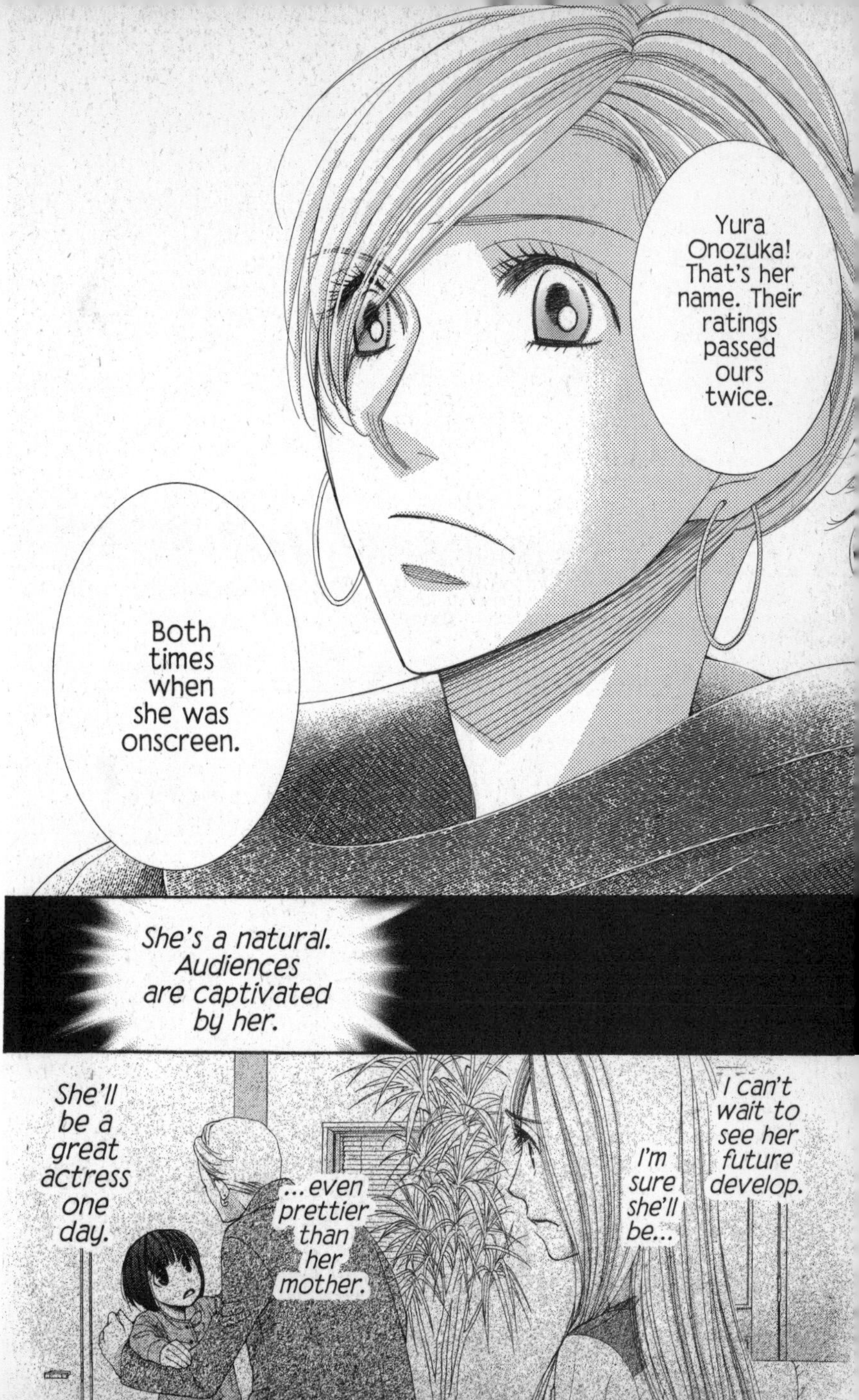
Yura Onozuka! That's her name. Their ratings passed ours twice.
Both times when she was onscreen.
She's a natural. Audiences are captivated by her.
I can't wait to see her future develop.
I'm sure she'll be...
...even prettier than her mother.
She'll be a great actress one day.

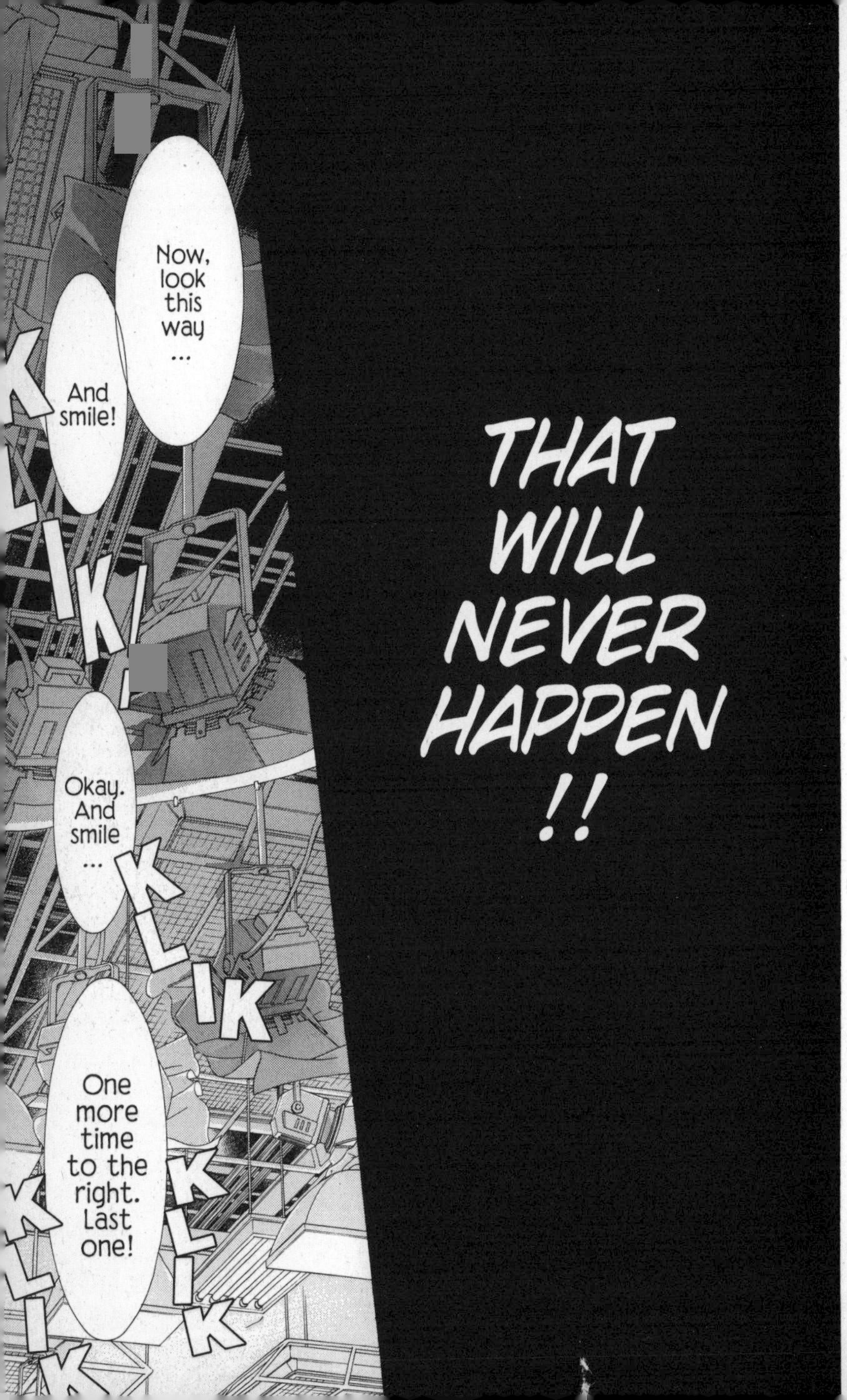
THAT WILL NEVER HAPPEN!!
Now, look this way...
And smile!
KLIK
Okay. And smile...
KLIK
One more time to the right. Last one!
KLIK
KLIK

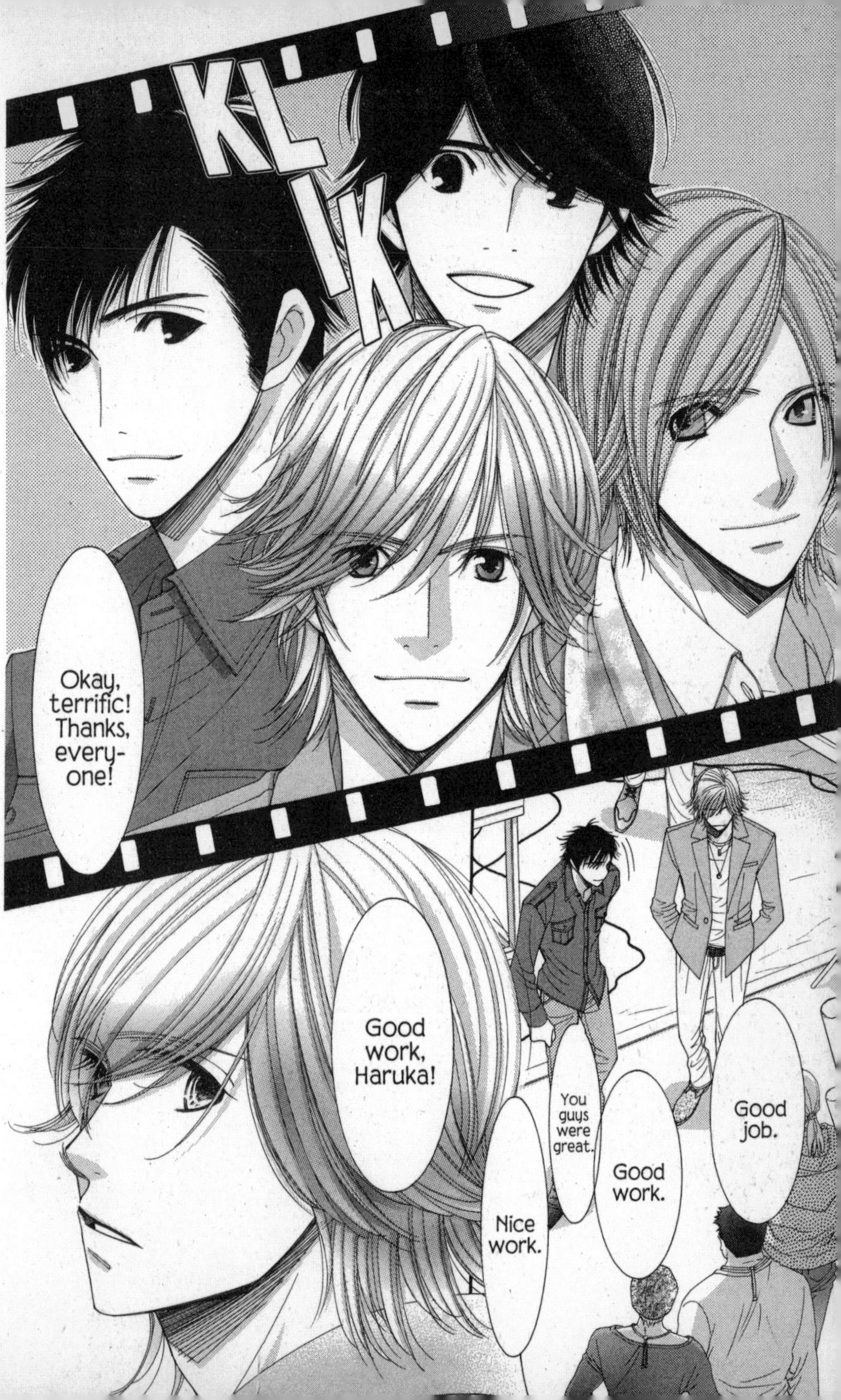
KLIK
Okay, terrific! Thanks, every-one!
Good job.
Good work.
You guys were great.
Nice work.
Good work, Haruka!

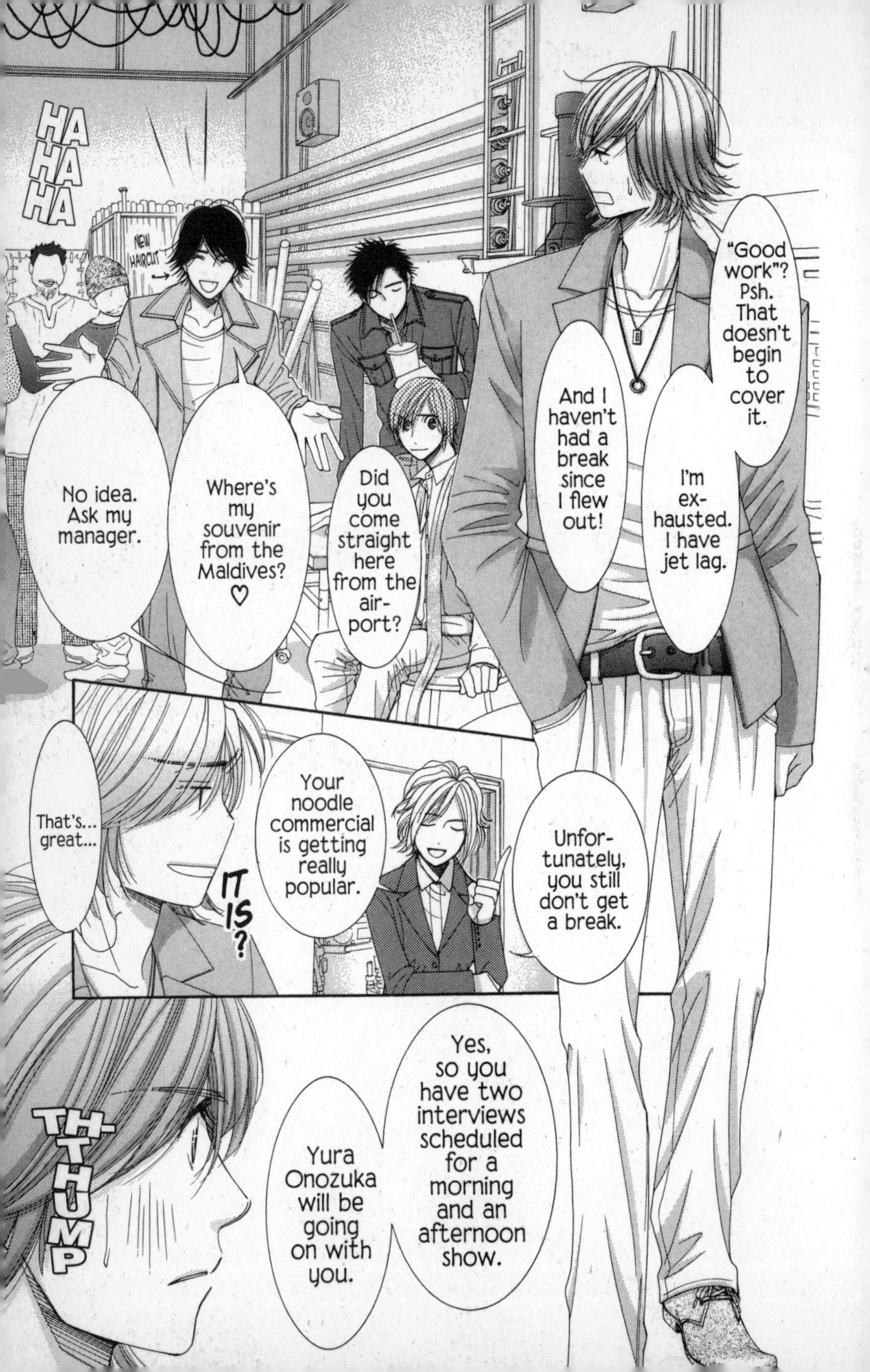
"Good work"? Psh. That doesn't begin to cover it.
I'm exhausted. I have jet lag.
And I haven't had a break since I flew out!
Did you come straight here from the airport?
Where's my souvenir from the Maldives? ♡
NEW HAIRCUT
HA HA HA
No idea. Ask my manager.
Unfortunately, you still don't get a break.
Your noodle commercial is getting really popular.
IT IS?
That's... great...
Yes, so you have two interviews scheduled for a morning and an afternoon show.
Yura Onozuka will be going on with you.
TH-THUMP

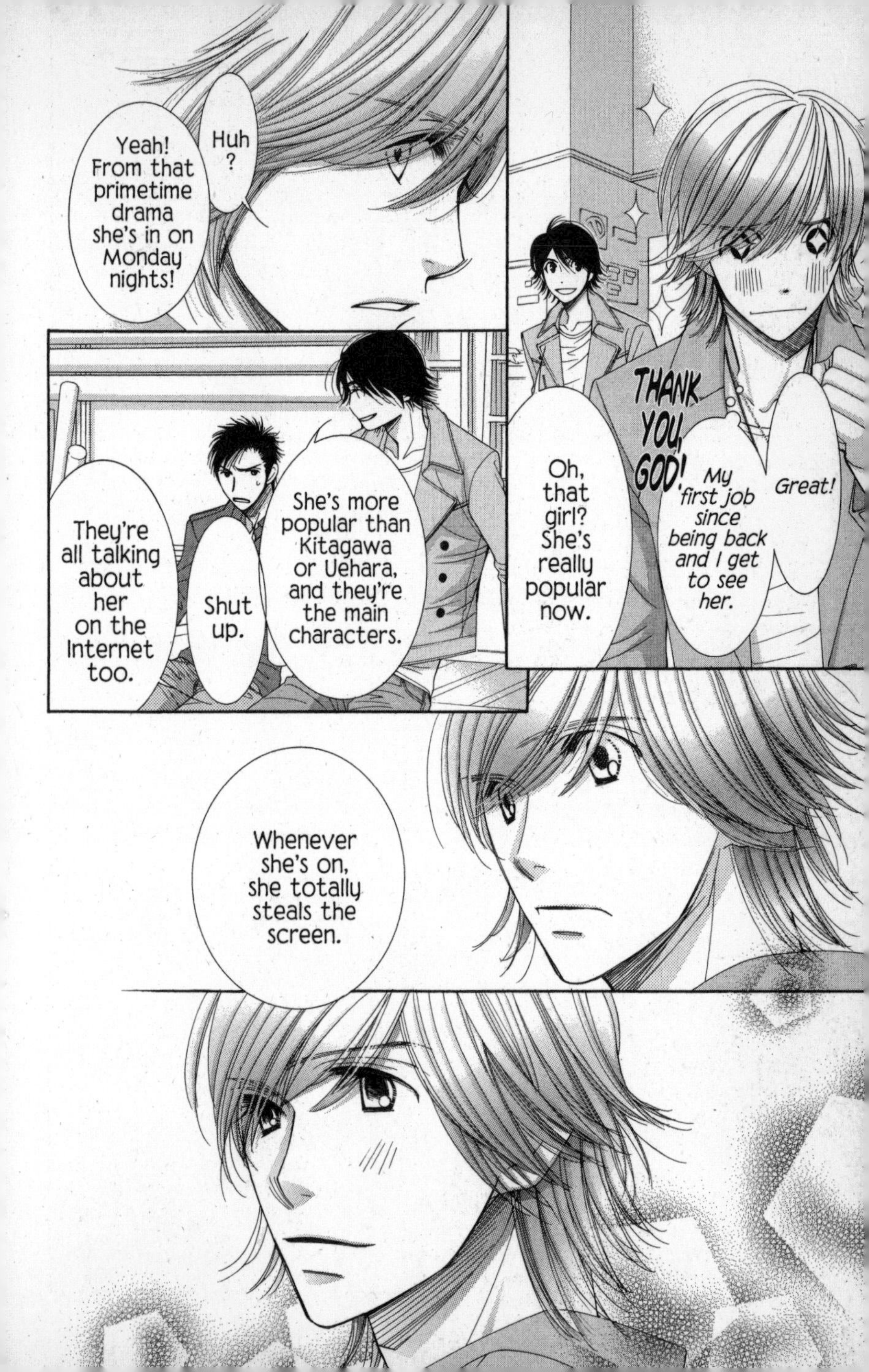
Great!
My first job since being back and I get to see her.
THANK YOU, GOD!
Oh, that girl? She's really popular now.
Huh?
Yeah! From that primetime drama she's in on Monday nights!
She's more popular than Kitagawa or Uehara, and they're the main characters.
Shut up.
They're all talking about her on the Internet too.
Whenever she's on, she totally steals the screen.

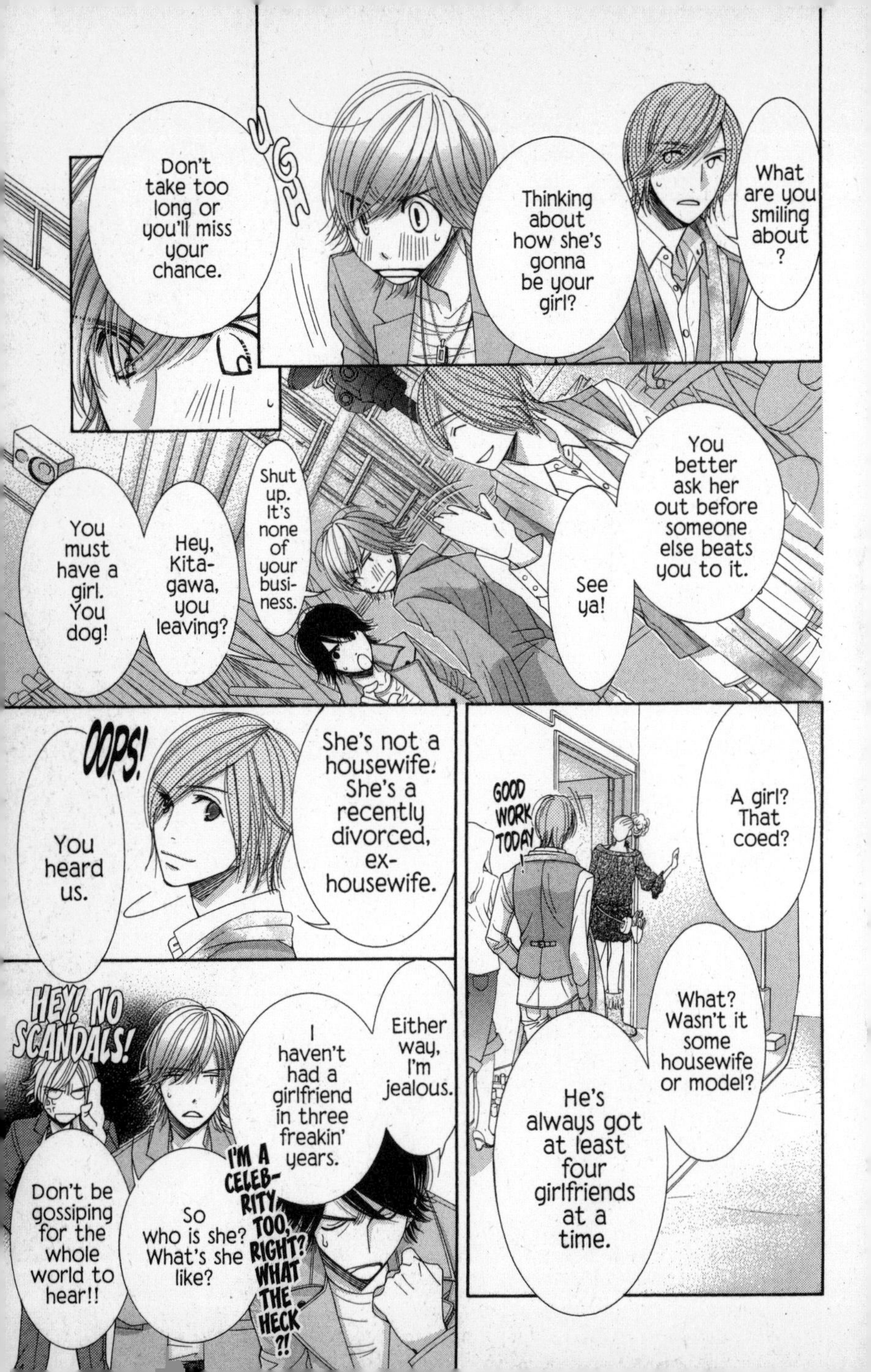
What are you smiling about?
Thinking about how she's gonna be your girl?
Don't take too long or you'll miss your chance.
You better ask her out before someone else beats you to it.
See ya!
Shut up. It's none of your business.
Hey, Kitagawa, you leaving?
You must have a girl. You dog!
A girl? That coed?
GOOD WORK TODAY!
What? Wasn't it some housewife or model?
He's always got at least four girlfriends at a time.
She's not a housewife. She's a recently divorced, ex-housewife.
OOPS!
You heard us.
Either way, I'm jealous.
I haven't had a girlfriend in three freakin' years.
I'M A CELEBRITY TOO, RIGHT? WHAT THE HECK?!
So who is she? What's she like?
HEY! NO SCANDALS!
Don't be gossiping for the whole world to hear!!

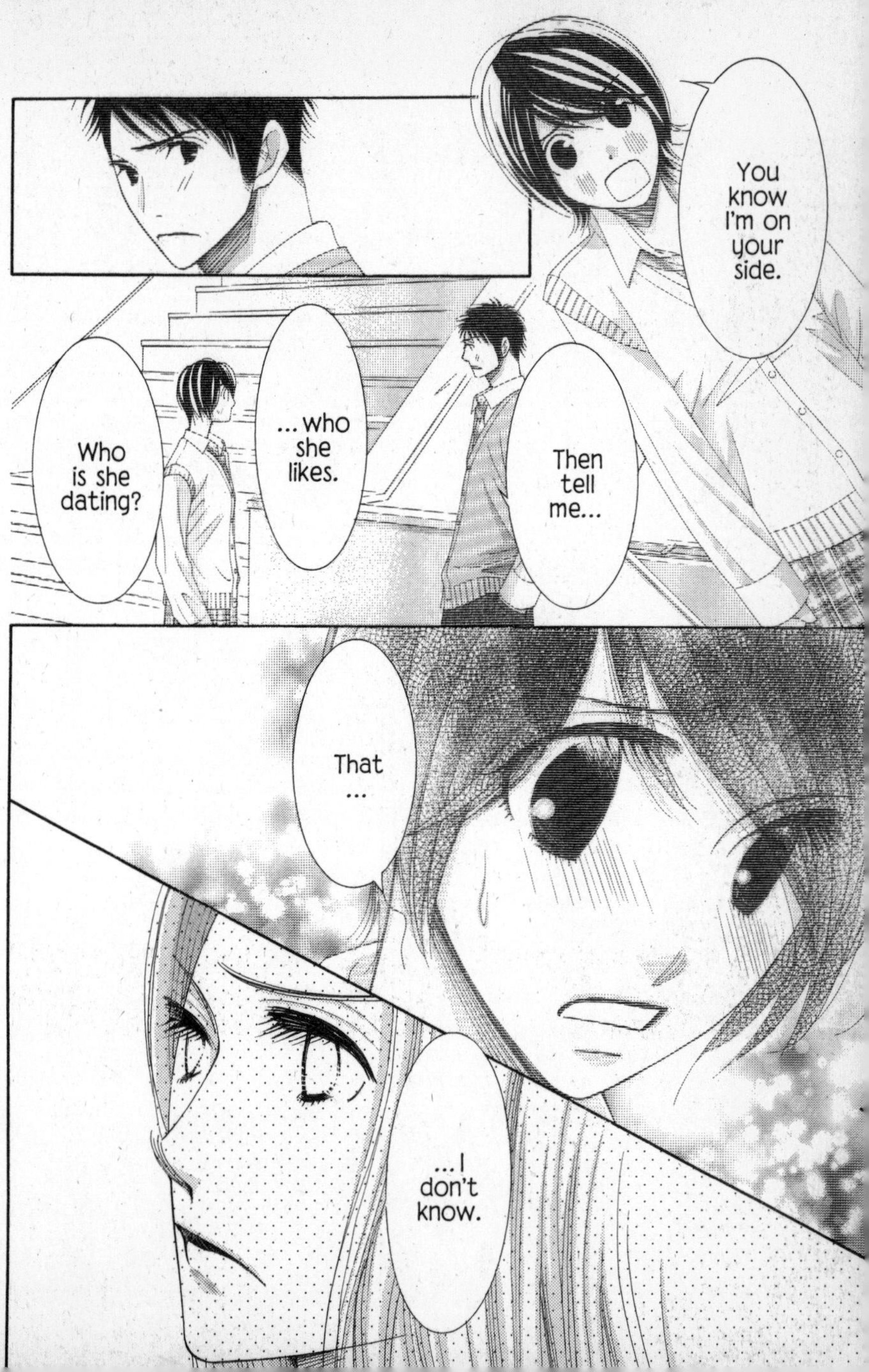

You know I'm on your side.
Then tell me...
...who she likes.
Who is she dating?
That ...
...I don't know.

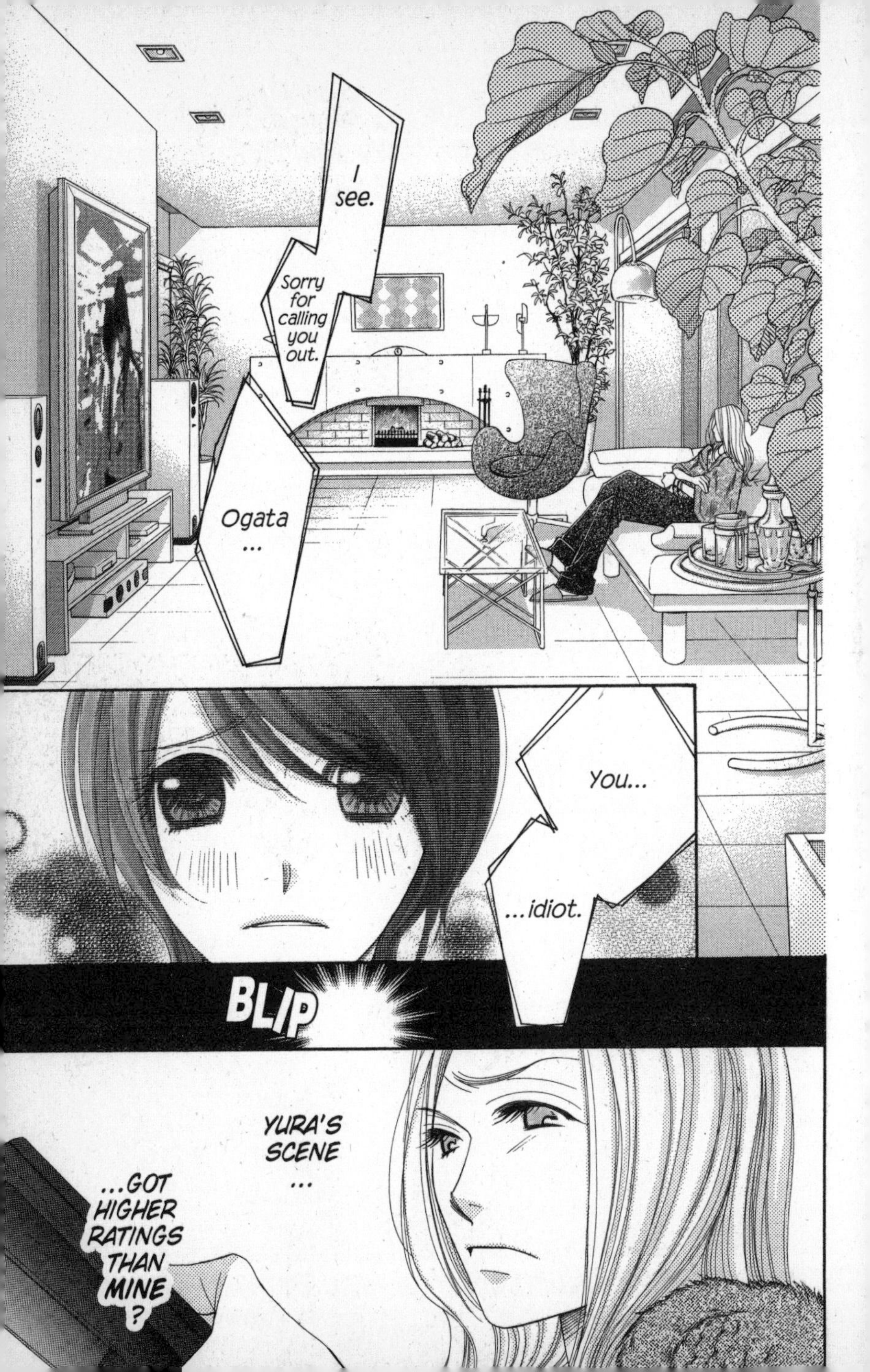
I see.
Sorry for calling you out.
Ogata...
You...
...idiot.
BLIP
YURA'S SCENE...
...GOT HIGHER RATINGS THAN MINE?

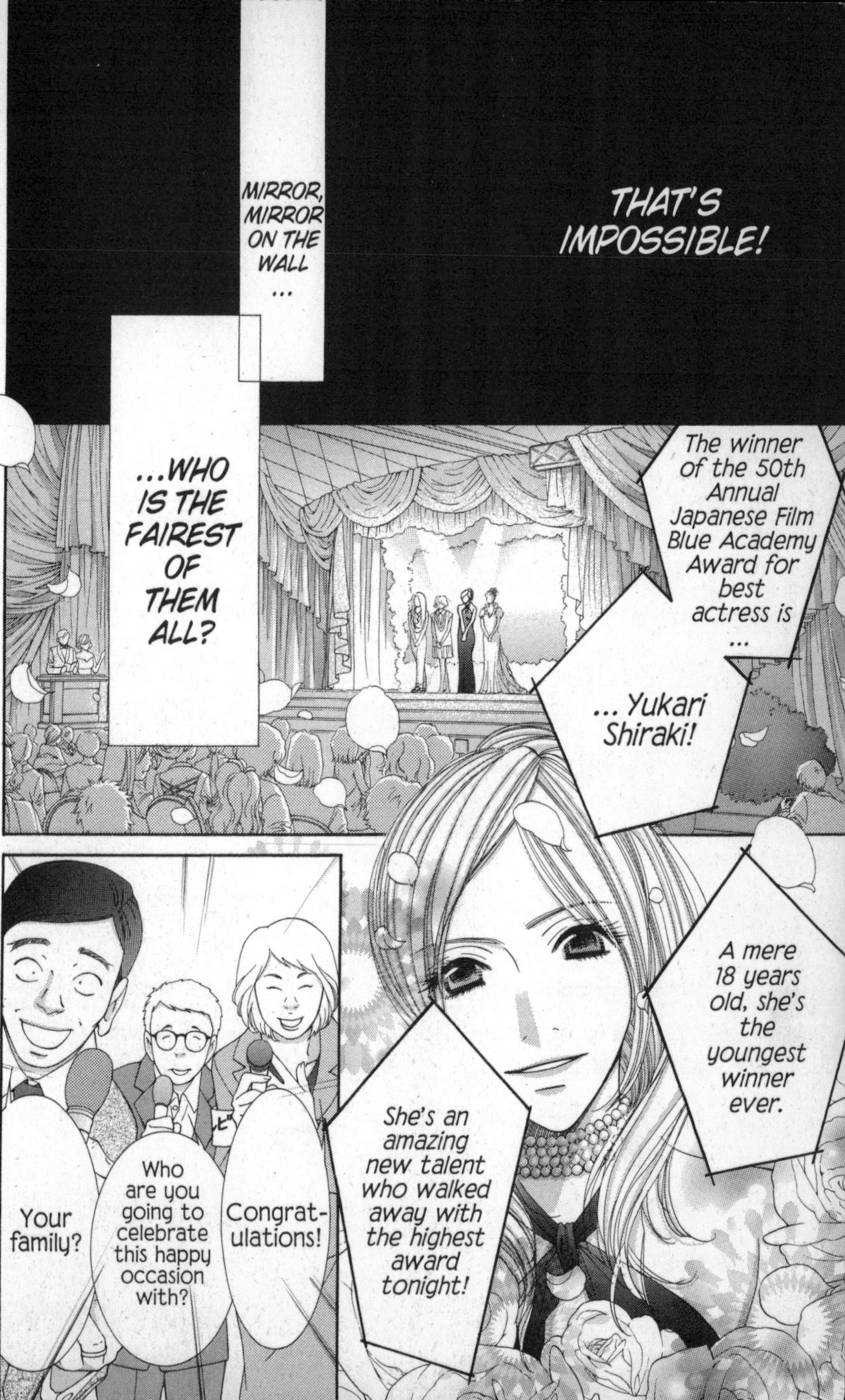
THAT'S IMPOSSIBLE!
MIRROR, MIRROR ON THE WALL ...
...WHO IS THE FAIREST OF THEM ALL?
The winner of the 50th Annual Japanese Film Blue Academy Award for best actress is ...
... Yukari Shiraki!
A mere 18 years old, she's the youngest winner ever.
She's an amazing new talent who walked away with the highest award tonight!
Congrat-ulations!
Who are you going to celebrate this happy occasion with?
Your family?

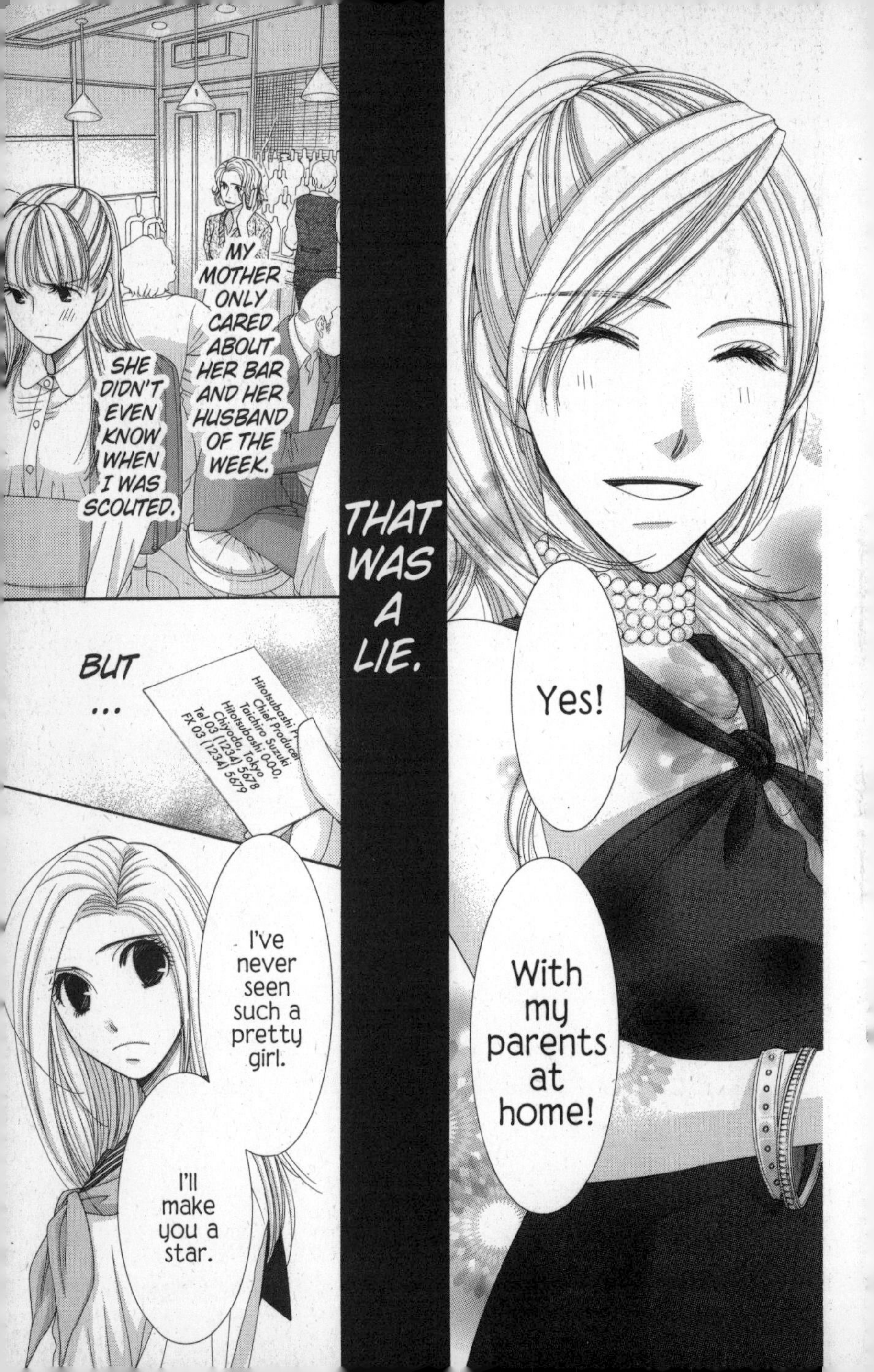
Yes!
With my parents at home!
THAT WAS A LIE.
MY MOTHER ONLY CARED ABOUT HER BAR AND HER HUSBAND OF THE WEEK.
SHE DIDN'T EVEN KNOW WHEN I WAS SCOUTED.
BUT ...
Chief Producer
Taichiro Suzuki
Hitotsubashi 0-0-0,
Chiyoda, Tokyo
Tel 03 (1234) 5678
FX 03 (1234) 5679
I've never seen such a pretty girl.
I'll make you a star.

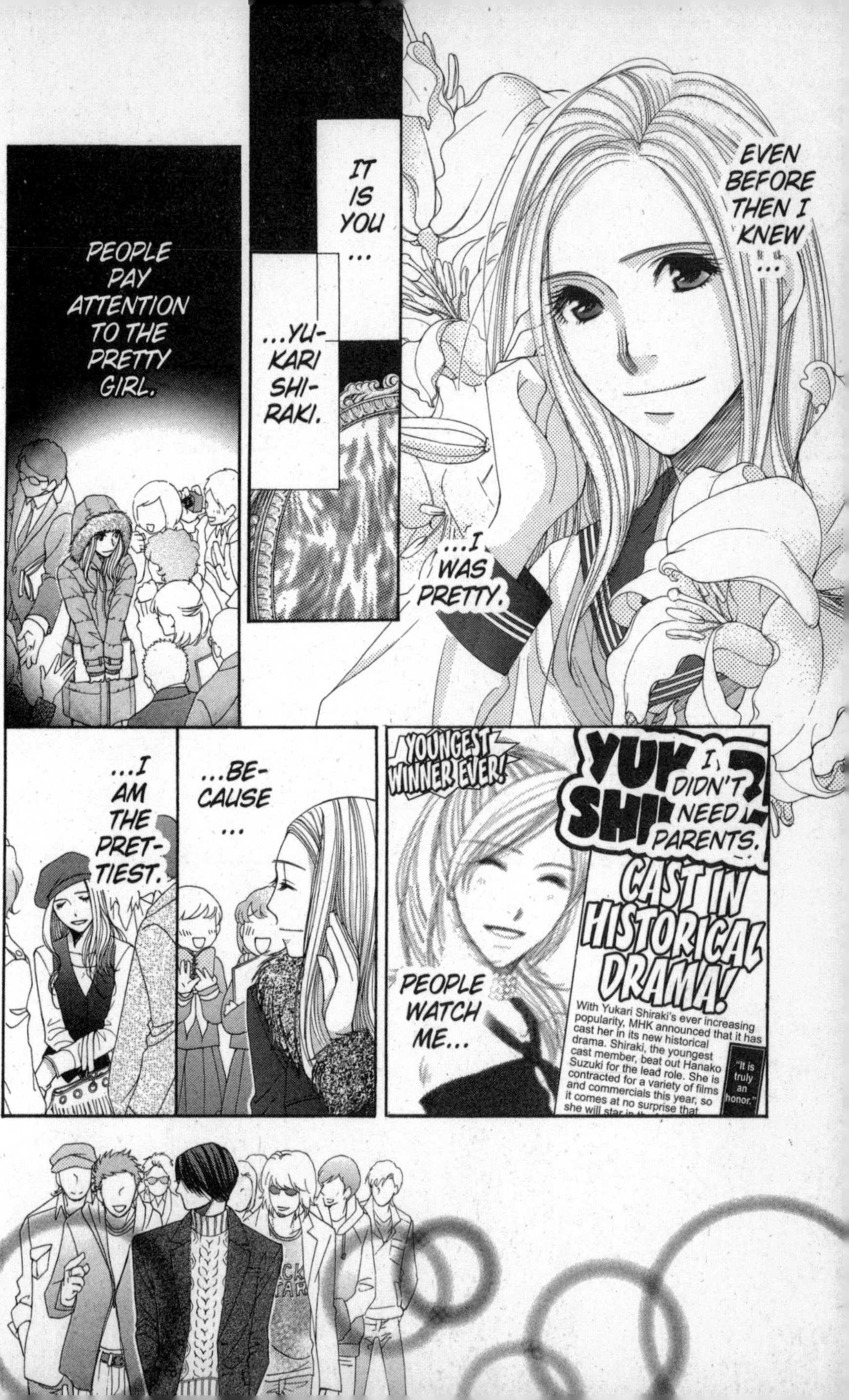
EVEN BEFORE THEN I KNEW...
...I WAS PRETTY.
IT IS YOU...
...YU-KARI SHI-RAKI.
PEOPLE PAY ATTENTION TO THE PRETTY GIRL.
I DIDN'T NEED PARENTS.
YOUNGEST WINNER EVER!
CAST IN HISTORICAL DRAMA!
With Yukari Shiraki's ever increasing popularity, MHK announced that it has cast her in its new historical drama. Shiraki, the youngest cast member, beat out Hanako Suzuki for the lead role. She is contracted for a variety of films and commercials this year, so it comes at no surprise that
"It is truly an honor."
PEOPLE WATCH ME...
...BE-CAUSE...
...I AM THE PRET-TIEST.

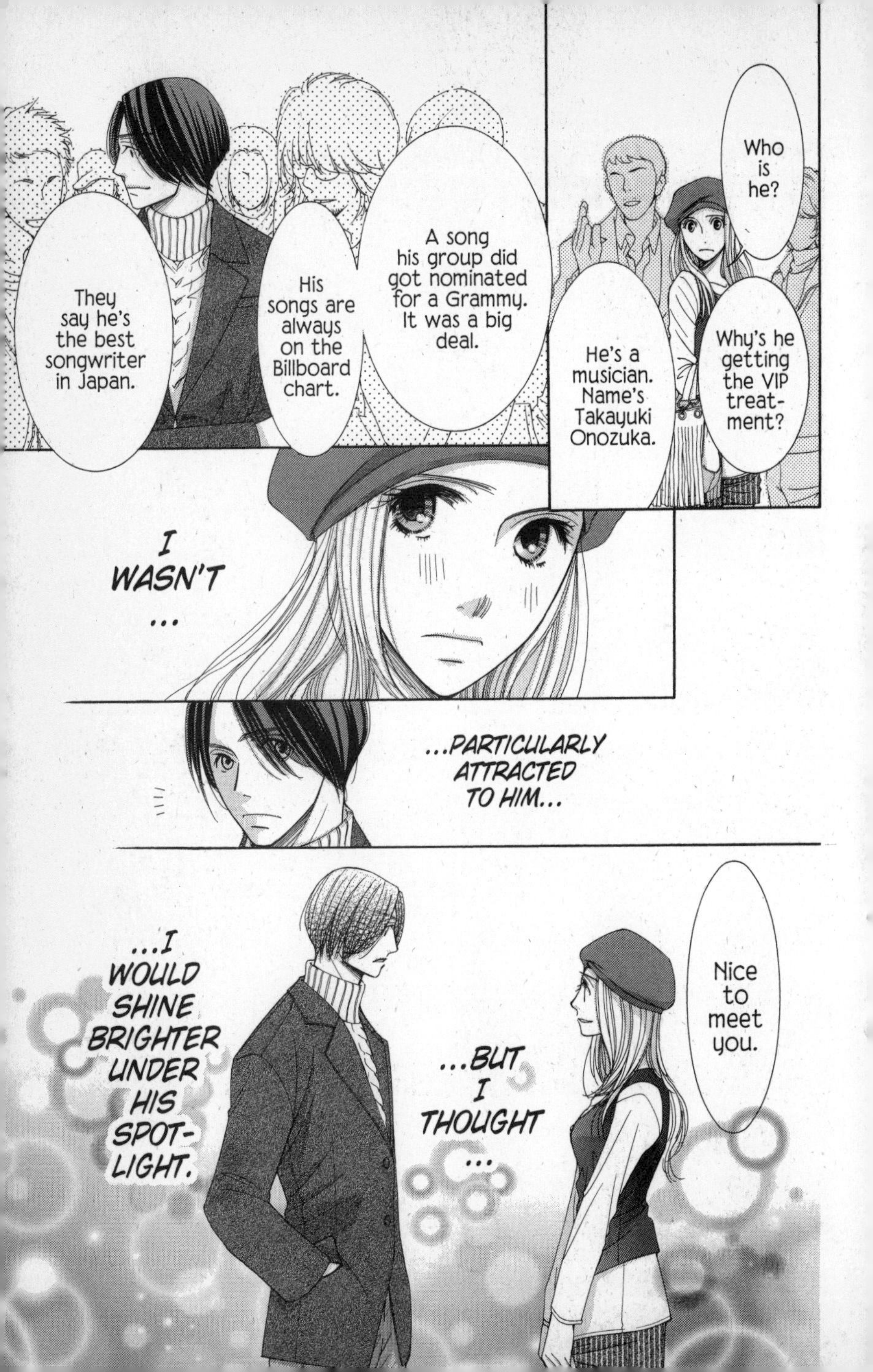
Who is he?
Why's he getting the VIP treat-ment?
He's a musician. Name's Takayuki Onozuka.
A song his group did got nominated for a Grammy. It was a big deal.
His songs are always on the Billboard chart.
They say he's the best songwriter in Japan.
I WASN'T ...
...PARTICULARLY ATTRACTED TO HIM...
Nice to meet you.
...BUT I THOUGHT ...
...I WOULD SHINE BRIGHTER UNDER HIS SPOT-LIGHT.

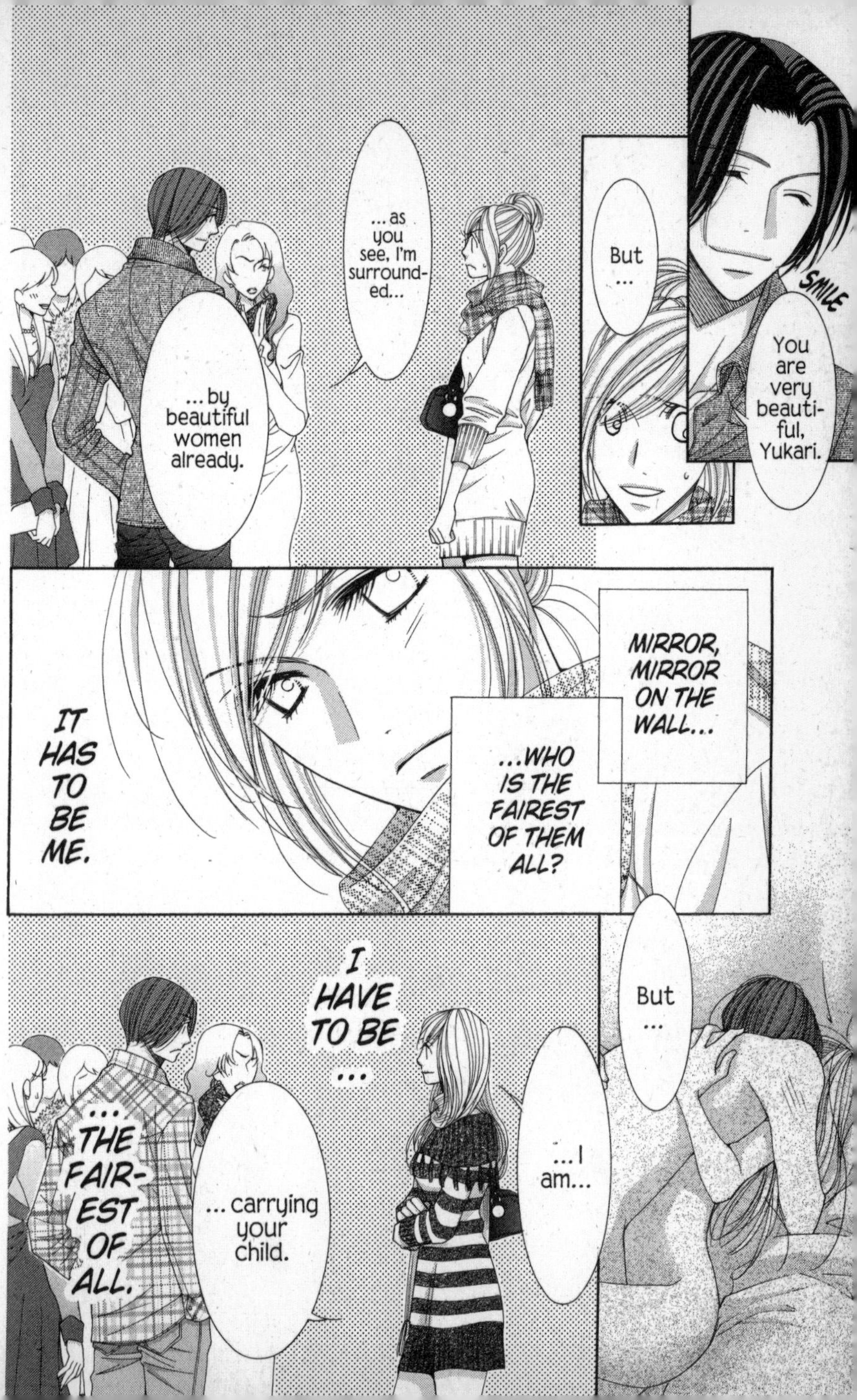
SMILE
You are very beautiful, Yukari.
But ...
... as you see, I'm surrounded...
... by beautiful women already.
MIRROR, MIRROR ON THE WALL...
...WHO IS THE FAIREST OF THEM ALL?
IT HAS TO BE ME.
But ...
...I am...
I HAVE TO BE ...
... carrying your child.
... THE FAIREST OF ALL.

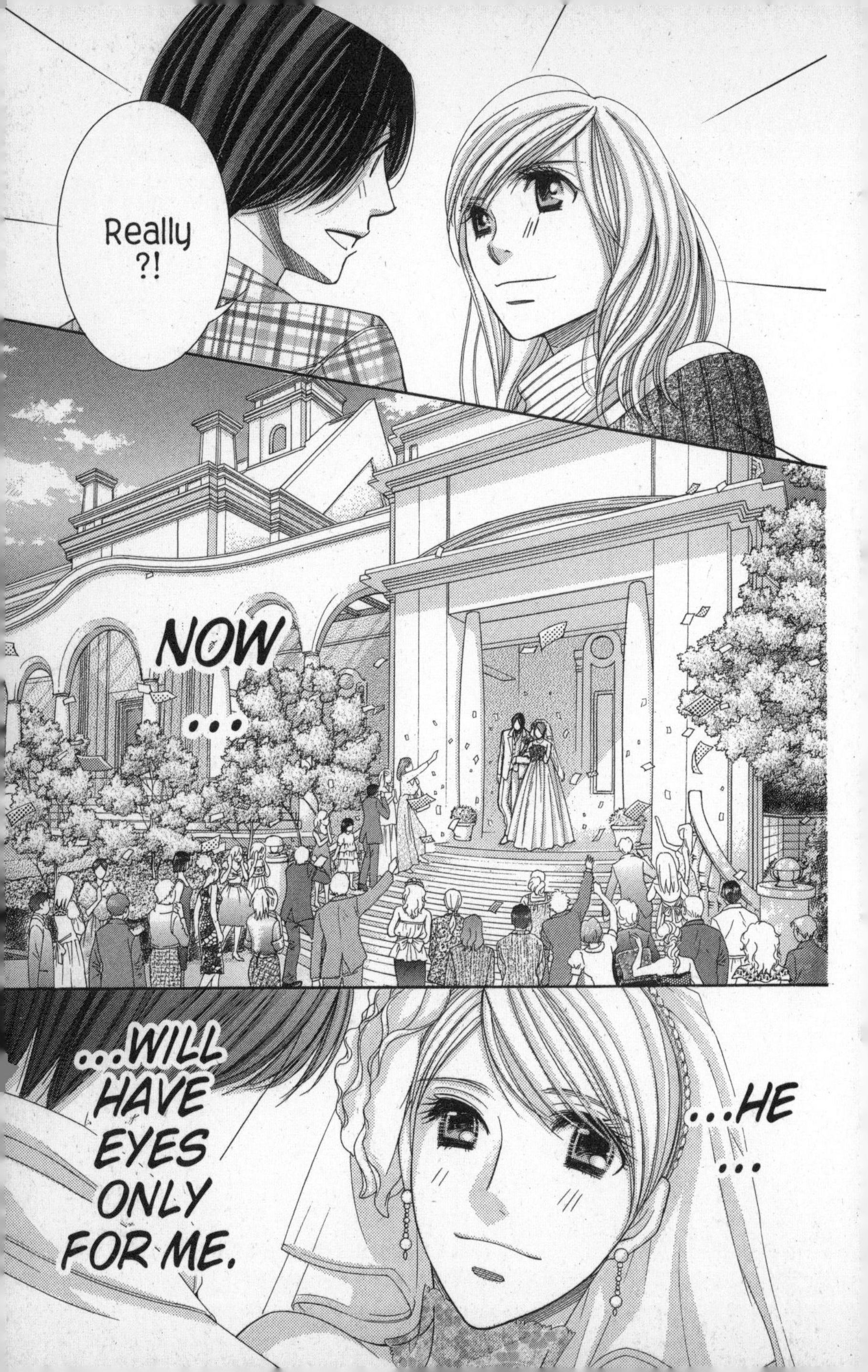
Really ?!
NOW ...
...HE ...
...WILL HAVE EYES ONLY FOR ME.

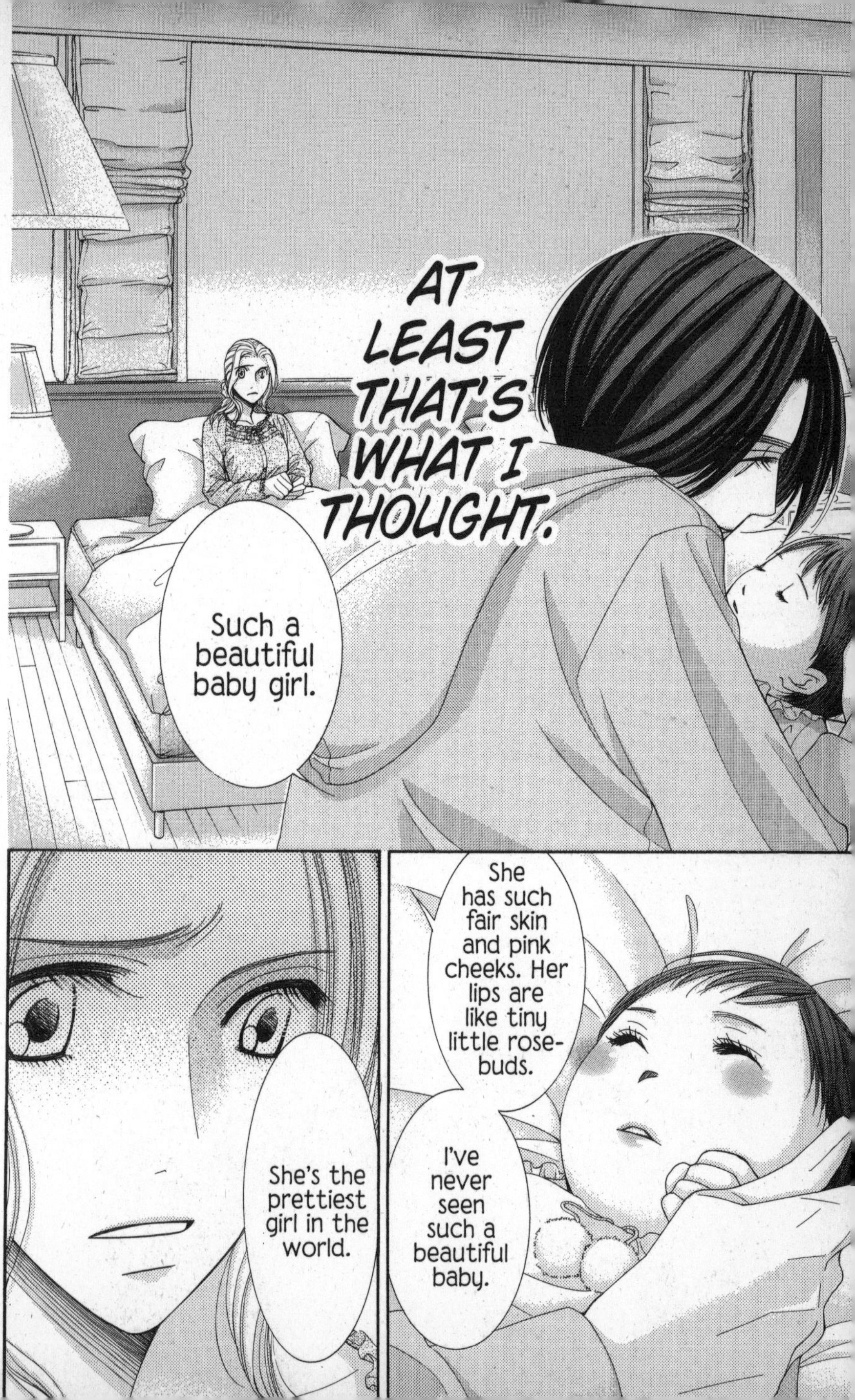
AT LEAST THAT'S WHAT I THOUGHT.
Such a beautiful baby girl.
She has such fair skin and pink cheeks. Her lips are like tiny little rose-buds.
I've never seen such a beautiful baby.
She's the prettiest girl in the world.

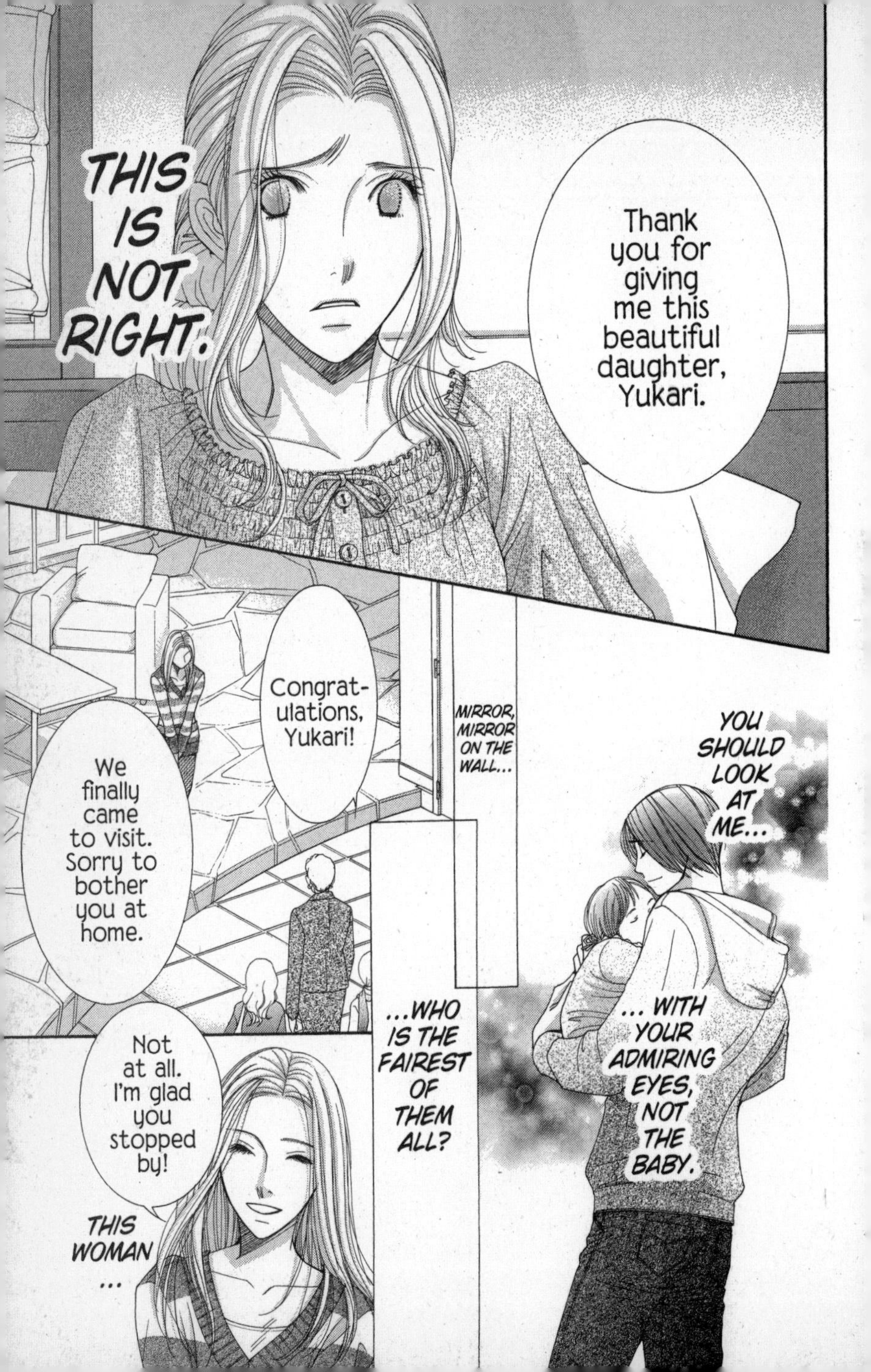
Thank you for giving me this beautiful daughter, Yukari.
THIS IS NOT RIGHT.
YOU SHOULD LOOK AT ME...
MIRROR, MIRROR ON THE WALL...
... WITH YOUR ADMIRING EYES, NOT THE BABY.
...WHO IS THE FAIREST OF THEM ALL?
Congrat-ulations, Yukari!
We finally came to visit. Sorry to bother you at home.
Not at all. I'm glad you stopped by!
THIS WOMAN ...

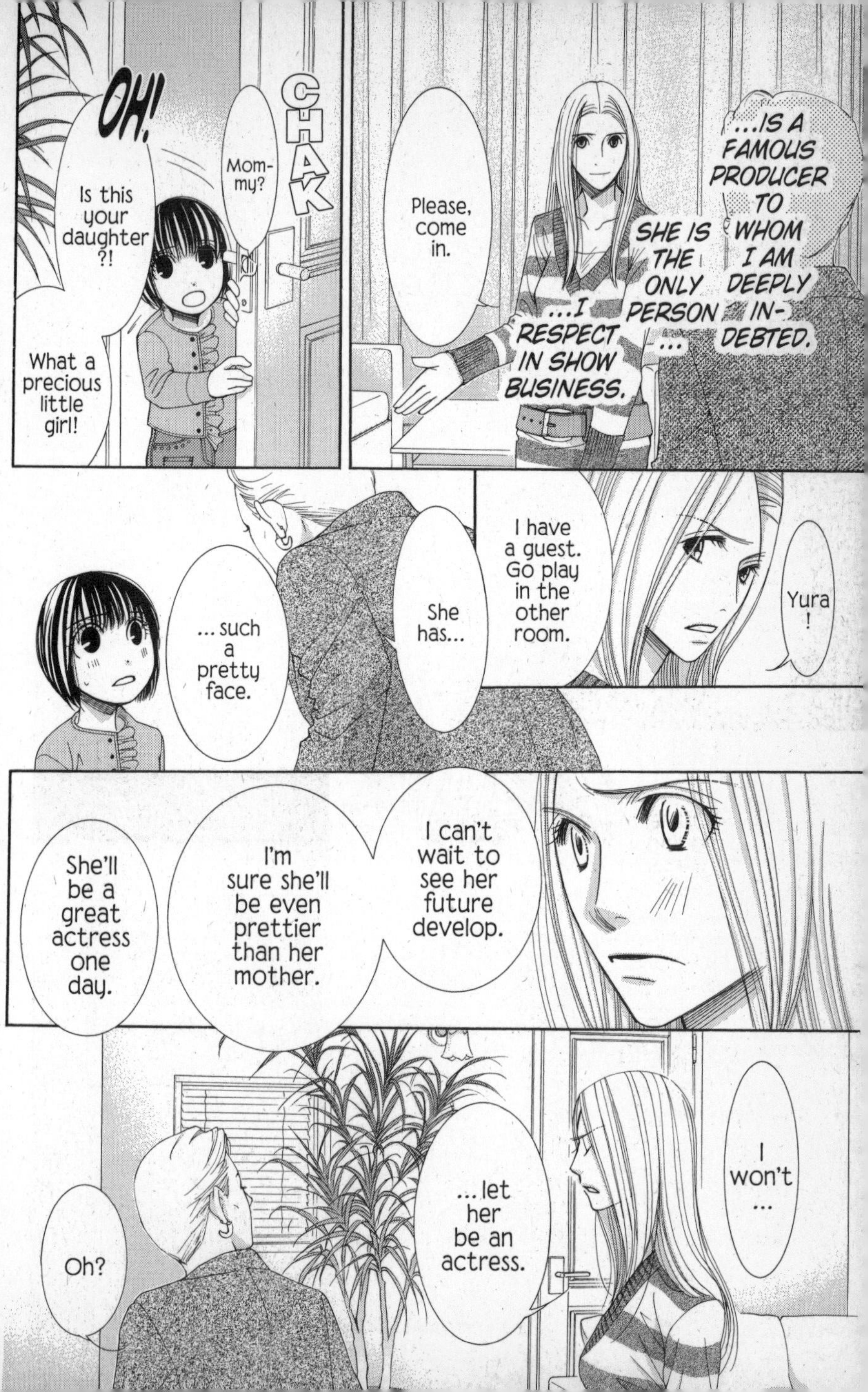
...IS A FAMOUS PRODUCER TO WHOM I AM DEEPLY IN-DEBTED.
SHE IS THE ONLY PERSON...
...I RESPECT IN SHOW BUSINESS.
Please, come in.
CHAK
Mom-my?
OH!
Is this your daughter?!
What a precious little girl!
Yura!
I have a guest. Go play in the other room.
She has...
...such a pretty face.
I can't wait to see her future develop.
I'm sure she'll be even prettier than her mother.
She'll be a great actress one day.
I won't...
...let her be an actress.
Oh?

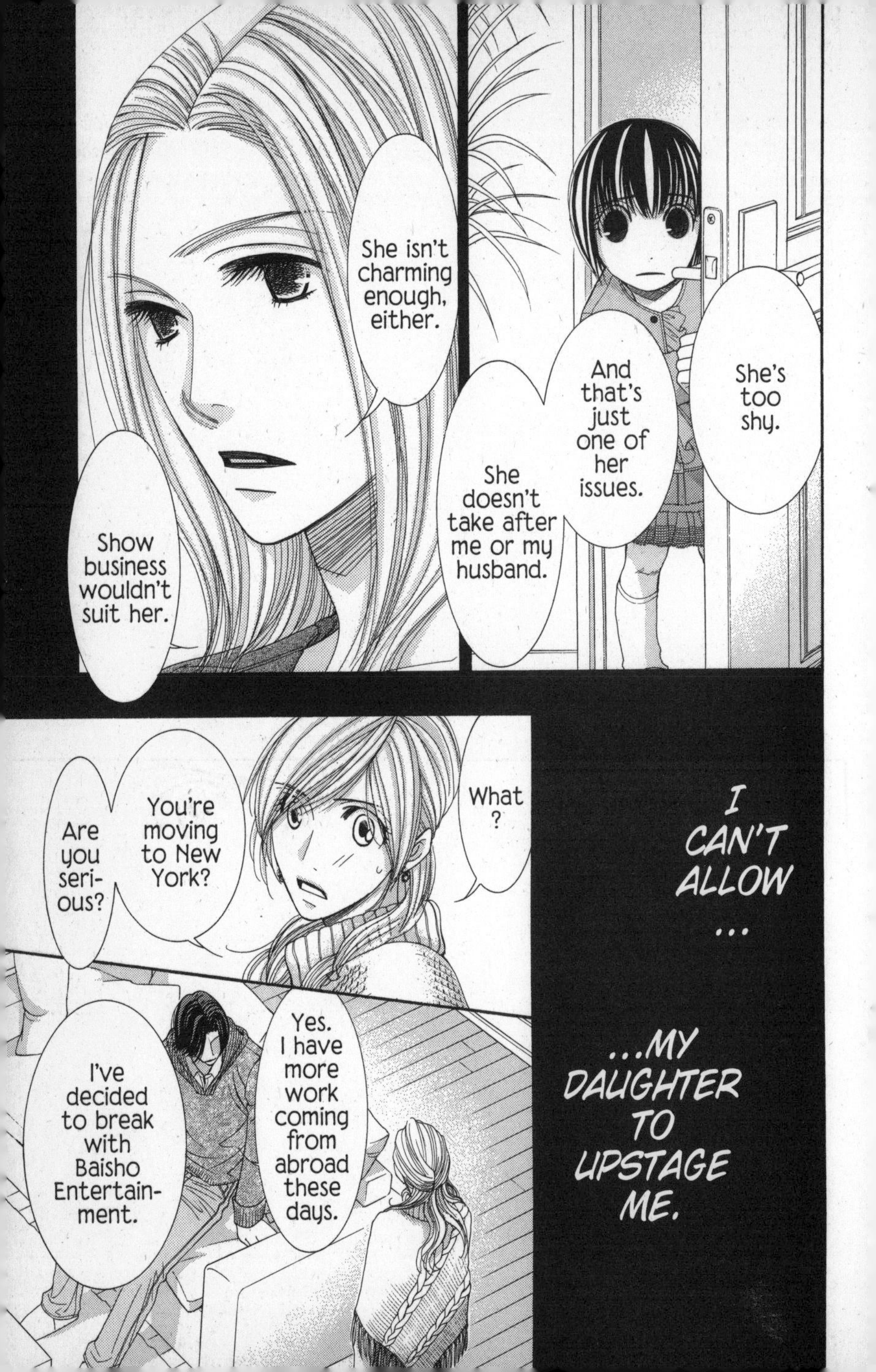
She's too shy.
And that's just one of her issues.
She doesn't take after me or my husband.
She isn't charming enough, either.
Show business wouldn't suit her.
I CAN'T ALLOW ...
...MY DAUGHTER TO UPSTAGE ME.
What?
You're moving to New York?
Are you seri-ous?
Yes. I have more work coming from abroad these days.
I've decided to break with Baisho Entertain-ment.

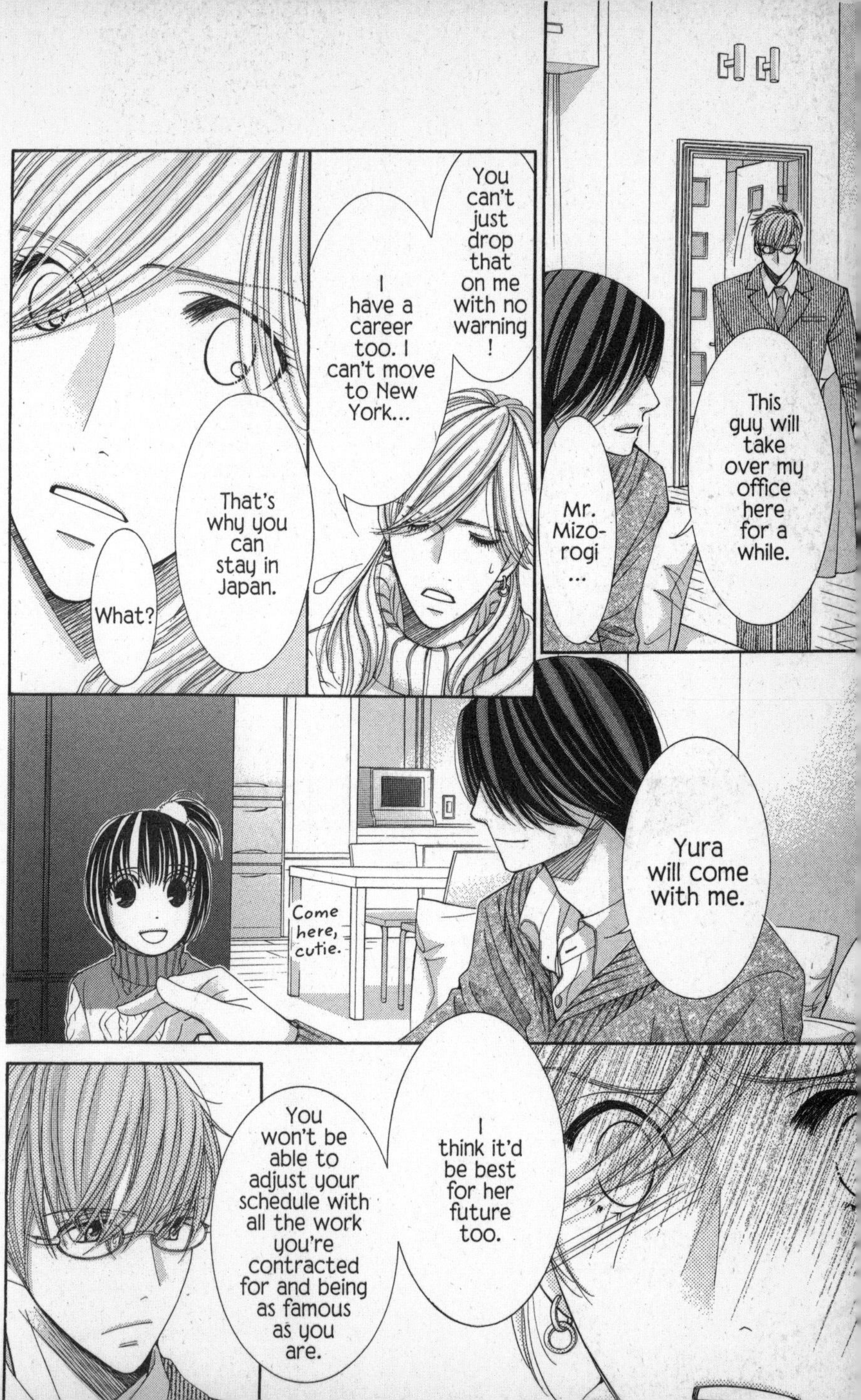
This guy will take over my office here for a while.
Mr. Mizorogi...
You can't just drop that on me with no warning!
I have a career too. I can't move to New York...
That's why you can stay in Japan.
What?
Yura will come with me.
Come here, cutie.
I think it'd be best for her future too.
You won't be able to adjust your schedule with all the work you're contracted for and being as famous as you are.

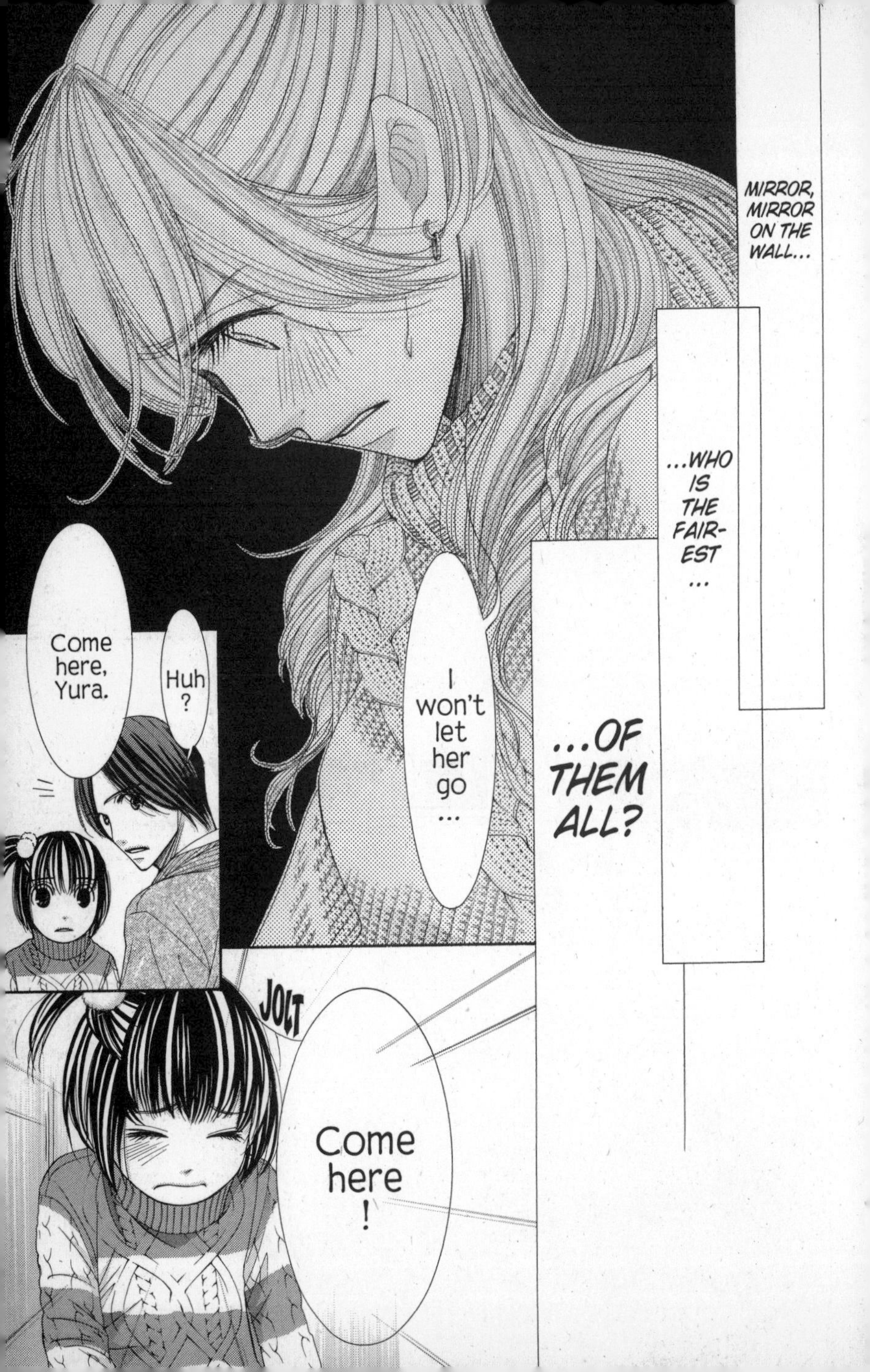
MIRROR, MIRROR ON THE WALL...
...WHO IS THE FAIREST...
...OF THEM ALL?
I won't let her go...
Come here, Yura.
Huh?
JOLT
Come here!

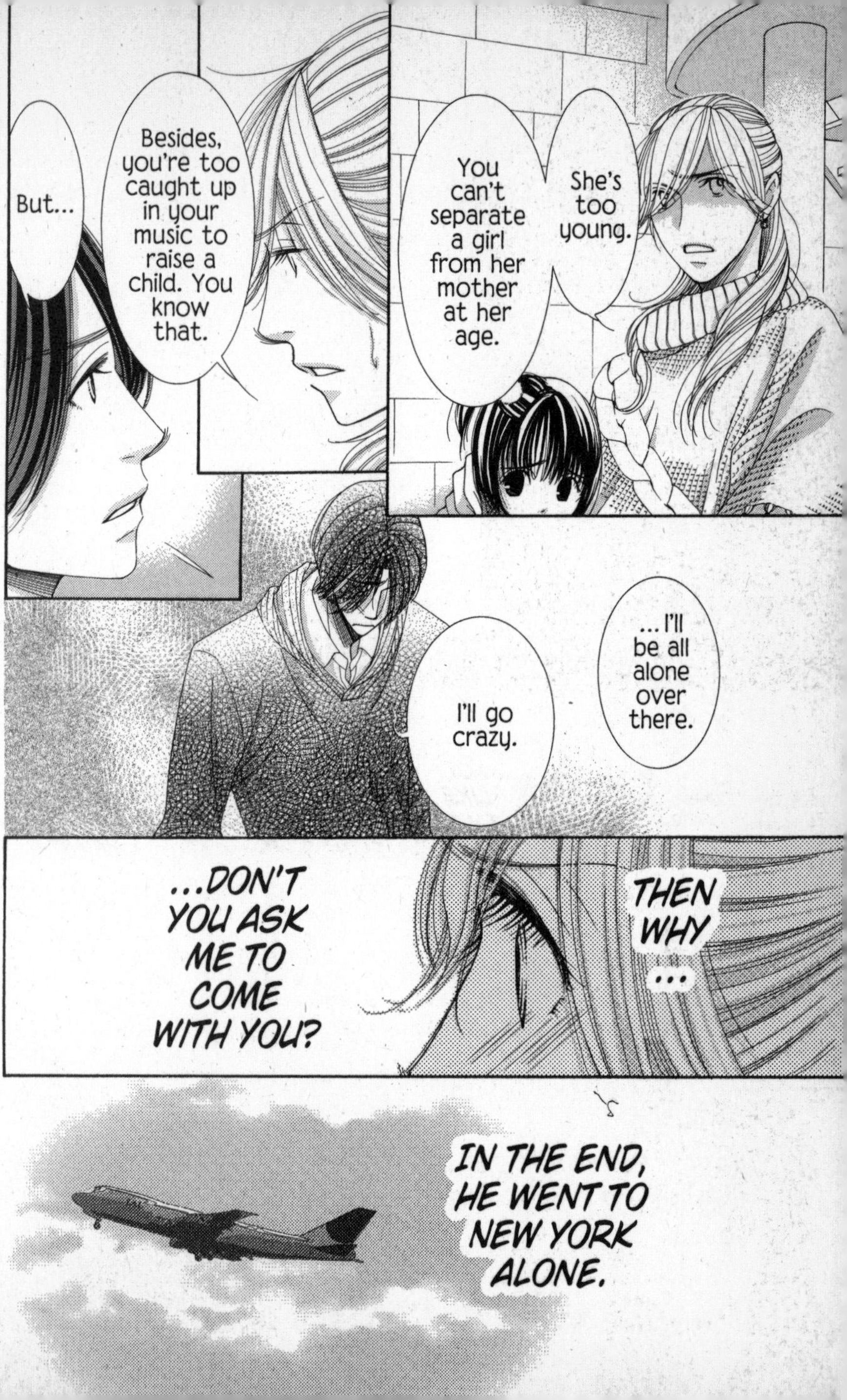
She's too young.
You can't separate a girl from her mother at her age.
Besides, you're too caught up in your music to raise a child. You know that.
But...
...I'll be all alone over there.
I'll go crazy.
THEN WHY...
...DON'T YOU ASK ME TO COME WITH YOU?
IN THE END, HE WENT TO NEW YORK ALONE.

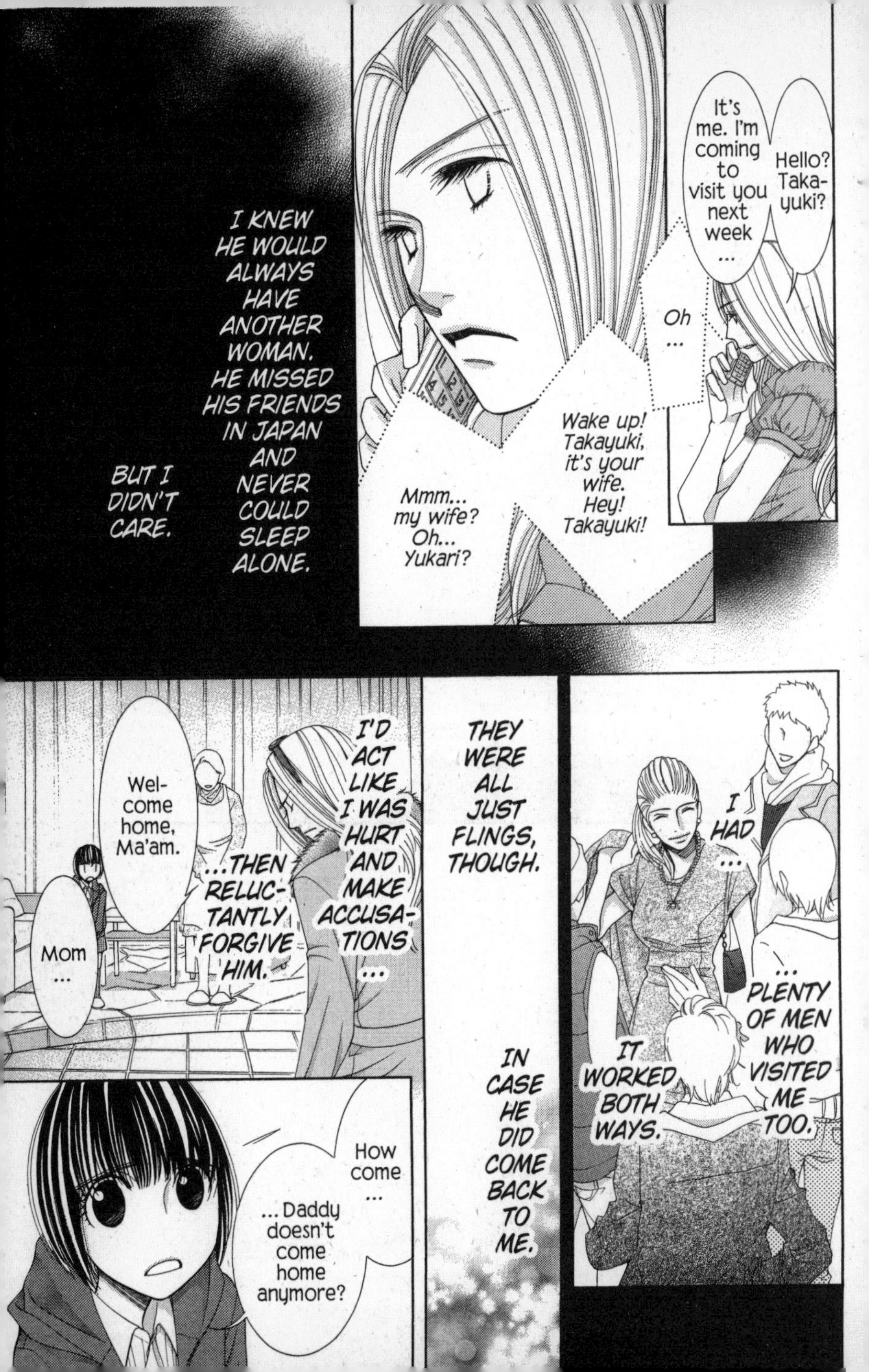
Hello? Taka-yuki?
It's me. I'm coming to visit you next week...
Oh...
Wake up! Takayuki, it's your wife. Hey! Takayuki!
Mmm... my wife? Oh... Yukari?
I KNEW HE WOULD ALWAYS HAVE ANOTHER WOMAN. HE MISSED HIS FRIENDS IN JAPAN AND NEVER COULD SLEEP ALONE.
BUT I DIDN'T CARE.
I HAD...
...PLENTY OF MEN WHO VISITED ME TOO.
IT WORKED BOTH WAYS.
THEY WERE ALL JUST FLINGS, THOUGH.
IN CASE HE DID COME BACK TO ME.
I'D ACT LIKE I WAS HURT AND MAKE ACCUSA-TIONS...
...THEN RELUC-TANTLY FORGIVE HIM.
Wel-come home, Ma'am.
Mom...
How come...
...Daddy doesn't come home anymore?

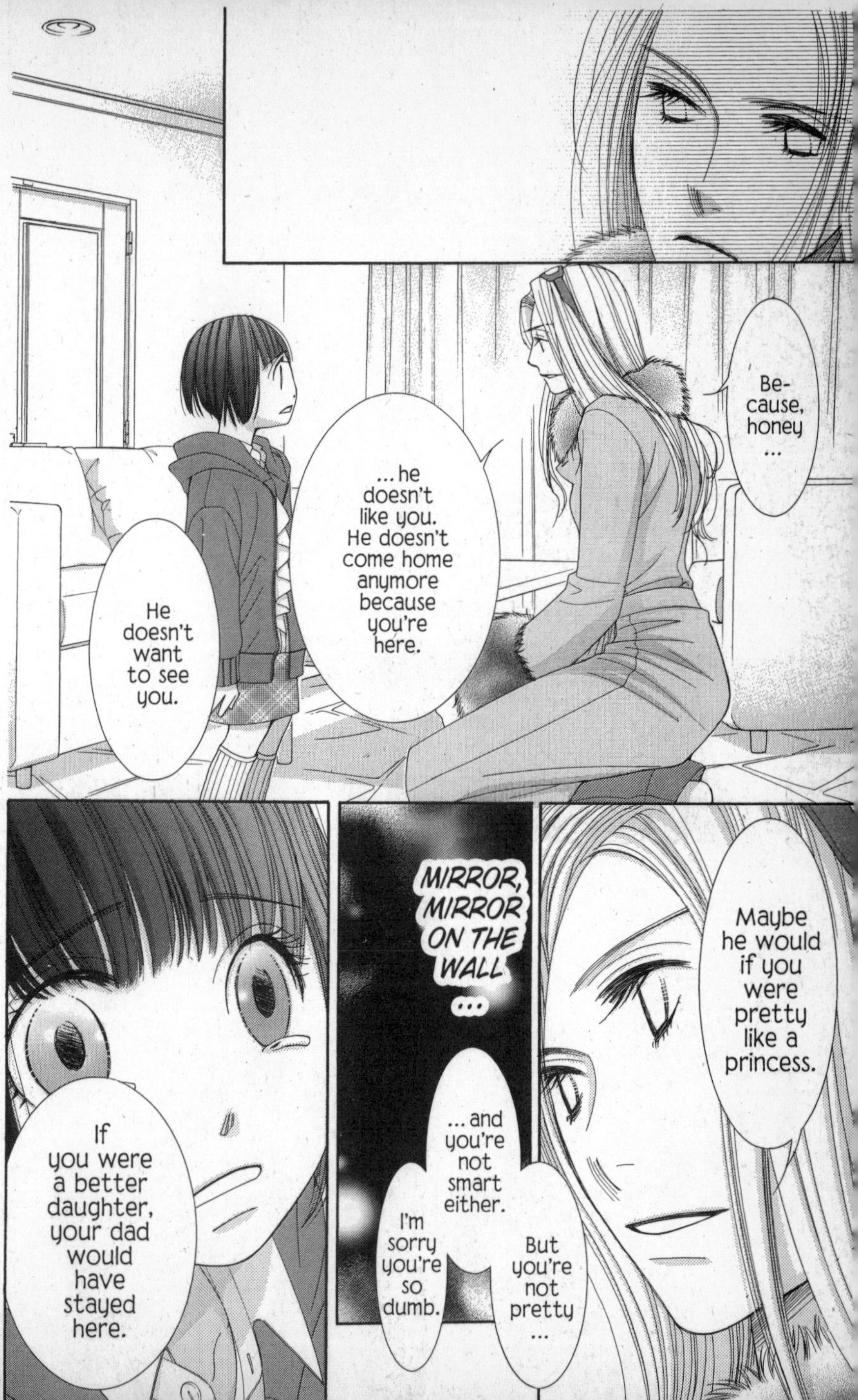
Be-cause, honey ...
... he doesn't like you. He doesn't come home anymore because you're here.
He doesn't want to see you.
Maybe he would if you were pretty like a princess.
But you're not pretty ...
... and you're not smart either.
I'm sorry you're so dumb.
MIRROR, MIRROR ON THE WALL ...
If you were a better daughter, your dad would have stayed here.

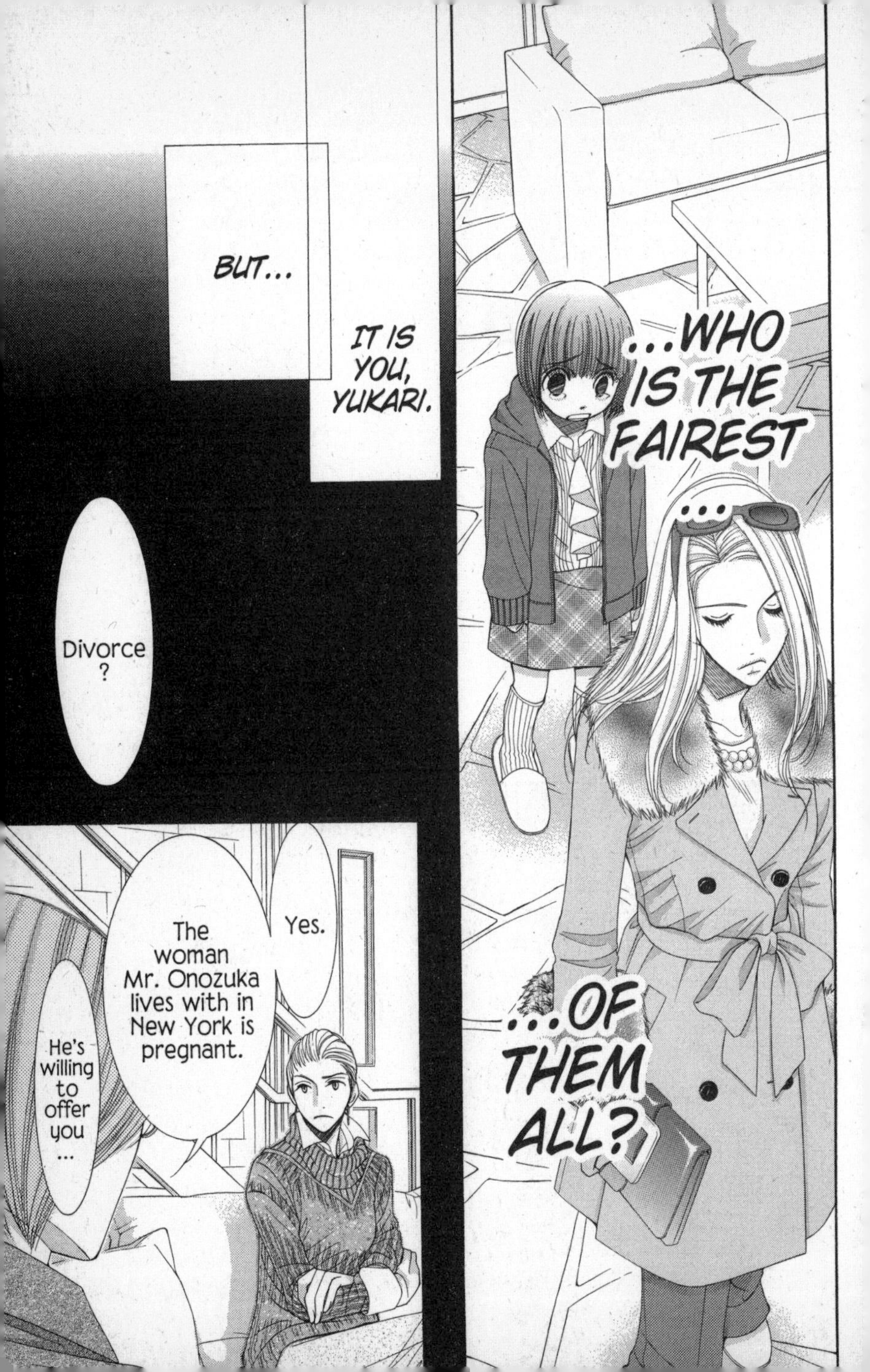
...WHO IS THE FAIREST ...
...OF THEM ALL?
BUT...
IT IS YOU, YUKARI.
Divorce?
Yes.
The woman Mr. Onozuka lives with in New York is pregnant.
He's willing to offer you ...

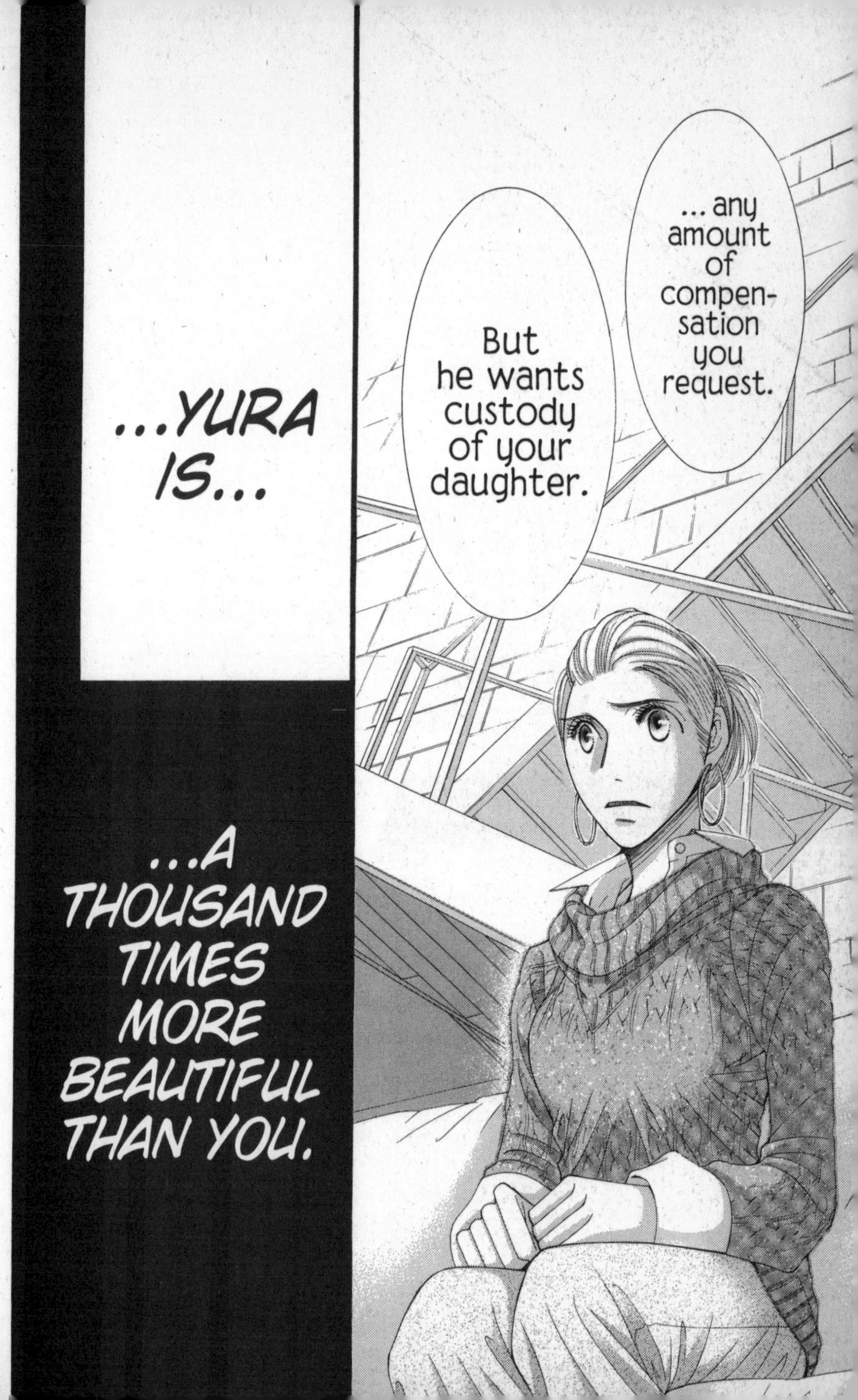
... any amount of compen- sation you request.
But he wants custody of your daughter.
...YURA IS...
...A THOUSAND TIMES MORE BEAUTIFUL THAN YOU.

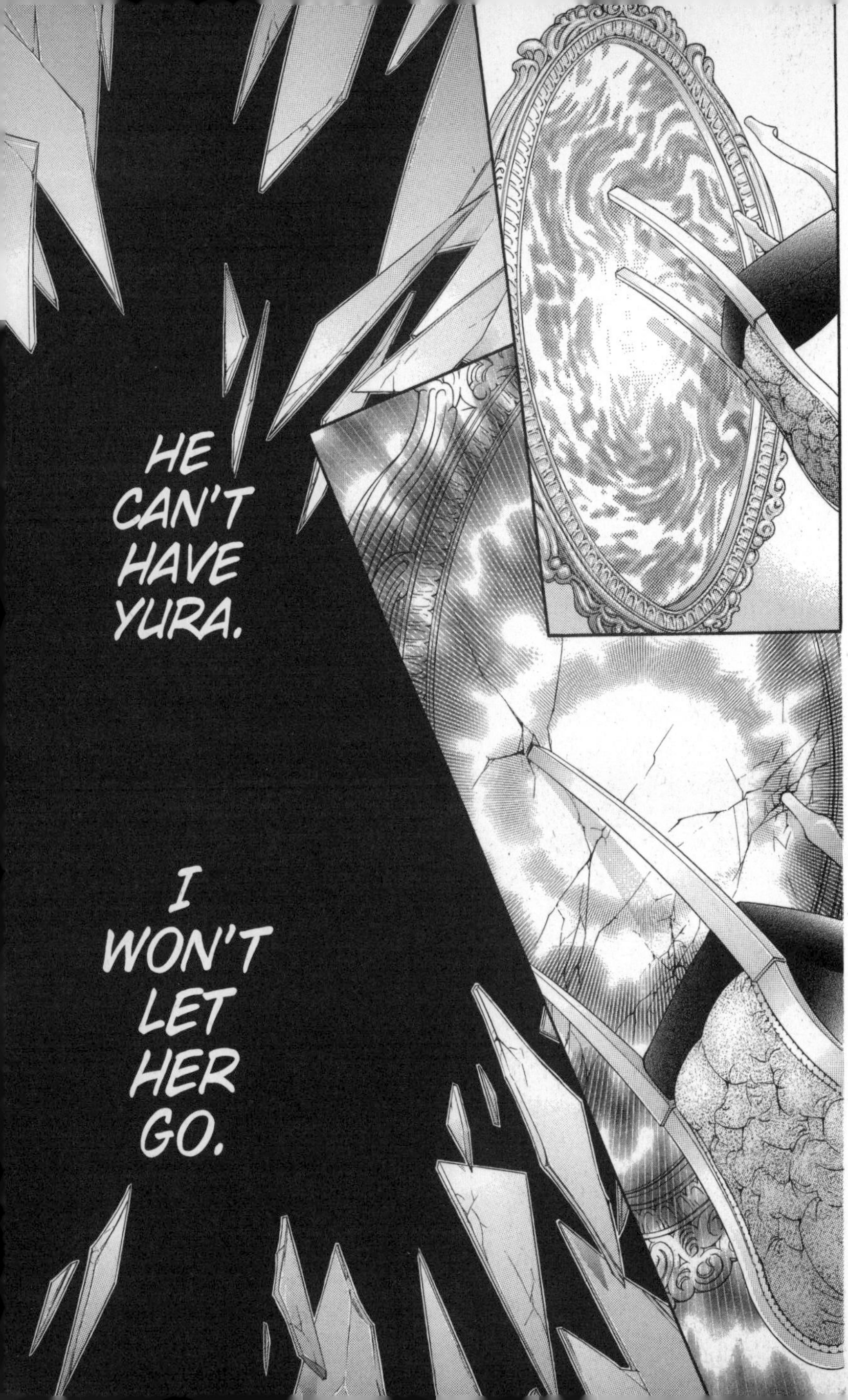
HE CAN'T HAVE YURA.
I WON'T LET HER GO.

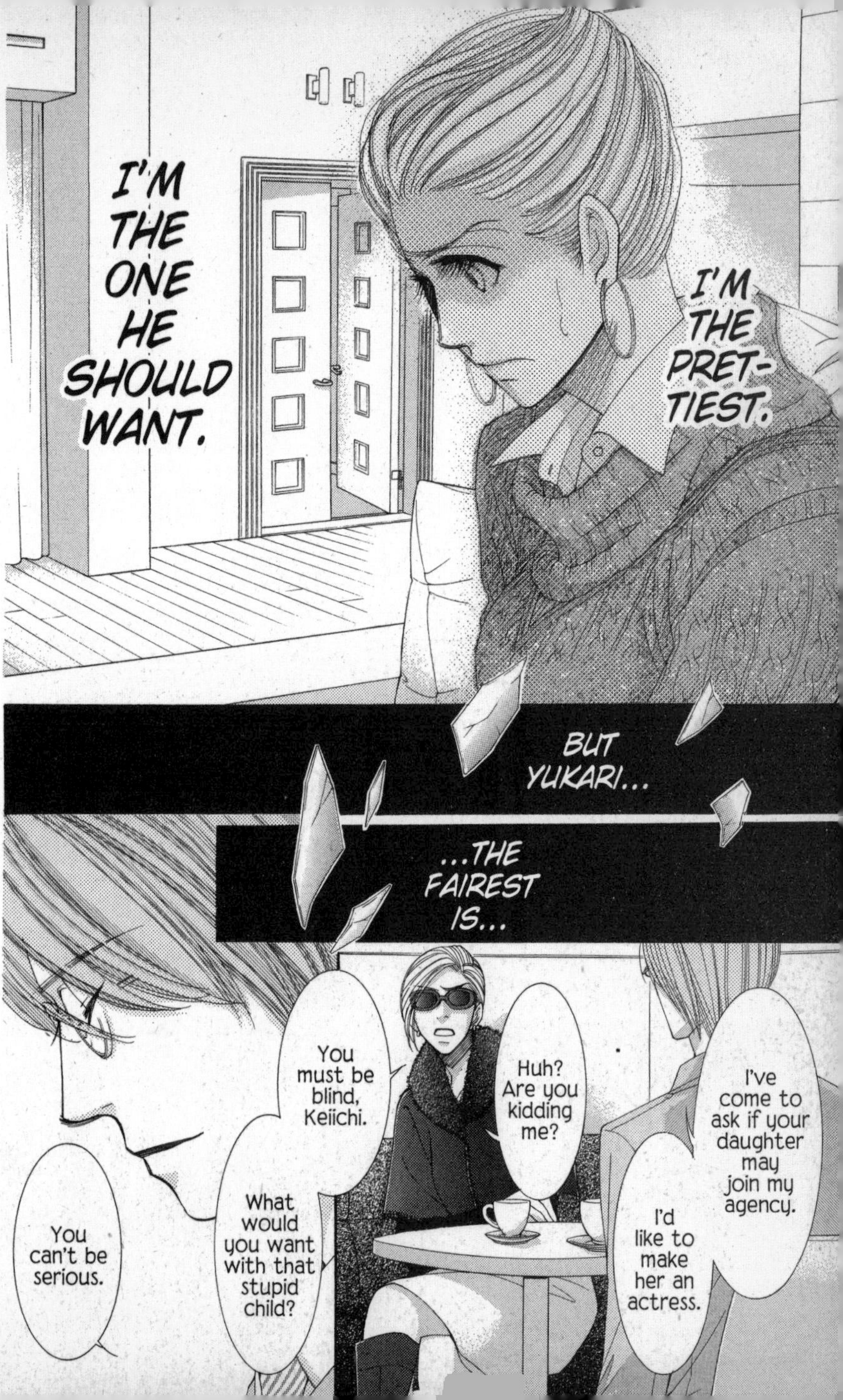
I'M THE PRETTIEST.
I'M THE ONE HE SHOULD WANT.
BUT YUKARI...
...THE FAIREST IS...
I've come to ask if your daughter may join my agency.
I'd like to make her an actress.
Huh? Are you kidding me?
You must be blind, Keiichi.
What would you want with that stupid child?
You can't be serious.

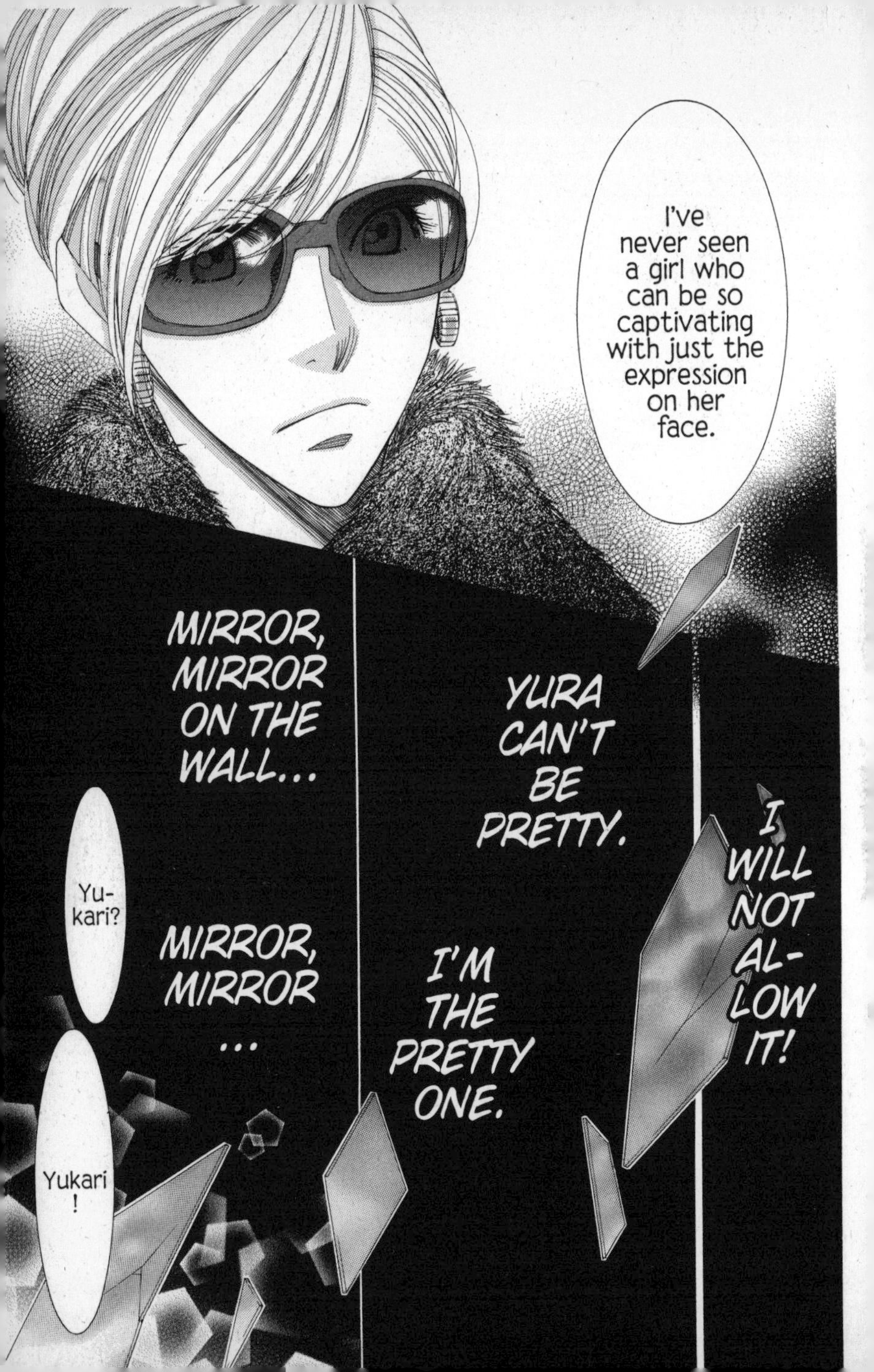
I've never seen a girl who can be so captivating with just the expression on her face.
I WILL NOT AL-LOW IT!
YURA CAN'T BE PRETTY.
I'M THE PRETTY ONE.
MIRROR, MIRROR ON THE WALL...
MIRROR, MIRROR ...
Yu-kari?
Yukari !

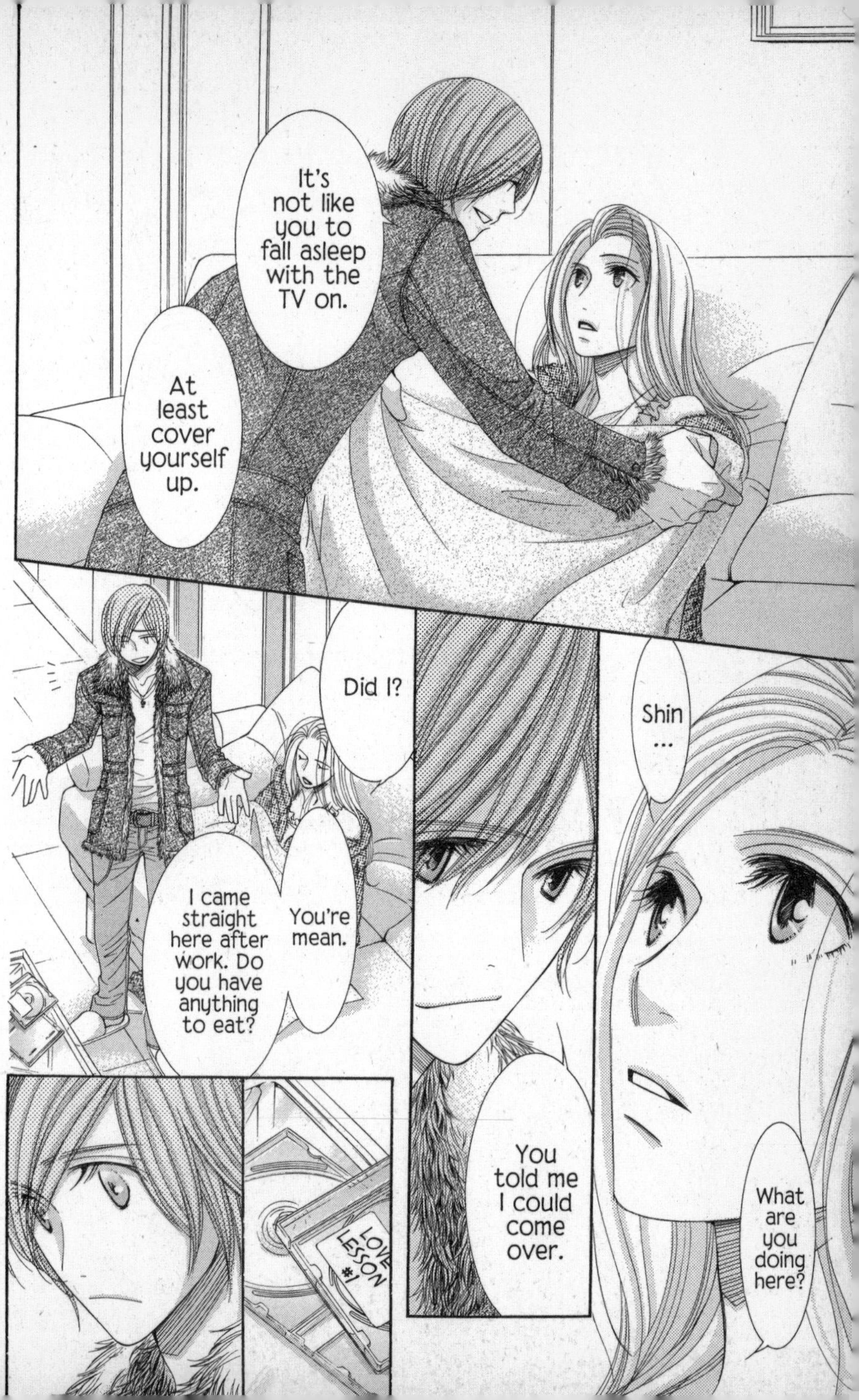
It's not like you to fall asleep with the TV on.
At least cover yourself up.
Shin ...
What are you doing here?
You told me I could come over.
Did I?
You're mean.
I came straight here after work. Do you have anything to eat?
LOVE LESSON #1

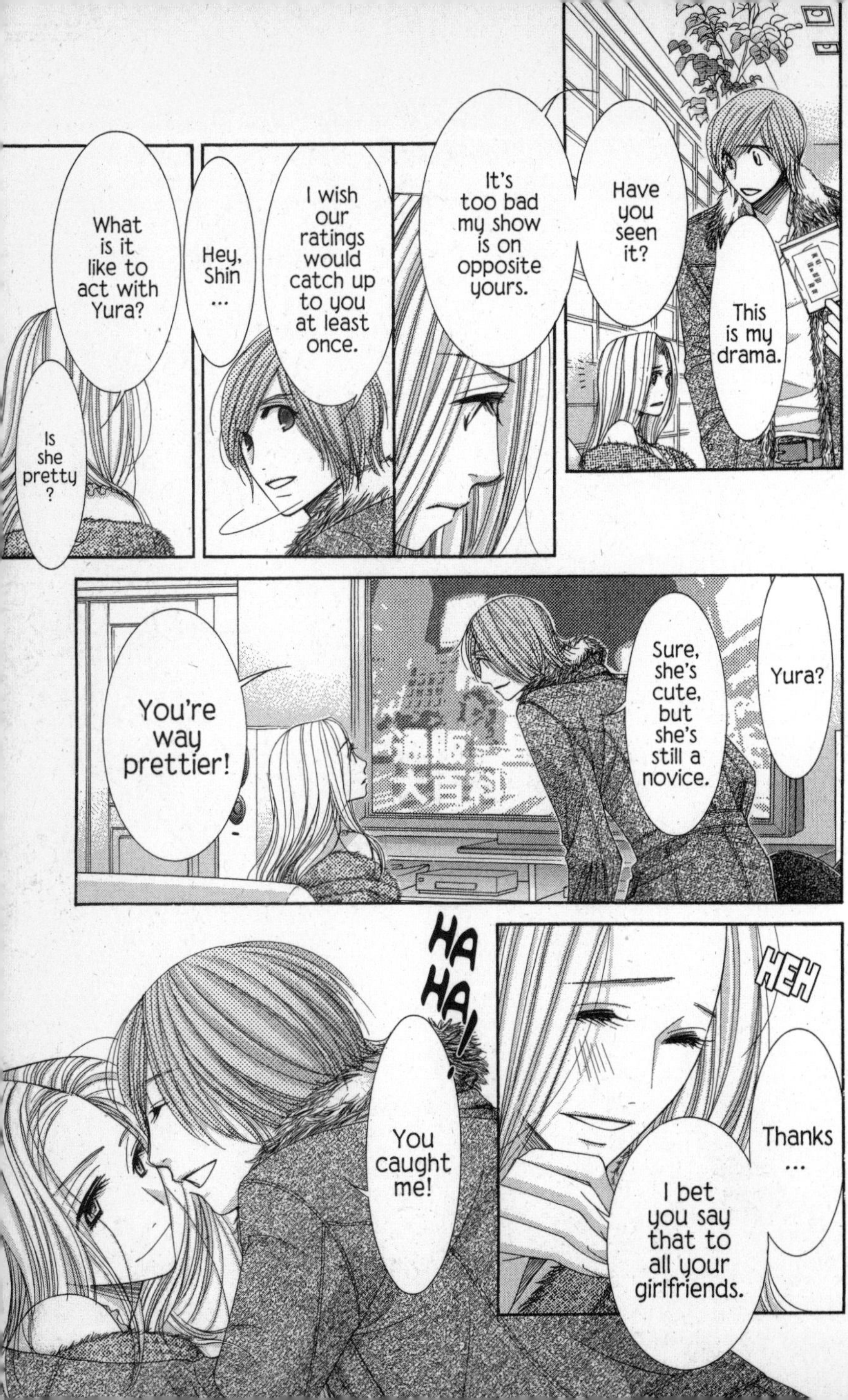
This is my drama.
Have you seen it?
It's too bad my show is on opposite yours.
I wish our ratings would catch up to you at least once.
Hey, Shin...
What is it like to act with Yura?
Is she pretty?
Yura?
Sure, she's cute, but she's still a novice.
通販大百科
You're way prettier!
HEH
Thanks...
I bet you say that to all your girlfriends.
HA HA!
You caught me!

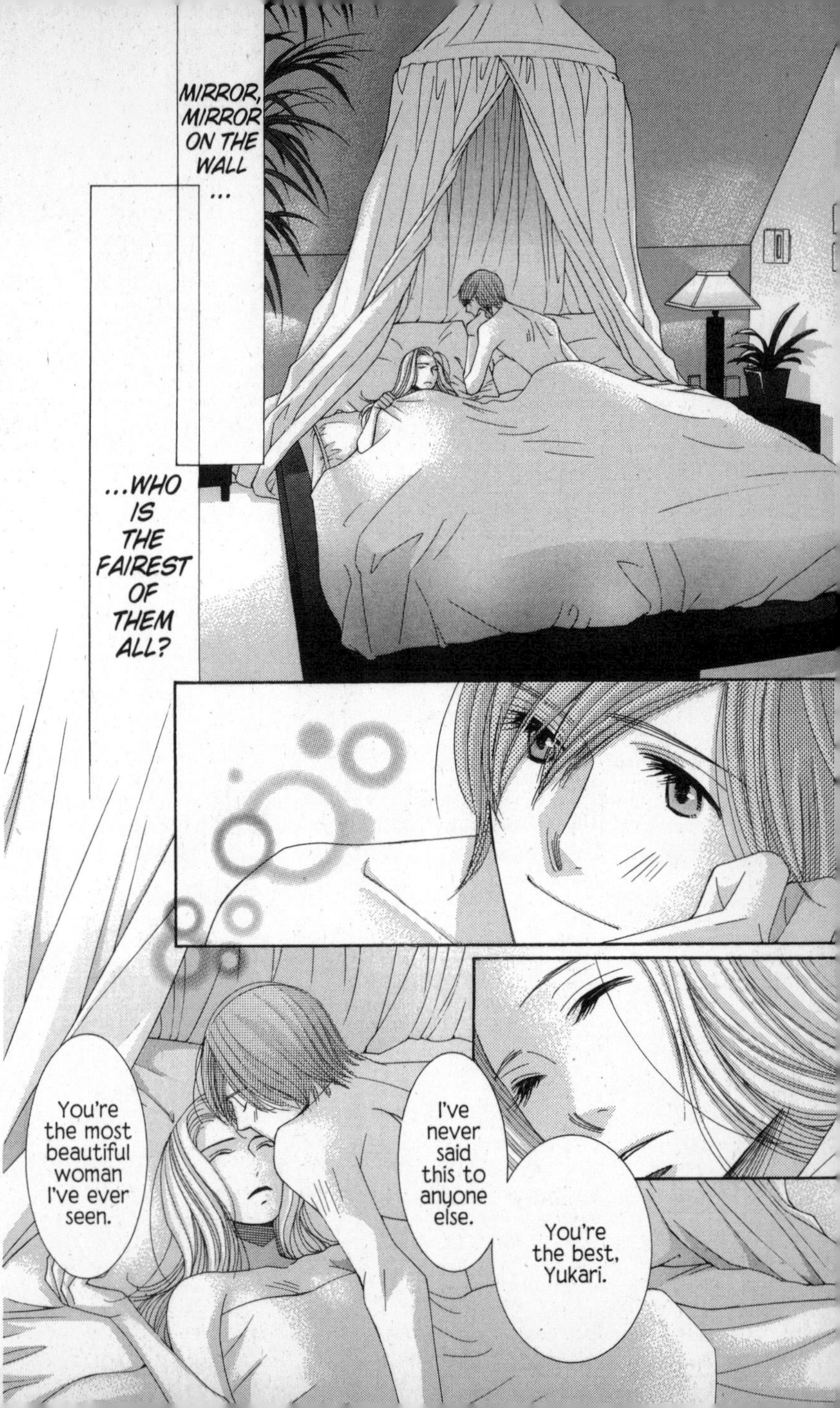
MIRROR, MIRROR ON THE WALL ...
...WHO IS THE FAIREST OF THEM ALL?
I've never said this to anyone else.
You're the best, Yukari.
You're the most beautiful woman I've ever seen.

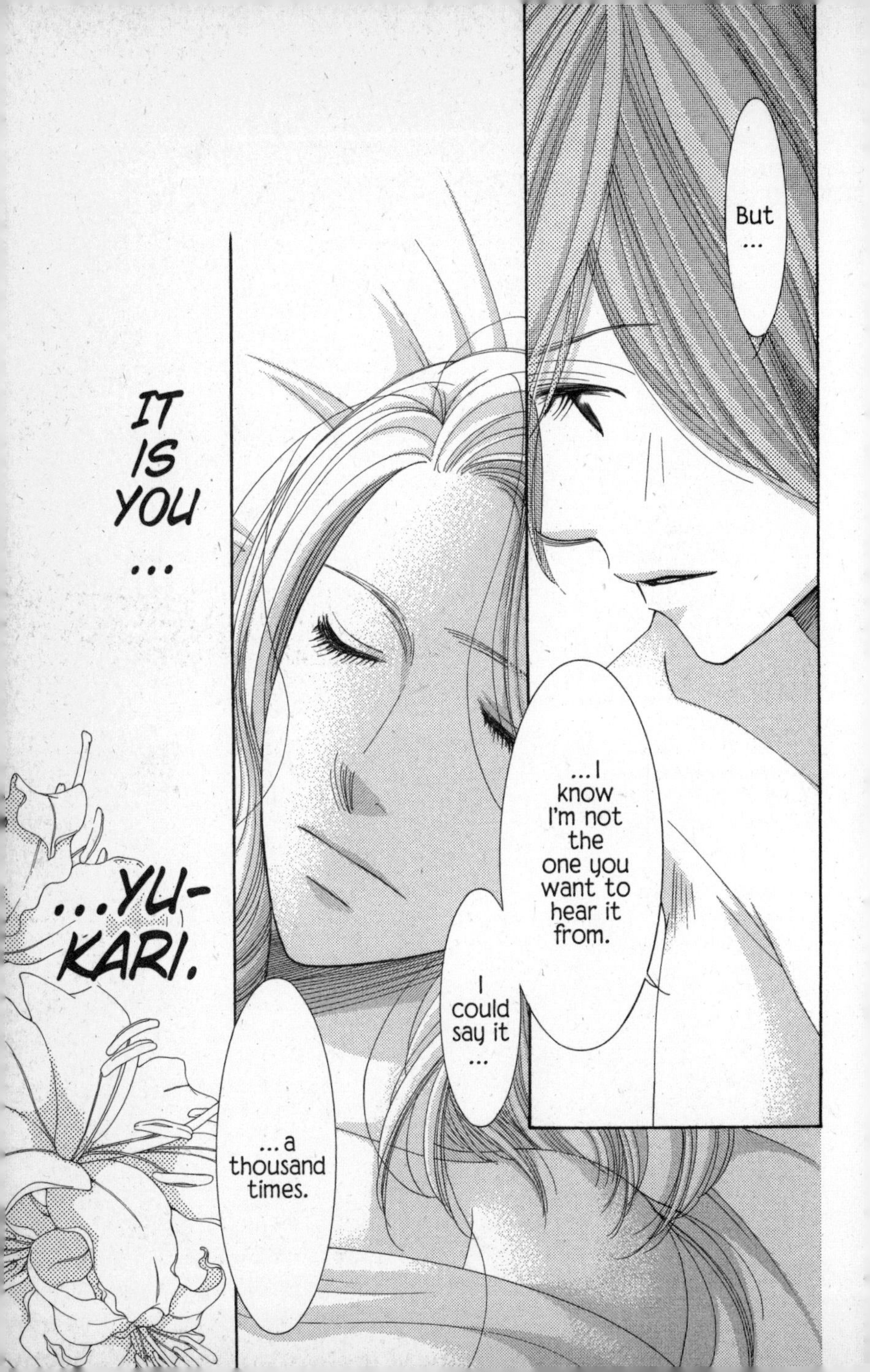
But ...
...I know I'm not the one you want to hear it from.
I could say it ...
...a thousand times.
IT IS YOU ...
...YU-KARI.

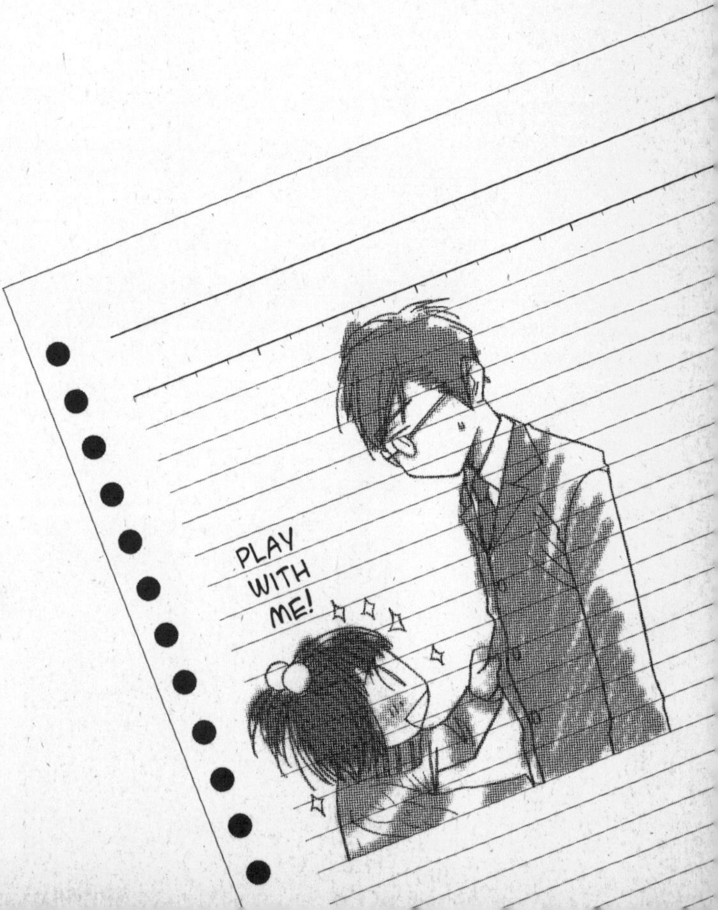
PLAY WITH ME!

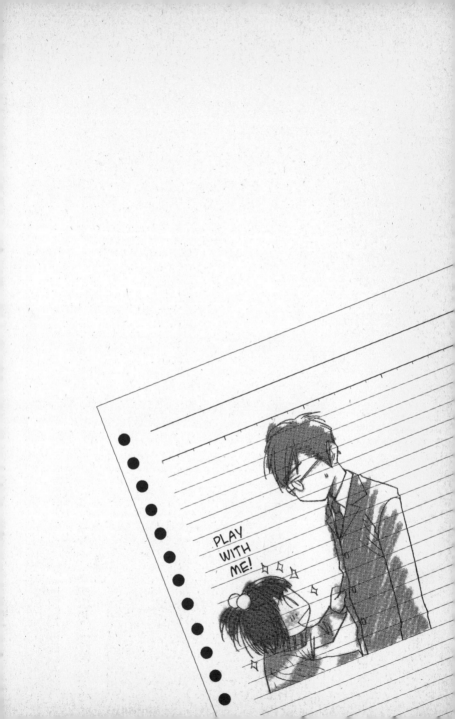

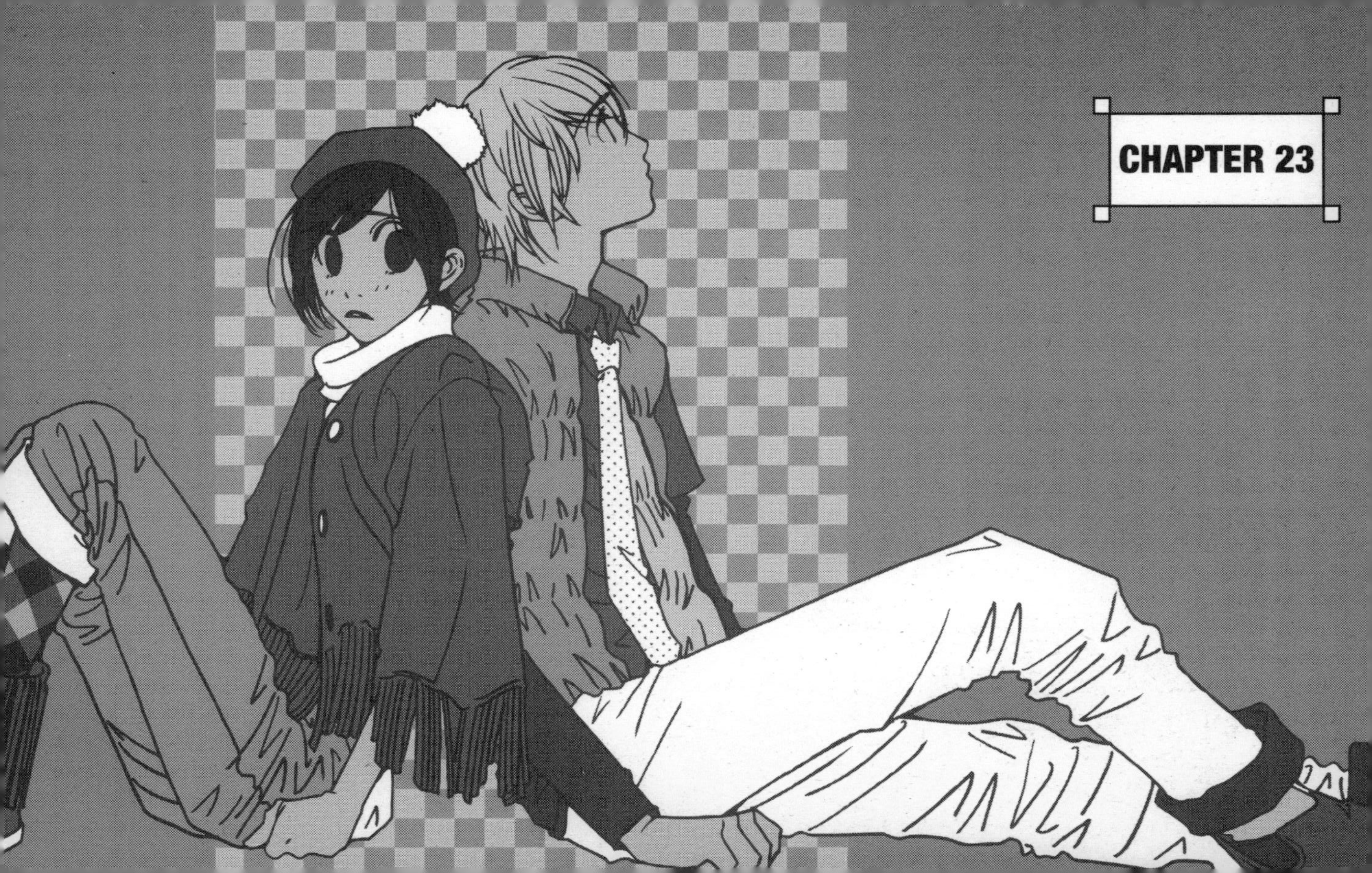
CHAPTER 23

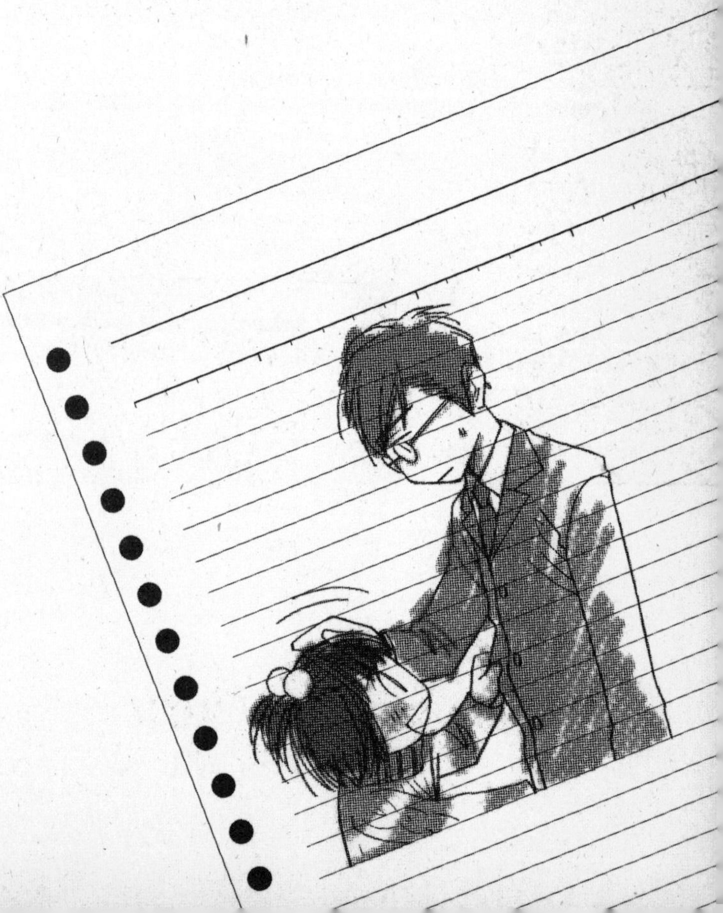

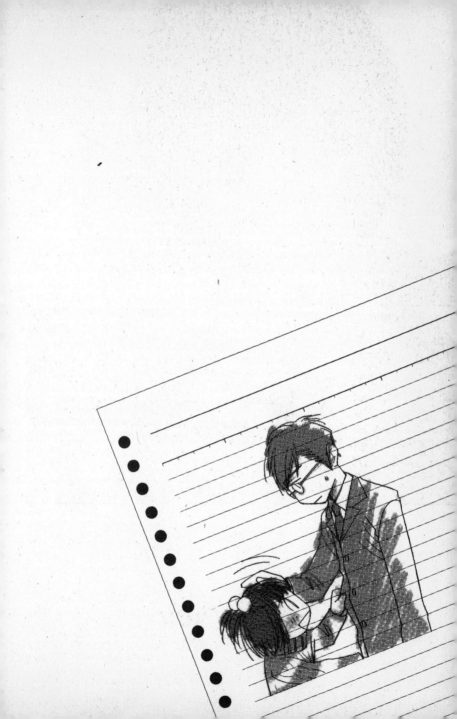

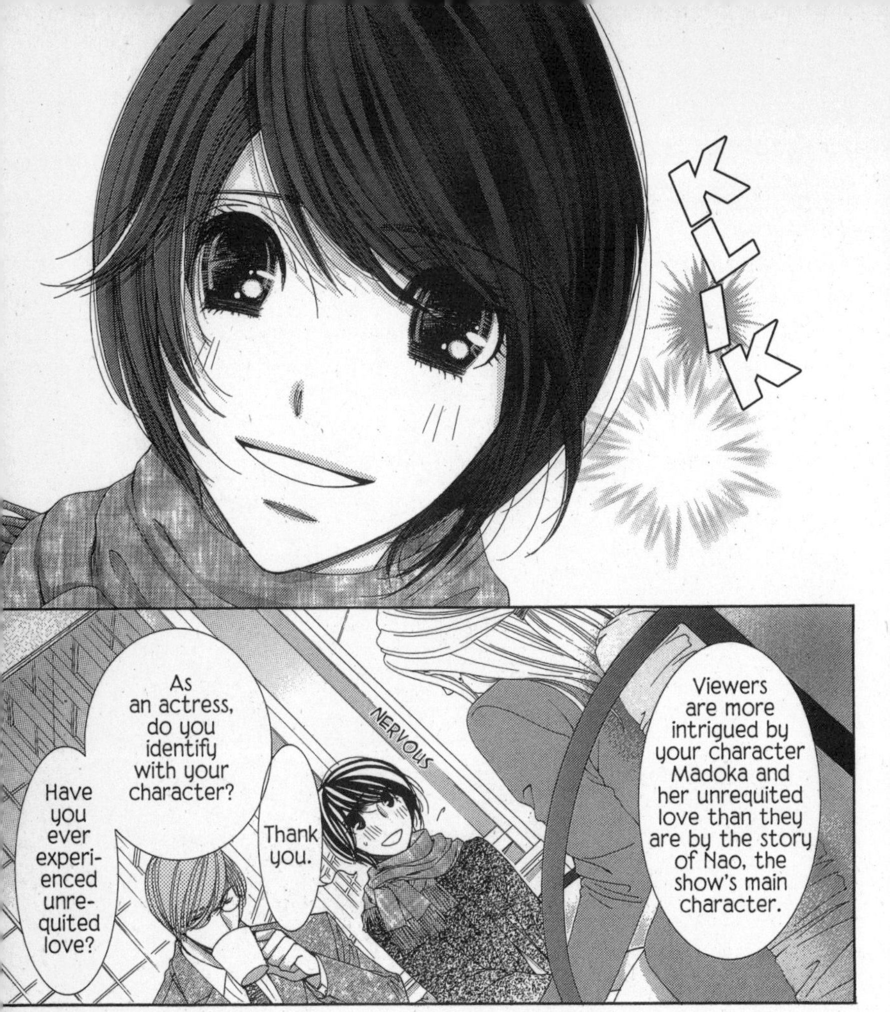
KLIK
Viewers are more intrigued by your character Madoka and her unrequited love than they are by the story of Nao, the show's main character.
NERVOUS
Thank you.
As an actress, do you identify with your character?
Have you ever experienced unrequited love?

Honey Hunt

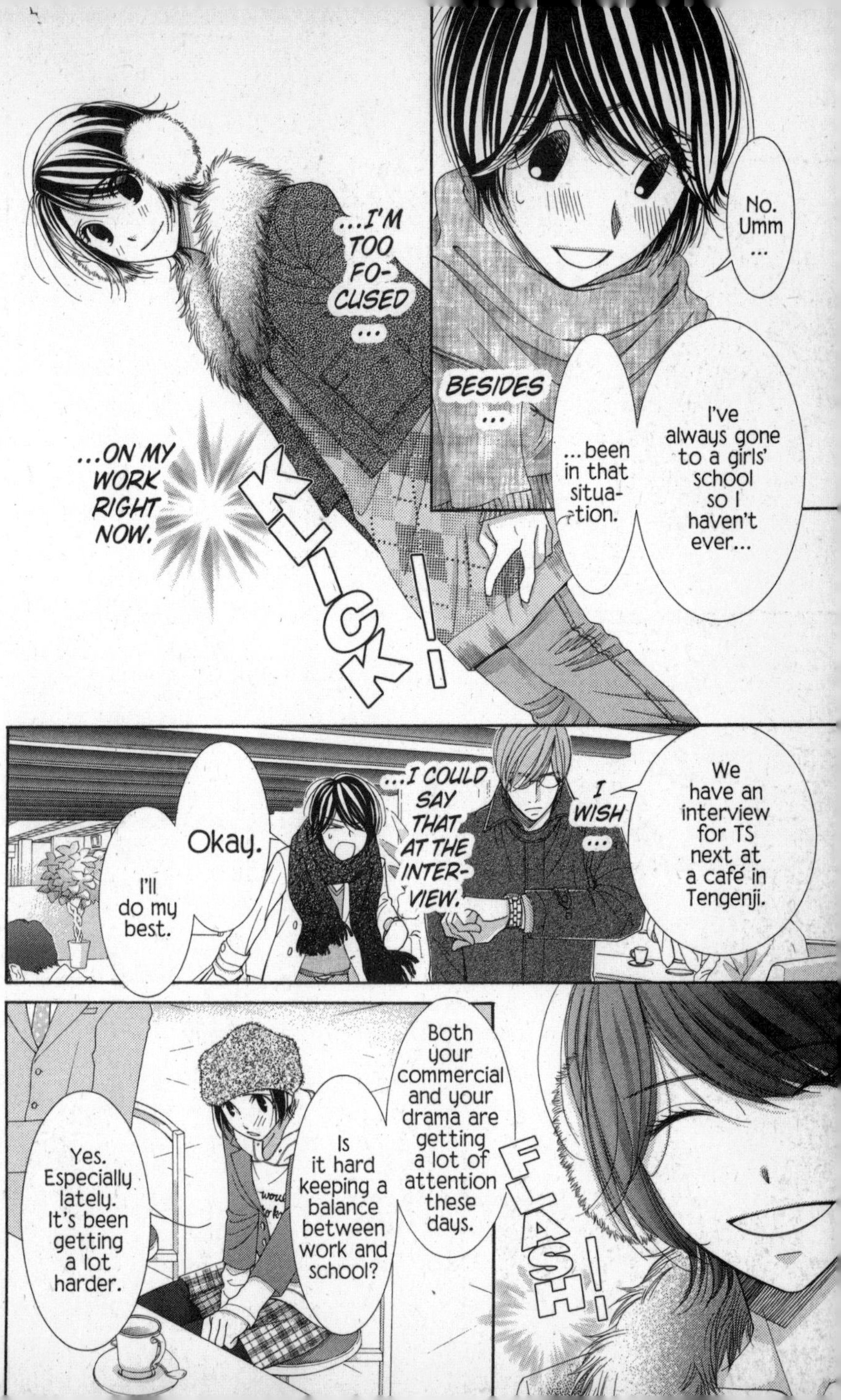
No. Umm ...
I've always gone to a girls' school so I haven't ever...
...been in that situation.
BESIDES ...
...I'M TOO FOCUSED ...
...ON MY WORK RIGHT NOW.
KLICK!!
We have an interview for TS next at a café in Tengenji.
I WISH ...
...I COULD SAY THAT AT THE INTERVIEW.
Okay.
I'll do my best.
FLASH!!
Both your commercial and your drama are getting a lot of attention these days.
Is it hard keeping a balance between work and school?
Yes. Especially lately. It's been getting a lot harder.

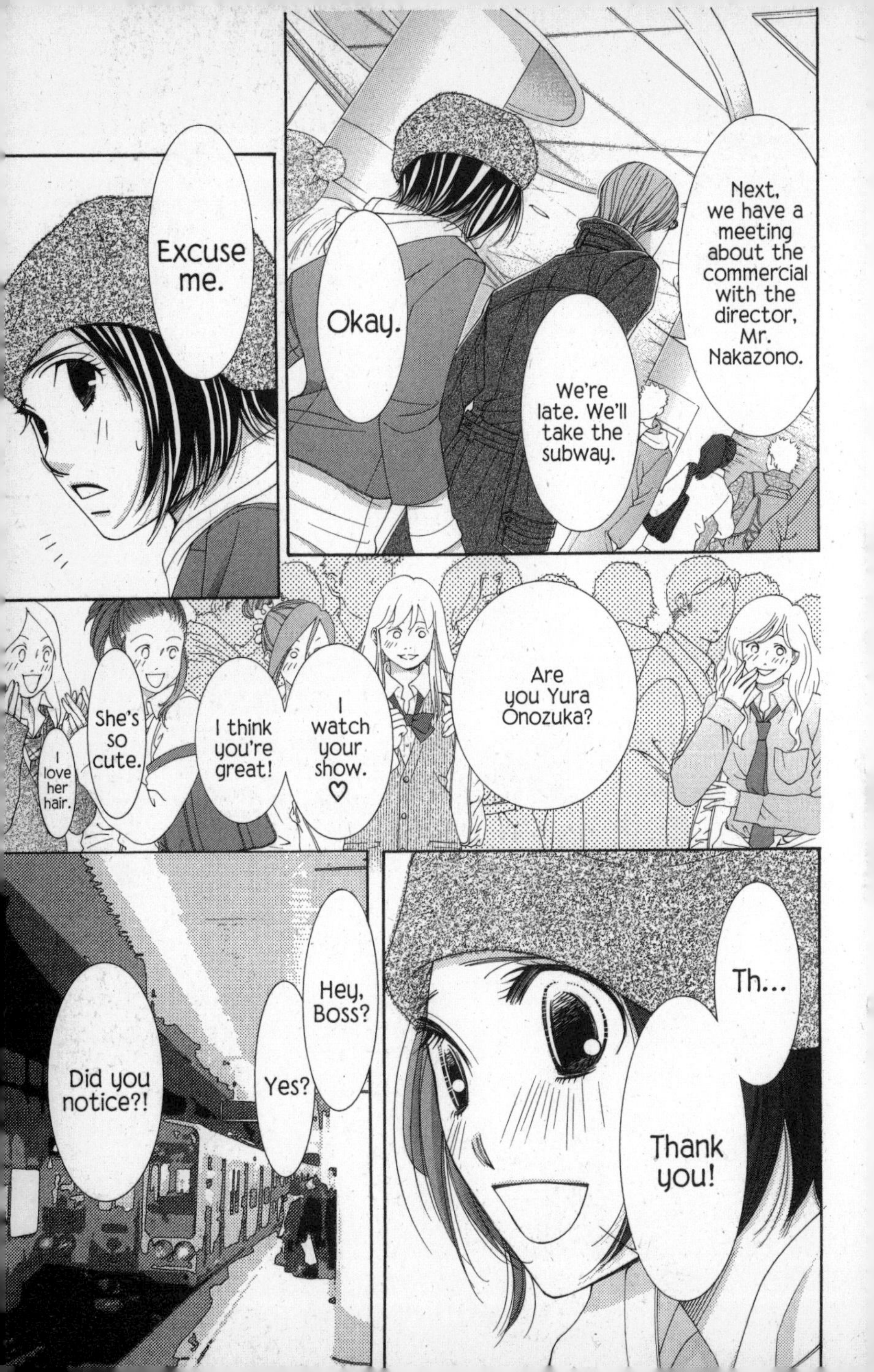
Next, we have a meeting about the commercial with the director, Mr. Nakazono.
We're late. We'll take the subway.
Okay.
Excuse me.
Are you Yura Onozuka?
I watch your show. ♡
I think you're great!
She's so cute.
I love her hair.
Th...
Thank you!
Hey, Boss?
Yes?
Did you notice?!

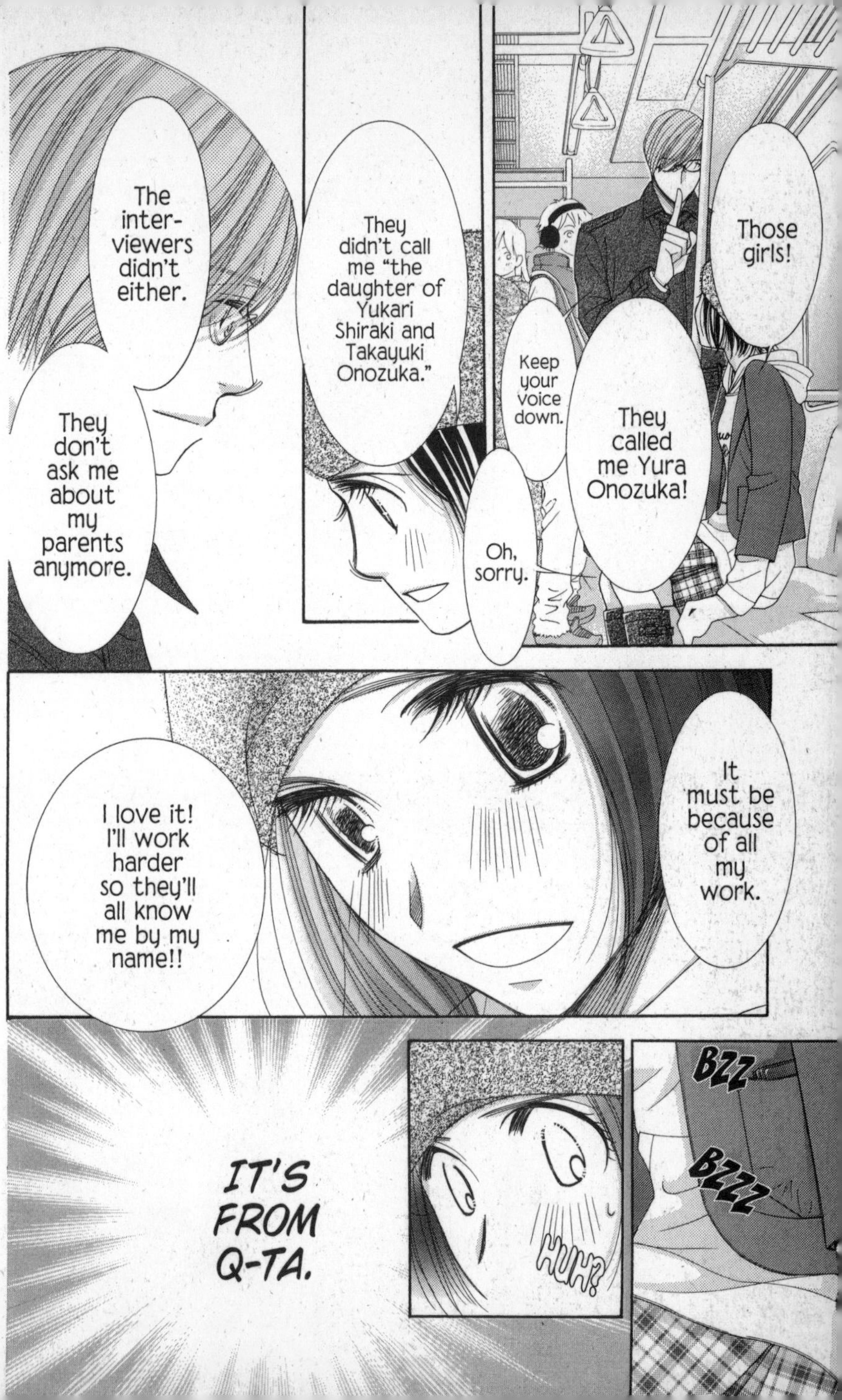
Those girls!
They called me Yura Onozuka!
Keep your voice down.
Oh, sorry.
They didn't call me "the daughter of Yukari Shiraki and Takayuki Onozuka."
The inter-viewers didn't either.
They don't ask me about my parents anymore.
It must be because of all my work.
I love it! I'll work harder so they'll all know me by my name!!
BZZ
BZZZ
HUH?
IT'S FROM Q-TA.

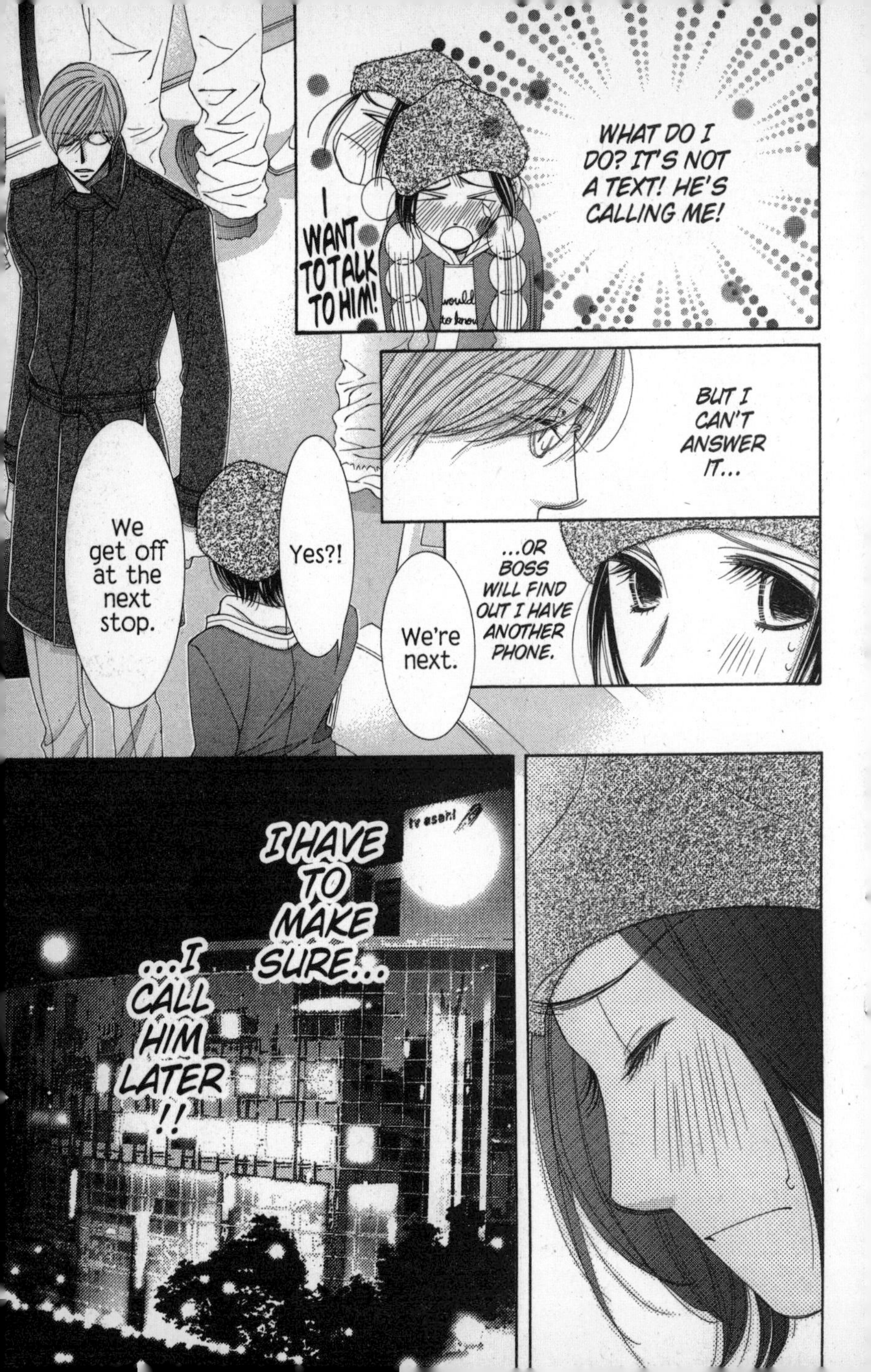
WHAT DO I DO? IT'S NOT A TEXT! HE'S CALLING ME!
I WANT TO TALK TO HIM!
BUT I CAN'T ANSWER IT...
...OR BOSS WILL FIND OUT I HAVE ANOTHER PHONE.
We get off at the next stop.
Yes?!
We're next.
I HAVE TO MAKE SURE...
...I CALL HIM LATER!!
tv asahi

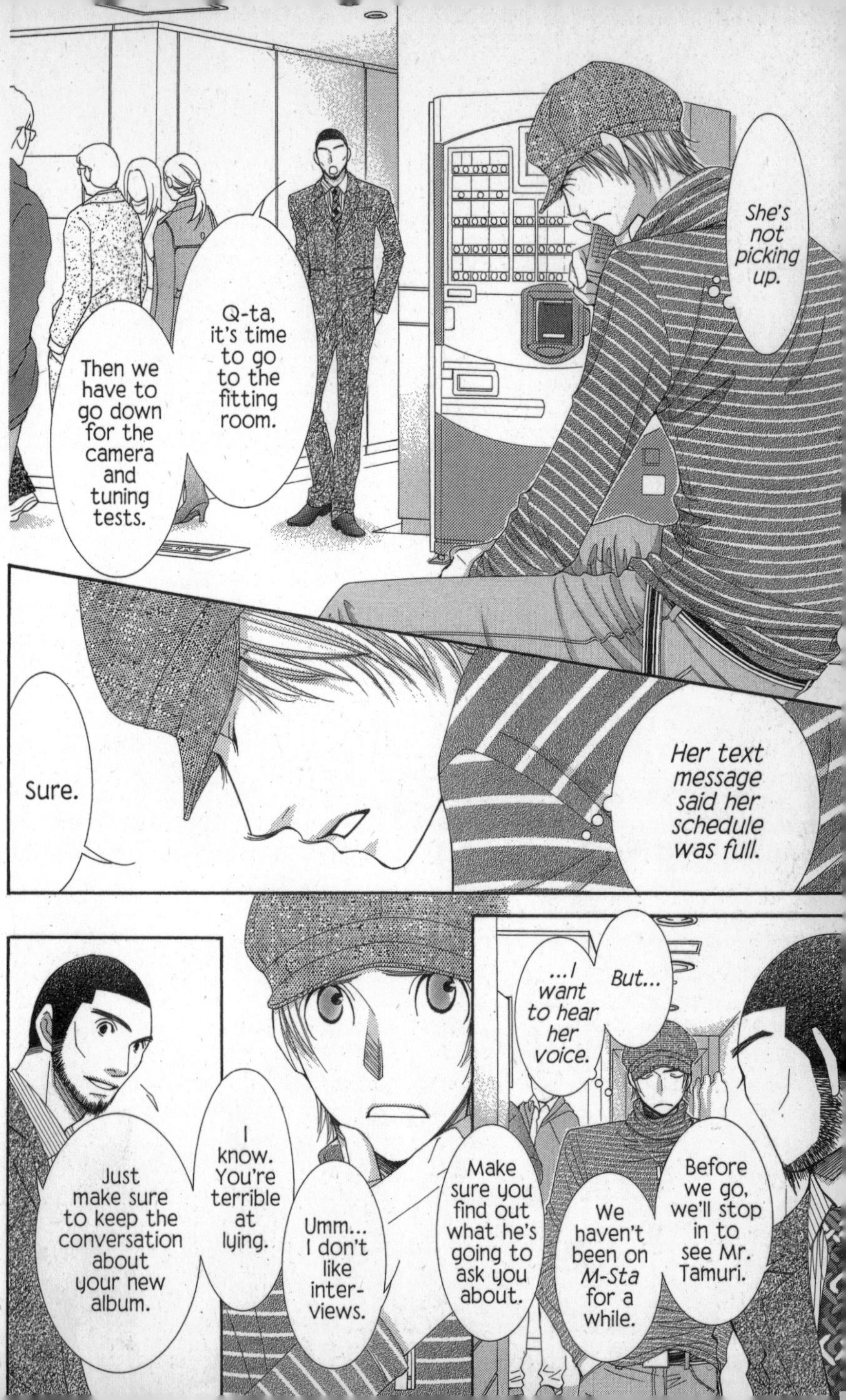
She's not picking up.
Q-ta, it's time to go to the fitting room.
Then we have to go down for the camera and tuning tests.
Her text message said her schedule was full.
Sure.
But...
...I want to hear her voice.
Before we go, we'll stop in to see Mr. Tamuri.
We haven't been on *M-Sta* for a while.
Make sure you find out what he's going to ask you about.
Umm... I don't like inter-views.
I know. You're terrible at lying.
Just make sure to keep the conversation about your new album.

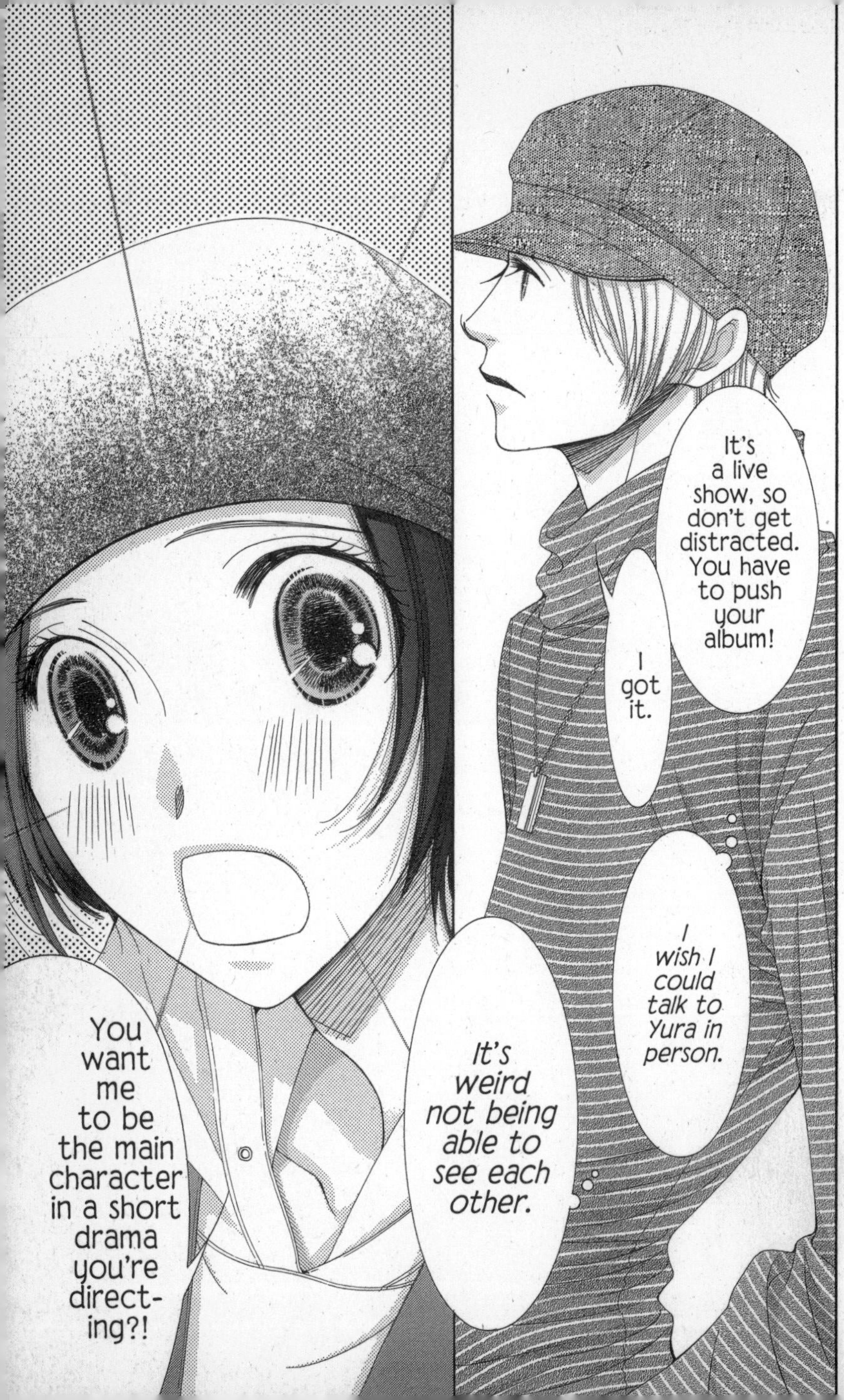
It's a live show, so don't get distracted. You have to push your album!
I got it.
I wish I could talk to Yura in person.
It's weird not being able to see each other.
You want me to be the main character in a short drama you're direct-ing?!

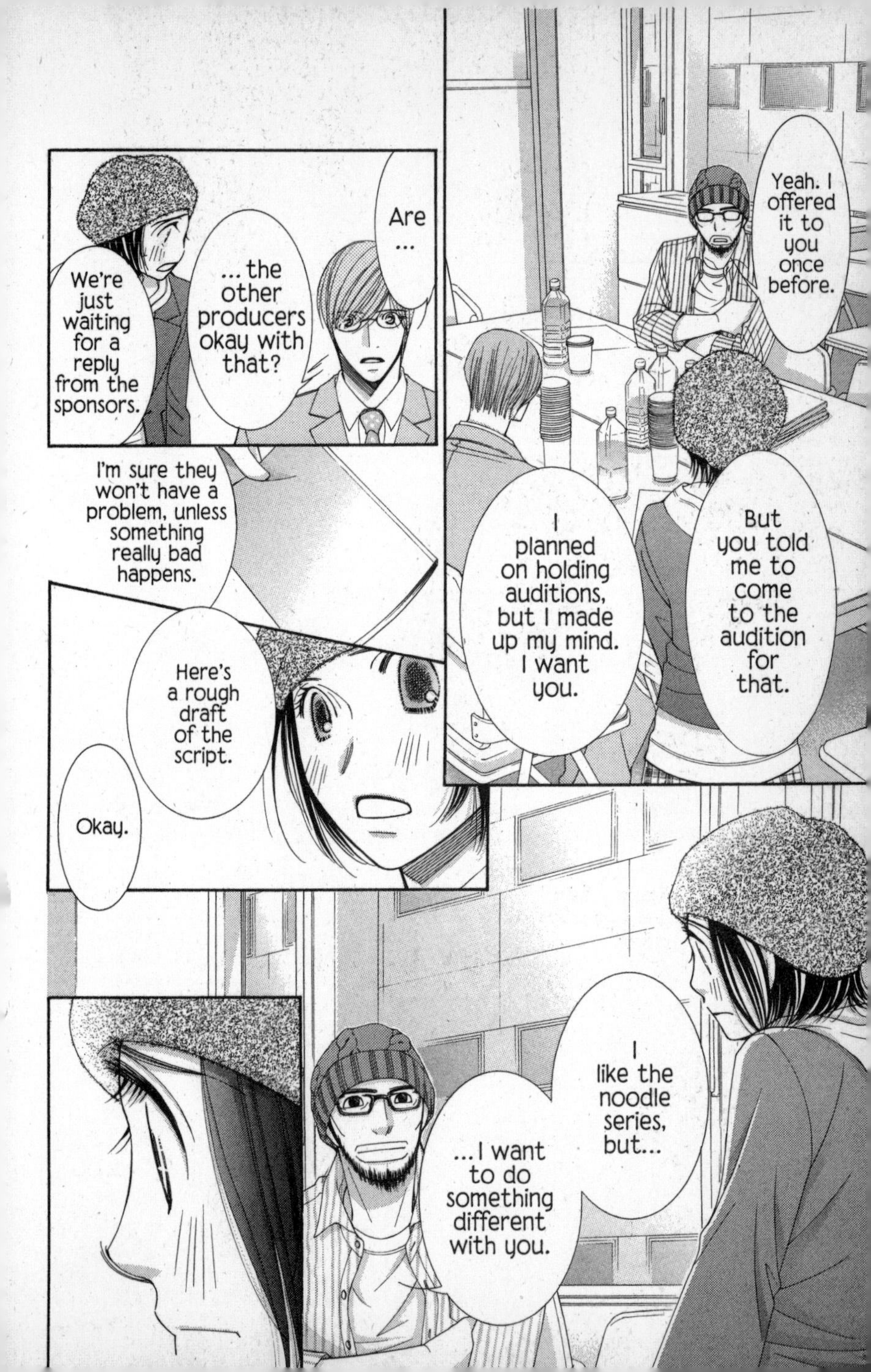
Yeah. I offered it to you once before.
But you told me to come to the audition for that.
I planned on holding auditions, but I made up my mind. I want you.
Are...
...the other producers okay with that?
We're just waiting for a reply from the sponsors.
I'm sure they won't have a problem, unless something really bad happens.
Here's a rough draft of the script.
Okay.
I like the noodle series, but...
...I want to do something different with you.

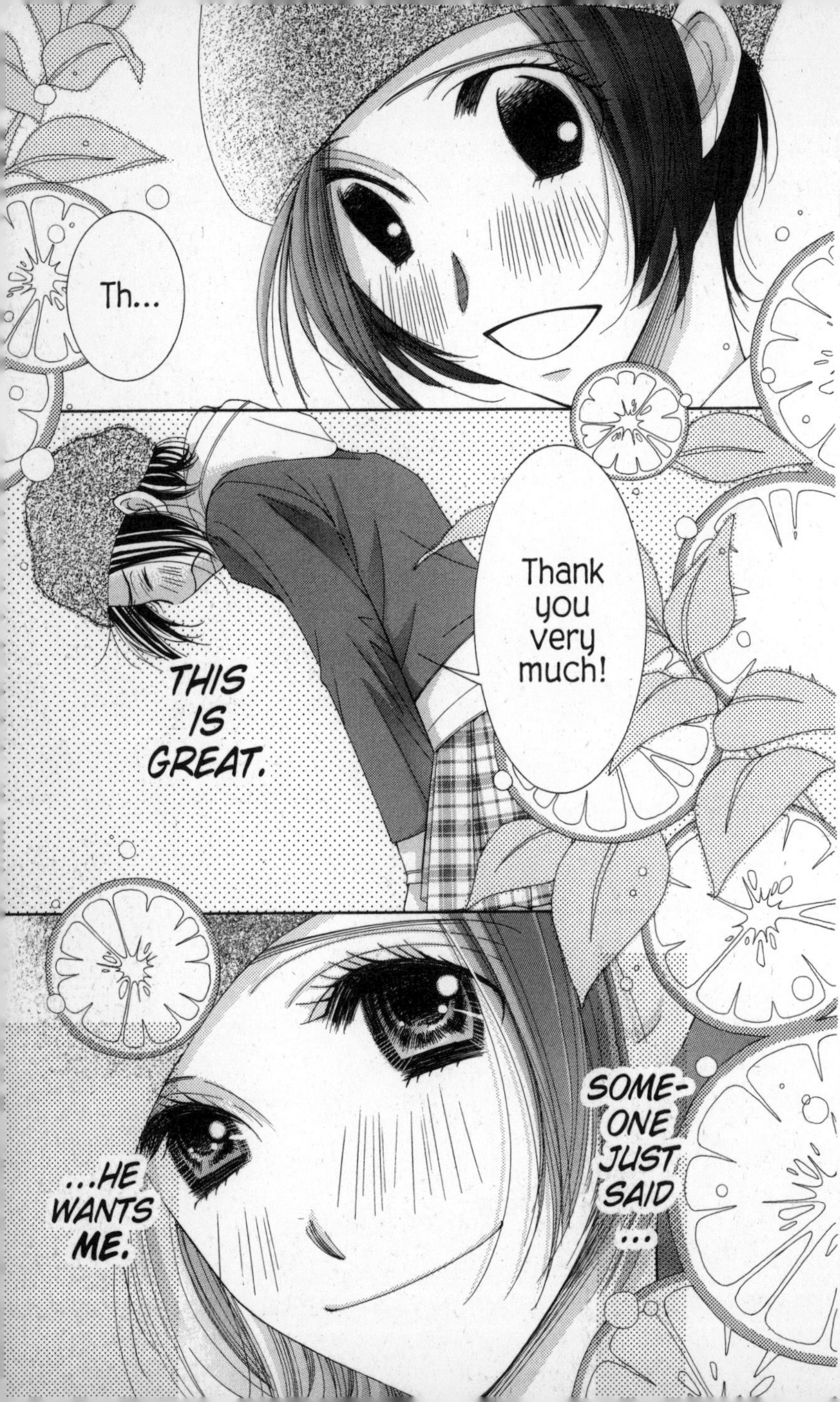
Th...
Thank you very much!
THIS IS GREAT.
SOME-ONE JUST SAID...
...HE WANTS ME.

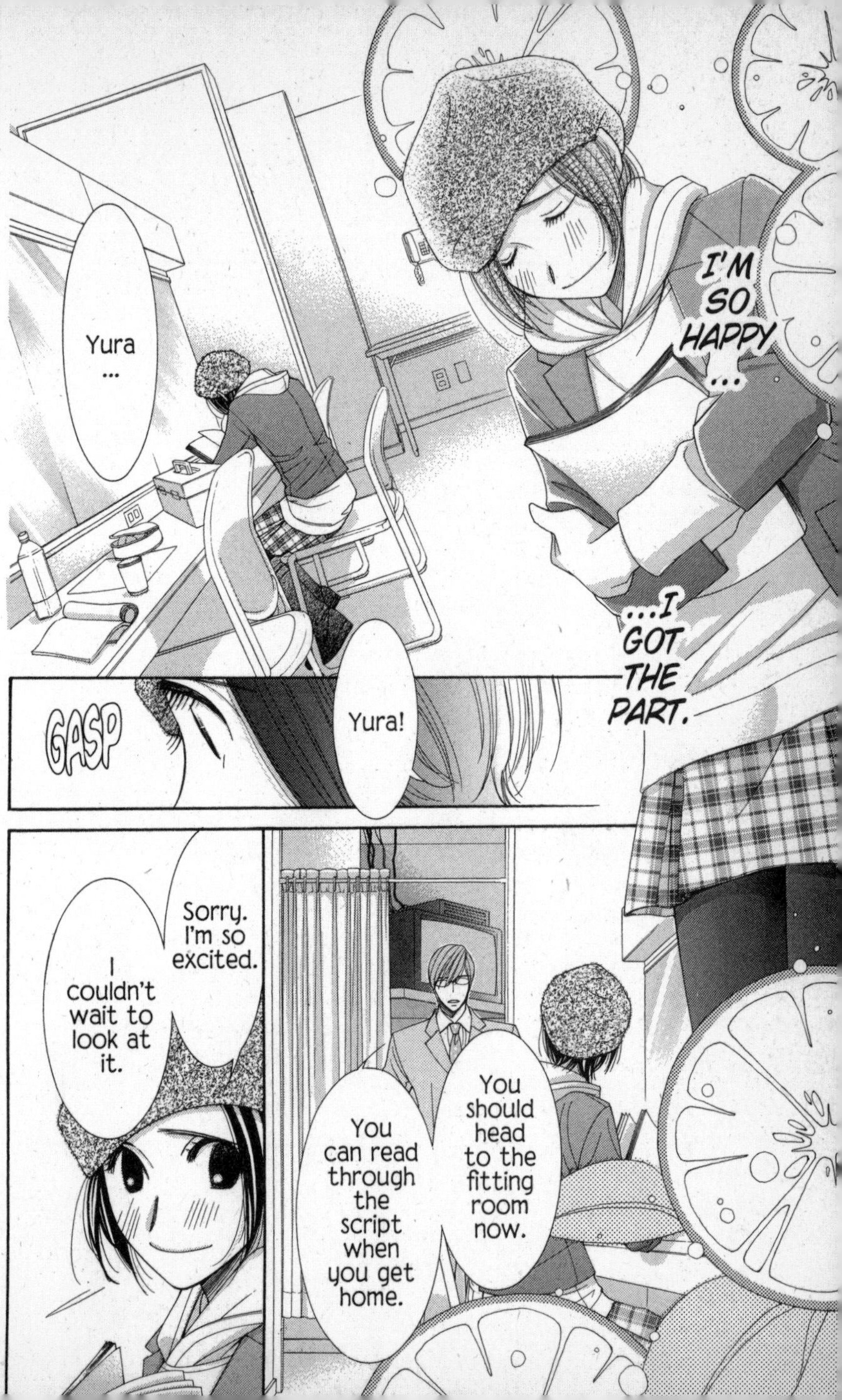

I'M SO HAPPY...
...I GOT THE PART.
Yura ...
Yura!
GASP
You should head to the fitting room now.
You can read through the script when you get home.
Sorry. I'm so excited.
I couldn't wait to look at it.

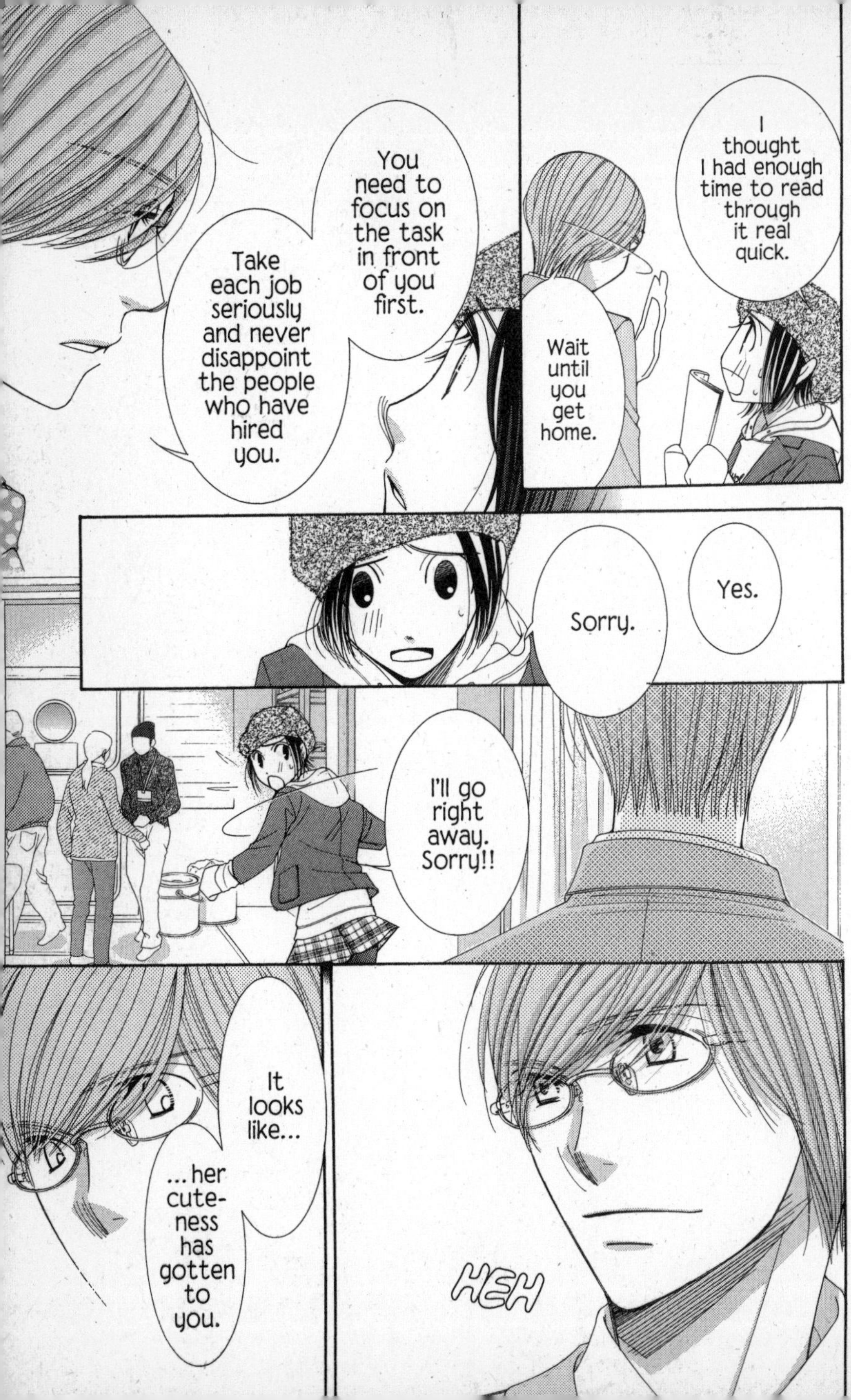
I thought I had enough time to read through it real quick.
Wait until you get home.
You need to focus on the task in front of you first.
Take each job seriously and never disappoint the people who have hired you.
Yes.
Sorry.
I'll go right away. Sorry!!
HEH
It looks like...
...her cuteness has gotten to you.

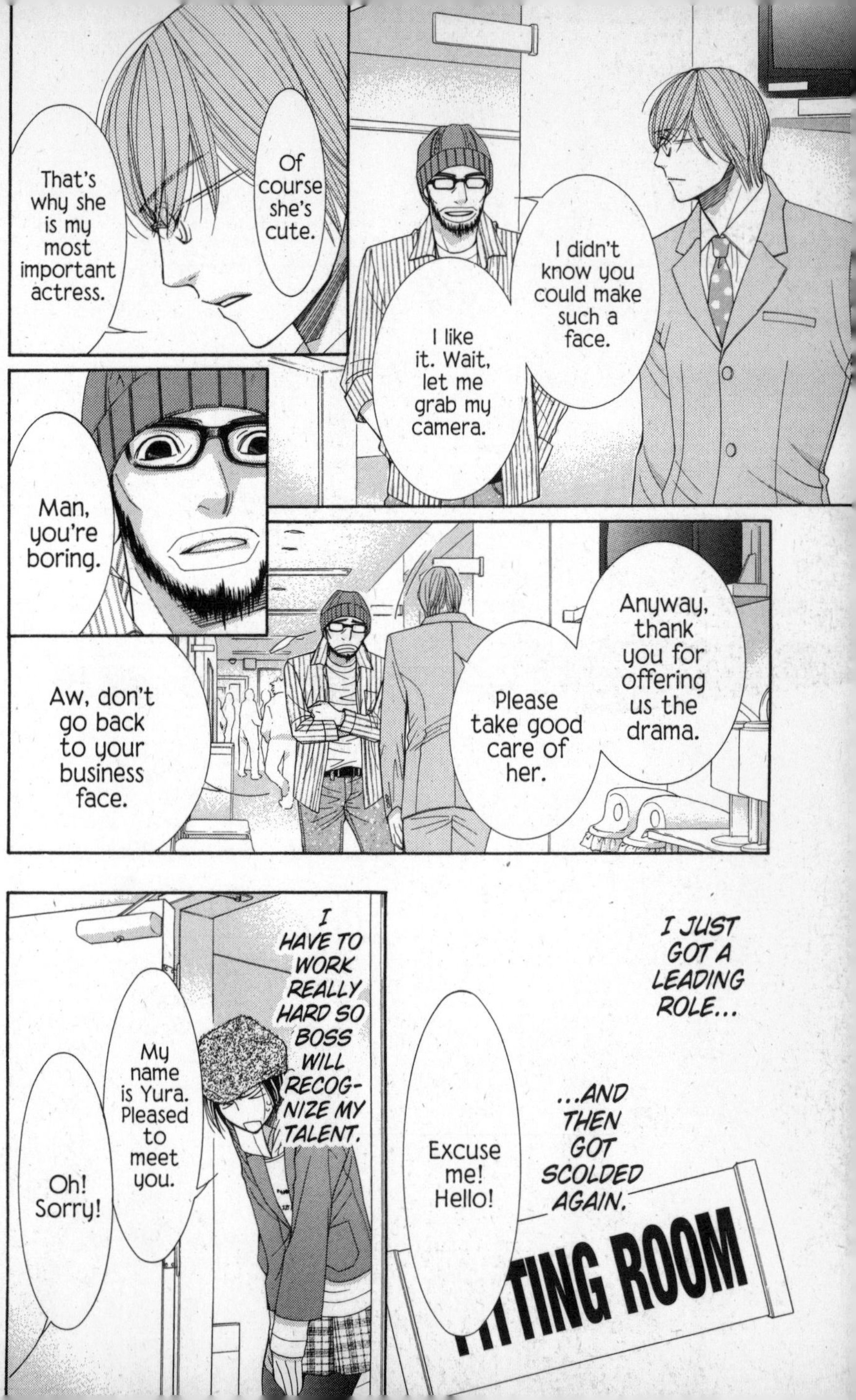
I didn't know you could make such a face.
I like it. Wait, let me grab my camera.
Of course she's cute.
That's why she is my most important actress.
Man, you're boring.
Anyway, thank you for offering us the drama.
Please take good care of her.
Aw, don't go back to your business face.
I JUST GOT A LEADING ROLE...
...AND THEN GOT SCOLDED AGAIN.
Excuse me! Hello!
TTING ROOM
I HAVE TO WORK REALLY HARD SO BOSS WILL RECOGNIZE MY TALENT.
My name is Yura. Pleased to meet you.
Oh! Sorry!

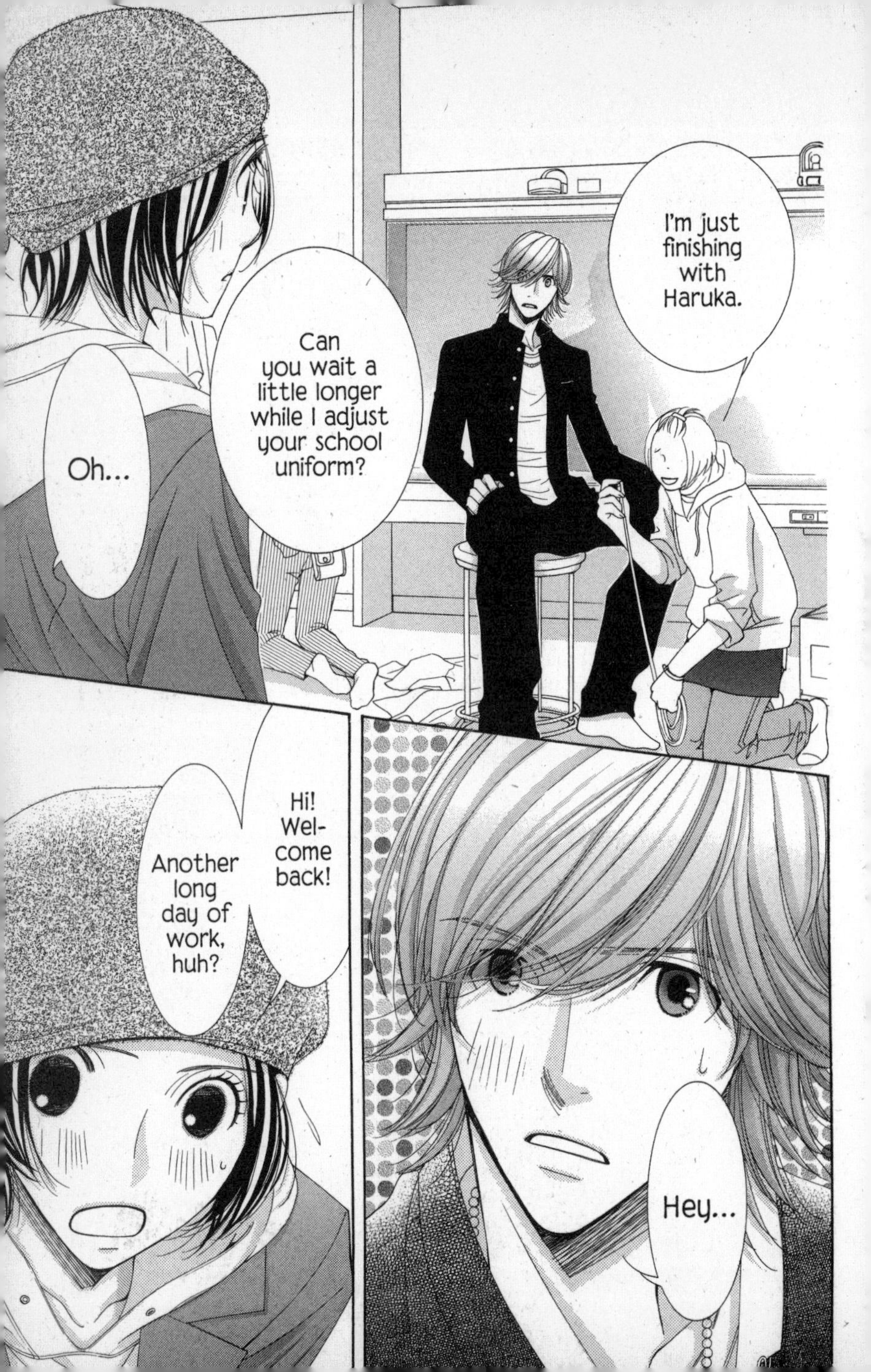
I'm just finishing with Haruka.
Can you wait a little longer while I adjust your school uniform?
Oh...
Hey...
Hi! Wel-come back!
Another long day of work, huh?

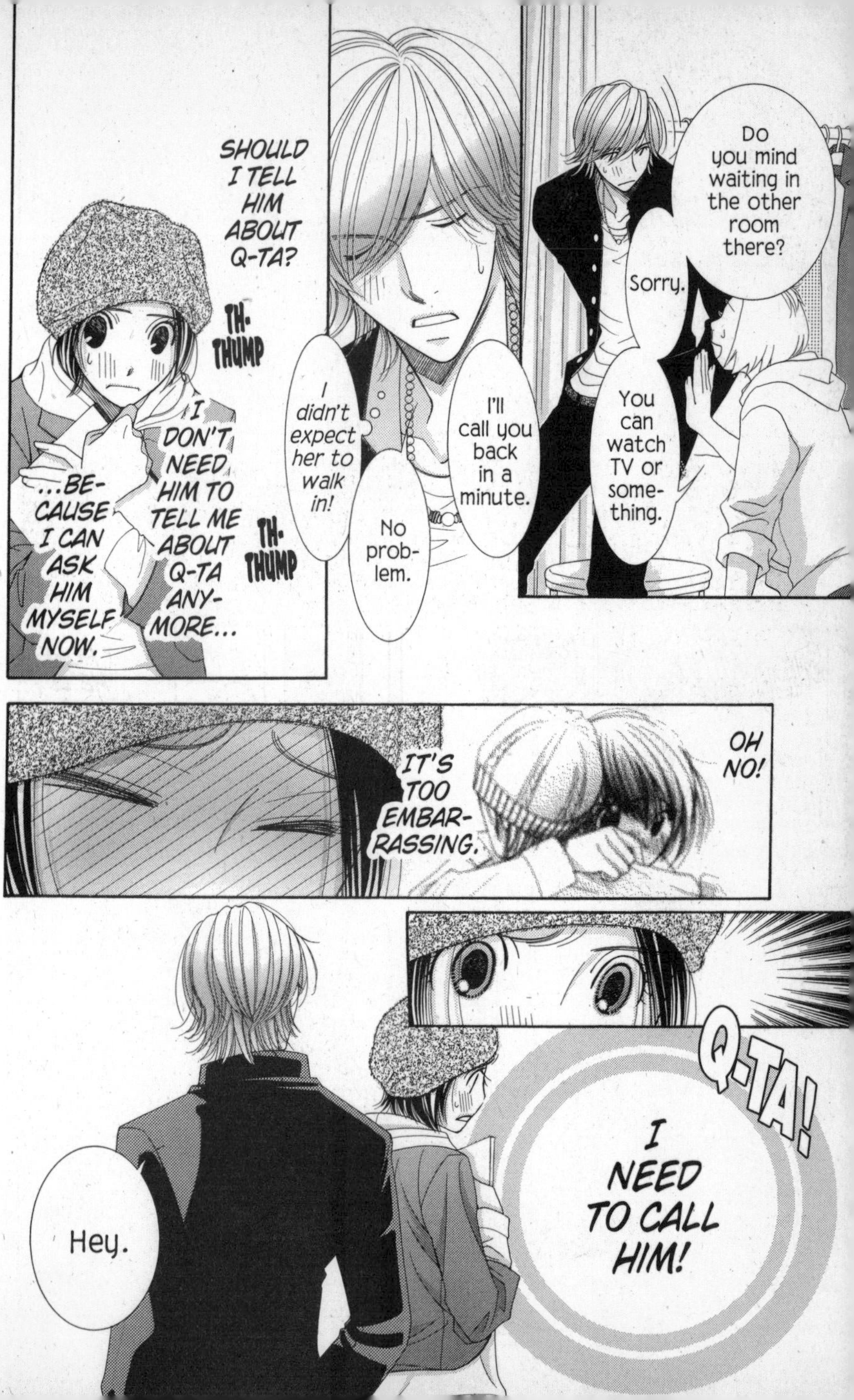
Do you mind waiting in the other room there?
Sorry.
You can watch TV or some-thing.
I'll call you back in a minute.
I didn't expect her to walk in!
No prob-lem.
SHOULD I TELL HIM ABOUT Q-TA?
TH-THUMP
I DON'T NEED HIM TO TELL ME ABOUT Q-TA ANY-MORE...
TH-THUMP
...BE-CAUSE I CAN ASK HIM MYSELF NOW.
OH NO!
IT'S TOO EMBAR-RASSING.
Q-TA!
I NEED TO CALL HIM!
Hey.

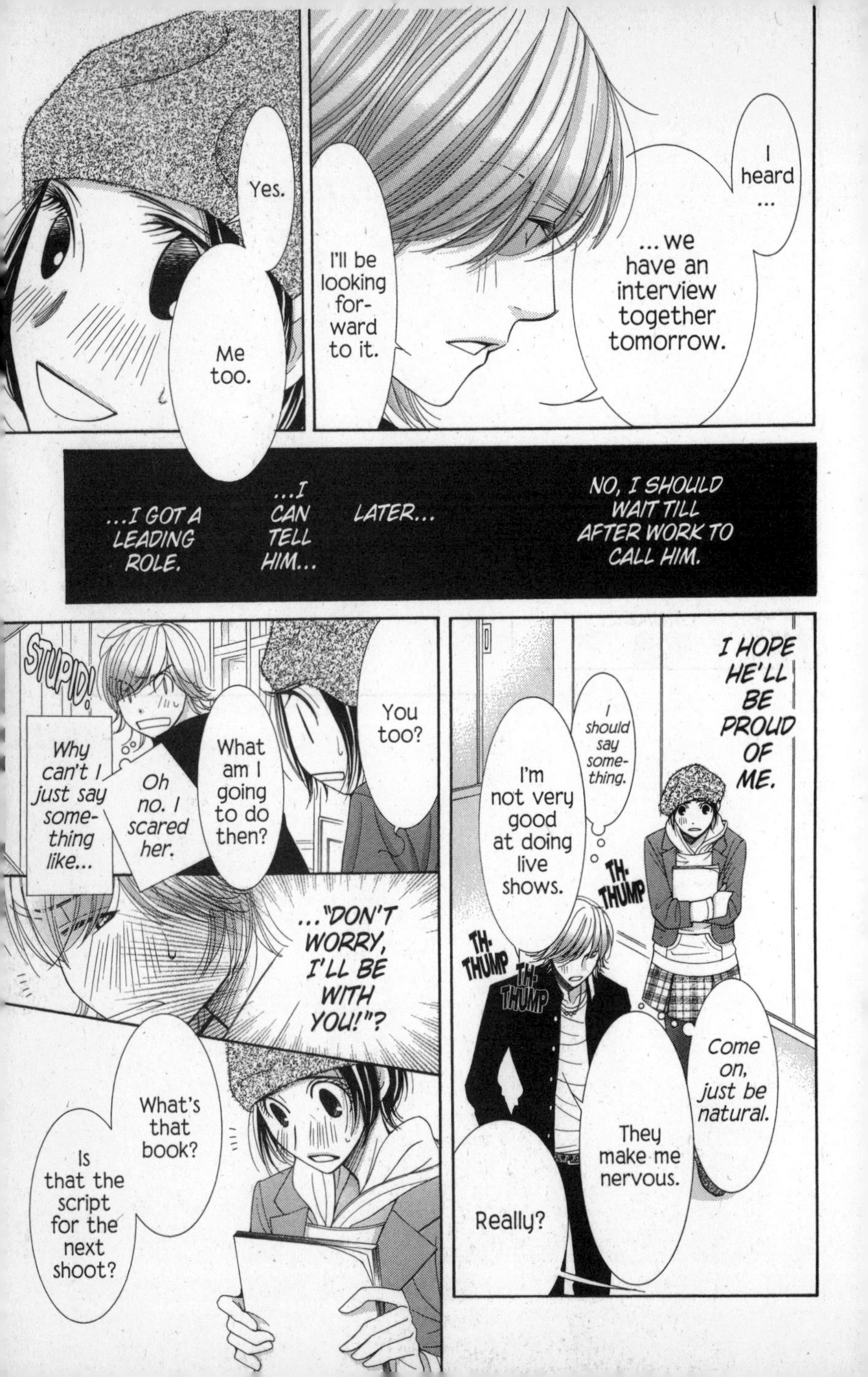
I heard ...
... we have an interview together tomorrow.
I'll be looking for-ward to it.
Yes.
Me too.
NO, I SHOULD WAIT TILL AFTER WORK TO CALL HIM.
LATER...
...I CAN TELL HIM...
...I GOT A LEADING ROLE.
I HOPE HE'LL BE PROUD OF ME.
I should say some-thing.
I'm not very good at doing live shows.
TH-THUMP
TH-THUMP
TH-THUMP
Come on, just be natural.
They make me nervous.
Really?
You too?
What am I going to do then?
Oh no. I scared her.
STUPID!
Why can't I just say some-thing like...
..."DON'T WORRY, I'LL BE WITH YOU!"?
What's that book?
Is that the script for the next shoot?

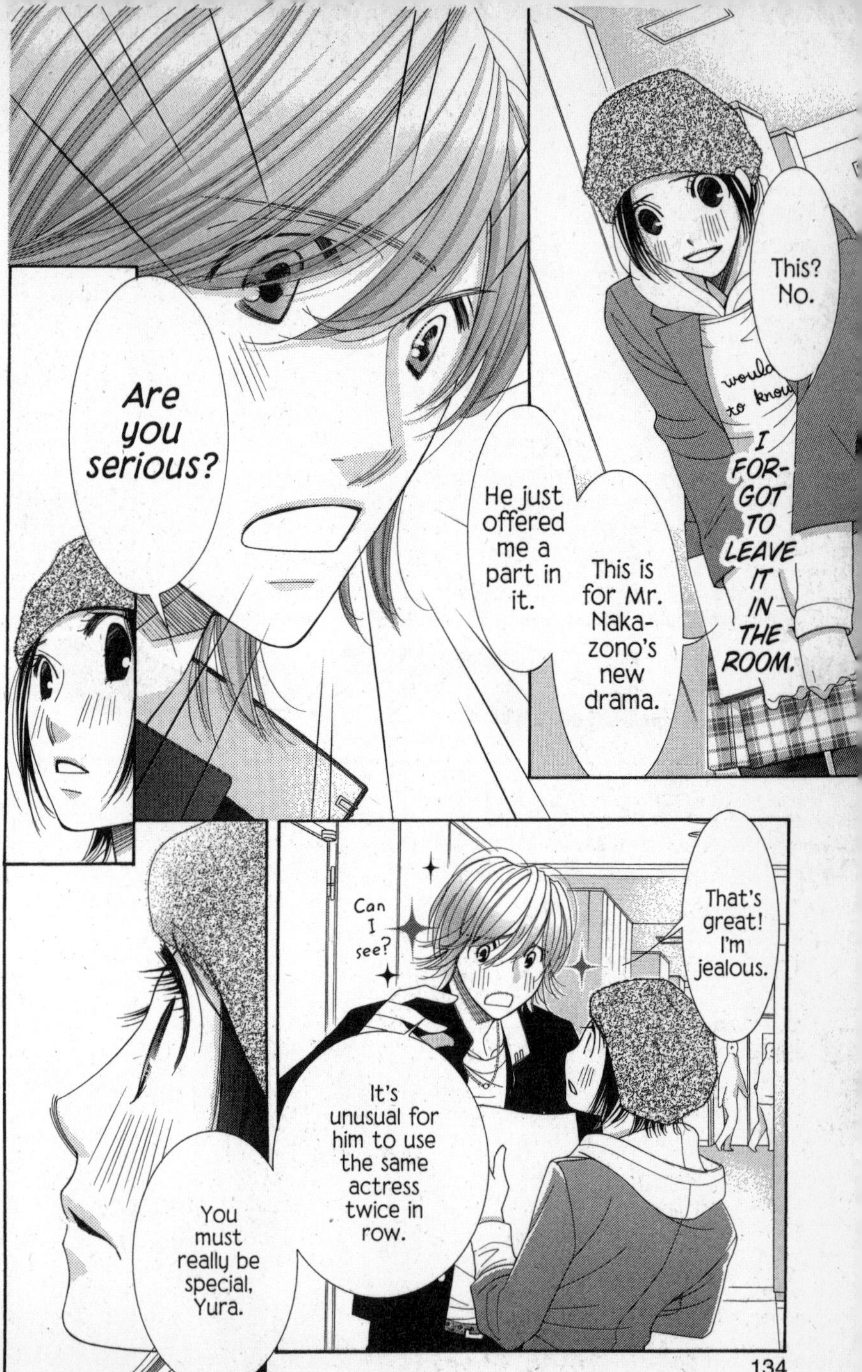
This? No.
I FORGOT TO LEAVE IT IN THE ROOM.
This is for Mr. Nakazono's new drama.
He just offered me a part in it.
Are you serious?
That's great! I'm jealous.
Can I see?
It's unusual for him to use the same actress twice in row.
You must really be special, Yura.

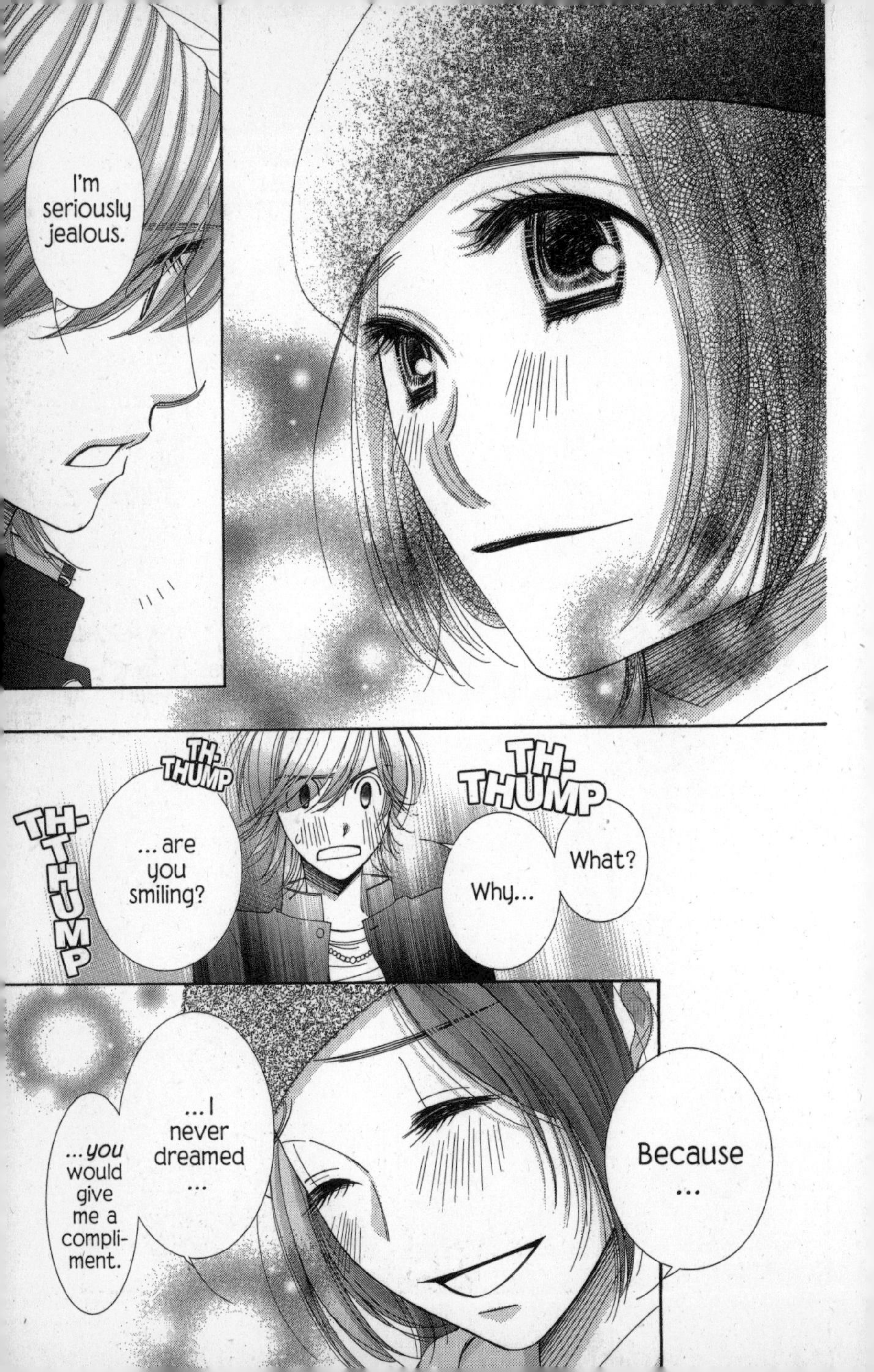
I'm seriously jealous.
TH-THUMP
What?
Why...
TH-THUMP
...are you smiling?
TH-THUMP
Because ...
...I never dreamed ...
...*you* would give me a compli-ment.

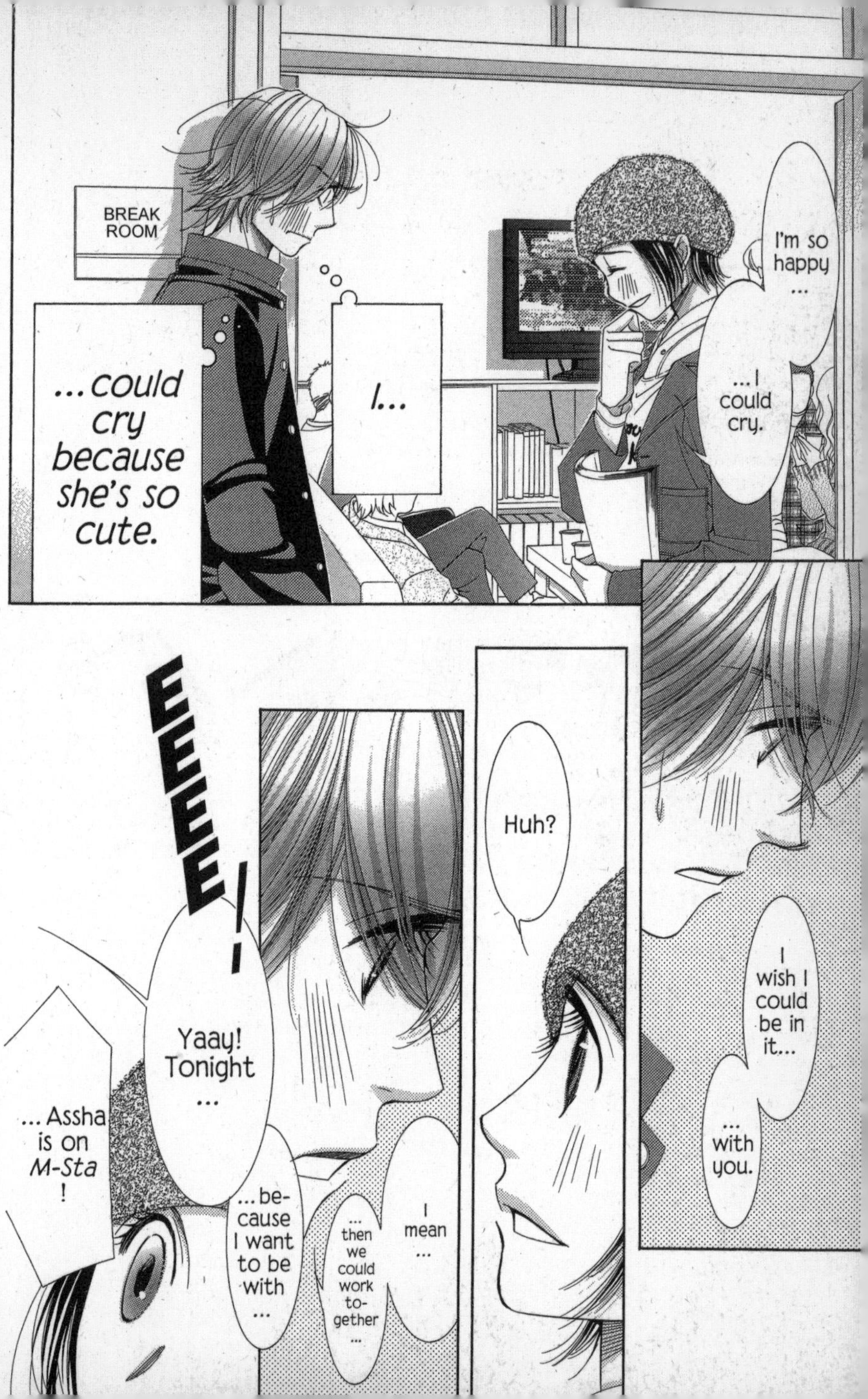
I'm so happy ...
... I could cry.
BREAK ROOM
I...
...could cry because she's so cute.
I wish I could be in it...
... with you.
Huh?
I mean ...
... then we could work to-gether ...
... be-cause I want to be with ...
EEEE!
Yaay! Tonight ...
... Assha is on *M-Sta* !

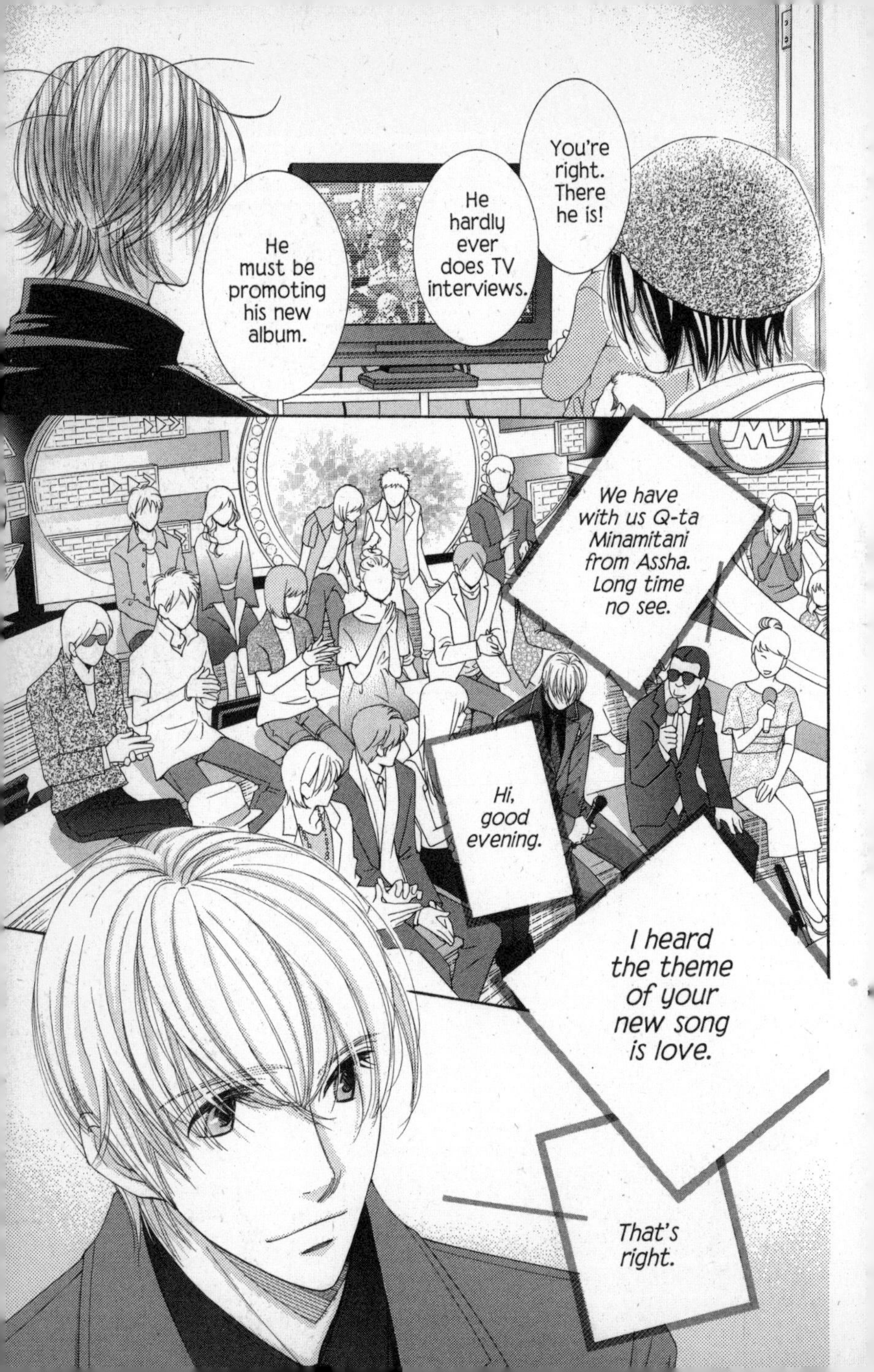
You're right. There he is!
He hardly ever does TV interviews.
He must be promoting his new album.
We have with us Q-ta Minamitani from Assha. Long time no see.
Hi, good evening.
I heard the theme of your new song is love.
That's right.

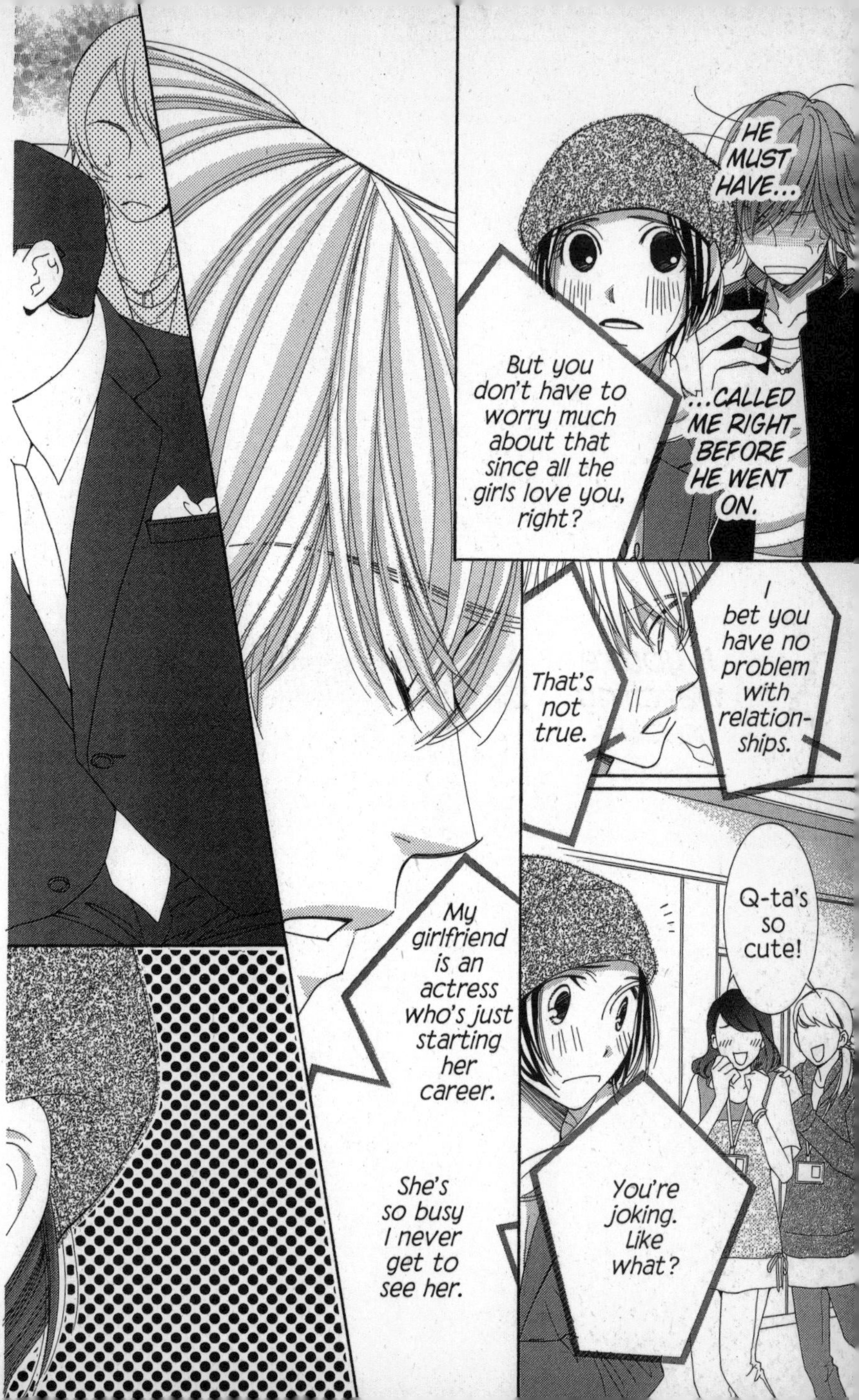
HE MUST HAVE...
...CALLED ME RIGHT BEFORE HE WENT ON.
But you don't have to worry much about that since all the girls love you, right?
I bet you have no problem with relationships.
That's not true.
Q-ta's so cute!
You're joking. Like what?
My girlfriend is an actress who's just starting her career.
She's so busy I never get to see her.

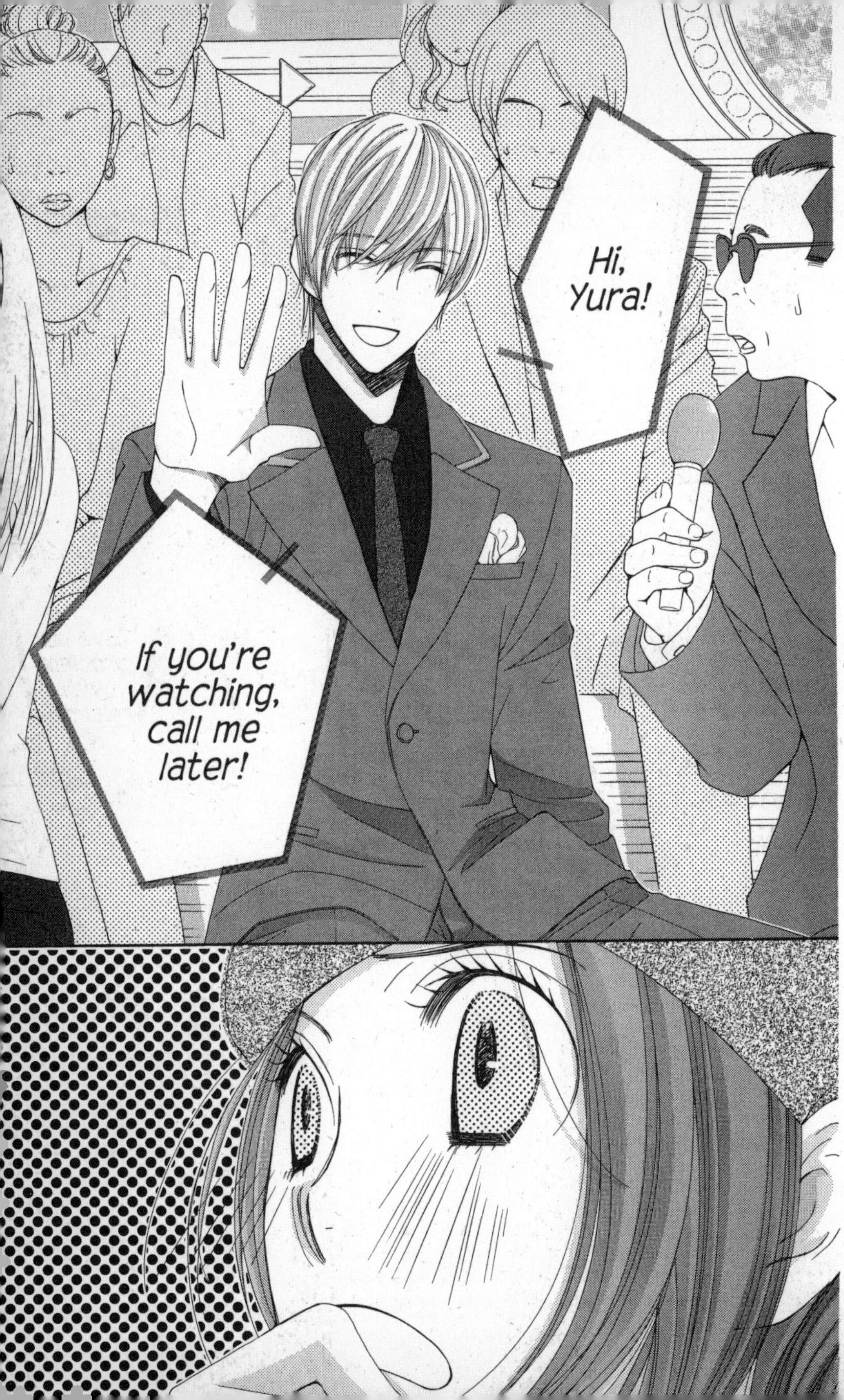
Hi, Yura!
If you're watching, call me later!

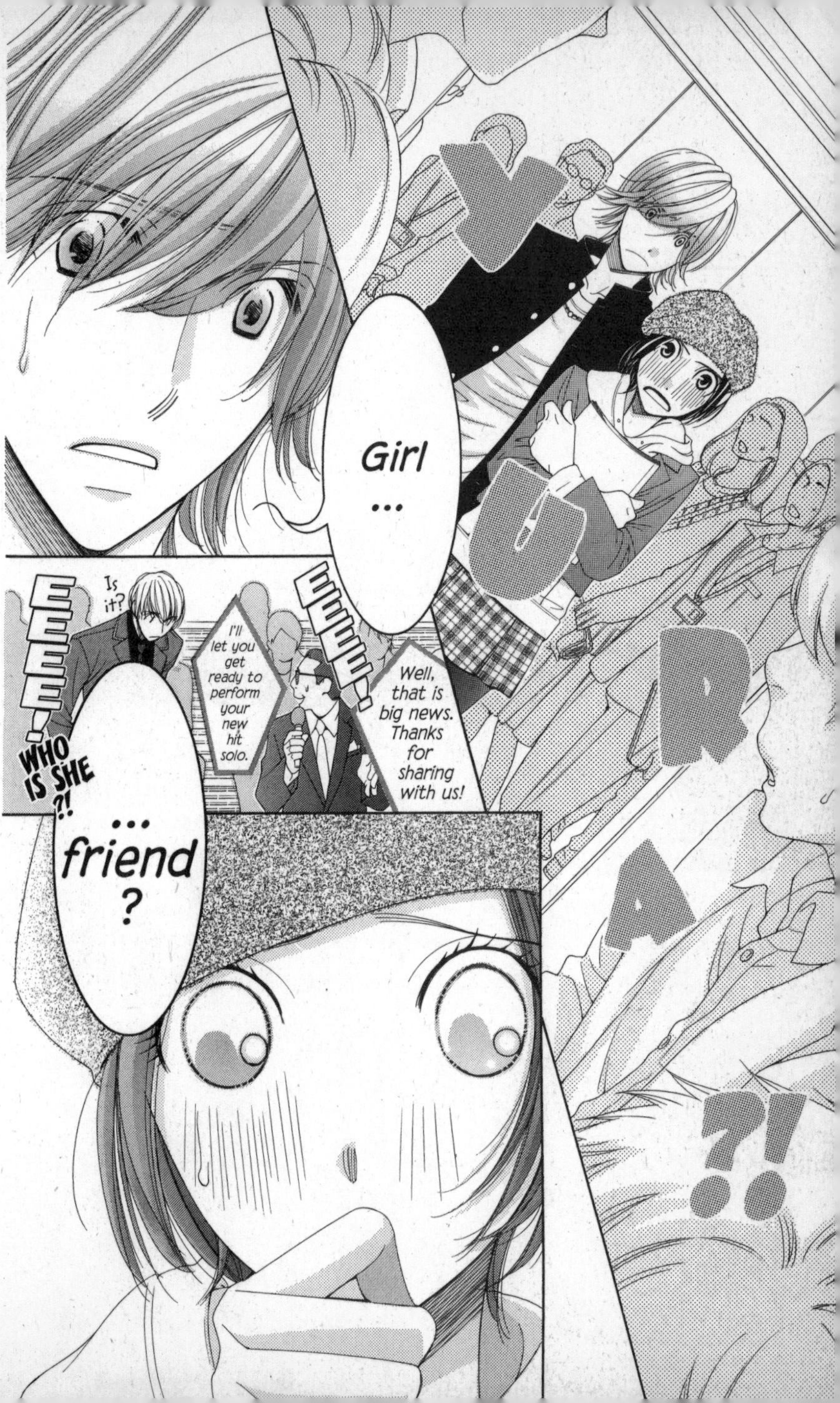

YURA ?!
Girl ...
Well, that is big news. Thanks for sharing with us!
I'll let you get ready to perform your new hit solo.
EEEE
Is it?
EEEE! WHO IS SHE ?!
... friend ?

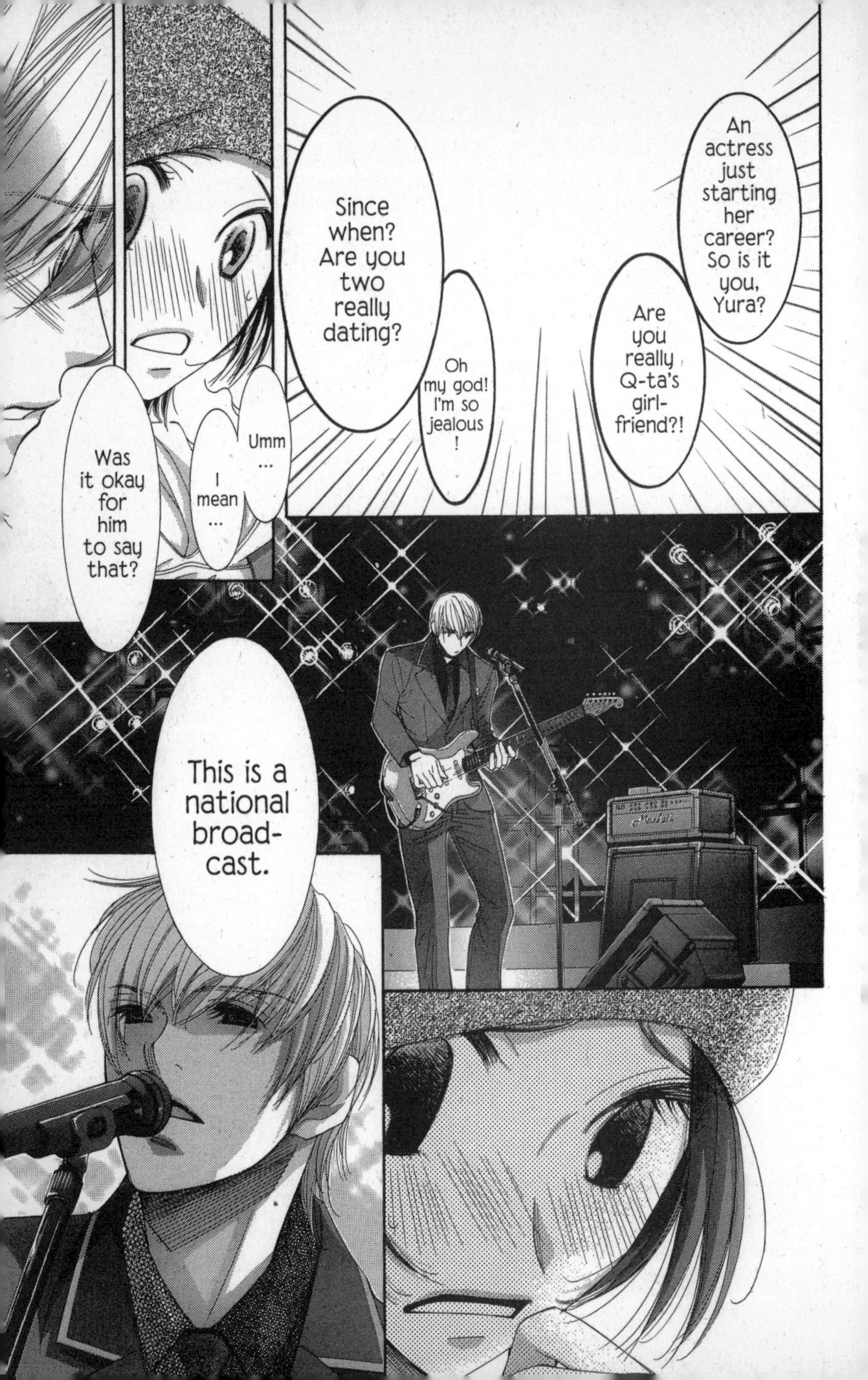
An actress just starting her career? So is it you, Yura?
Are you really Q-ta's girl-friend?!
Oh my god! I'm so jealous!
Since when? Are you two really dating?
Umm...
I mean...
Was it okay for him to say that?
This is a national broad-cast.

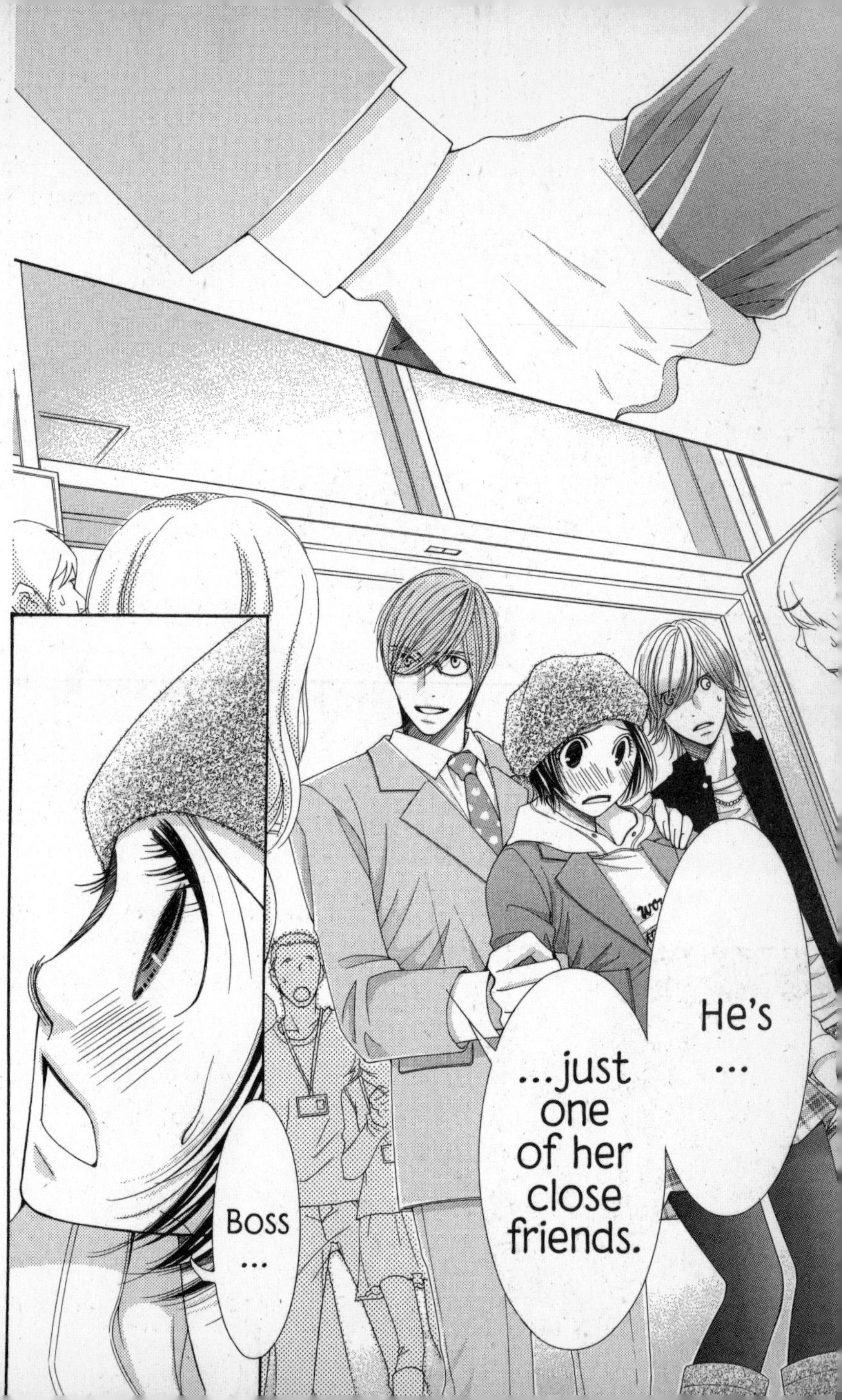
He's ...
...just one of her close friends.
Boss ...

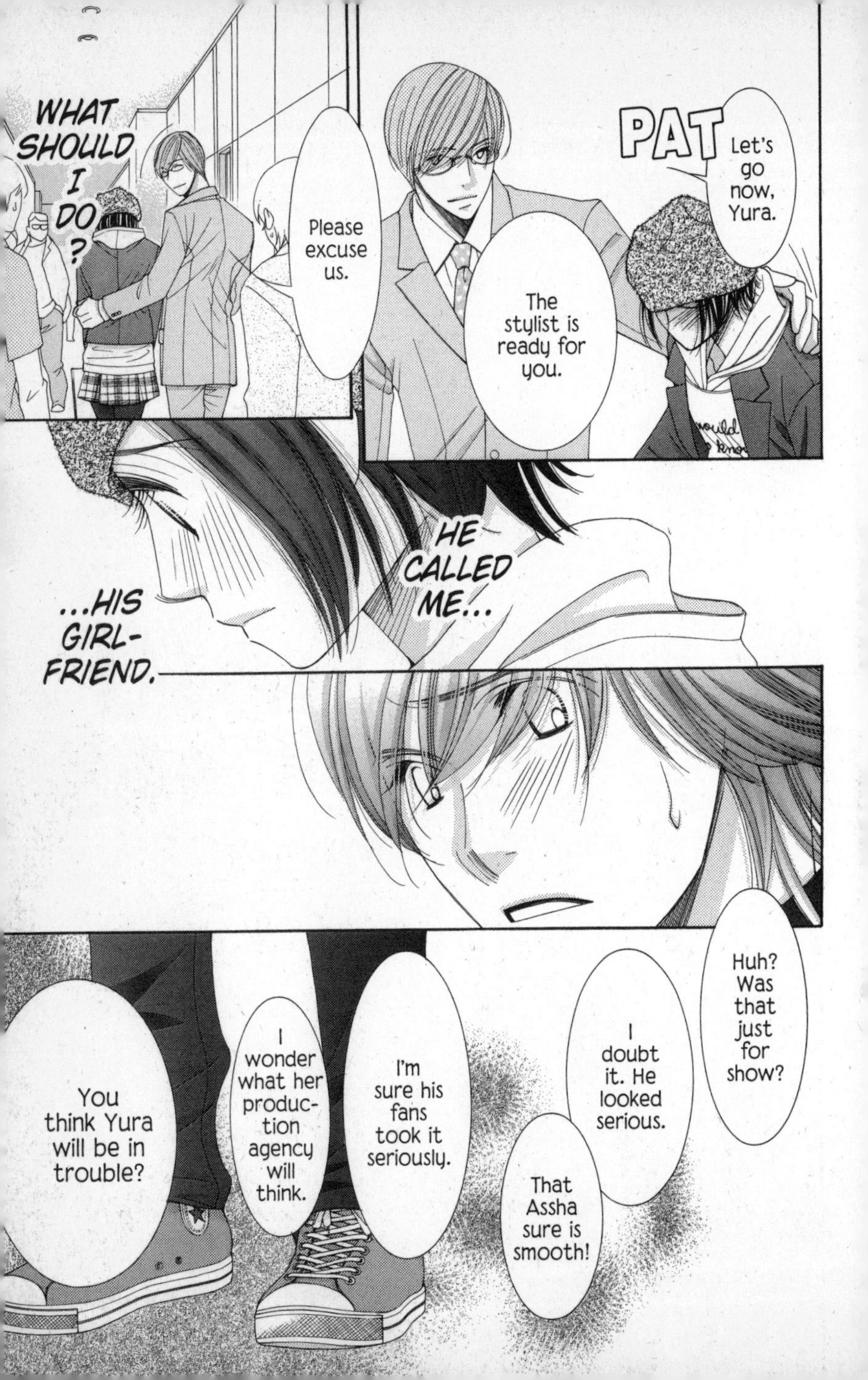
PAT
Let's go now, Yura.
The stylist is ready for you.
Please excuse us.
WHAT SHOULD I DO?
HE CALLED ME...
...HIS GIRL-FRIEND.
Huh? Was that just for show?
I doubt it. He looked serious.
That Assha sure is smooth!
I'm sure his fans took it seriously.
I wonder what her production agency will think.
You think Yura will be in trouble?

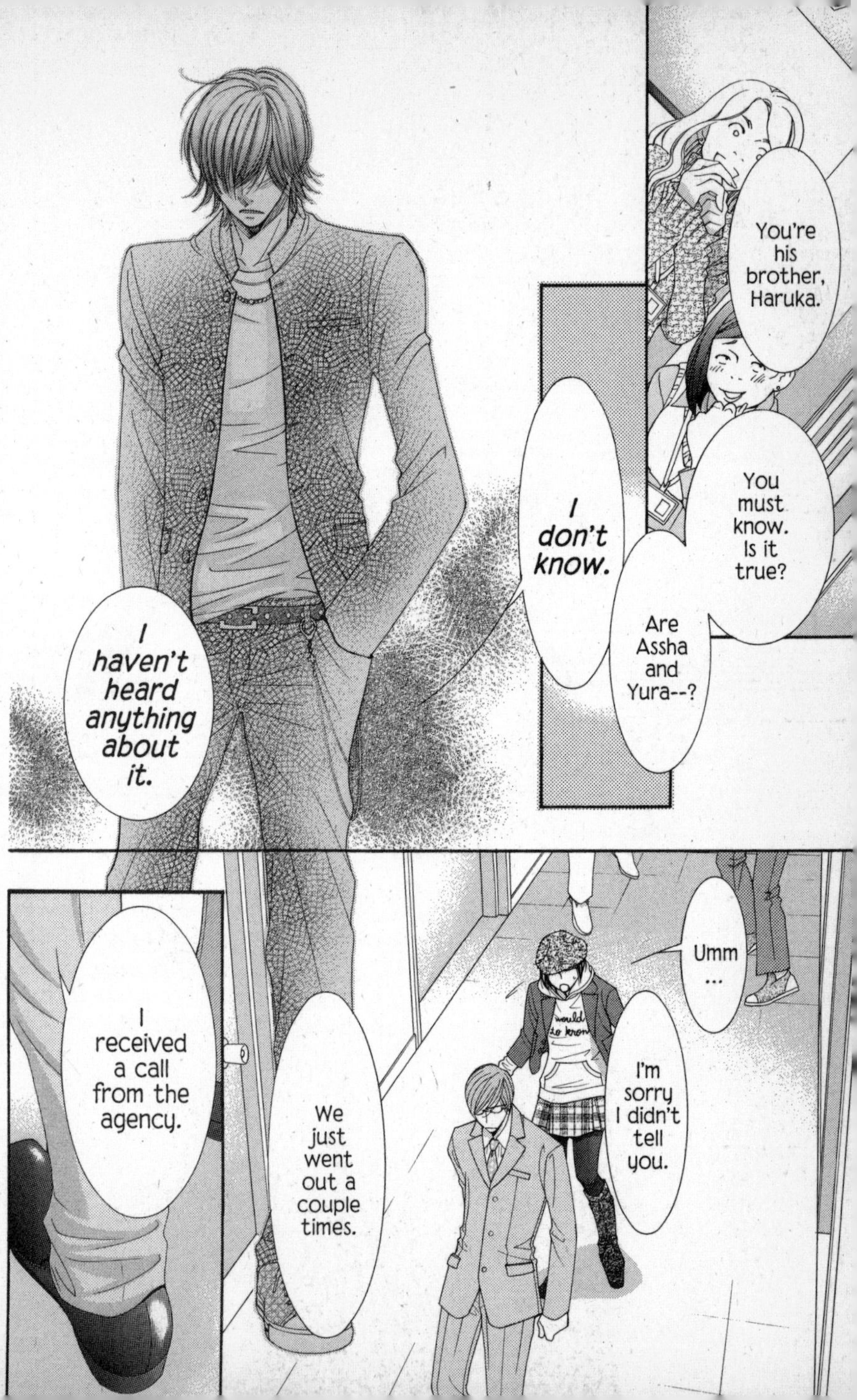
You're his brother, Haruka.
You must know. Is it true?
Are Assha and Yura--?
I don't know.
I haven't heard anything about it.
Umm ...
I'm sorry I didn't tell you.
We just went out a couple times.
I received a call from the agency.

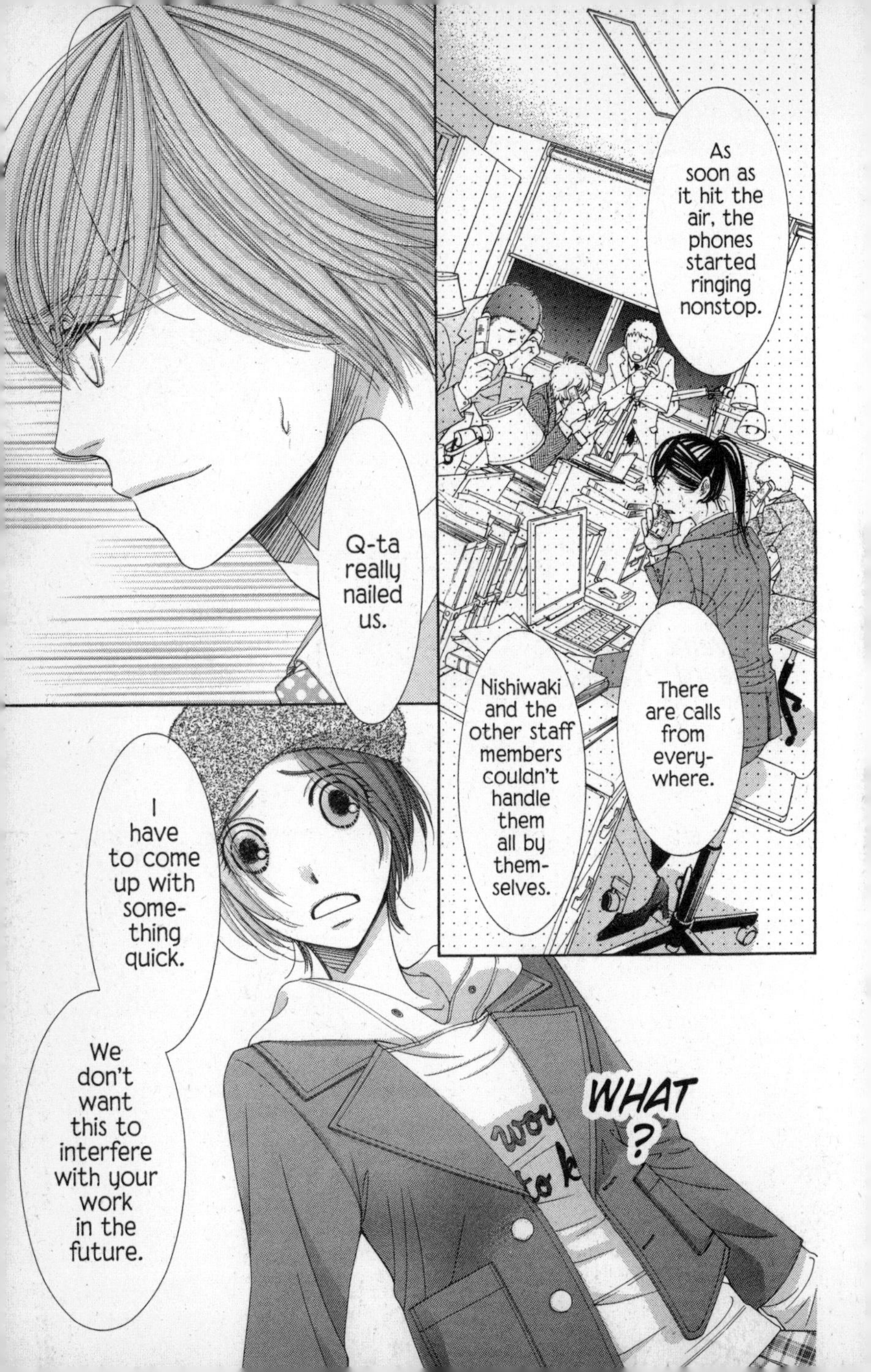
As soon as it hit the air, the phones started ringing nonstop.
There are calls from every-where.
Nishiwaki and the other staff members couldn't handle them all by them-selves.
Q-ta really nailed us.
I have to come up with some-thing quick.
We don't want this to interfere with your work in the future.
WHAT?

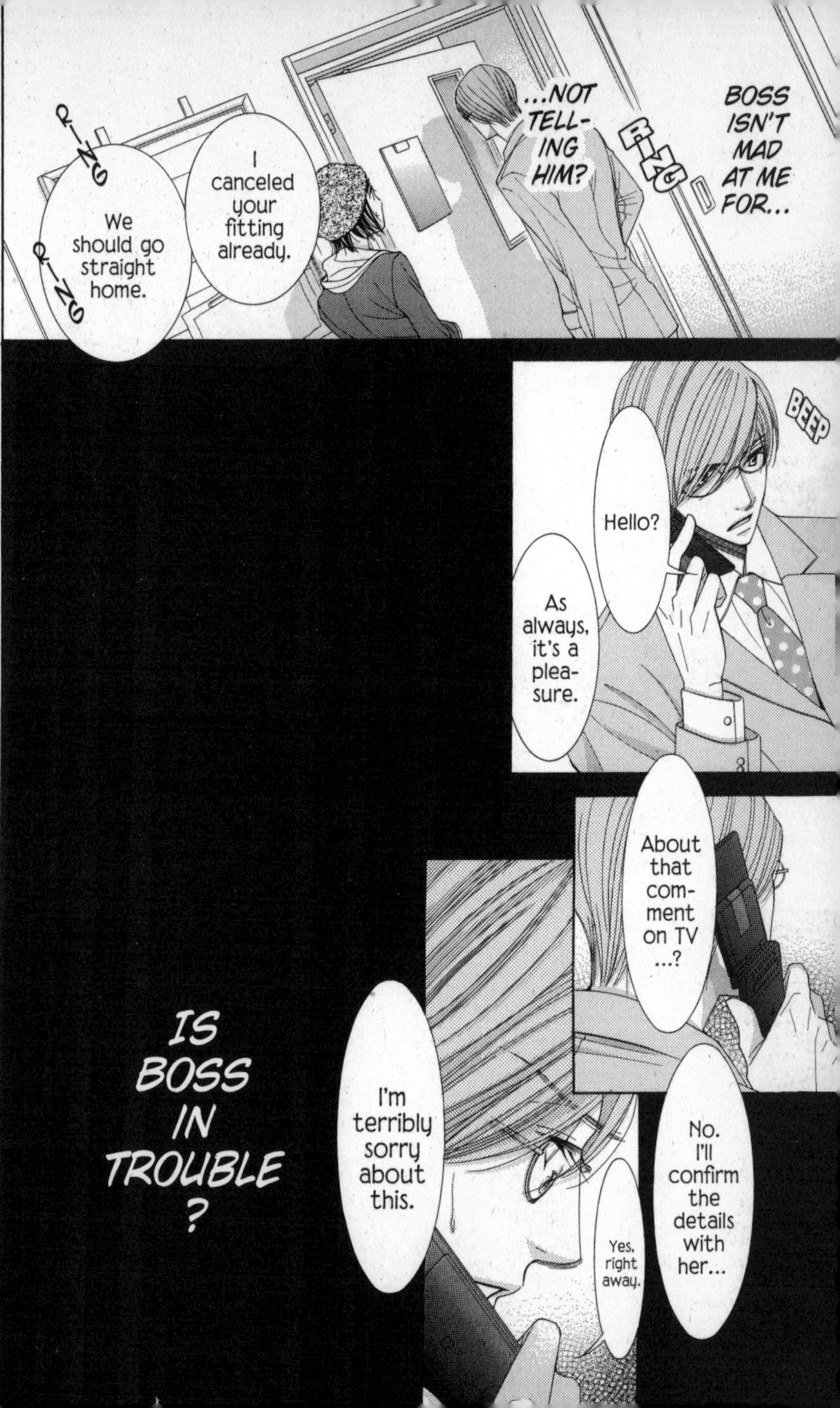
BOSS ISN'T MAD AT ME FOR...
RING
...NOT TELLING HIM?
I canceled your fitting already.
We should go straight home.
R-ING
R-ING
BEEP
Hello?
As always, it's a plea-sure.
About that com-ment on TV ...?
No. I'll confirm the details with her...
Yes, right away.
I'm terribly sorry about this.
IS BOSS IN TROUBLE ?

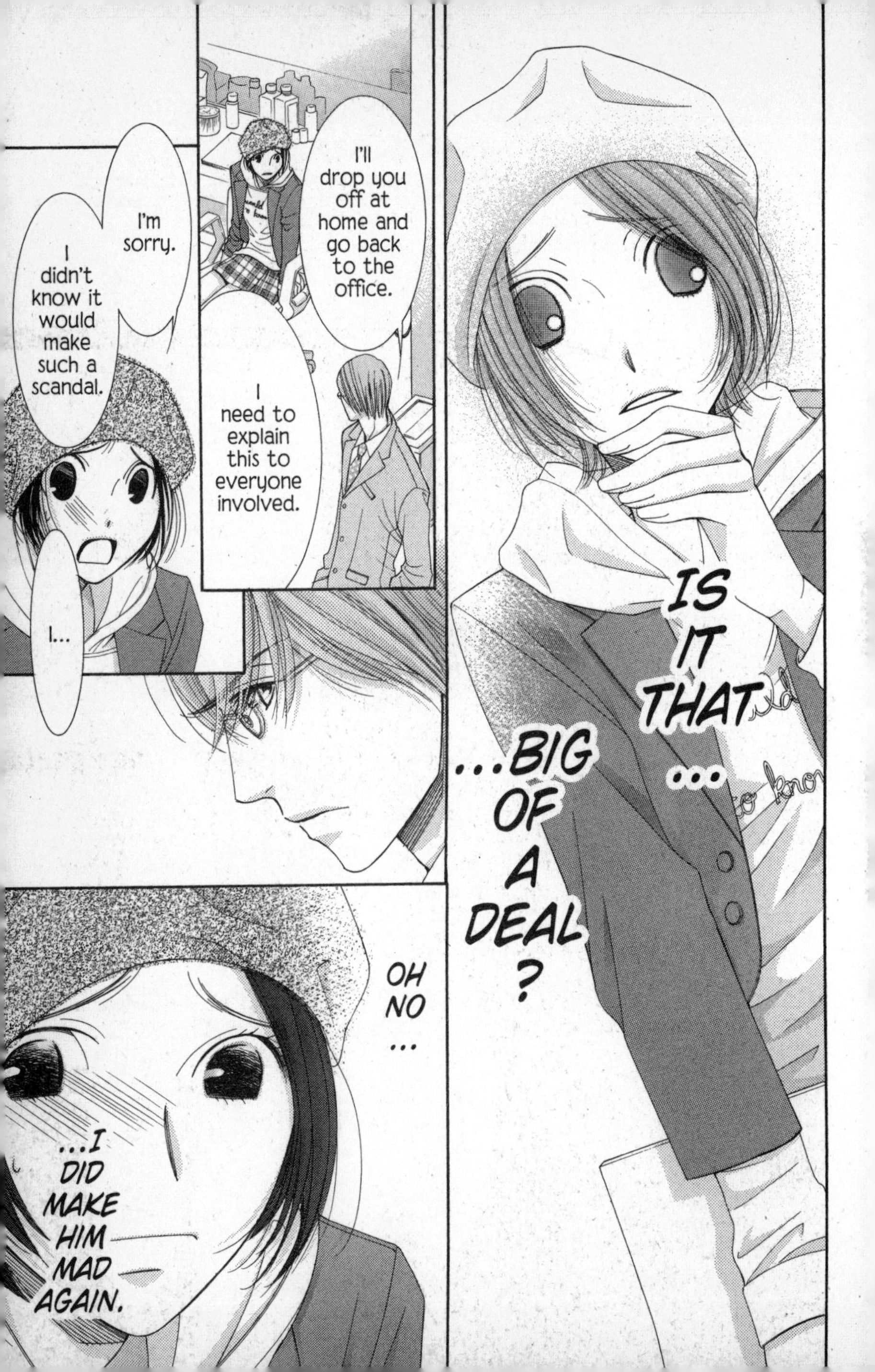
IS IT THAT...
...BIG OF A DEAL?
I'll drop you off at home and go back to the office.
I need to explain this to everyone involved.
I'm sorry.
I didn't know it would make such a scandal.
I...
OH NO...
...I DID MAKE HIM MAD AGAIN.

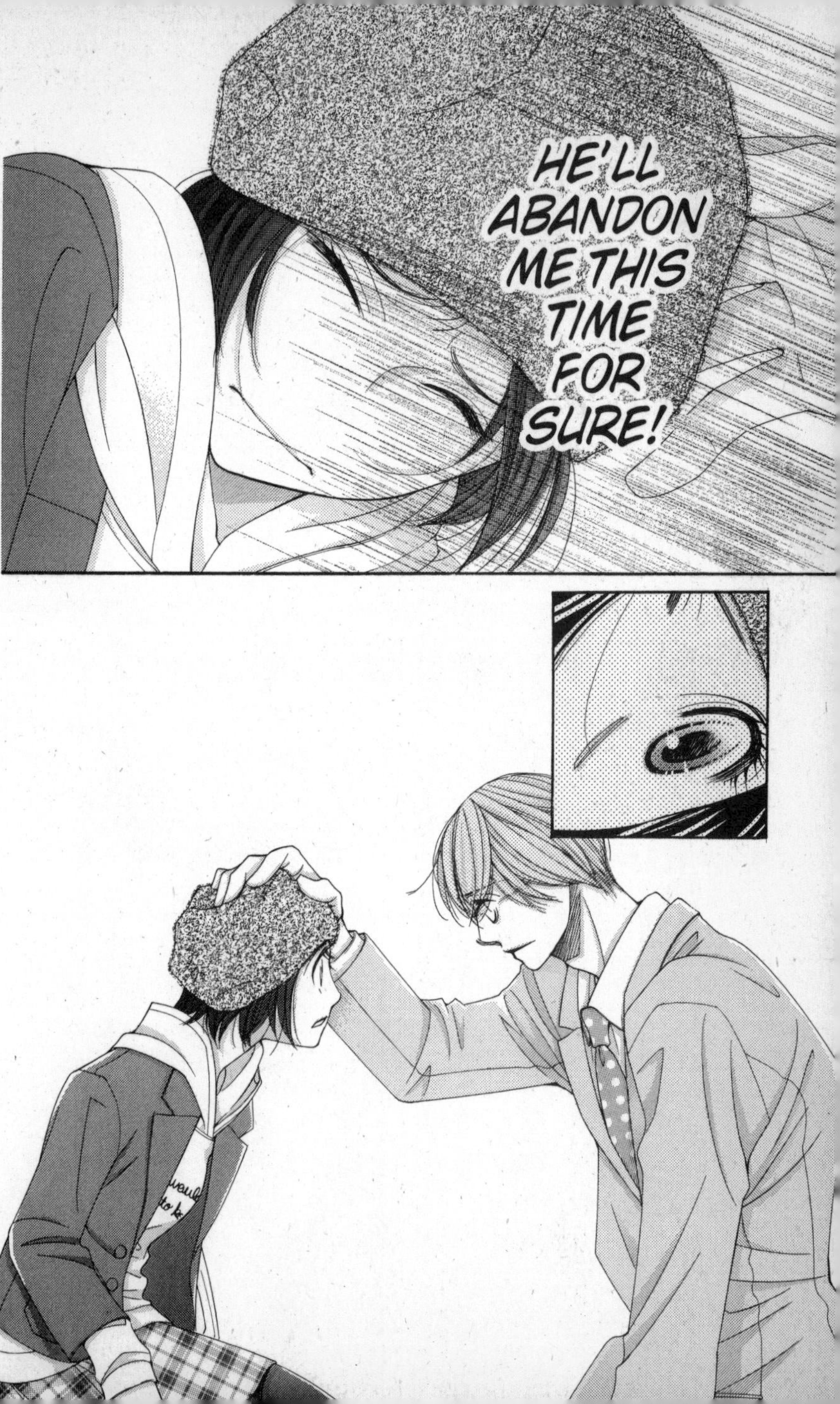
HE'LL ABANDON ME THIS TIME FOR SURE!

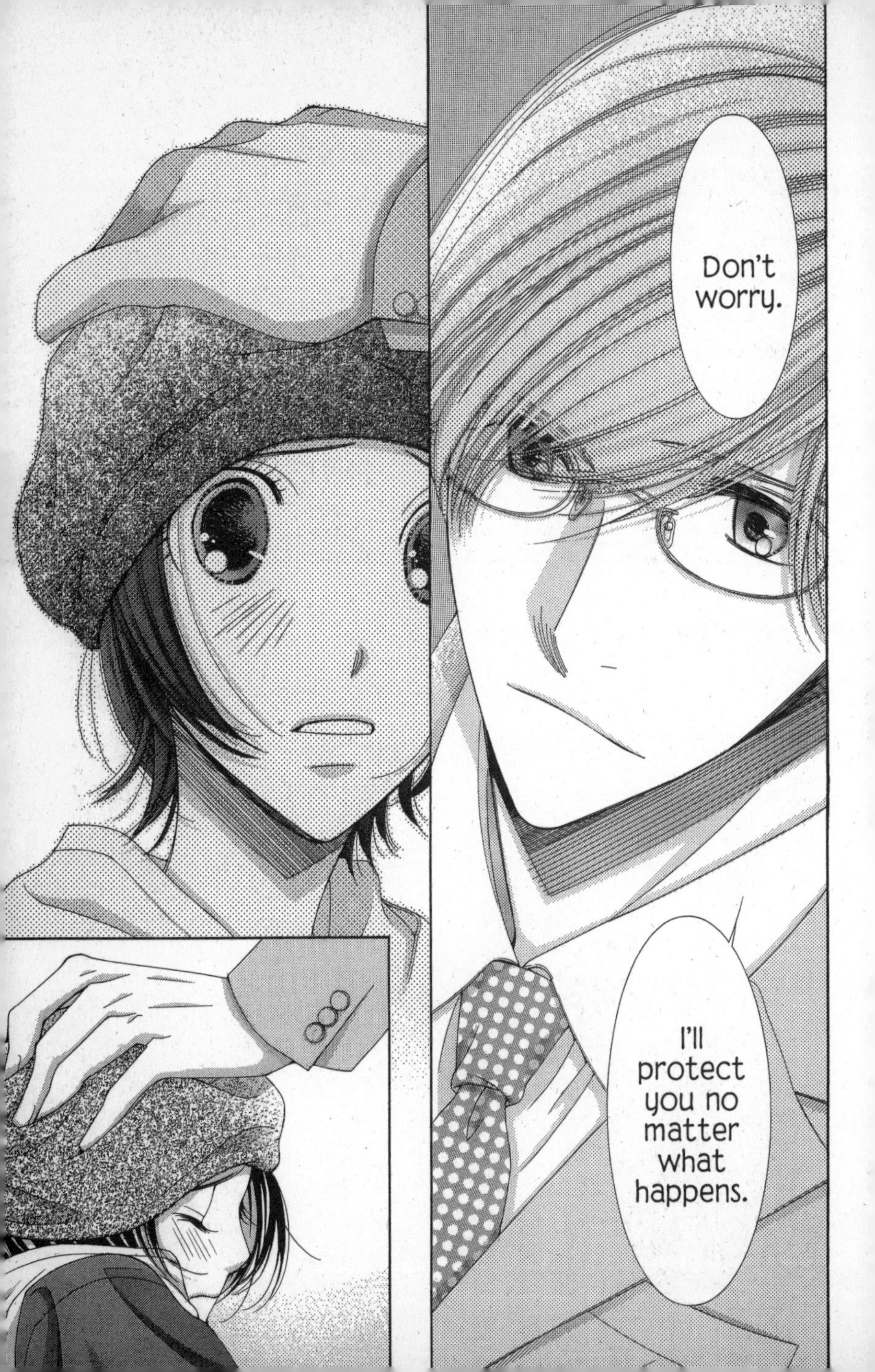
Don't worry.
I'll protect you no matter what happens.

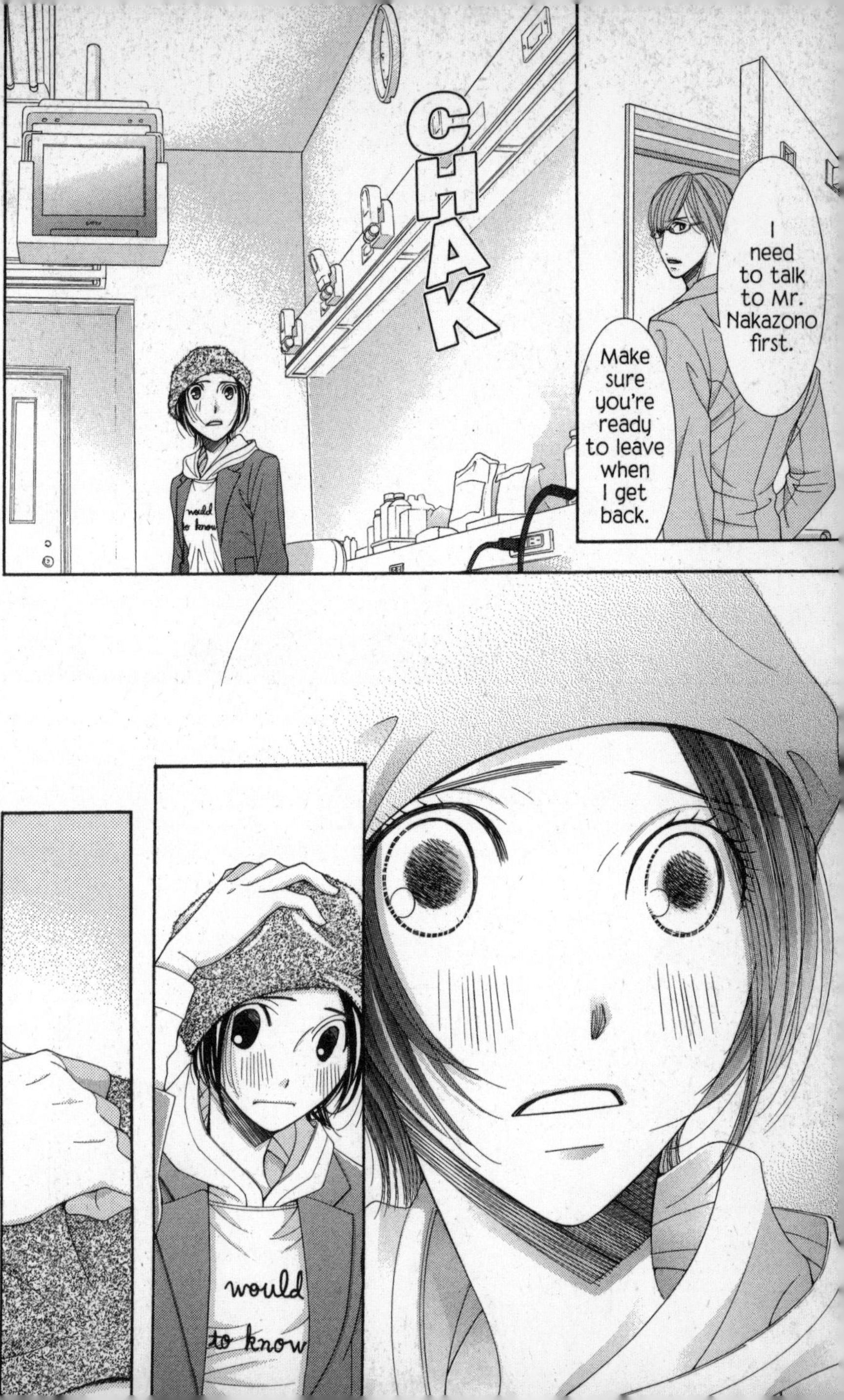
I need to talk to Mr. Nakazono first.
Make sure you're ready to leave when I get back.
CHAK

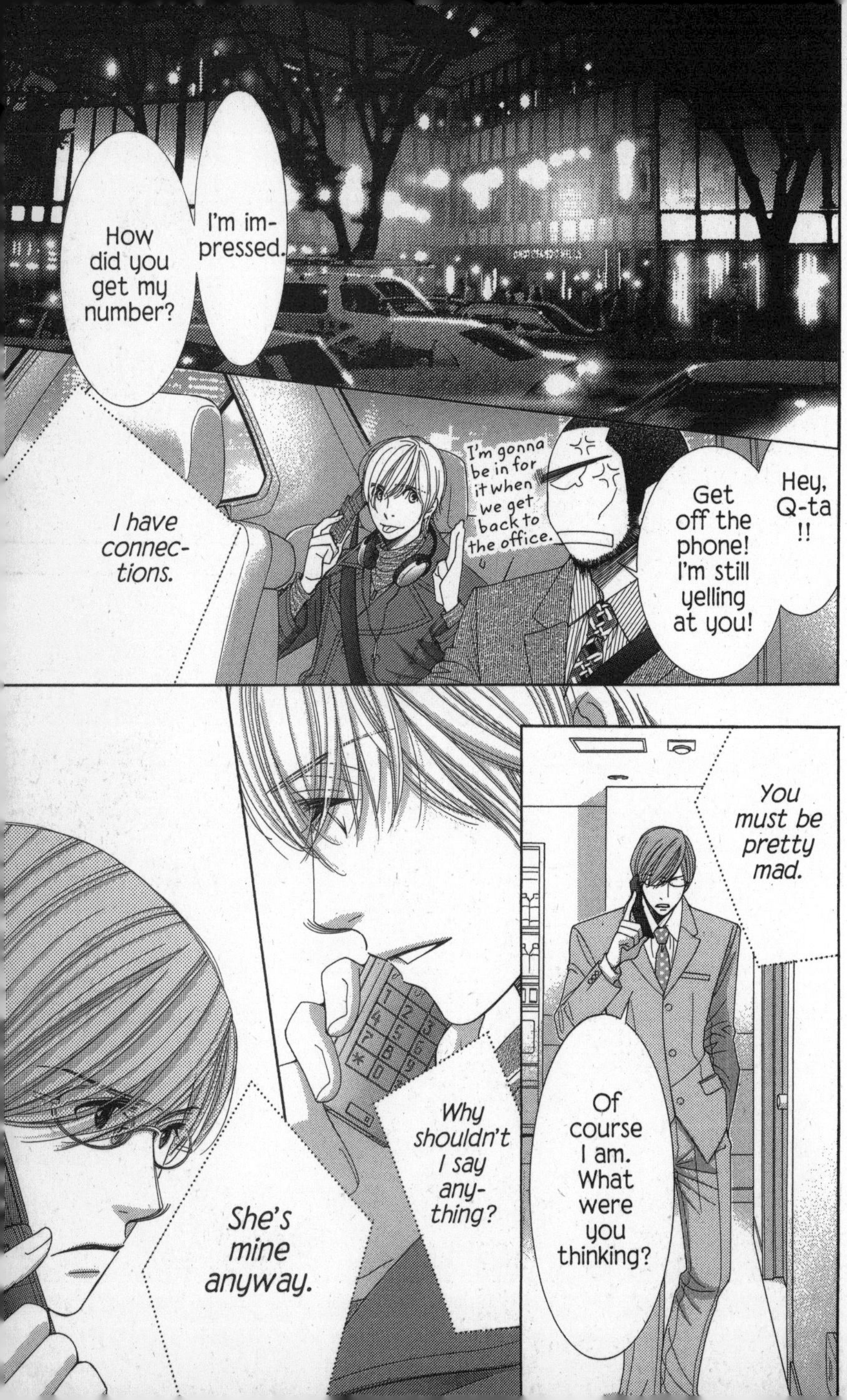
I'm impressed.
How did you get my number?
Hey, Q-ta !!
Get off the phone! I'm still yelling at you!
I'm gonna be in for it when we get back to the office.
I have connections.
You must be pretty mad.
Of course I am. What were you thinking?
Why shouldn't I say anything?
She's mine anyway.

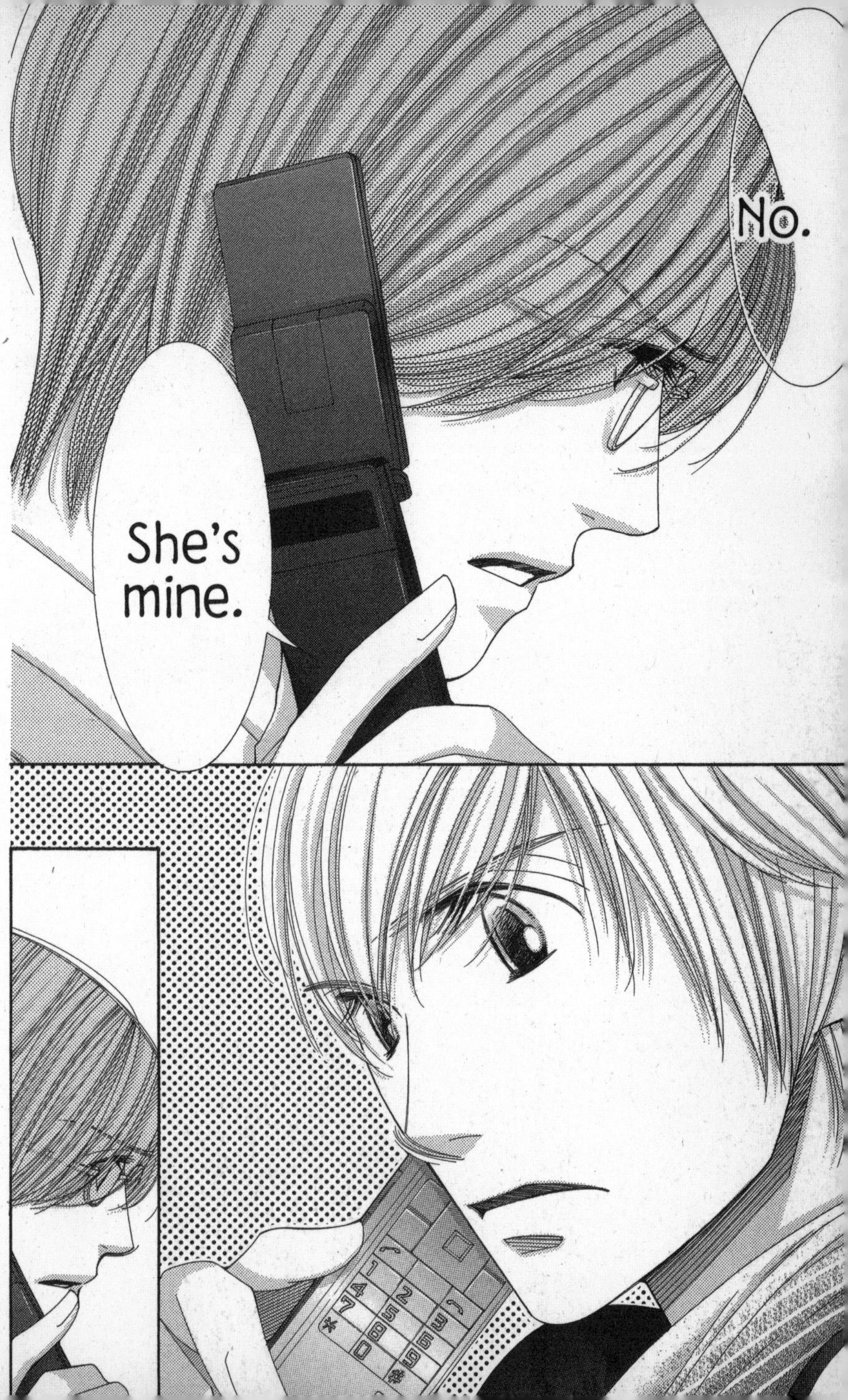
No.
She's mine.

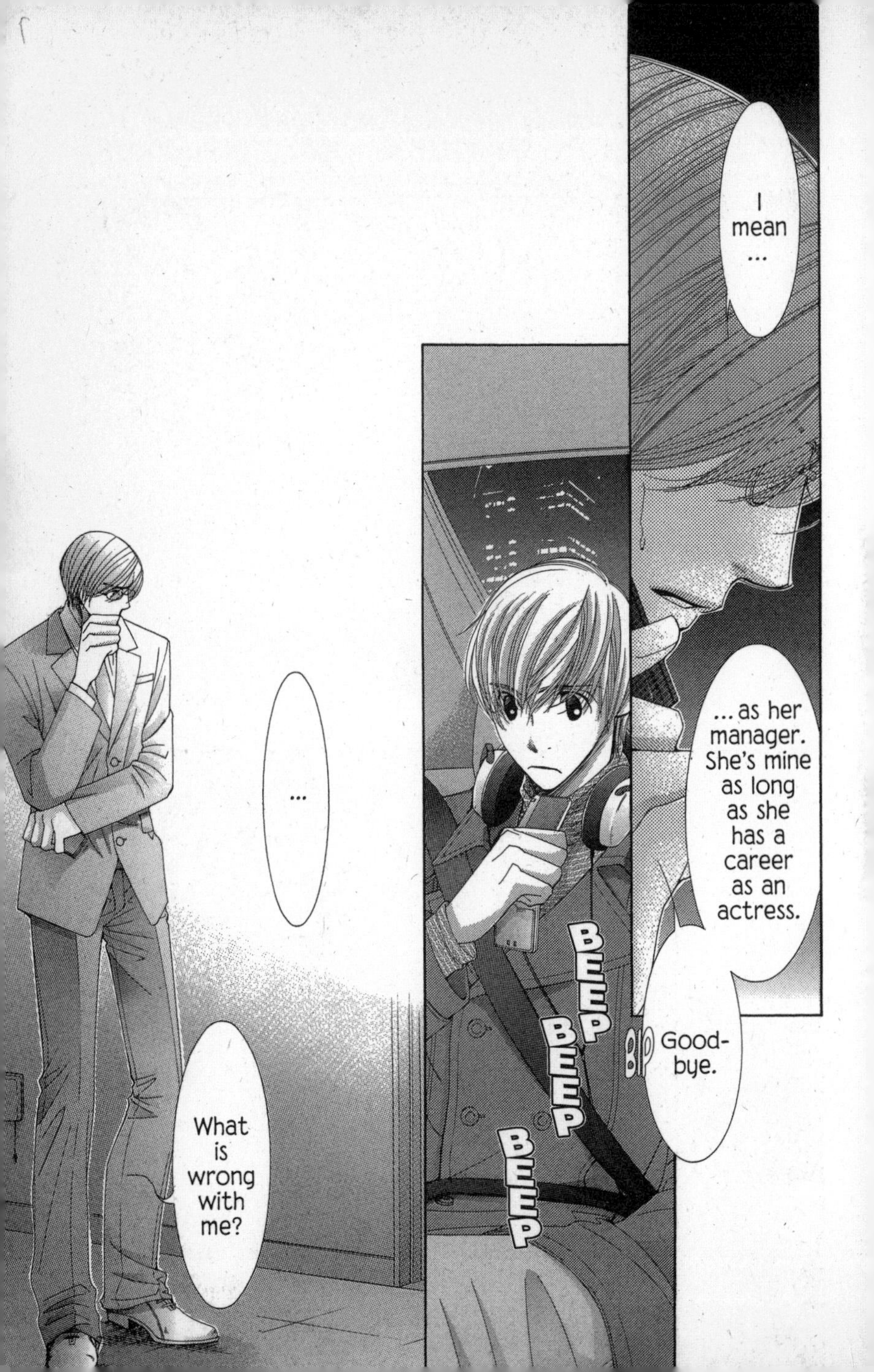
I mean ...
... as her manager. She's mine as long as she has a career as an actress.
BIP
Good-bye.
BEEP
BEEP
BEEP
...
What is wrong with me?

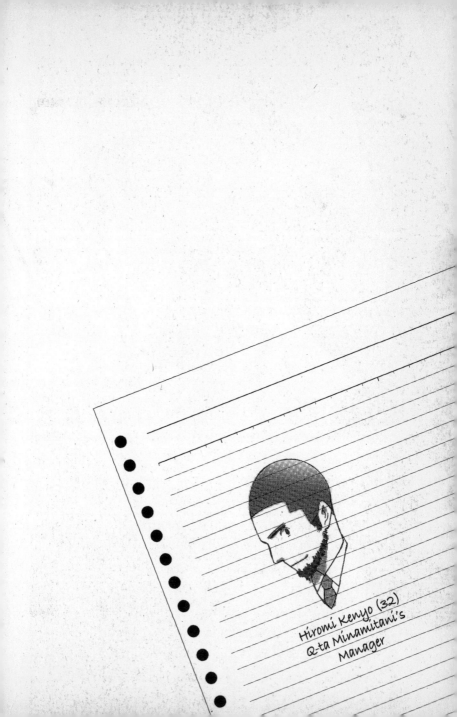

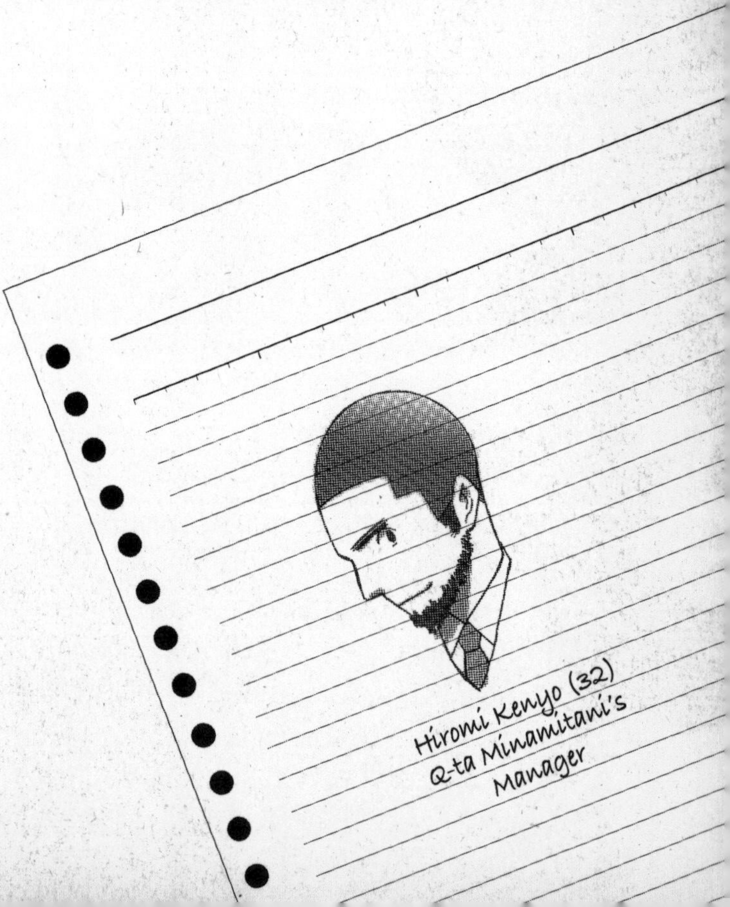
Hiromi Kenyo (32)
Q-ta Minamitani's
Manager

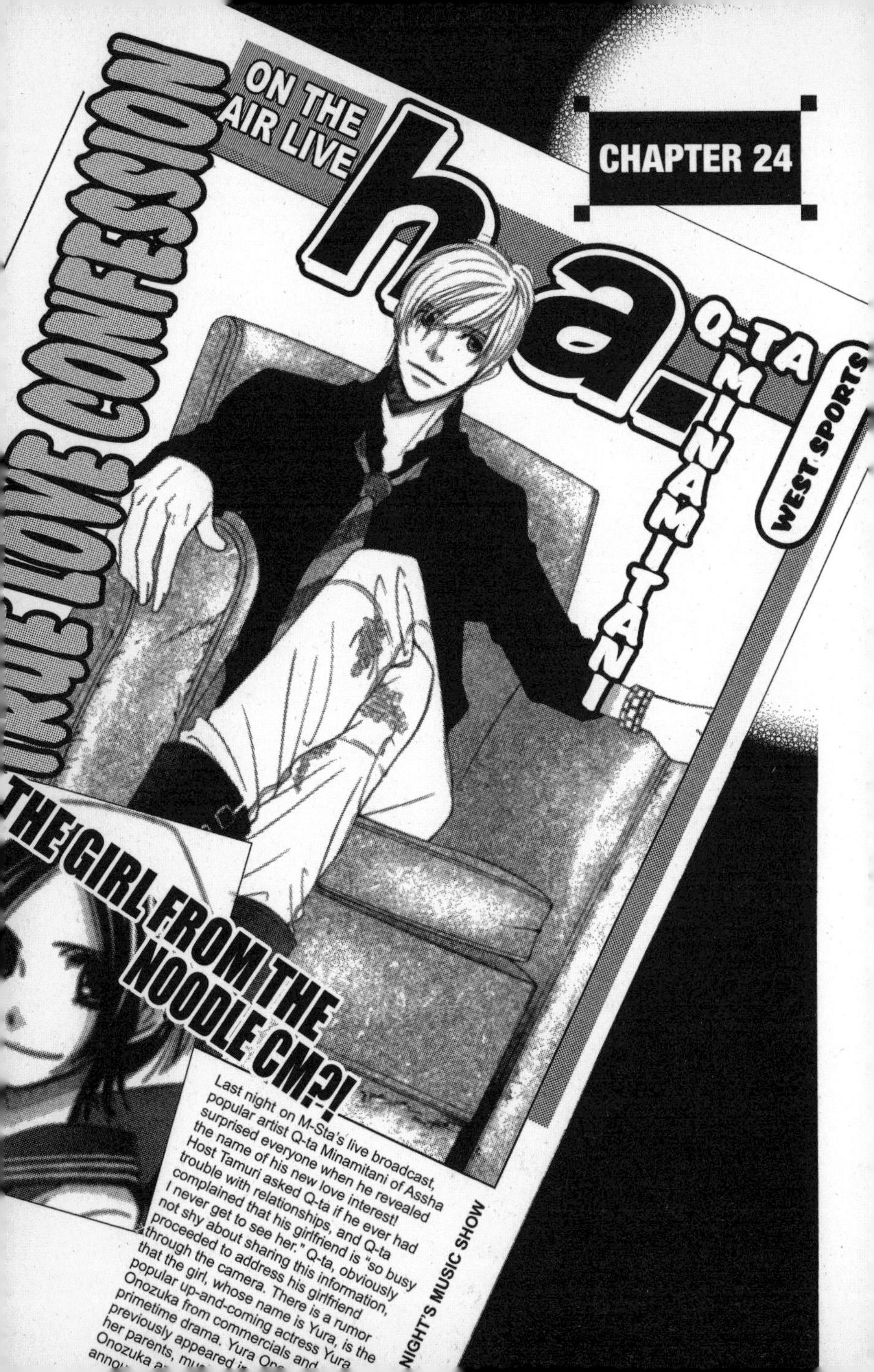
CHAPTER 24
LOVE CONFESSION
ON THE AIR LIVE
ha
Q-TA MINAMITANI
WEST SPORTS
THE GIRL FROM THE NOODLE CM?!
Last night on M-Sta's live broadcast, popular artist Q-ta Minamitani of Assha surprised everyone when he revealed the name of his new love interest! Host Tamuri asked Q-ta if he ever had trouble with relationships, and Q-ta complained that his girlfriend is "so busy I never get to see her." Q-ta, obviously not shy about sharing this information, proceeded to address his girlfriend through the camera. There is a rumor that the girl, whose name is Yura, is the popular up-and-coming actress Yura Onozuka from commercials and primetime drama. Yura
NIGHT'S MUSIC SHOW

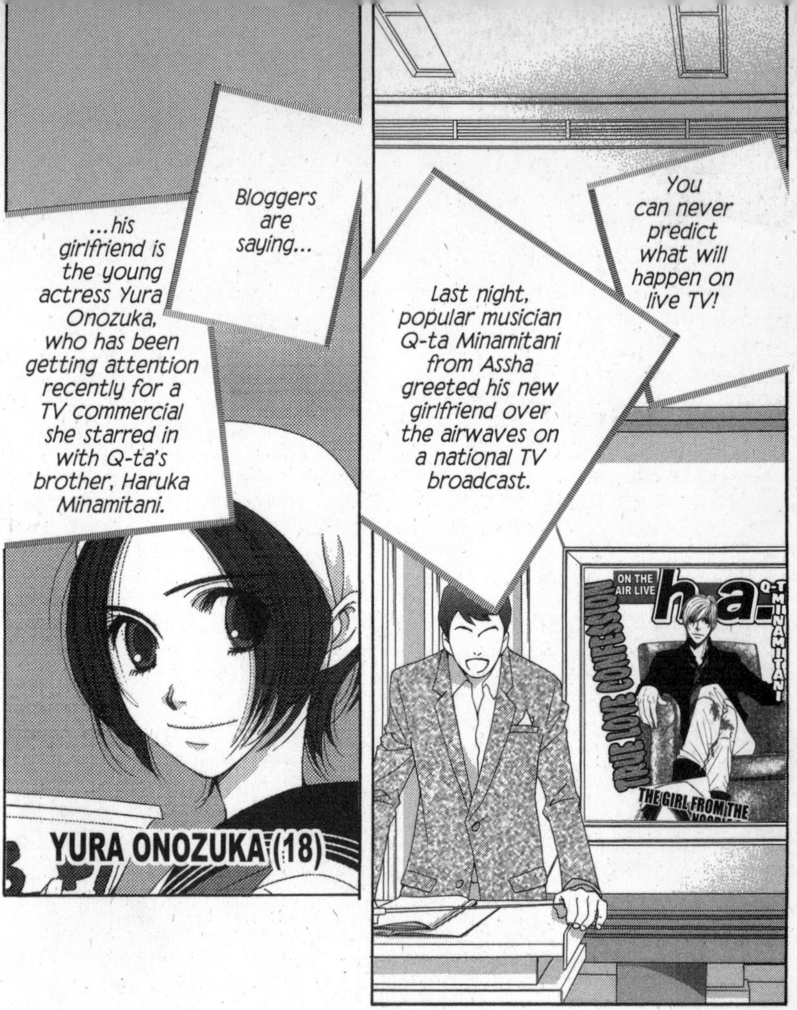
You can never predict what will happen on live TV!
Last night, popular musician Q-ta Minamitani from Assha greeted his new girlfriend over the airwaves on a national TV broadcast.
ON THE AIR LIVE
TRUE LOVE CONFESSION
THE GIRL FROM THE
Bloggers are saying...
...his girlfriend is the young actress Yura Onozuka, who has been getting attention recently for a TV commercial she starred in with Q-ta's brother, Haruka Minamitani.
YURA ONOZUKA (18)

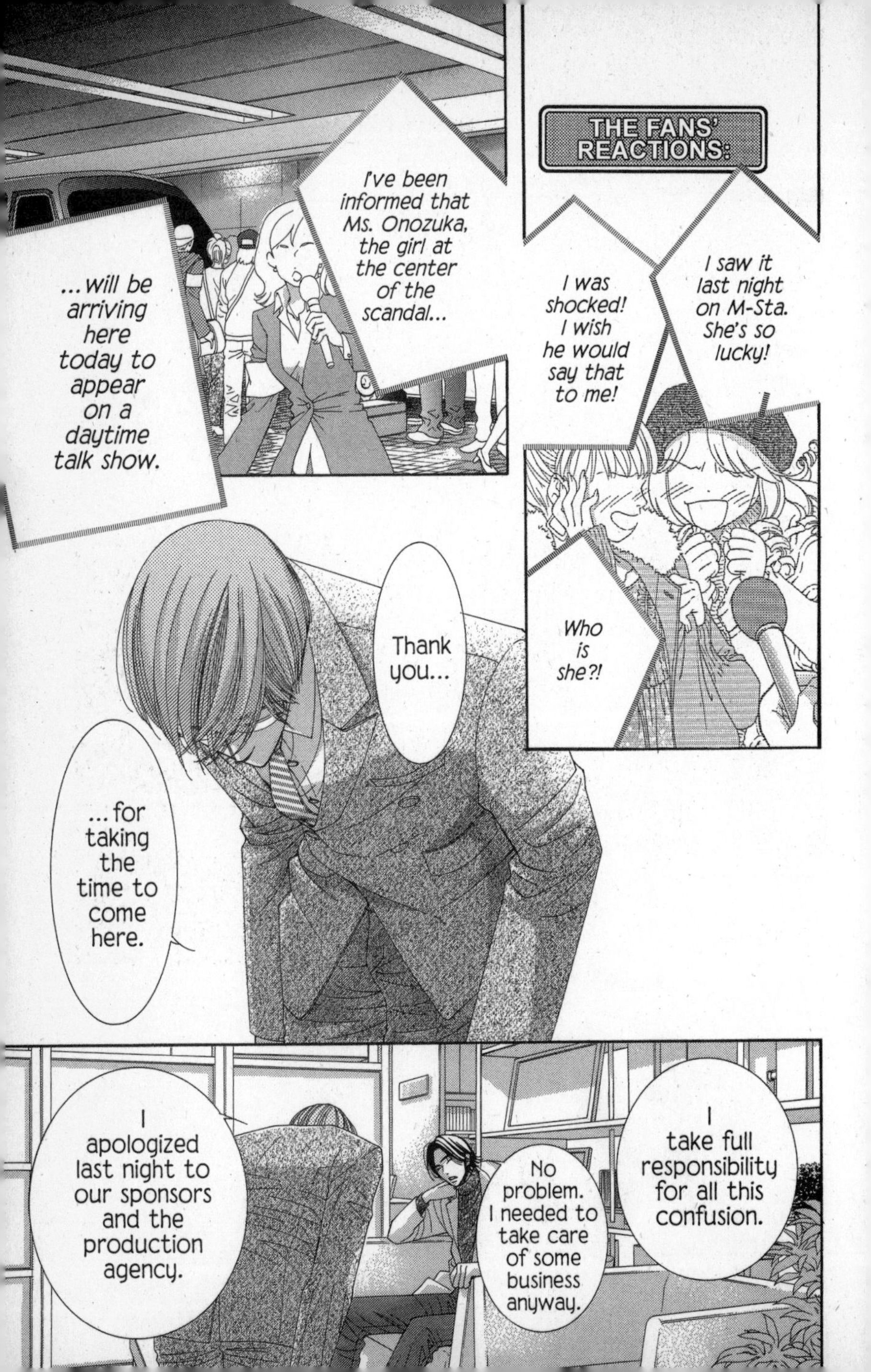
THE FANS' REACTIONS:
I saw it last night on M-Sta. She's so lucky!
I was shocked! I wish he would say that to me!
Who is she?!
I've been informed that Ms. Onozuka, the girl at the center of the scandal...
...will be arriving here today to appear on a daytime talk show.
Thank you...
...for taking the time to come here.
I take full responsibility for all this confusion.
No problem. I needed to take care of some business anyway.
I apologized last night to our sponsors and the production agency.

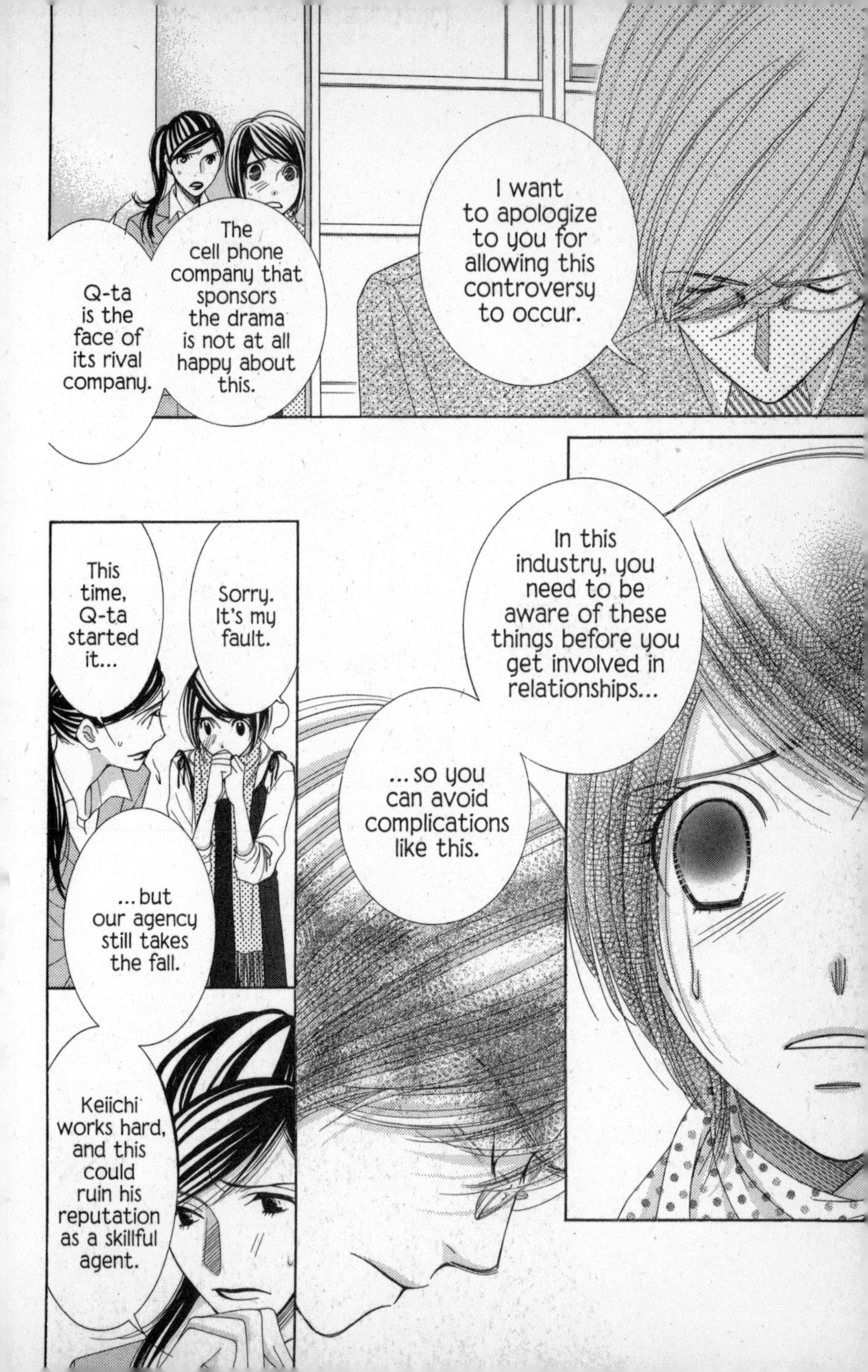
I want to apologize to you for allowing this controversy to occur.
The cell phone company that sponsors the drama is not at all happy about this.
Q-ta is the face of its rival company.
In this industry, you need to be aware of these things before you get involved in relationships...
...so you can avoid complications like this.
Sorry. It's my fault.
This time, Q-ta started it...
...but our agency still takes the fall.
Keiichi works hard, and this could ruin his reputation as a skillful agent.

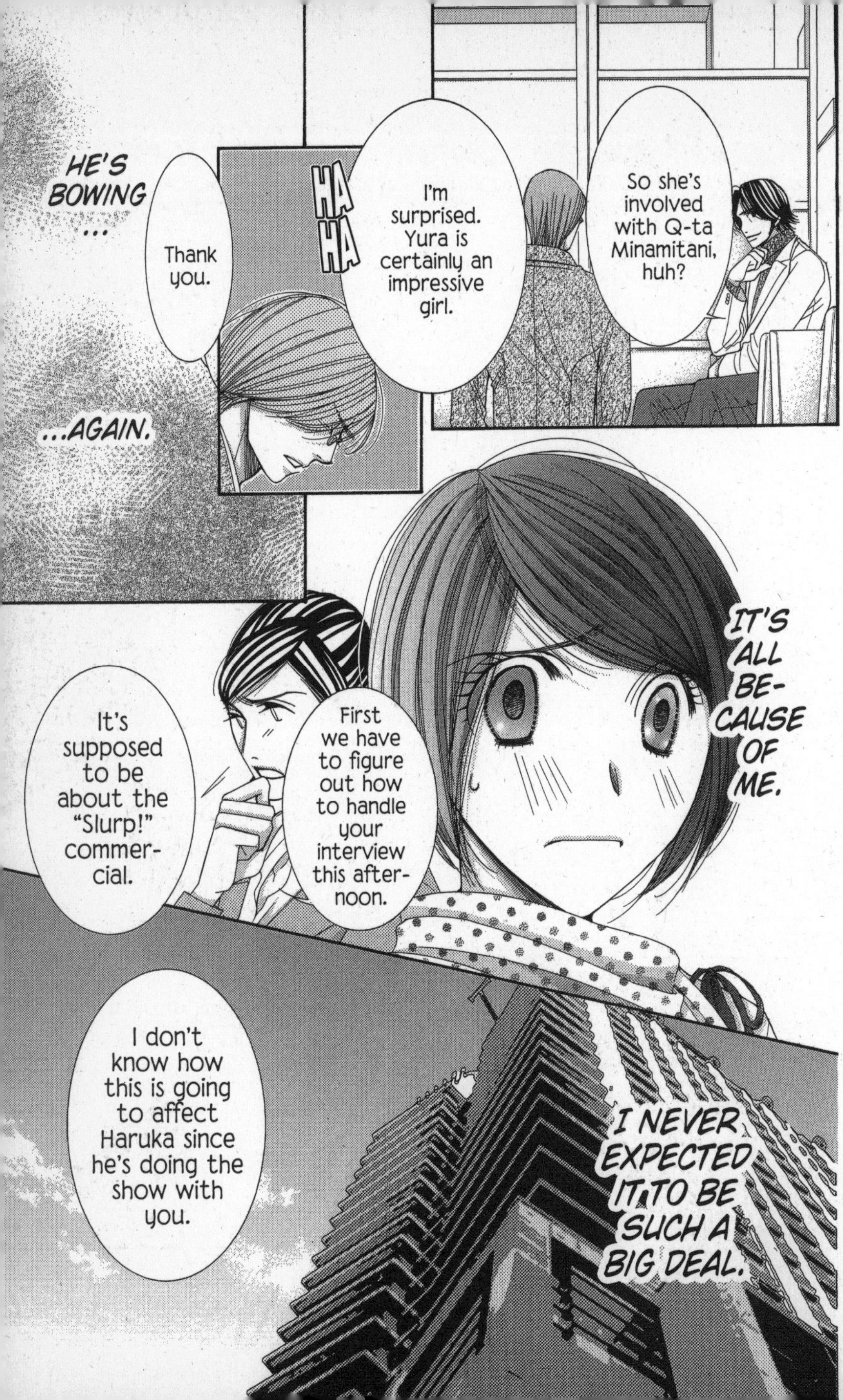
So she's involved with Q-ta Minamitani, huh?
HA HA
I'm surprised. Yura is certainly an impressive girl.
Thank you.
HE'S BOWING...
...AGAIN.
IT'S ALL BE-CAUSE OF ME.
First we have to figure out how to handle your interview this after-noon.
It's supposed to be about the "Slurp!" commer-cial.
I NEVER EXPECTED IT TO BE SUCH A BIG DEAL.
I don't know how this is going to affect Haruka since he's doing the show with you.

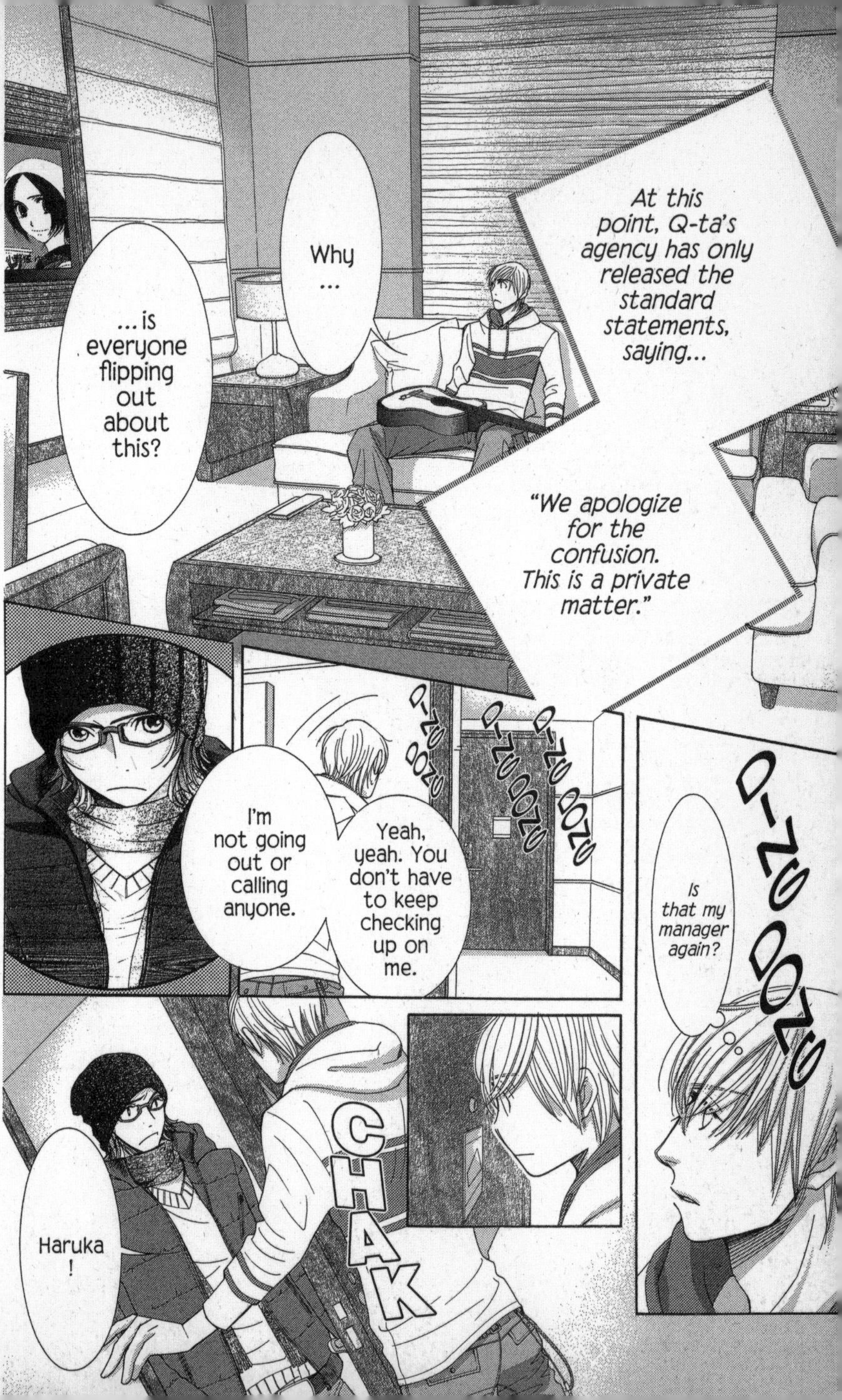
At this point, Q-ta's agency has only released the standard statements, saying...
"We apologize for the confusion. This is a private matter."
Why ...
... is everyone flipping out about this?
Q-ZU DOZU
Is that my manager again?
Q-ZU DOZU
Q-ZU DOZU
Q-ZU DOZU
I'm not going out or calling anyone.
Yeah, yeah. You don't have to keep checking up on me.
CHAK
Haruka!

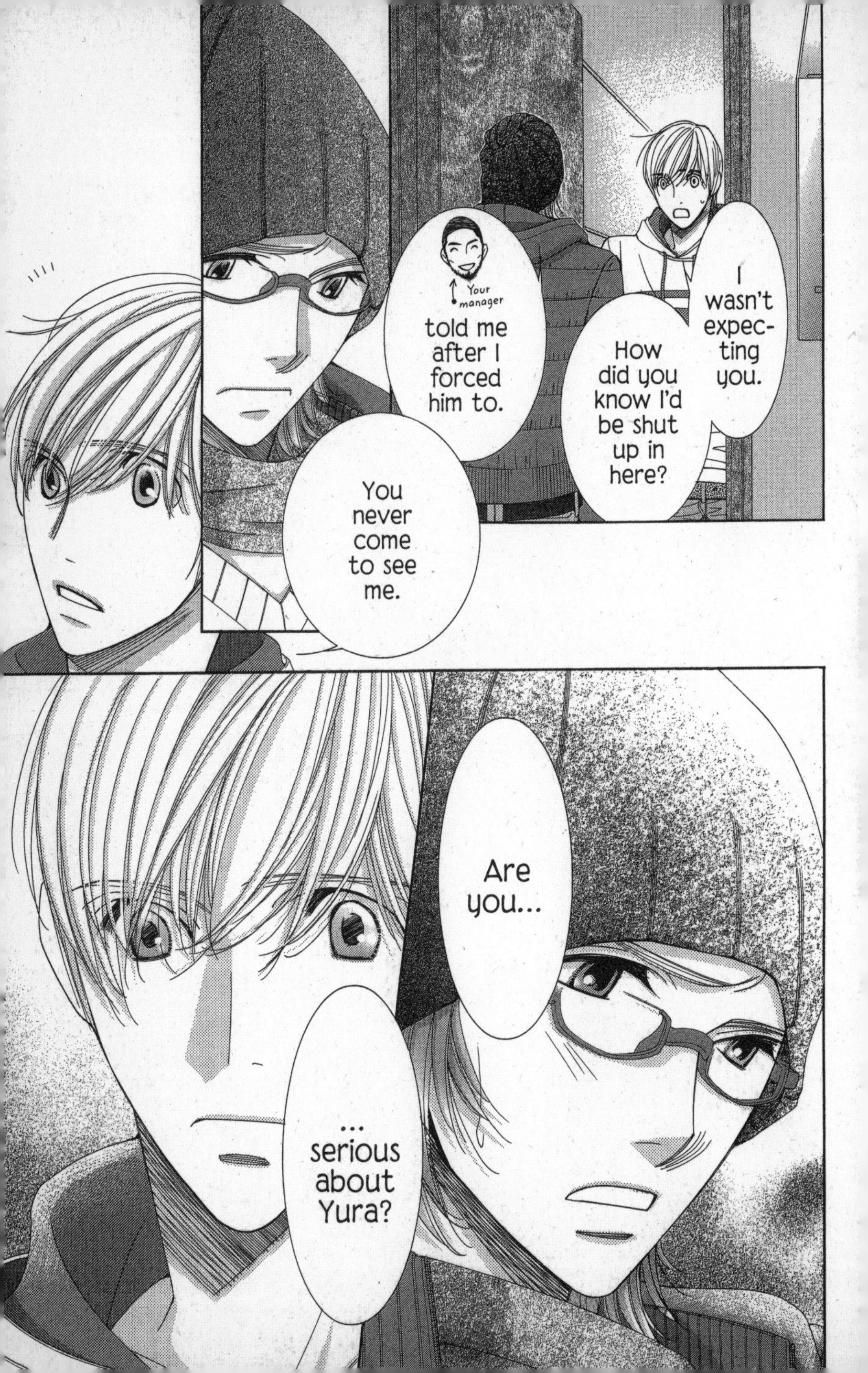
I wasn't expecting you.
How did you know I'd be shut up in here?
Your manager
told me after I forced him to.
You never come to see me.
Are you...
...serious about Yura?

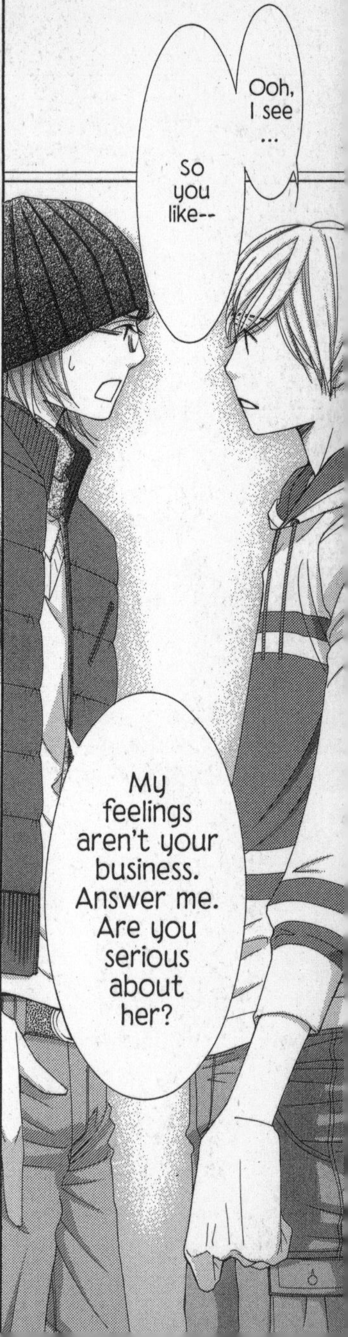
Ooh, I see ...
So you like--
My feelings aren't your business. Answer me. Are you serious about her?

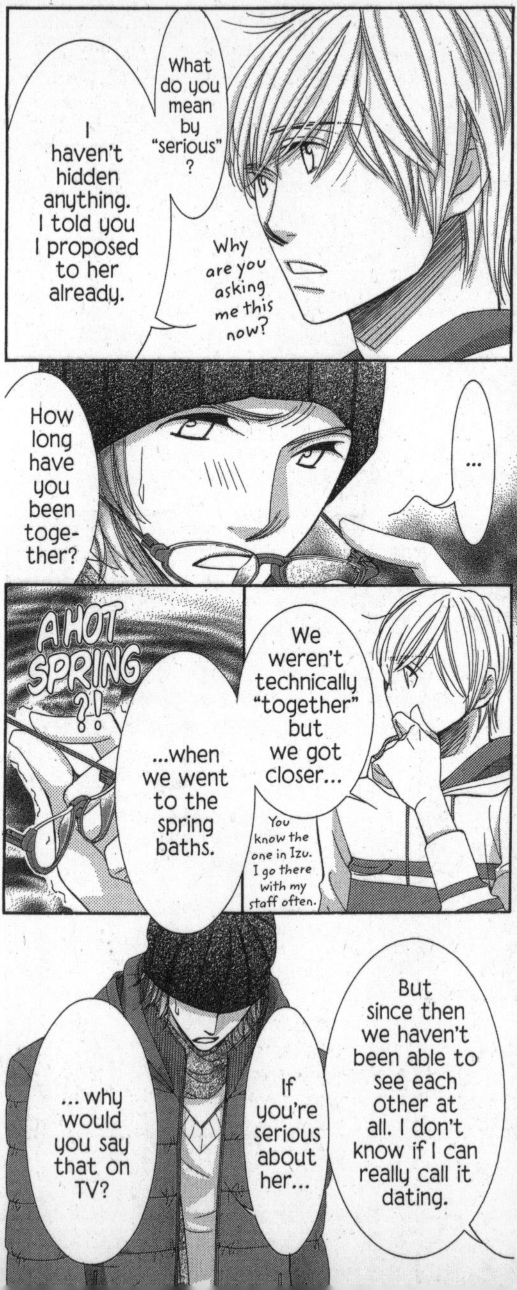
What do you mean by "serious"?
Why are you asking me this now?
I haven't hidden anything. I told you I proposed to her already.
...
How long have you been toge-ther?
We weren't technically "together" but we got closer...
You know the one in Izu. I go there with my staff often.
...when we went to the spring baths.
A HOT SPRING ?!
But since then we haven't been able to see each other at all. I don't know if I can really call it dating.
If you're serious about her...
...why would you say that on TV?

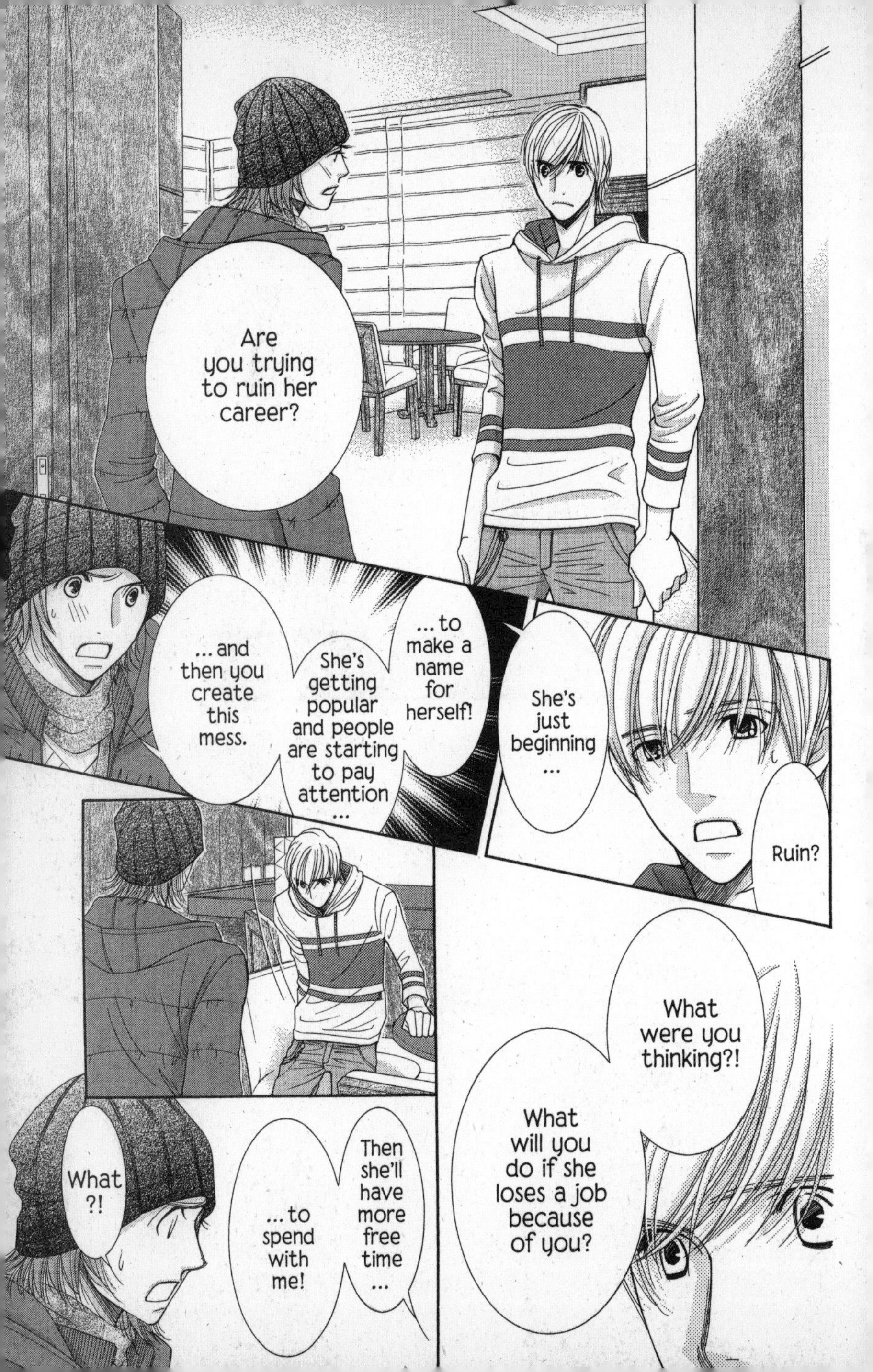
Are you trying to ruin her career?
Ruin?
She's just beginning ...
... to make a name for herself!
She's getting popular and people are starting to pay attention ...
... and then you create this mess.
What were you thinking?!
What will you do if she loses a job because of you?
Then she'll have more free time ...
... to spend with me!
What ?!

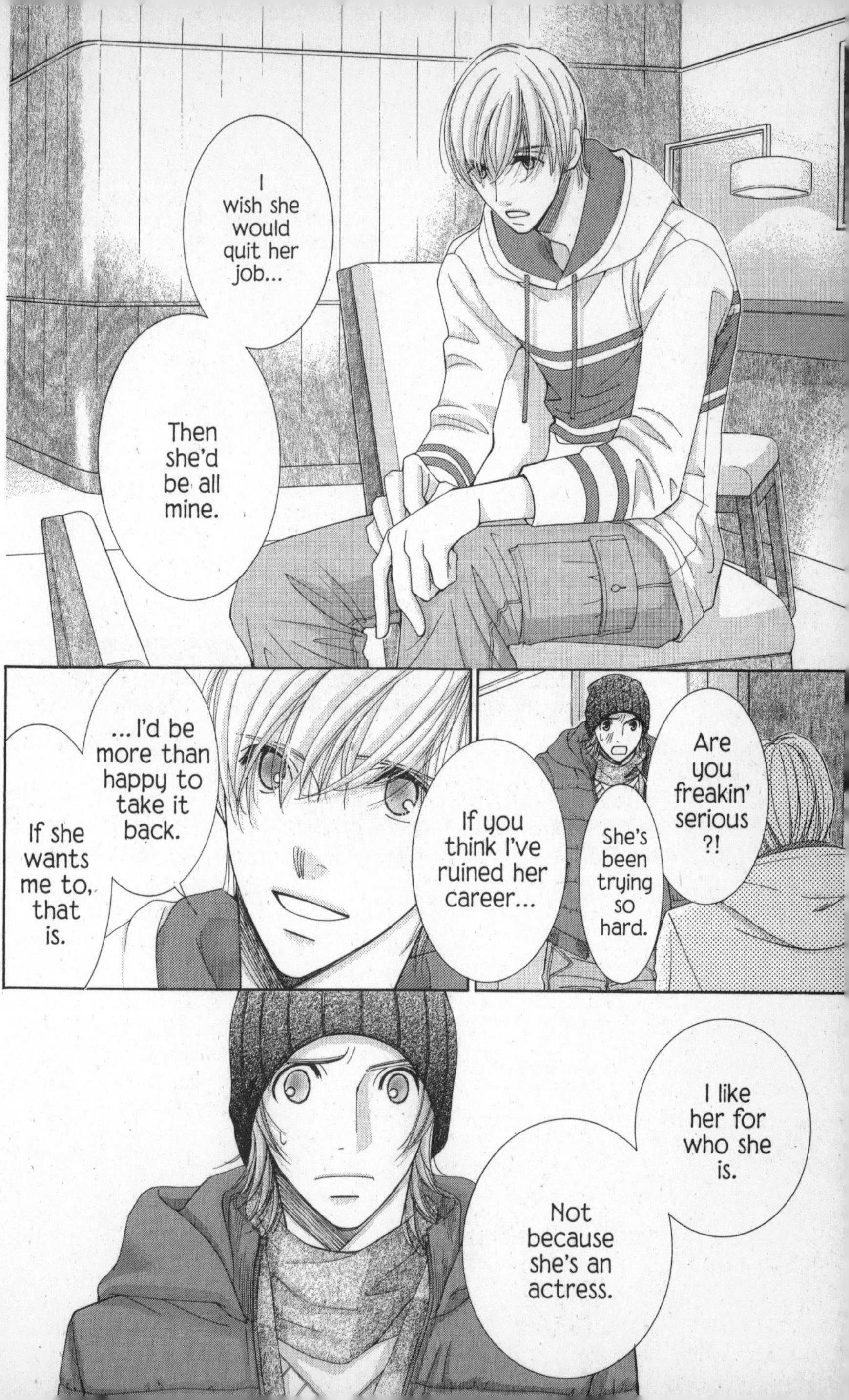
I wish she would quit her job...
Then she'd be all mine.
Are you freakin' serious?!
She's been trying so hard.
If you think I've ruined her career...
...I'd be more than happy to take it back.
If she wants me to, that is.
I like her for who she is.
Not because she's an actress.

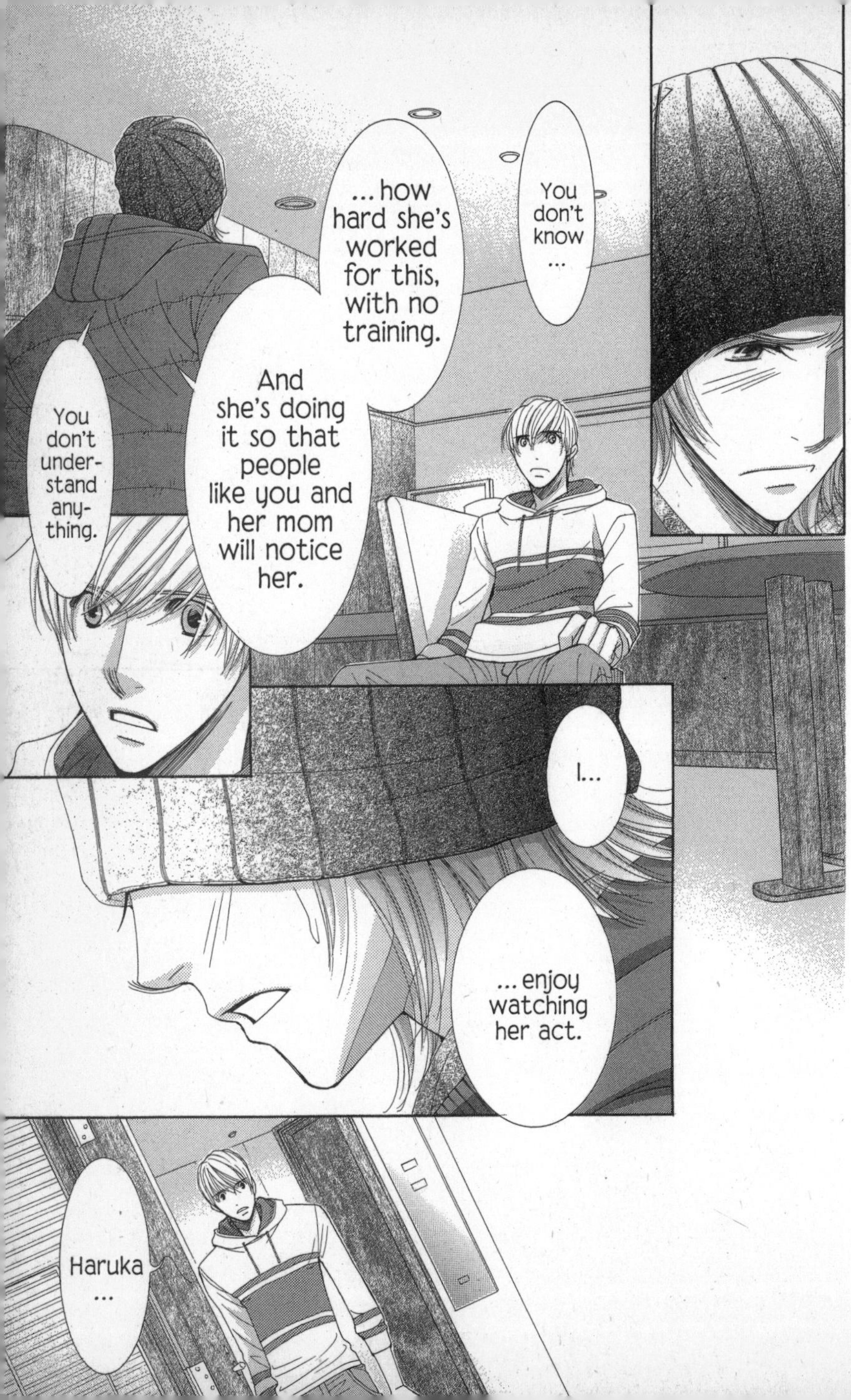
You don't know ...
... how hard she's worked for this, with no training.
And she's doing it so that people like you and her mom will notice her.
You don't under-stand any-thing.
I...
... enjoy watching her act.
Haruka ...

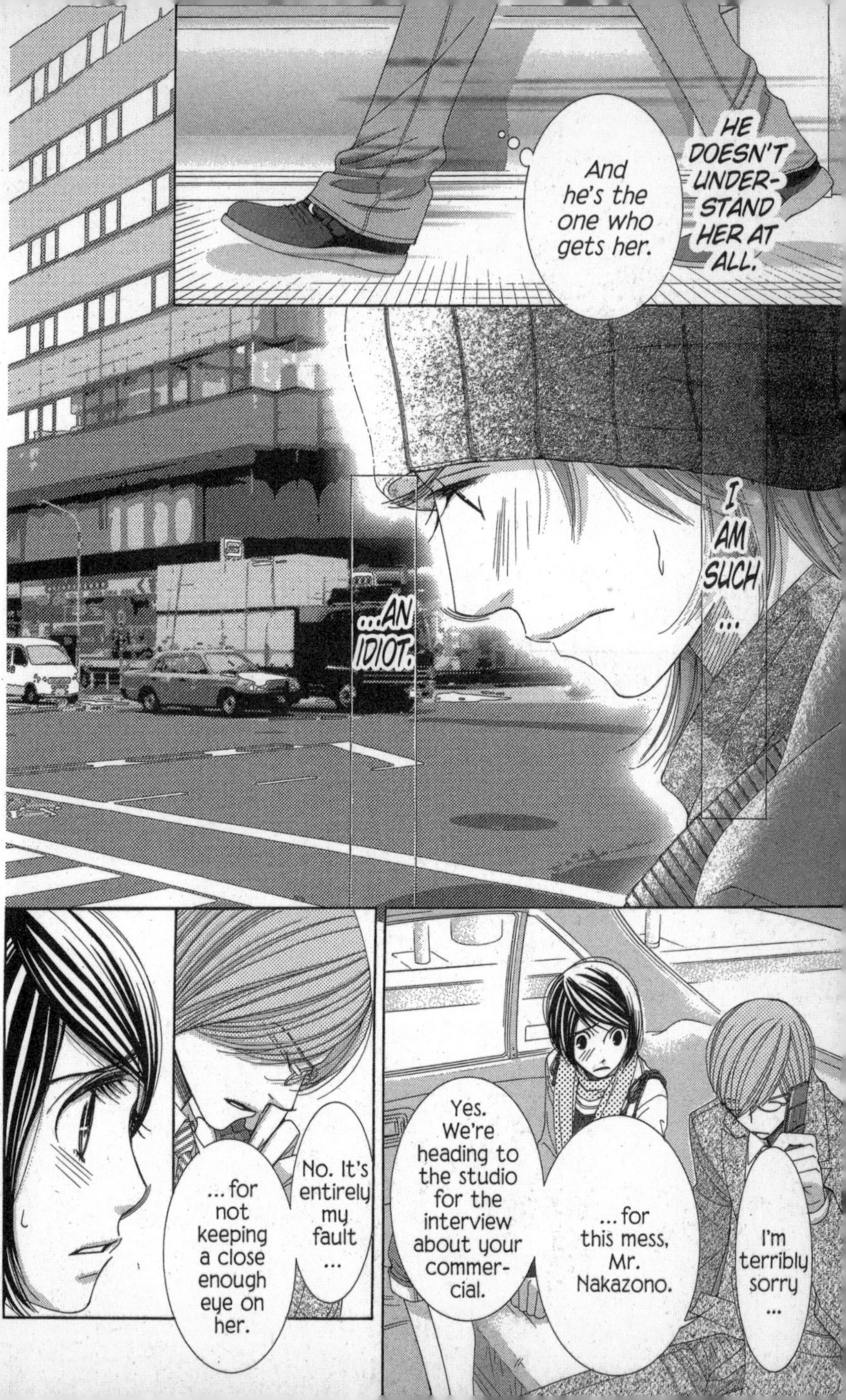
HE DOESN'T UNDERSTAND HER AT ALL.
And he's the one who gets her.
I AM SUCH...
...AN IDIOT.
I'm terribly sorry...
...for this mess, Mr. Nakazono.
Yes. We're heading to the studio for the interview about your commercial.
No. It's entirely my fault...
...for not keeping a close enough eye on her.

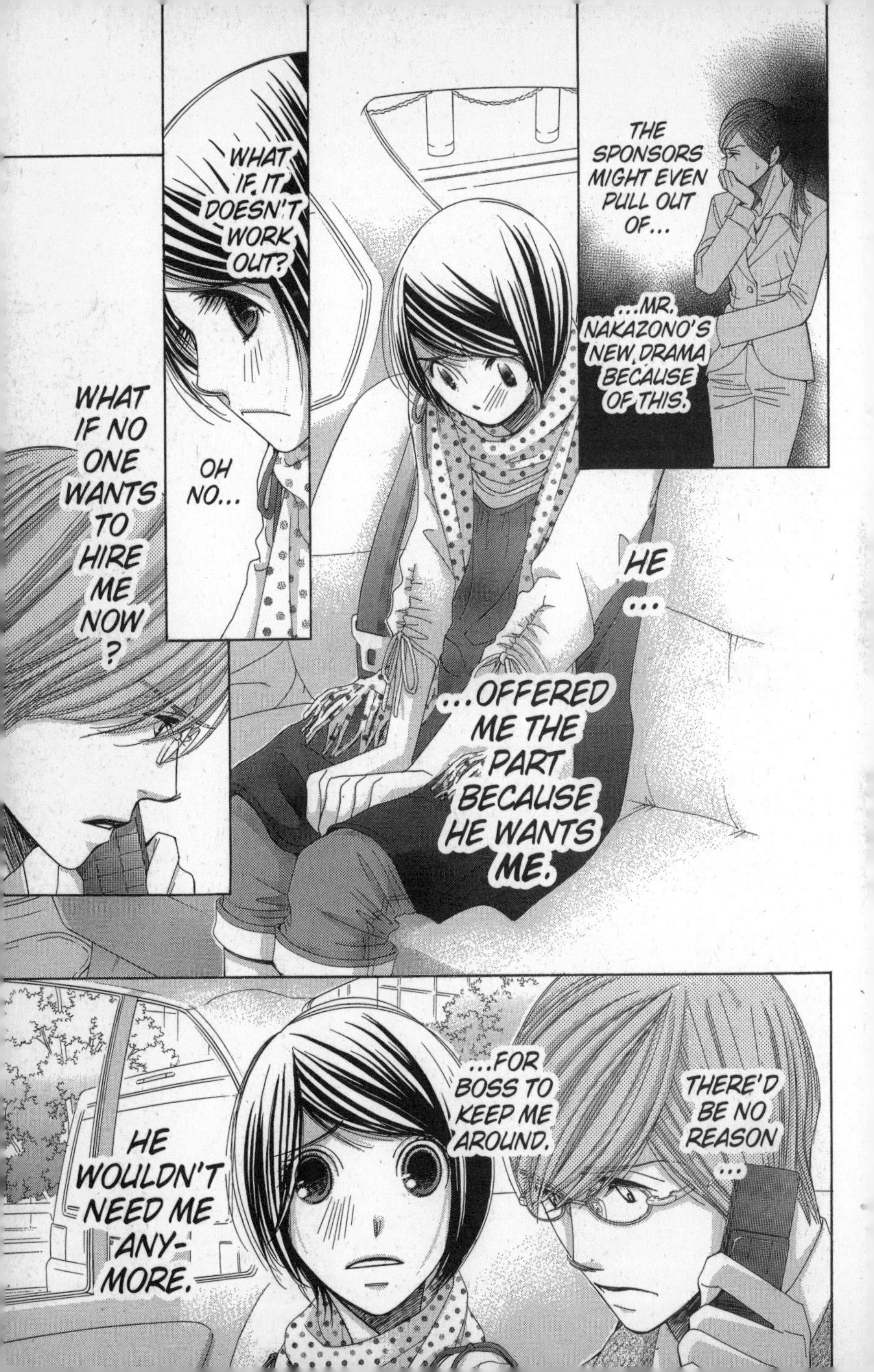
THE SPONSORS MIGHT EVEN PULL OUT OF...
...MR. NAKAZONO'S NEW DRAMA BECAUSE OF THIS.
WHAT IF IT DOESN'T WORK OUT?
OH NO...
WHAT IF NO ONE WANTS TO HIRE ME NOW?
HE ...
...OFFERED ME THE PART BECAUSE HE WANTS ME.
THERE'D BE NO REASON ...
...FOR BOSS TO KEEP ME AROUND.
HE WOULDN'T NEED ME ANY-MORE.

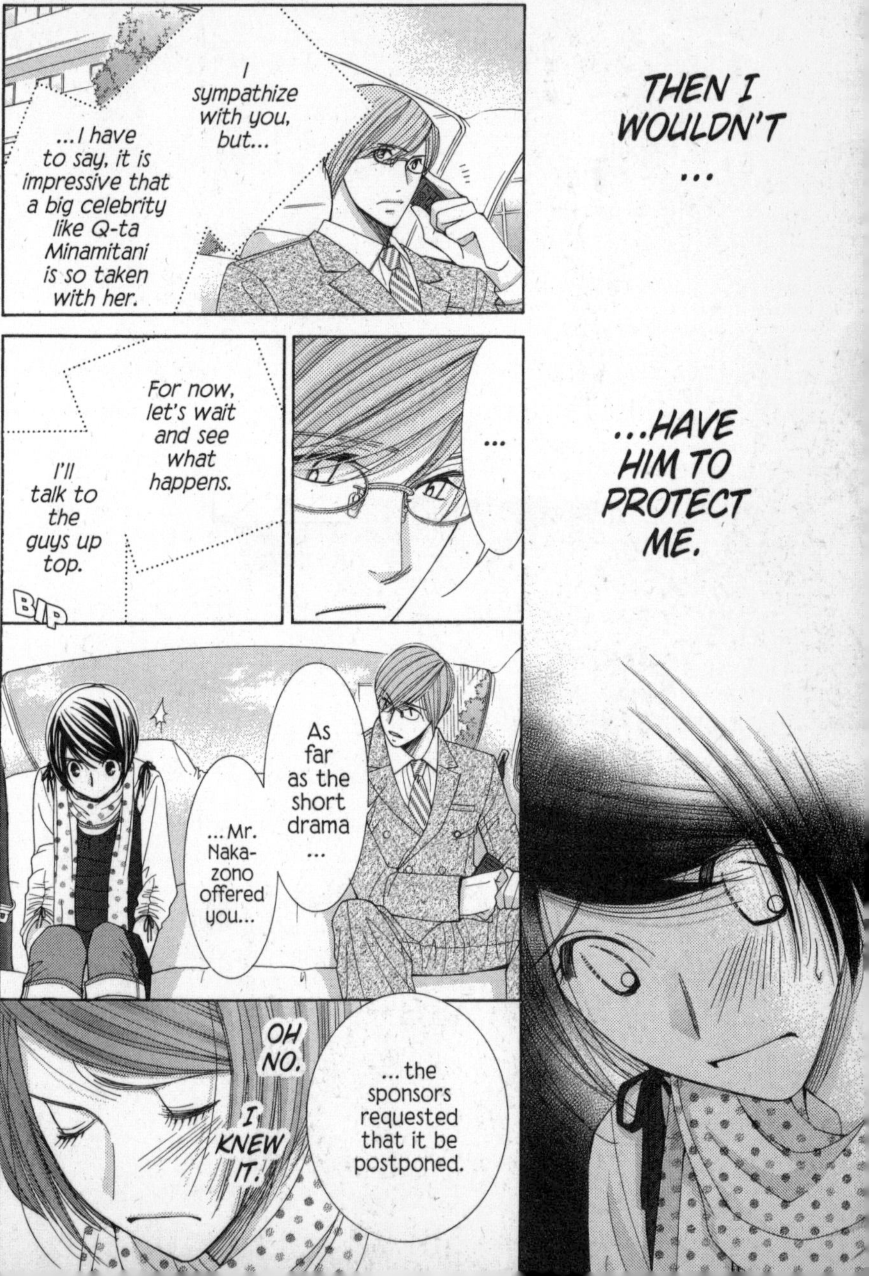
THEN I WOULDN'T ...
...HAVE HIM TO PROTECT ME.
I sympathize with you, but...
...I have to say, it is impressive that a big celebrity like Q-ta Minamitani is so taken with her.
...
For now, let's wait and see what happens.
I'll talk to the guys up top.
BIP
As far as the short drama ...
...Mr. Nakazono offered you...
...the sponsors requested that it be postponed.
OH NO.
I KNEW IT.

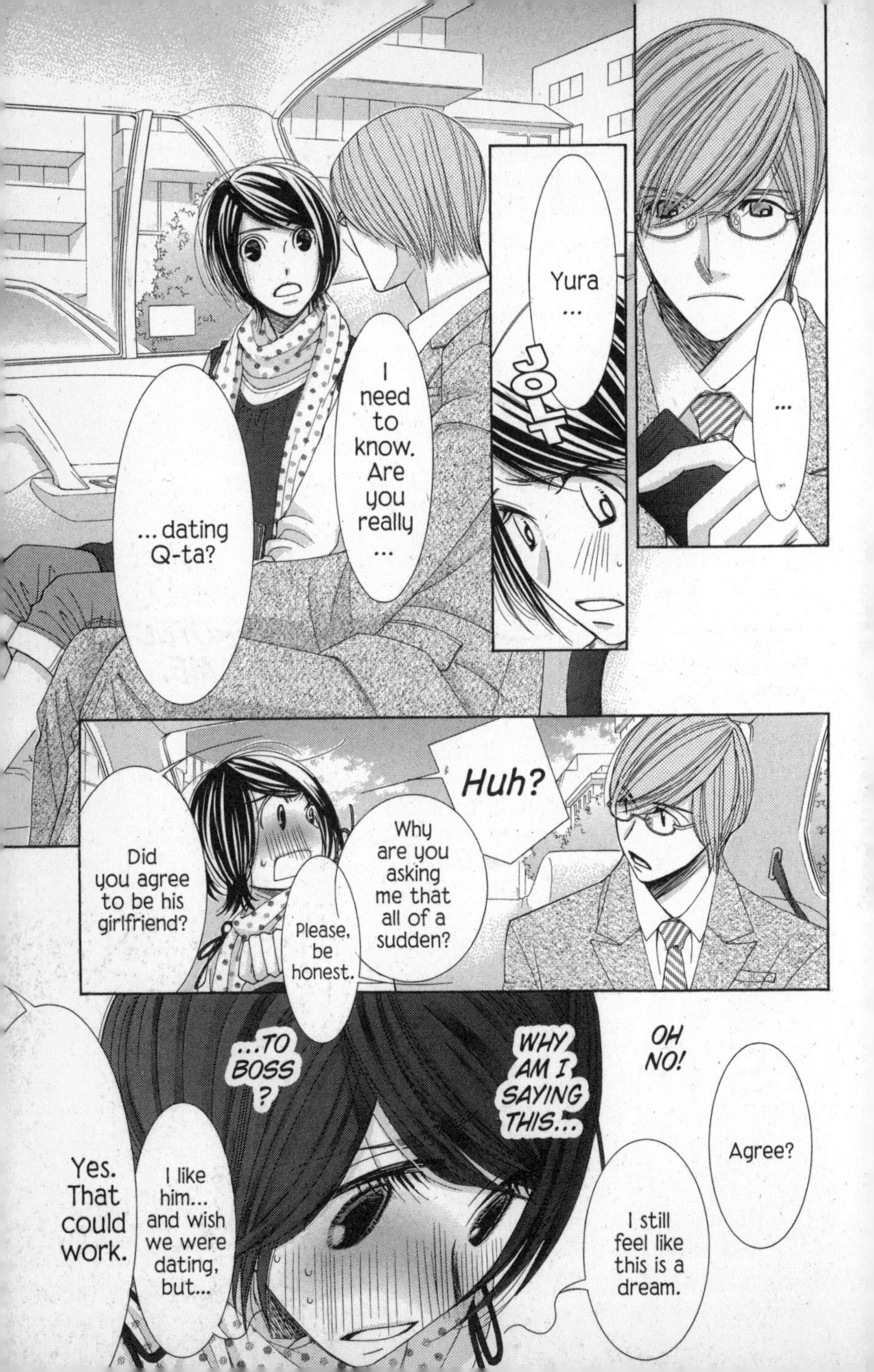
...
Yura ...
JOLT
I need to know. Are you really ...
... dating Q-ta?
Huh?
Why are you asking me that all of a sudden?
Did you agree to be his girlfriend?
Please, be honest.
OH NO!
Agree?
WHY AM I SAYING THIS...
I still feel like this is a dream.
...TO BOSS?
I like him... and wish we were dating, but...
Yes. That could work.

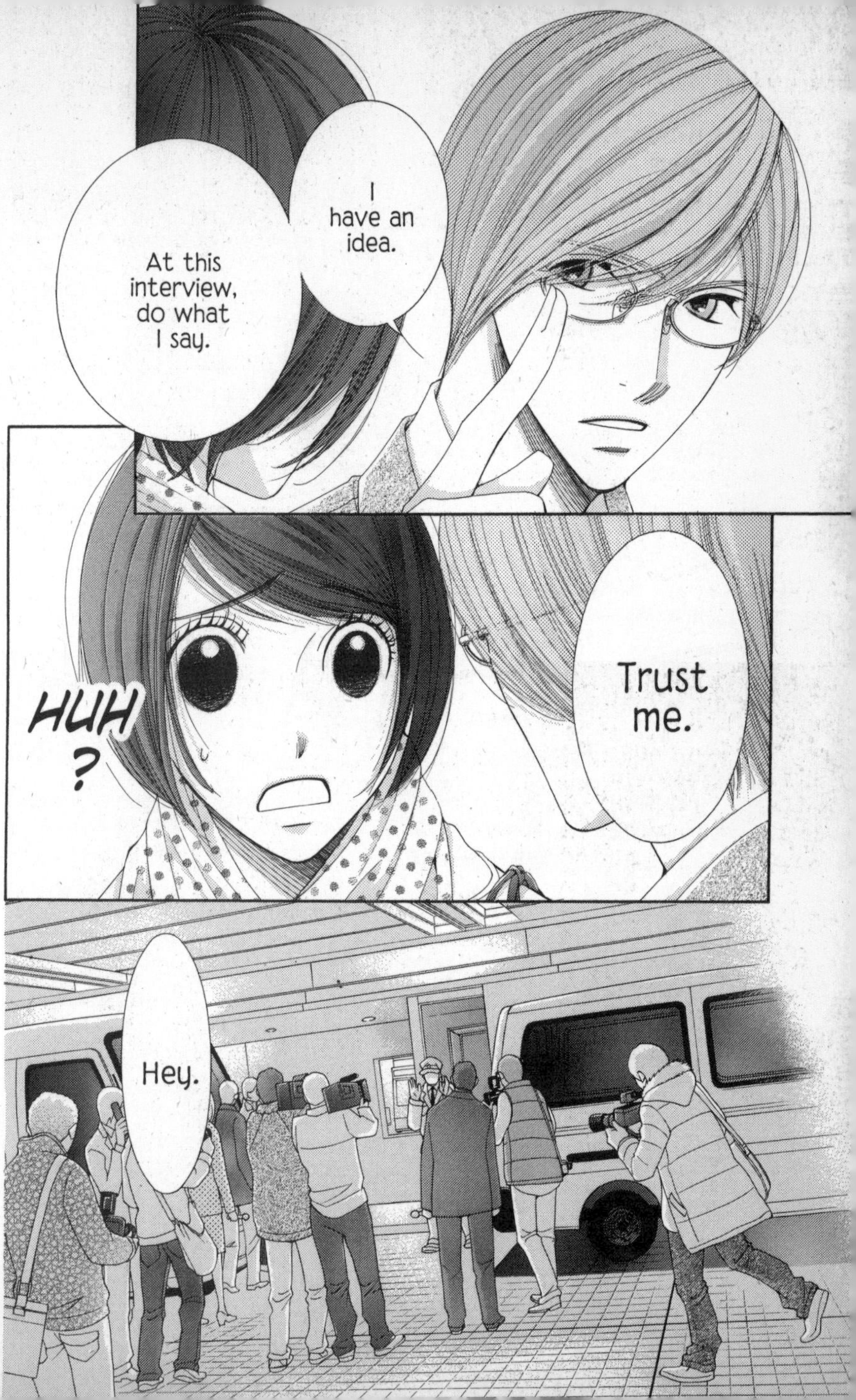
I have an idea.
At this interview, do what I say.
Trust me.
HUH?
Hey.

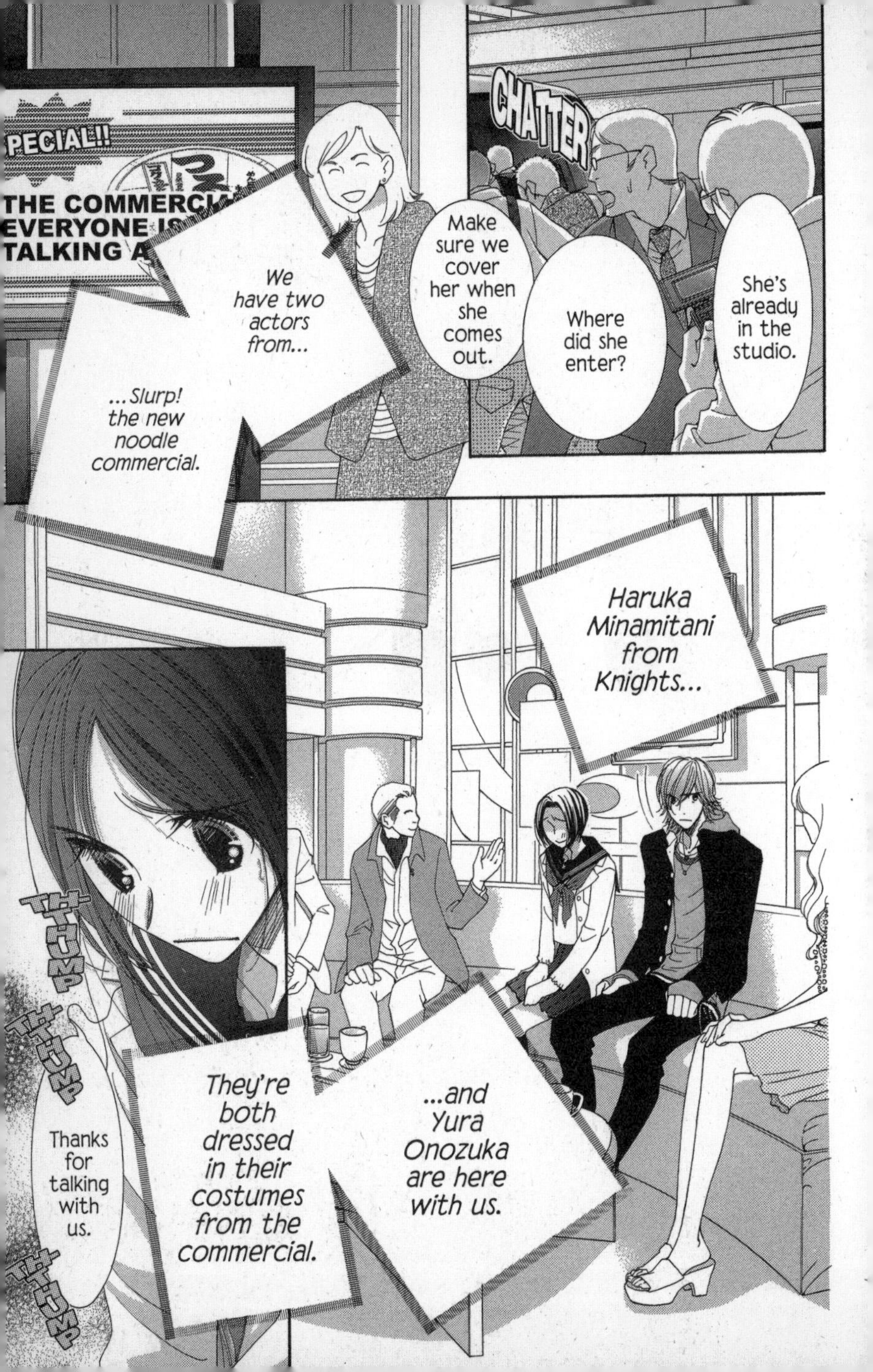
CHATTER
She's already in the studio.
Where did she enter?
Make sure we cover her when she comes out.
PECIAL!!
THE COMMERCI
EVERYONE IS
TALKING A
We have two actors from...
...Slurp! the new noodle commercial.
Haruka Minamitani from Knights...
...and Yura Onozuka are here with us.
They're both dressed in their costumes from the commercial.
Thanks for talking with us.
TH-THUMP
TH-THUMP
TH-THUMP

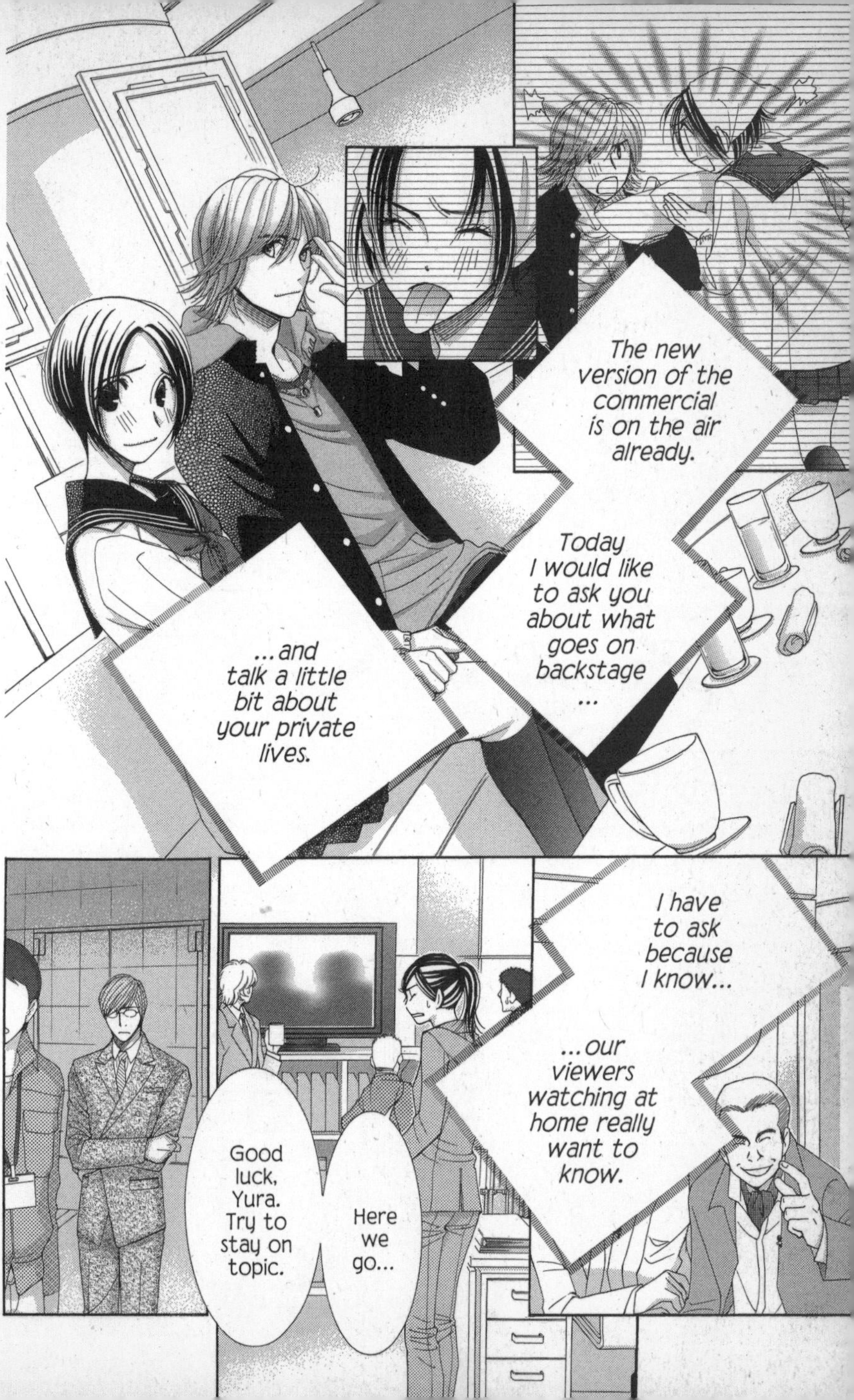
The new version of the commercial is on the air already.
Today I would like to ask you about what goes on backstage...
...and talk a little bit about your private lives.
I have to ask because I know...
...our viewers watching at home really want to know.
Here we go...
Good luck, Yura. Try to stay on topic.

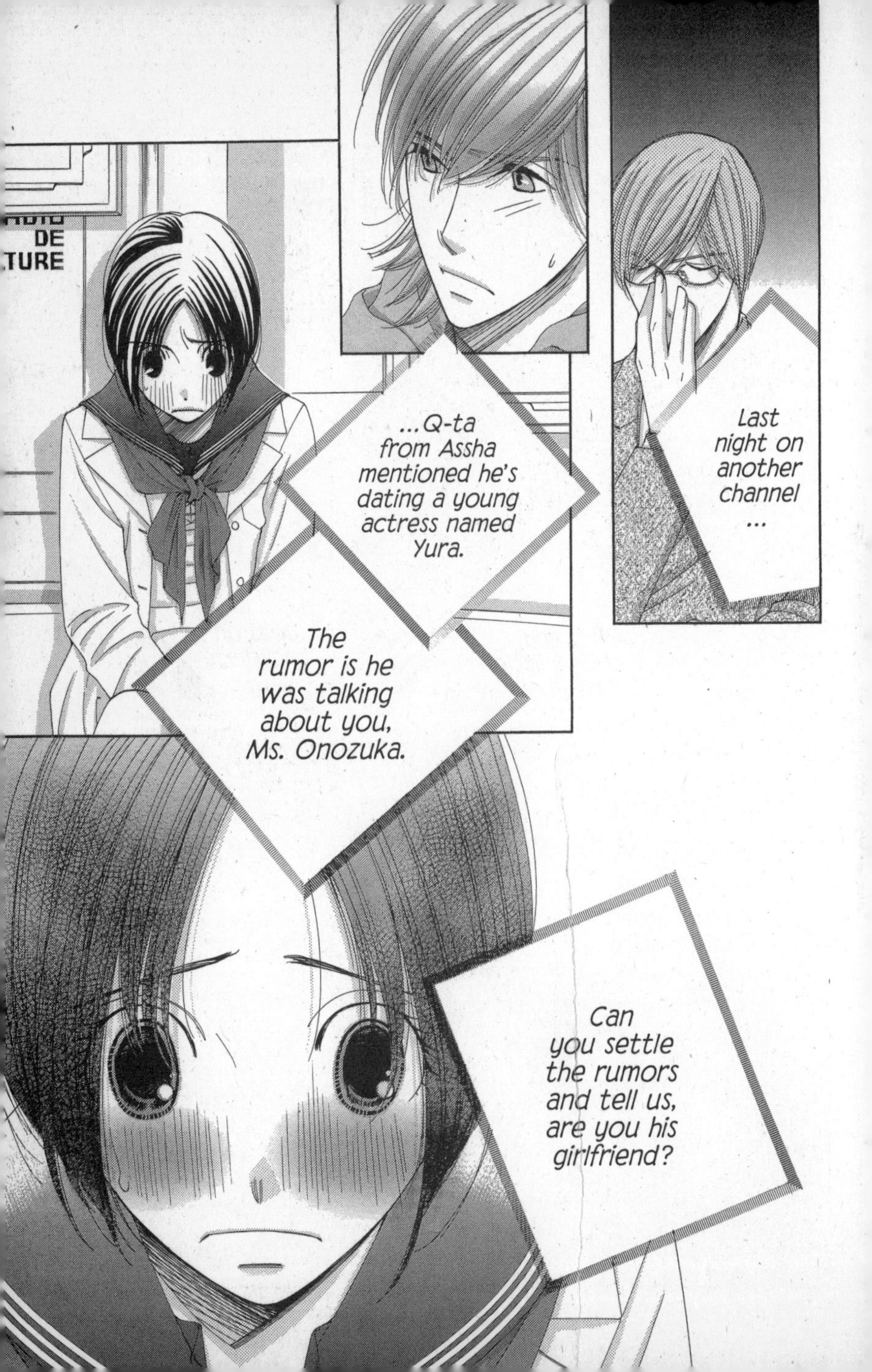
Last night on another channel ...
...Q-ta from Assha mentioned he's dating a young actress named Yura.
The rumor is he was talking about you, Ms. Onozuka.
Can you settle the rumors and tell us, are you his girlfriend?

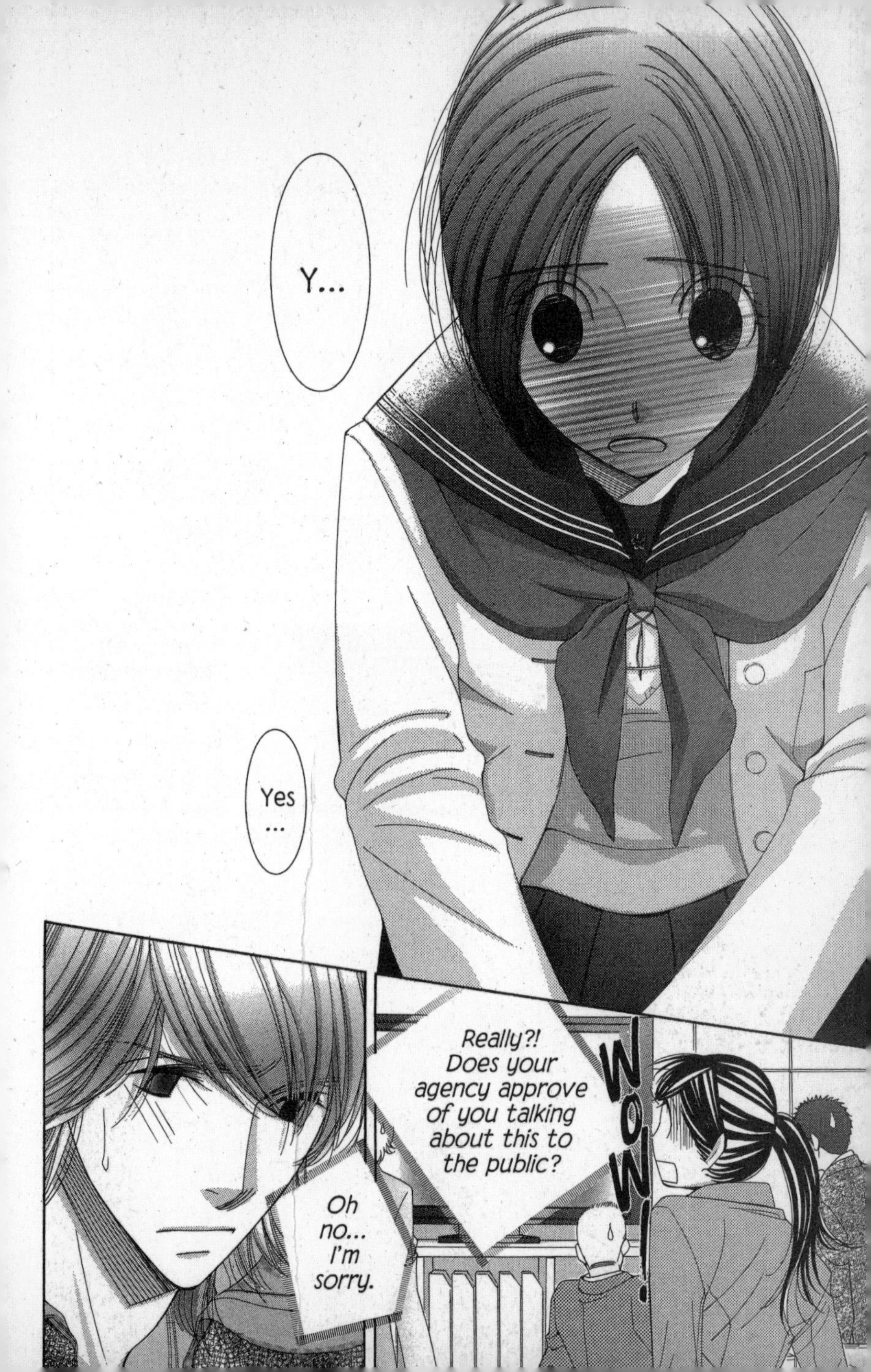
Y...
Yes ...
Really?! Does your agency approve of you talking about this to the public?
WOW!
Oh no... I'm sorry.

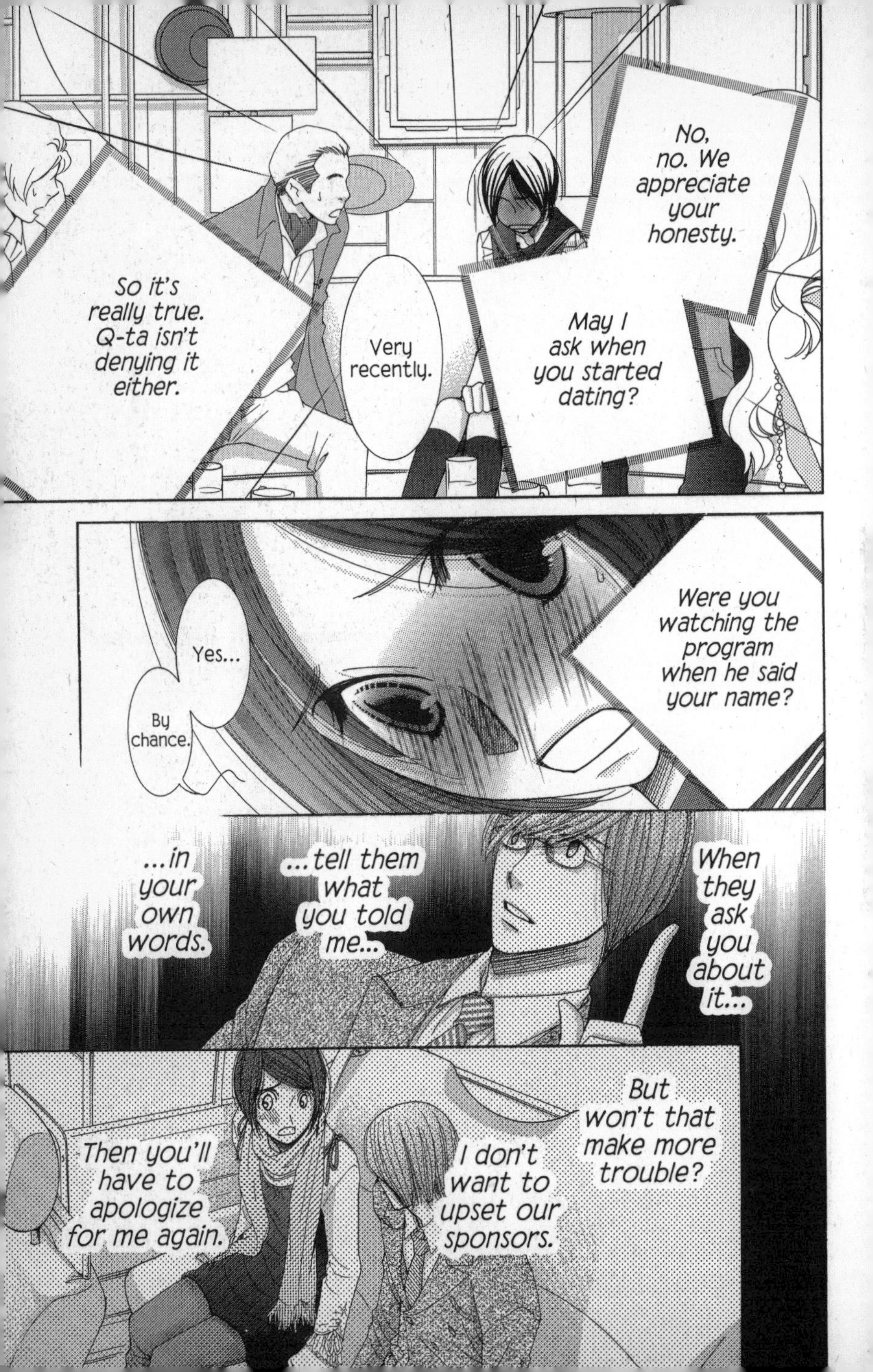
No, no. We appreciate your honesty.
May I ask when you started dating?
Very recently.
So it's really true. Q-ta isn't denying it either.
Were you watching the program when he said your name?
Yes...
By chance.
When they ask you about it...
...tell them what you told me...
...in your own words.
But won't that make more trouble?
I don't want to upset our sponsors.
Then you'll have to apologize for me again.

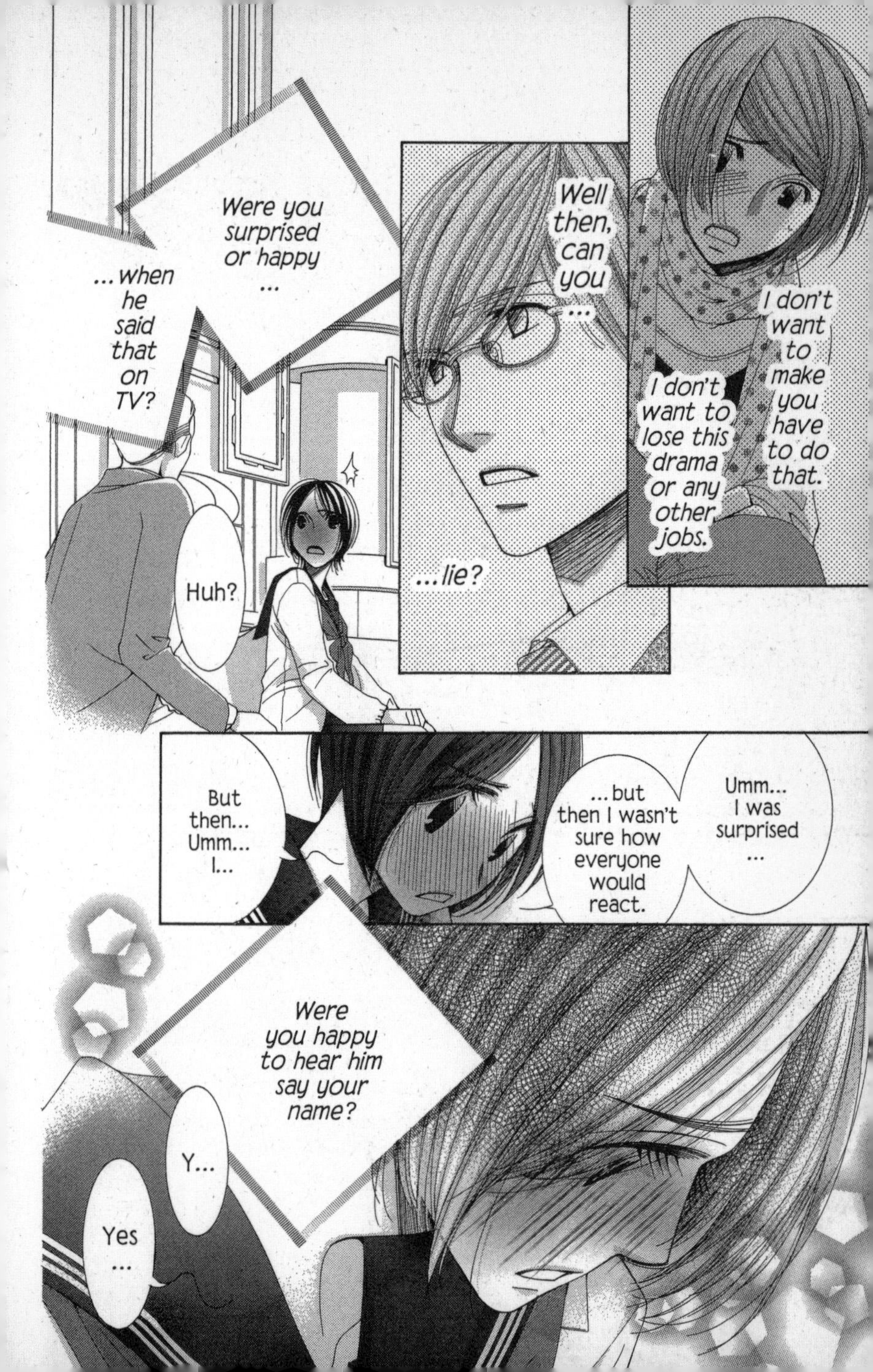
I don't want to make you have to do that.
I don't want to lose this drama or any other jobs.
Well then, can you...
...lie?
Were you surprised or happy...
...when he said that on TV?
Huh?
Umm... I was surprised...
...but then I wasn't sure how everyone would react.
But then... Umm... I...
Were you happy to hear him say your name?
Y...
Yes...

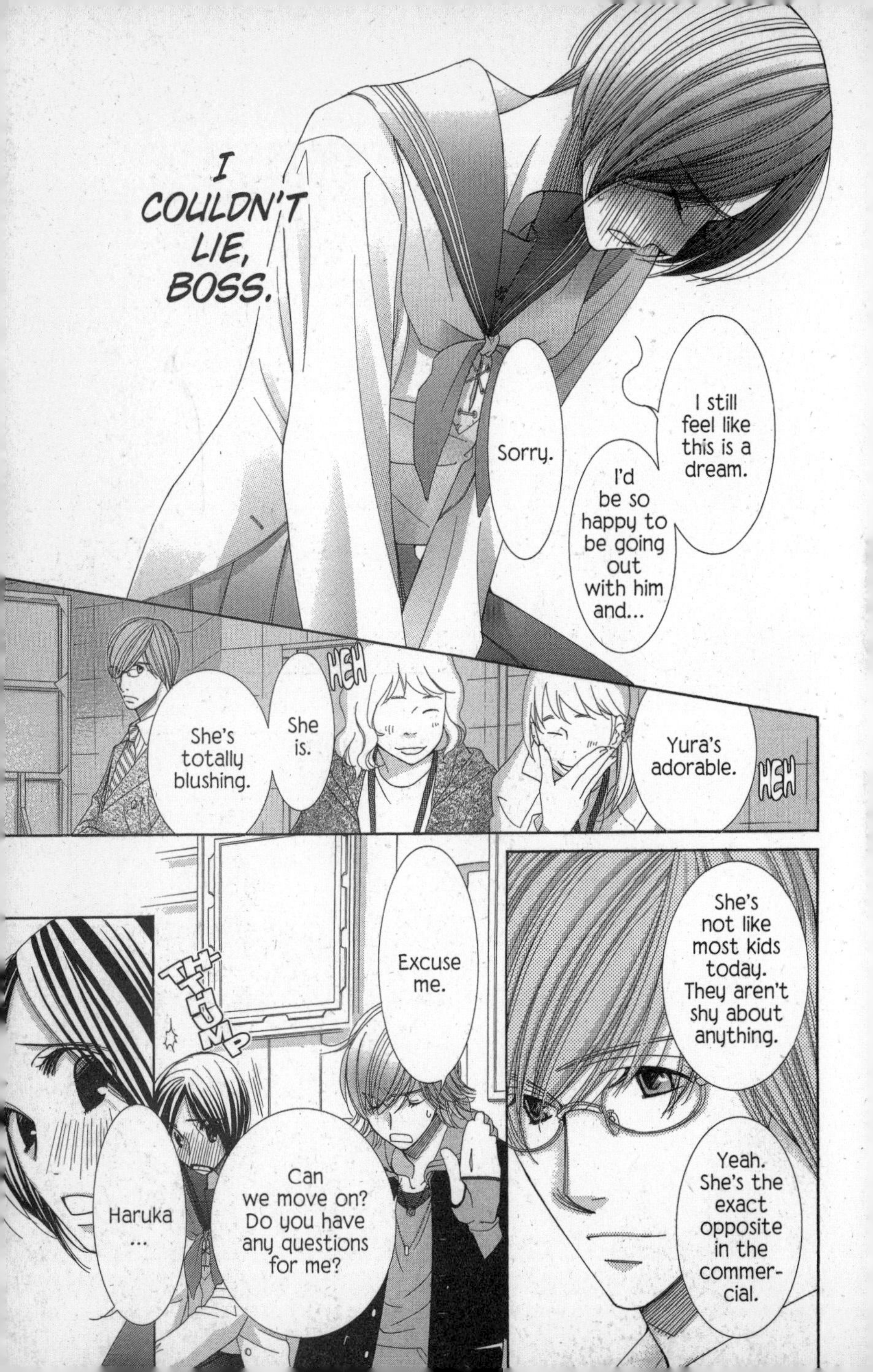
I still feel like this is a dream.
I'd be so happy to be going out with him and...
Sorry.
I COULDN'T LIE, BOSS.
HEH
Yura's adorable.
HEH
She is.
She's totally blushing.
She's not like most kids today. They aren't shy about anything.
Yeah. She's the exact opposite in the commercial.
Excuse me.
Can we move on? Do you have any questions for me?
TH-THUMP
Haruka ...

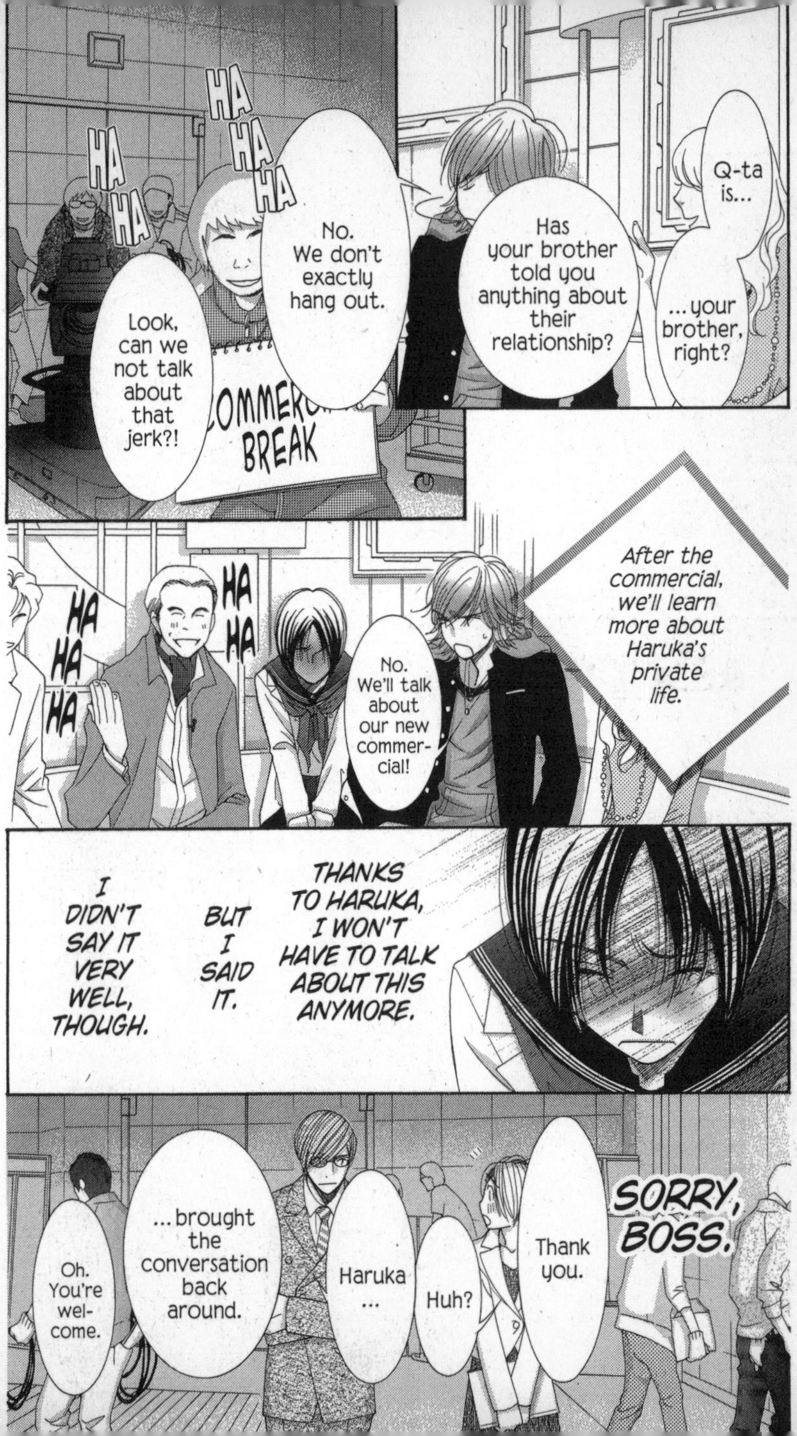
Q-ta is...
...your brother, right?
Has your brother told you anything about their relationship?
No. We don't exactly hang out.
HA HA HA HA
HA HA HA
Look, can we not talk about that jerk?!
BREAK
After the commercial, we'll learn more about Haruka's private life.
No. We'll talk about our new commercial!
HA HA
HA HA HA
THANKS TO HARUKA, I WON'T HAVE TO TALK ABOUT THIS ANYMORE.
BUT I SAID IT.
I DIDN'T SAY IT VERY WELL, THOUGH.
SORRY, BOSS.
Thank you.
Huh?
Haruka...
...brought the conversation back around.
Oh. You're welcome.

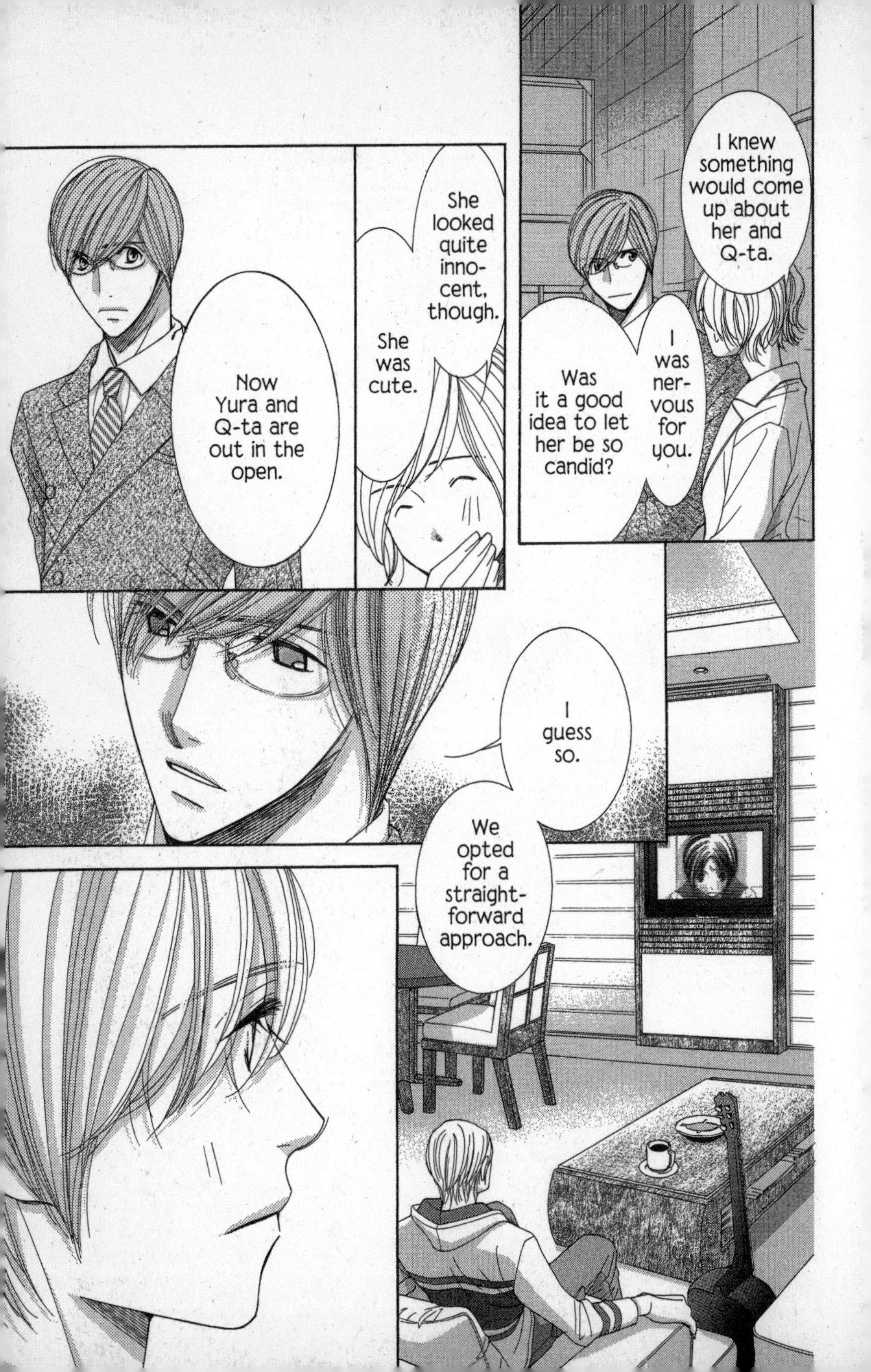
I knew something would come up about her and Q-ta.
I was nervous for you.
Was it a good idea to let her be so candid?
She looked quite innocent, though.
She was cute.
Now Yura and Q-ta are out in the open.
I guess so.
We opted for a straightforward approach.

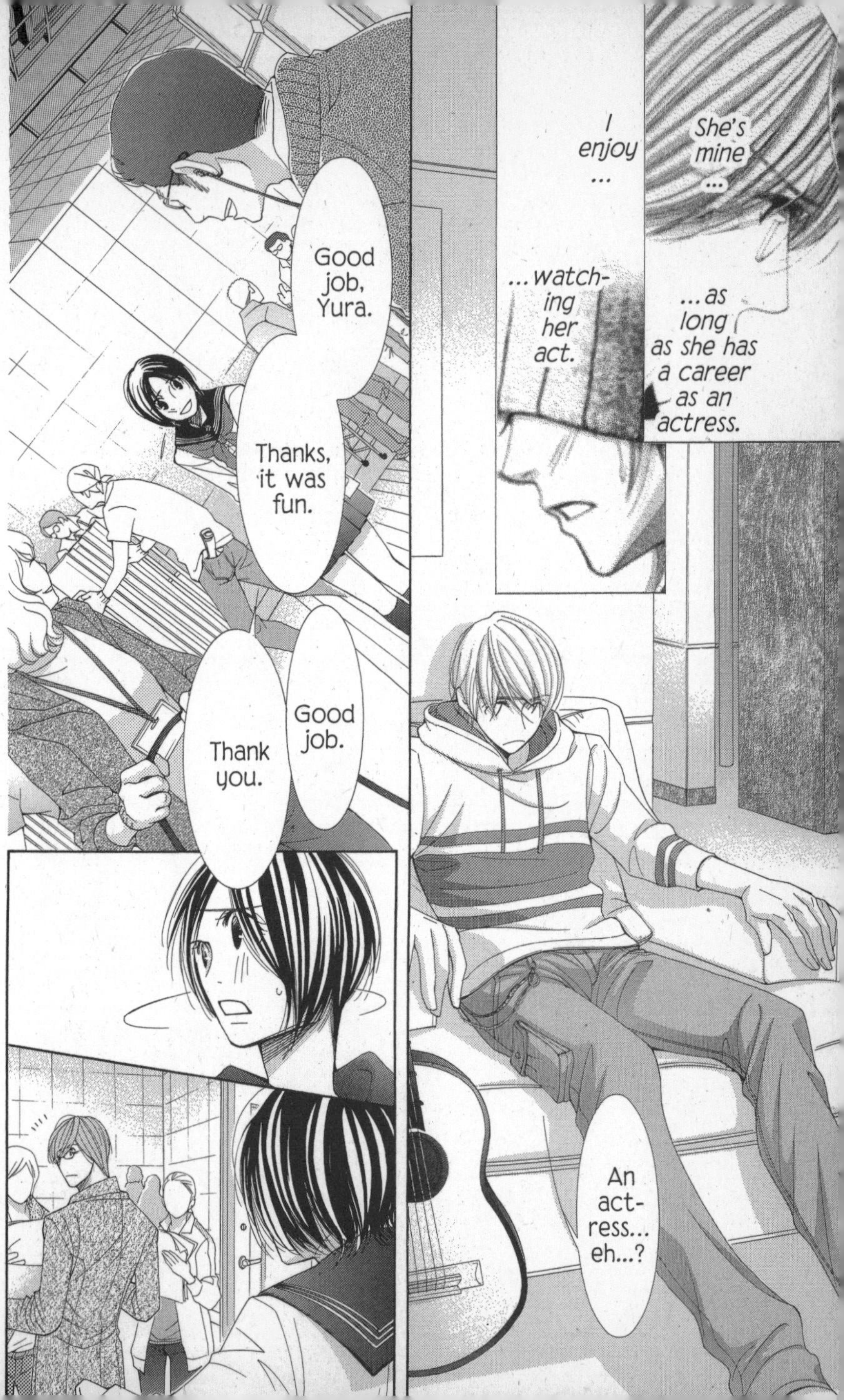
She's mine ...
...as long as she has a career as an actress.
I enjoy ...
...watching her act.
An actress... eh...?
Good job, Yura.
Thanks, it was fun.
Good job.
Thank you.

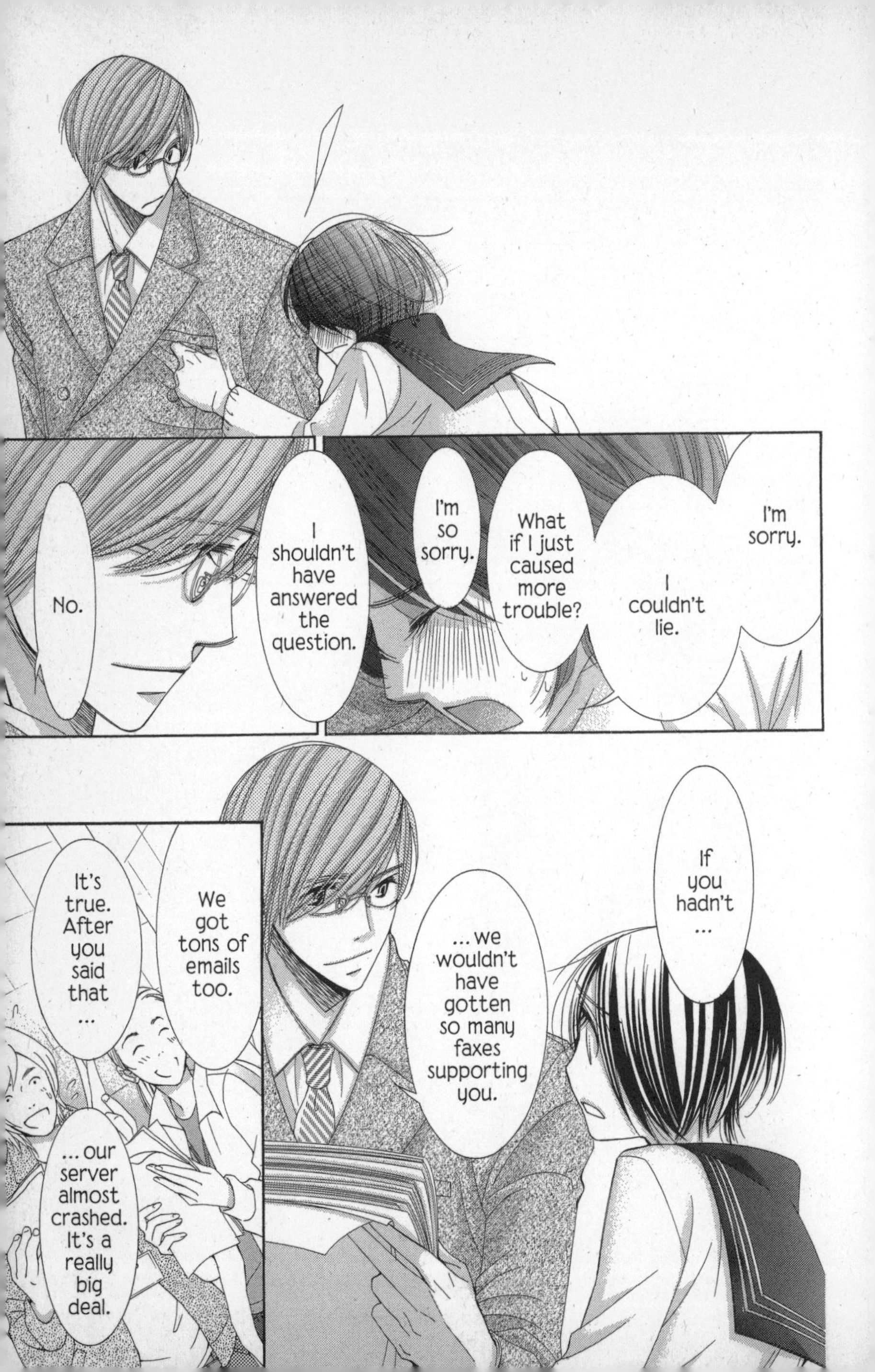
I'm sorry.
I couldn't lie.
What if I just caused more trouble?
I'm so sorry.
I shouldn't have answered the question.
No.
If you hadn't ...
... we wouldn't have gotten so many faxes supporting you.
We got tons of emails too.
It's true. After you said that ...
... our server almost crashed. It's a really big deal.

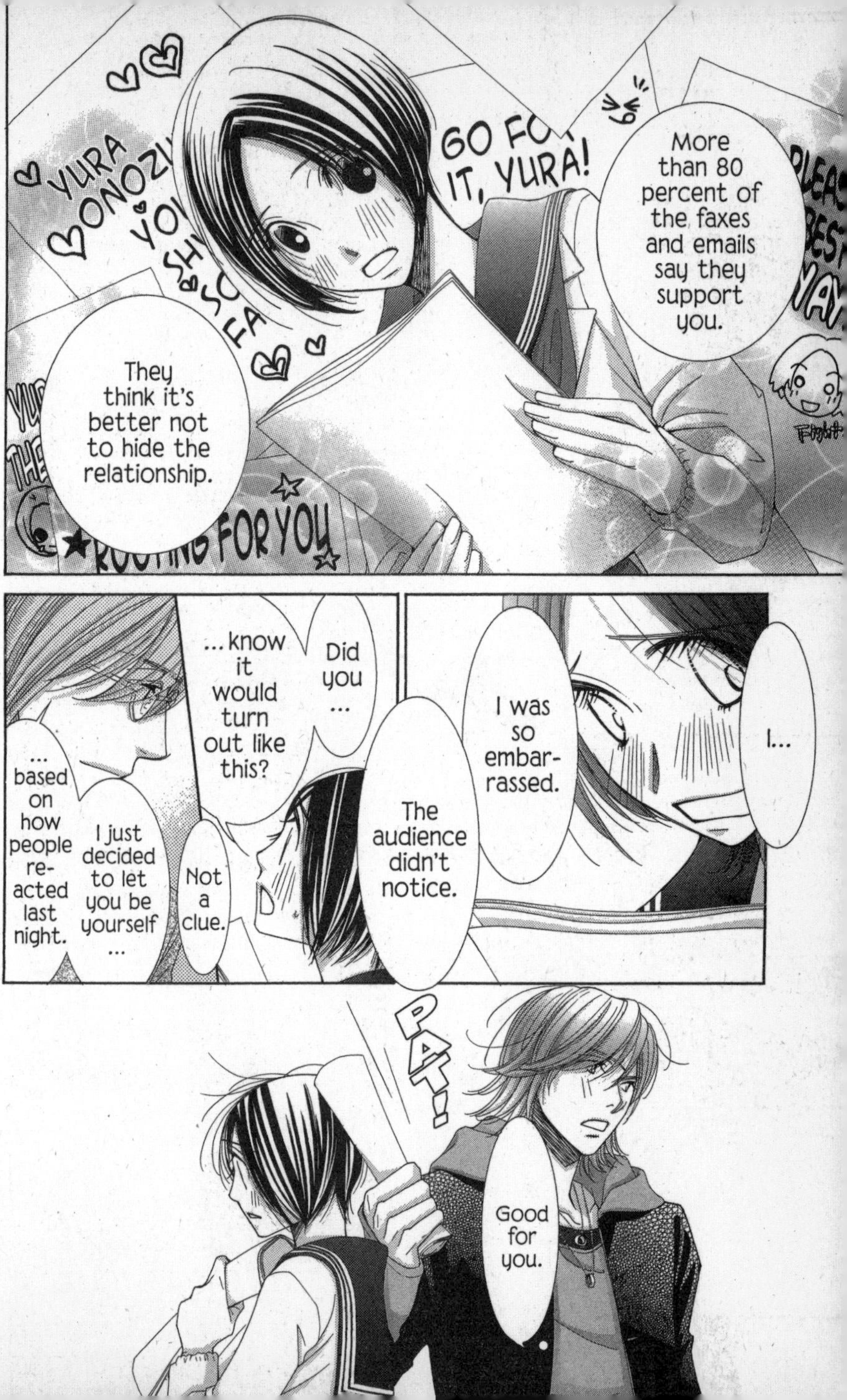
More than 80 percent of the faxes and emails say they support you.
They think it's better not to hide the relationship.
I...
I was so embar-rassed.
The audience didn't notice.
Not a clue.
Did you ...
... know it would turn out like this?
I just decided to let you be yourself ...
... based on how people re-acted last night.
PAT!
Good for you.

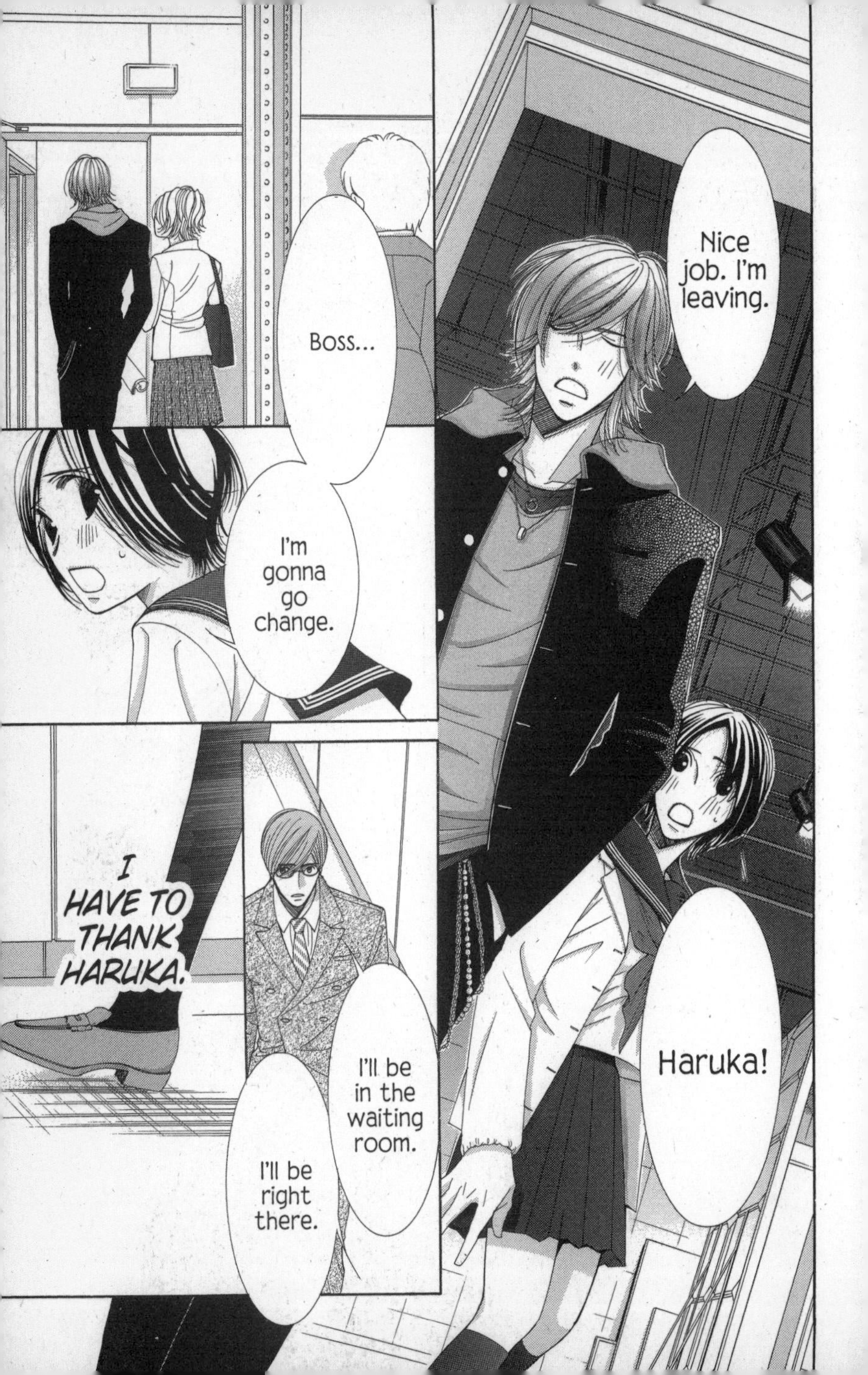
Nice job. I'm leaving.
Haruka!
Boss...
I'm gonna go change.
I'll be in the waiting room.
I'll be right there.
I HAVE TO THANK HARUKA.

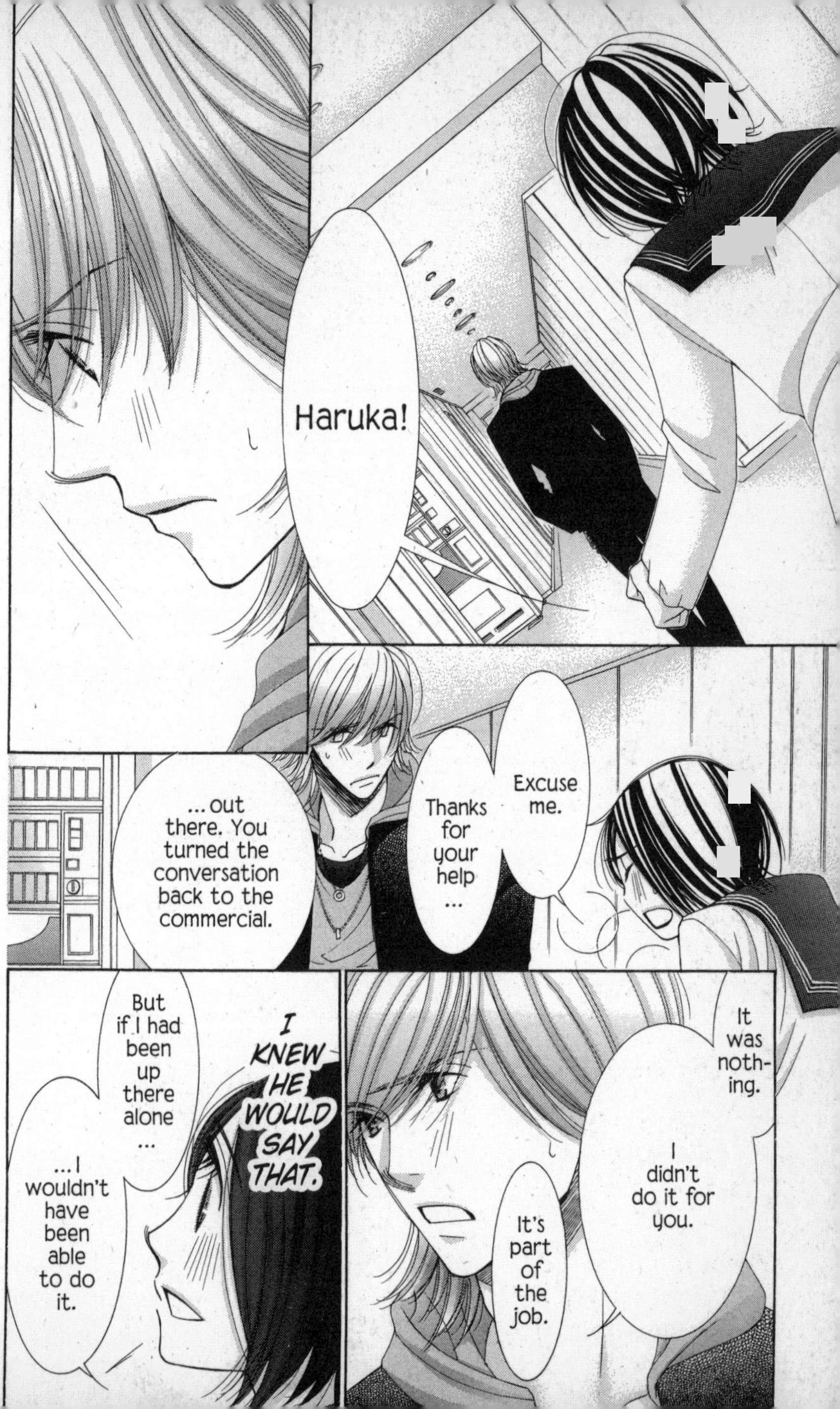
Haruka!
Excuse me.
Thanks for your help ...
... out there. You turned the conversation back to the commercial.
It was nothing.
I didn't do it for you.
It's part of the job.
But if I had been up there alone ...
I KNEW HE WOULD SAY THAT.
... I wouldn't have been able to do it.

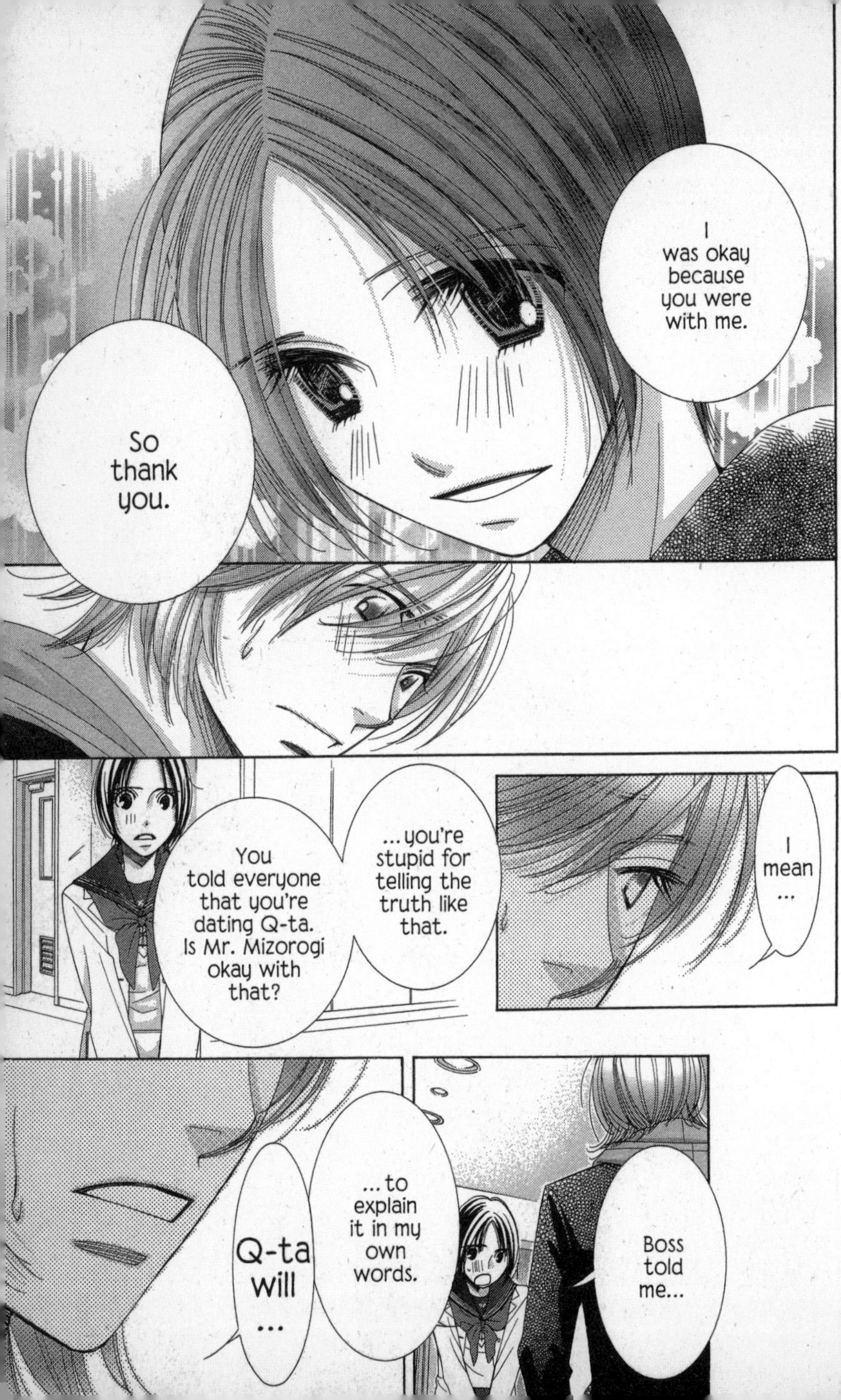
I was okay because you were with me.
So thank you.
I mean ...
...you're stupid for telling the truth like that.
You told everyone that you're dating Q-ta. Is Mr. Mizorogi okay with that?
Boss told me...
...to explain it in my own words.
Q-ta will ...

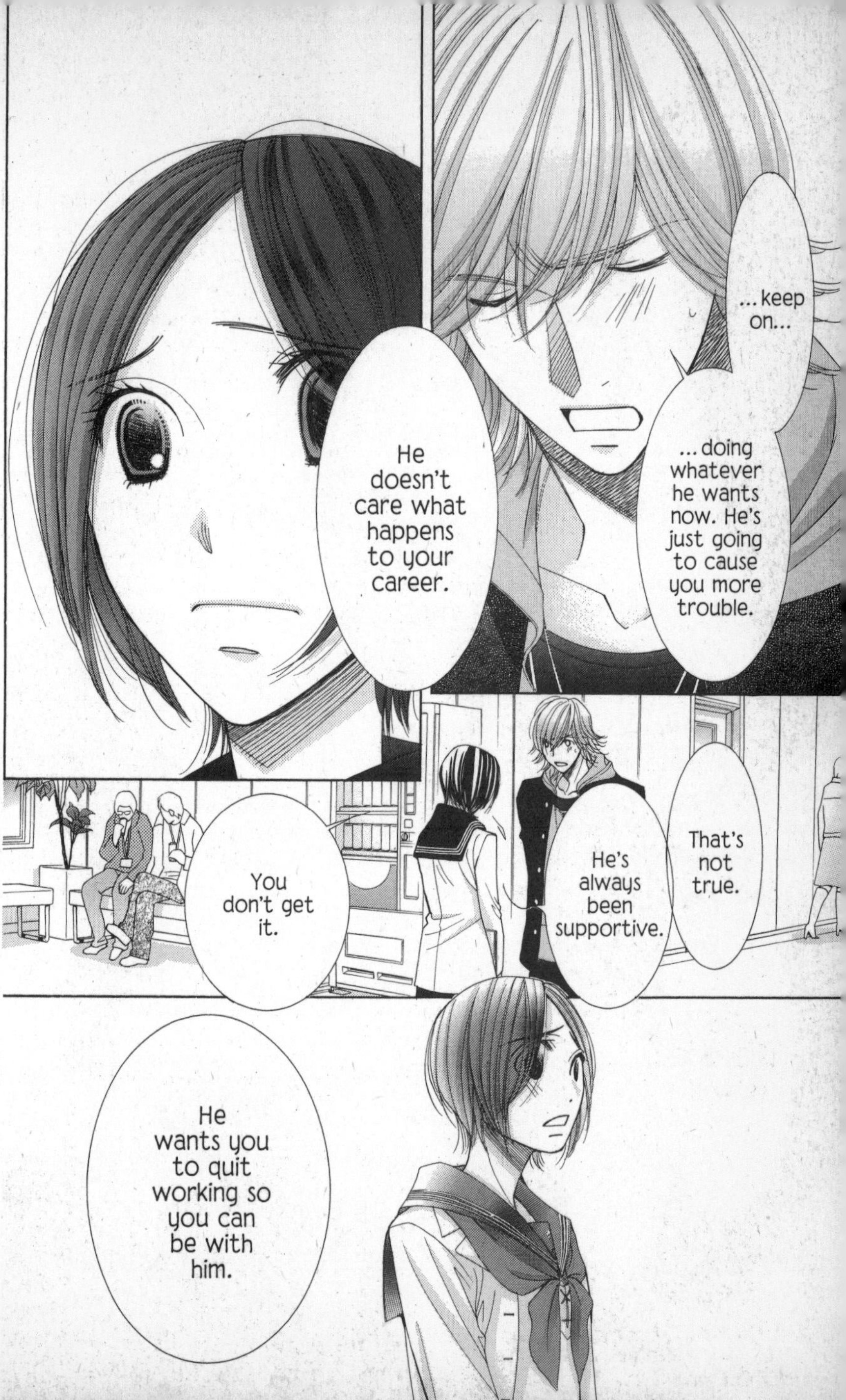
...keep on...
...doing whatever he wants now. He's just going to cause you more trouble.
He doesn't care what happens to your career.
That's not true.
He's always been supportive.
You don't get it.
He wants you to quit working so you can be with him.

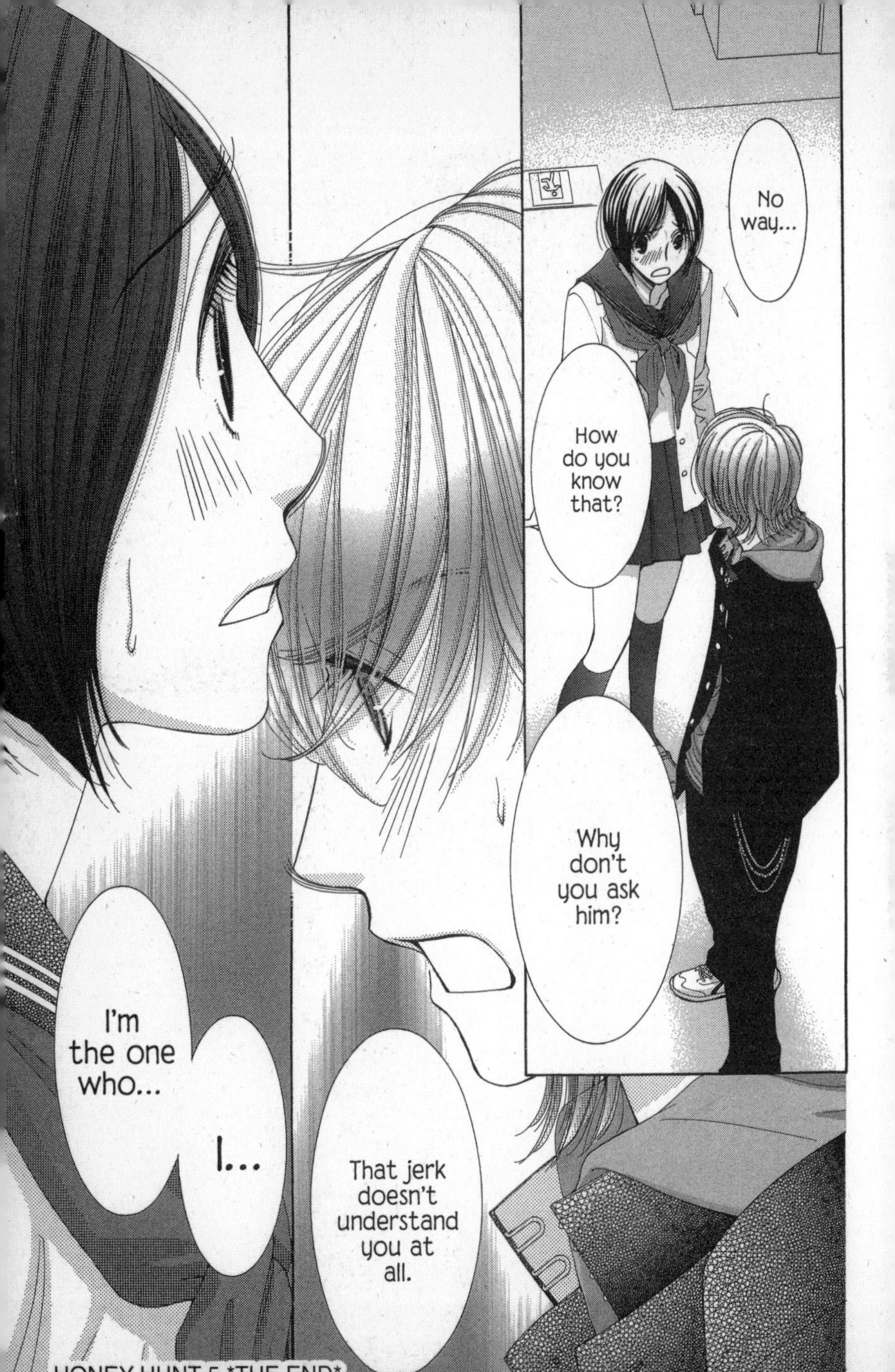
No way...
How do you know that?
Why don't you ask him?
That jerk doesn't understand you at all.
I'm the one who...
I...

HONEY HUNT 5 *THE END*

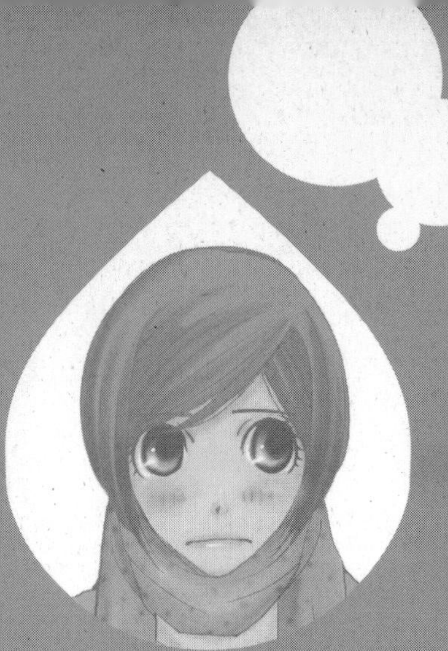

MIKI AIHARA

Here we go with the fifth volume! I had always wanted to write about Yura's mother, Yukari. I use the theme from the first version of *Snow White* in *Grimm's Fairy Tales*. In the more familiar version, Snow White's stepmother throws her out of the castle and poisons her with an apple. In the original version, it is Snow White's birth mother who does this. The story is kind of sad that way, but I love this sort of messy human drama!

Miki Aihara, from Shizuoka Prefecture, is the creator of the manga series *Hot Gimmick*. She began her career with *Lip Conscious!*, which ran in *Bessatsu Shojo Comic*. Her other work includes *Seiten Taisei* (The Clear, Wide Blue Sky), *So Bad!*, and *Tokyo Boys & Girls*. She's a Gemini whose hobbies include movies and shopping.

HONEY HUNT
VOL.5

Shojo Beat Edition

STORY AND ART BY MIKI AIHARA

© 2007 Miki AIHARA/Shogakukan
All rights reserved.
Original Japanese edition "HONEY HUNT" published by SHOGAKUKAN Inc.

English Adaptation/Liz Forbes
Translation/Ari Yasuda, HC Language Solutions, Inc.
Touch-up Art & Lettering/Rina Mapa
Design/Ronnie Casson
Editor/Alexis Kirsch

VP, Production/Alvin Lu
VP, Sales & Product Marketing/Gonzalo Ferreyra
VP, Creative/Linda Espinosa
Publisher/Hyoe Narita

Printed in Canada

Published by VIZ Media, LLC
P.O. Box 77010
San Francisco, CA 94107

10 9 8 7 6 5 4 3 2 1
First printing, August 2010

www.viz.com   www.shojobeat.com

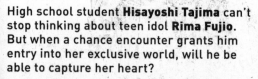

Change Your PERSPECTIVE

From Miki Aihara,
Creator of *Honey Hunt* and
Tokyo Boys & Girls

Watch Hatsumi's life get turned
upside down BIG time with
VIZBIG Editions of *Hot Gimmick!*
Each volume features:

- Three volumes in one
- Larger trim size
- Exclusive cover designs
- Color artwork
- Bonus content

A great way to introduce new readers to a series

See why **Bigger is Better**

Start your VIZBIG collection today!

RATED
T+
FOR OLDER
TEEN
ratings.viz.com

Shojo Beat

MANGA from the HEART

OTOMEN
STORY AND ART BY
AYA KANNO

VAMPIRE KNIGHT
STORY AND ART BY
MATSURI HINO

Natsume's BOOK of FRIENDS
STORY AND ART BY
YUKI MIDORIKAWA

Want to see more of what you're looking for?

Let your voice be heard!

shojobeat.com/mangasurvey

Help us give you more manga from the heart!

RATED T FOR TEEN ratings.viz.com
RATED T+ FOR OLDER TEEN ratings.viz.com
VIZ media
www.viz.com